Views of the Borough of Catasauqua, 1852

A HISTORY

OF

CATASAUQUA

IN

LEHIGH COUNTY

PENNSYLVANIA

BY

James F Lambert and Henry J Reinhard

1914
The Searle & Dressler Co , Inc
Allentown Pa

TO
THE MEMORY
OF THE CHARACTER
AND ACHIEVEMENTS
OF OUR NOBLE TOWNSMEN
PAST AND PRESENT
AND AS AN INSPIRATION
TO THE POSTERITY OF CATASAUQUA
IS THIS VOLUME
DEDICATED

James F. Lambert

Henry J. Reinhard

DeAlton F. Gould

Gus. E. Oswald

Alfred C. Lewis

FOREWORD

At a regularly called meeting of the Historical Committee of the Old Home Week Association, held in the parlors of the Phoenix Fire Co, November 29, 1913, James F Lambert and Henry J Reinhard were unanimously elected editors of a proposed History of Catasauqua, which it was resolved to publish

At a meeting of the same Committee held in the Directors' Room of the High School Building, May 6, 1914, it was resolved that one thousand copies of the History be printed

History is a written statement of what is known; an account of that which exists or has existed The task of the historian lies in his search for authenticity The editors of this volume addressed letters and series of questions to practically every industry and individual in Catasauqua, inquiring after definite data, in order that they might make the subject-matter authoritative "Many men, many minds," is verified by the fact that more than once have they heard two persons of equal intelligence relate the same incident along such vastly different lines that it did not at all seem like the same incident May the reader who will discover fancied inaccuracies be sure to balance well his own mind and recollect that there are other minds, both clear and strong, that see or recall the incident from a different angle

Furthermore, the editors of this book did not write an essay on the subject assigned them They have not expanded on the philosophy of the theme They have striven diligently to tell the true story of the life of Catasauqua, and her people, in the briefest form possible This they did and nothing more

For the prompt and many courteous replies to their inquiries they are truly grateful They deem it a privilege to acknowledge the benevolent courtesy of Mr William H Glace, Esq, who favored them with his recent book (1914) on "Early History and Reminiscences of Catasauqua," with permission to "take all or such portions as you desire in the preparation of your pamphlet for Old Home Week" They beg further to acknowledge worthy contributions by James S.

Stillman, Frank M Horn, Wm H Schneller, Esq, J S Elverson, Dr. Charles Milson, Sarah J McIntyre, the Clergy of Catasauqua, and others whose suggestions they valued most highly In response to the solicitation of the editors the firm of Geo V Millar and Company, Printers and Publishers, of Scranton, Pa, loaned them the free use of certain cuts of scenes in and about town, which are inserted in this Volume Attention was drawn to them through a beautiful *Souvenir of Catasauqua,* published by this progressive firm, and for sale by Messrs A J Etheredge & Co The editors hereby express their cordial gratitude to Messrs Geo V. Millar & Co. for their courtesy

For obvious reasons the editors were not in a position to begin their work until the middle of March Their regular duties, as Pastor of a large parish in one instance, and Supervising Principal of the Schools in the other, could not be neglected. Therefore, they prevailed upon their friends Gus. E Oswald, Principal of the High School, Alfred C Lewis, Instructor in the Commercial Department, and De Alton F Gould of the Department of English in the High School to assist them in their work, so as to enable them to bring forth this book in ample time for the Celebration. They have chosen to express their cordial appreciation of the valuable services of these gentlemen by placing their cuts on the editorial page

If time and space did not forbid they would most gladly have inserted many more biographies and reminiscences No doubt some persons and incidents will come to mind, after the last proof will have been returned to the printers, which should have been inserted by all means But, human work is never perfect

That the perusal of this volume may prove both pleasing and profitable to all is their ardent wish

THE EDITORS

June 1, 1914

CONTENTS

CHAPTER I—CATASAUQUA

	Page
Boundary Adjusted	6
Bridges	7
Bridge, Crane Company	9
Change of Name	5
Canal	13
Communication (Telephones)	33
Charity Society	35
Civic League	36
Drinking Fountains	23
Early Settlers	2
Extension	6
Expressage and Telegraphy	16
Four Families	2
Fire Protection	23
Phoenix Fire Company	24
Southwark Hose Company No 9	26
Charotin Hose Company No. 1	28
East End Independent Hose and Chemical Company No 1	29
Incorporation	4
Light, Heat and Power	30
Mail Service	14
Pumping Station	22
Police Force	34

CHAPTER II.—INDUSTRIES

	Page
Auto Service, Peerless	72
Boiler Compound, Young's	69
Boiler Works, Catasauqua	67
Brewery, Eagle	59
Brewery, Catasauqua	60
Crane Iron Works	38
Corporate Existence	42
Acquisition of Rights	43
Empire Steel and Iron Company	45
Car, Wheel and Axle Works, Lehigh	57
Davies and Thomas Company	53
Dispatch, Catasauqua	63
Emanuel and Company	67
F W. Wint and Company	51
Fire Brick Works, Lehigh	62

IX

	Page
Furniture Company, Herrington	72
Grist Mill, Mauser and Cressman	49
Garage, Catasauqua	71
Horse Shoe Company, Bryden	64
Iron Company, Thomas	46
Ice Company, Crystal	73
Motor Car Works, Catasauqua	72
Planing Mill, Goldsmith	68
Pine Olein Company	53
Rubber Company, Leicester	70
Silk Company, Wahnetah	65
Silk Mill, Dery	66
Silk Company, Catasauqua	71
Thermometer Works, Keys	71

CHAPTER III — CHURCHES.

	Page
Congregational, Bethel Welsh	118
Evangelical, Immanuel	79
Episcopal, St Stephen's	119
Greek Catholic	122
Lutheran, St Paul's	89
Lutheran, Holy Trinity	116
Methodist Episcopal, Grace	108
Presbyterian, First	74
Presbyterian, Bridge Street	84
Presbyterian, Hokendauqua	113
Reformed, Salem	96
Roman Catholic, St. Mary's	101
Roman Catholic, St Lawrence	106
Roman Catholic, St Andrew's Slovak	125
United Evangelical, St. John's	121

CHAPTER IV. — SCHOOLS

	Page
Buildings	128
Bible in Schools	140
Current Accounts and Salaries	134
Colored Children	139
Clock and Bell	143
Class Day	143
Deaths in the Board	144
High School	136
Lectures	143
Music	142
Museum	142
Night School	144
Organization and Enrollment	134

	Page
Patriotism	140
Physical Culture	142
Reports, Monthly	142
School Board, Present	145
Tunnel	143
Teachers' Meeting	141
Teachers, Present Corps of	145
Teachers, Complete List of	146
Valuation and Assessments	134
The North Catasauqua Schools	148

CHAPTER V—FRATERNAL AND SOCIAL ORGANIZATIONS

	Page
Auquasat Club	165
Charotin Club	165
Catasauqua Club	164
Choral Society, The Catasauqua	179
Degree of Pocahontas	168
I O O F, Catasauqua Lodge No 269	150
I. O O F, Fraternity Encampment No 156	153
Jr O U A. M.	161
Knights of Friendship	160
Knights of Golden Eagle, Catasauqua Castle No 241	158
Knights of Malta	163
Lyceum Club	166
Masons, F and A, Porter Lodge No 284	152
Moose, Loyal Order of	169
P. O S of A, No 301	154
Pioneer Band	171
Rebekah Lodge, No 159	158
Red Men, Improved Order of	156
Royal Arch Chapter No. 278	163
Russian Orthodox Society, St Syril	163
Shepherds of Bethlehem, Order of	164
St Peter and St Paul Society	165
St Andrew's Societies	170
T A. B. Society, St Lawrence	161
Temperance Society	169
Woodmen of the World	168
The Soldiers	
G. A. R., Fuller Post	171
Soldiers' Monument	172
46th Regiment	174
47th Regiment	174
Other Volunteers	175
Spanish American War Volunteers	176

CHAPTER VI.—BANKS

	Page
The National Bank of Catasauqua	180
The Lehigh National Bank	186
Building and Loan Associations.	
Home, The	188
Catasauqua, The	189
Lehigh, The	189

CHAPTER VII.—TRADESMEN AND CRAFTSMEN

	Page		Page
Acme Beef Company	203	Goldsmith, George C D.	194
Applegate, J. & Sons	190	Graffin Brothers	206
Bachman, Ammon H	206	Granite Works, Catasauqua	222
Baumer, Robert	226	Hauser, A A	203
Beck and Frey	212	Hauser, H. O	204
Beitel & Son, Time Pieces	216	Harris, Henry	195
Benko, Martin	196	Heckenberger Drug Store	215
Bowen Grocery	194	Heffelfinger, Mrs James	199
Bower, C D W	202	Hersh Hardware Company	210
Boyer, E J	192	Hoch, John W	207
Buss, William J.	208	Hoffman & Follweiler	221
Campbell, F J.	213	Holtzleicer, William T	196
Case, Titus R	220	Ice Cream	198
Catasauqua Mercantile Company	192		
Clark, William B	209	Johnston, William E	227
Childs Grocery Company	194	Keener, Elvin	204
		Kemp, Charles	212
Deemer and Litzenberger	206	Kibler, A H	198
Deily, George B F.	190	Klingler, Frank	204
Donkel, Mrs Winfield S	200	Koch and Younger	198
Dotterer, D. M.	196	Kozlowski, Mrs. Wanda	196
Eckensberger, Harry F	220	Kuehner, William F	203
Edgar, Mrs Mary	200	Kurtz, Philip F	196
Edgar Brothers	200		
Erdman, Elmer E	219	Laubach, John J	202
		Lawall Brothers	214
Feenstra, John K.	221	Lipsky, Jacob W.	212
Fehr, Clinton	199		
Fisher, John	216	Matchette, Joseph & Son	206
Fitzhugh, George W	223	Mark, William B	208
Five and Ten Cent Store	198	Miller, Alfred L	213
Frederick and Scherer	218	Miller, Ira H	214
Frey, Charles W	208	Milson, Daniel, Jr	207
Fuller Oil & Supply Company	205	Milkmen	197
		Missmer, James E	191
Geiger, Peter	197	Missmer, John H	226
Gemmel, Samuel P	209	Moyer, Morris H	200
Giering, Oliver H	225		
Gillespie, David, Jr	191	Newhard, Frank H D.	220

	Page		Page
O'Donnell, Anthony	195	Smith, George	195
Onushak, Harry	195	Smith, Owen J	201
Oldt, Edwin	221	Smith, W. J Company	205
Ostheimer, A	211	Snyder, Frank	201
		Steinhilber, W B	191
		Streham, John	211
Peters, Calvin D.	222		
		Taylor, Joseph, and Sons	190
Reitzler, Nicholas	201	Theatre, The Majestic	227
Roth, C. F	214	Theatre, The Palace	228
Roth, Samuel A	226		
Roxberry, William	225	Walker, Philip F.	202
		Walp Shoe, The	211
		Weaver, Oscar	201
Sacks, John G	201	Weisley, William	191
Sacks, William A.	201	Weiss, Edwin	226
Schick and Hausman	212	Webber, Matthew F	193
Schieler, A. E Company	213	Wertman, Henry J	208
Schifreen, Solomon	213	Williams, William S.	197
Schneller, John P	210	Wotring, H S	193
Schneller, Charles W	209	Wotring, Milton D	193
Schneider, Charles	210		
Seyfried, James J	193	Young, Frank A	200
Sharpe, Robert	217	Zellers	223
Sheckler, Charles E, Jr	221		
Smith, Quintus H	224	Zieser, E J	195

CHAPTER VIII—HOTELS

	Page
American	229
Biery's	229
Bottling Plant	237
Catasauqua Brewery Saloon, The	235
Catasauqua House, The	233
Eagle, The	230
Farmers, The	233
Horse Shoe House, The	236
Imperial, The	234
Liquor Store	237
Mansion House, The	236
Northampton House, The	234
Oriental, The	236
Pennsylvania, The	231
St. George's, The	234
Union Hotel, The	235
Walker, The	237

CHAPTER IX —PROFESSIONAL MEN

	Page
Becker, Dr. Alfred J	247
Dentistry	250
Glace, William H	252
Glick, Austin A.	258
Heckenberger, Dr William A	249
Hornbeck, Dr M E	242
Hornbeck, Dr James L	243
Hammersly, R. Clay	256
Keim, Dr C J	244
Keim, Dr H J S	245
Koons and Son	260
McIntyre, Dr George	238
Milson, Dr. Charles E	246
Quig, Dr Frederick W	238
Quinn, Thomas	261
Rehrig, J Edward, D. D S	251
Riegel, Dr H H.	238
Riegel, Dr W A	240
Roth, Cornelius F	262
Schneller, Dr John S.	249
Schneller, William H	259
Stine, Oscar J	257
Scherer, Dr Thomas A	246
Ulrich, Alexander N	257
Ulrich, Charles N	258
Willoughby, Wesley, D. D S	250
Yoder, Dr Daniel	241

CHAPTER X.—BIOGRAPHICAL SKETCHES

	Page		Page
Beitel, James C	308	Eberhard, Frederick	283
Biery, Jonas	263	Eberhard, Peter J	285
Biery, Solomon	263	Eberhard, Ferdinand	284
Biery, Daniel	263	Faust, John Philip	264
Breinig, George	265	Faust, Jonas	264
Breinig, Simon	265	Frederick, George	277
Buck, Henry H.	338	Frederick, Owen	277
Chapman, Charles W	301	Frederick, Ogden E	278
Davis, David	317	Frederick, T F	278
Davis, Daniel	319	Fuller, James W, 1st	285
Davies, George	321	Fuller, James W, 2nd	286
Deily, Jacob	266	Gillespie, David	293
Deily, George	267	Gilbert, Mrs Ellen C	345
Deily, Francis J	267	Graffin, Charles	310
Dery, D George	336	Griffith, David R	337

	Page		Page
Holton, George E	343	Nevins, James	298
Horn, Col. Melchior H	295		
Horn, Frank M	294	Peckitt, Leonard	344
Hudders, John	283	Peter, John	268
Hunt, David	313	Phillips, William	282
Hunt, Joshua	311	Randall, Edmund	315
Hunter, John	282	Roberts, Jacob	340
Jones, Thomas	291	Schneller, Charles G	290
Kildare, William M	328	Seaman, Henry J	342
Kohler, Richard O	341	Snyder, Jonathan	268
Kostenbader, Herman	313	Snyder, William T	289
Kurtz, John George	266	Storm, Philip	305
		Swartz, Benjamin F	333
Lawall, Jacob	299		
Lackey, James	295	Thomas, David	268
Leibert, John	297	Thomas, Samuel	271
Lewis, Arnold C	302	Thomas, Edwin	273
Lewis, William G	303	Thomas, William R	274
Matchette, Capt Joseph	306	Thomas, James	275
McKee, William W.	336	Weaver, Valentine W	323
McIntyre, John	281	Weaver, Benjamin H	325
McIntyre, Robert	280	Williams, David R	320
McClellan, William	282	Williams, John	328
Milson, Daniel	298	Williams, Robert E	330
Morrison, John	323	Williams, Oliver	331
Moyer, Jonas F	334	Younger, William	326

CHAPTER XI.—REMINISCENCES

	Page
Breinig Buys a Farm	351
Conrad Weiser Letter	355
Canal Excursion	357
Choral Society	361
David Thomas Letter	347
Dramatic Club	353
Early Ordinances	347
Emanuel Employment	349
Esther Hudders	350
Furnace Visitors	359
Floods	359
Friday in School	361
Gas Bags	349
Game of Ball	362
Grave Diggers	364
Irish Parade	352
Indian Relics	355
Maggie Jones and the Circus	350
Municipal Bake Ovens	352

	Page
Mexican War Veterans	354
"Mexicon John"	355
Opening L. V. R. R.	358
Old Buildings	367
Presbyterian Grove Services	353
Potato Sales	354
Piggery	360
Sulphur Matches	352
Schneller Letter	356
Steel Pens	361
Sundry Quotations	365
Tuyeres	359
The Corpse	364
The Last Day of School	362
Water Fight	358
Whip in School	361

CHAPTER XII—BOROUGH OFFICIALS

	Page
Program and Views	369
Officers of the Old Home Week Association	371
Program	372-373
Views	375-408

HISTORY OF CATASAUQUA.

CHAPTER I.—CATASAUQUA

The Iron Borough, as it is frequently termed, was originally known as Biery's Port. It is situated on a portion of a 10,000 acre tract of land devised by the Proprietary of Pennsylvania, Sir William Penn, to his daughter Letitia, who with her husband, William Aubrey, of London, England, granted and conveyed the same to John Page, in 1731. A few months later, Page secured a warrant dated at London, Oct 10, 1731, to take up 2,723 acres of his grant which was surveyed and set apart for him by Nicholas Scull, on Oct 10, 1736.

The patent reads as follows, "And we do further by these presents and by virtue of the power and authorities granted by the Royal Charter to our Father William Penn, Esq, by his majesty, Charles the Second, erect said tract into a manor and to call it 'Chawton' and so from henceforth we will have it called, and reposing trust and confidence in the prudence and ability and integrity of the said Page and his loyalty to our sovereign, Lord George the Second, do give and grant unto the said John Page, his heirs and assigns, full power and authority to erect and constitute with the said manor a Court Baron with all things whatsoever which to a Court Baron do belong, and to have and to hold view of Frank Pledges, for the consideration of the peace and better government of the inhabitants within the said Manor by the said John Page, his heirs and assigns, or his or their stewards lawfully deputed and generally to do and to use all things which to the view of Frank Pledges do belong, or may or ought to belong. To be holden of us, our successors, proprietors of Pennsylvania, as of the signory of 'Windsor' in free and common socage by fealty or in lieu of all other services, yielding and paying therefor yearly unto us, ourselves and successors, one red rose on the 24th day of June in every year from hereafter in the City of Philadelphia to such person or persons as shall from time to time be appointed to receive the same."

This instrument calls the Manor "Chawton." There are deeds on record in the office at Easton showing that the word has also been written "Charotin." Local antiquarians seem to agree that "Charotin" is the result of a faulty scrivener, who either misspelled the word or wrote so poorly that the "w" of Chawton looked like the "ro" of Charotin.

EARLY SETTLERS.

Among the early settlers of this tract were Thomas Armstrong, Robert Gibson, Robert Clendennin, Joseph Wright, John Elliott, Andrew Mann, George and Nathaniel Taylor, all Irish names, showing that the town is situated within the bounds of the original Irish settlement which extended from Siegfried's to Koehler's locks, along the Lehigh, and eastward, along irregular lines, to the vicinage of Bath.

The advent of the Pennsylvania German however soon brought about many changes. While his Irish neighbors were discussing the possibilities of impending wars, he was content to toil and dig. This enabled him soon to offer prices for the land about him. By the beginning of the nineteenth century, not a single Irish land-owner was left along the river, nor within two or three miles of it.

The Irish having sold out, moved westward. Some settled in Central Pennsylvania while others found locations in the neighboring state of Ohio. Here land was much cheaper.

THE FOUR FAMILIES

The Irish, having sold out, moved westward. Some settled in Central Penn-should be mentioned.

Frederick and Henry Biery bought the old stone mill located where the Catasauqua Mills now stand, and the former built several of the stone structures still remaining on Race Street. Henry sold out to his brother and moved to New York.

John Peter, a weaver by trade, moved from Heidelberg in 1823 and located at Front and Bridge Streets on a small farm which he bought from Andrew Hower, and into a house built by John Zoundt

The Faust family, whose first representative here was John Philip Faust, lived at the old homestead now in possession of the Bryden Horse Shoe Company The foundation walls of the once stately mansion may still be traced in the yards of the Horse Shoe Works

Henry Breisch, a stone mason, occupied a small farm of ten acres of land in the vicinity of Third and Bridge Streets

East of the Biery farm, and beyond the Catasauqua creek, lay the farm acquired by John George Kurtz during 1760 Much of this is now occupied by the Third Ward of Catasauqua

To the north of the Kurtz farm lay a farm of 245 acres, purchased from the estate of Peter Beisel by George Breinig, on April 4, 1831

PUBLIC HIGHWAYS

Four public highways lay within the confines here described

One extended from the north via the Hokendauqua dam, along the banks of the Lehigh as far south as Chapel Street, thence eastward crossing Front Street on Chapel, and running along in a direction toward the chapel of the First Presbyterian Church, Third and Bridge Streets, and the Howertown Road, near Peach Street

Another road extended from the lower or Race Street bridge, called Biery's bridge, in an easterly direction This is still the old Bethlehem road

The Howertown Road forked from the Bethlehem Road at a point near Biery's bridge and ran almost due north along a course still marking this popular thoroughfare

The fourth road was a short connecting link from the mill race across the county bridge at the Davies and Thomas foundry

CHANGE OF NAME

After the organization of the Lehigh Crane Iron Company, Jan 10, 1839, the town was called "Craneville" in honor of George Crane of Wales, who was the owner of the iron works where David Thomas had been employed before coming to America.

In New Jersey, however, twenty miles from New York City, was a "Craneville" to which much mail matter, intended for this Craneville, went. This caused constant annoyance.

Another change of name was agitated. According to the fertile mind of some ripe scholar, the thought of "Iron City" was to be expressed in euphonious Greek, and the town called "Sideropolis."

Application had actually been made to the Postmaster-General in 1845, to have the post-office name changed from Craneville to Sideropolis, but for some unexplained reason the change was never made.

Owen Rice, chief clerk at the Crane Iron Works, wrote deeds for many people in and about town. Through these services, he learned from drafts made as early as 1735, and from later drawings, that the creek flowing along the eastern and southern limits of the town was called "Cattosoque." In the dialect of the Lenni-Lenape tribe of the Indians who first inhabited this section of country, it was named "Gattoshoci," which is said to mean *wants rain.* Others defined the term as signifying *dry* or *burnt ground,* and, as *sinking waters.* The word *Lecha* (Lehigh) is of similar origin.

INCORPORATION

The suggestion by Mr. Rice, that the town be named Catasauqua, was generally adopted, and application was made to the court of Quarter Sessions of the County of Lehigh, April 3, 1851, for incorporation into a Borough.

The decree of the court was rendered Feb. 1, 1853, and provided:

"That the village of Catasauqua and the territory in and around the same as comprised within the following boundaries, to wit: Beginning at a point in the River Lehigh at low water mark, thence through land of Paul Faust, on the line dividing the said county of Lehigh from the county of Northampton, to the public road leading from Bridge to Howertown, thence down the said road in the middle thereof, to a stone corner between lands of George Breinig and Henry Kurtz, thence on the line between the said lands of the said Breinig and Kurtz to Catasauqua creek, thence down said creek the several courses and distances thereof to its junction with the River Lehigh, thence up the said River Lehigh, the several courses and distances thereof at low water mark to the place of beginning, be and the same is hereby declared a body corporate in law, under and subject to the provisions, requirements and enactments of the Act of Assembly, entitled 'An Act regulating boroughs,' approved April 3, 1851, to be known and designated in law and otherwise as the borough of Catasauqua, and shall constitute a separate Election and School District, subject to all the laws now in force regulating such districts The election for borough officers is hereby directed to be held on the third Friday of March annually, at the public house now in the o cupancy of Charles Nolf, until removed therefrom according to law ''

The maiden election of officials for the new corporation resulted as follows

Chief Burgess—David Thomas

Town Council—Jesse Knauss, William Biery, Joshua Hunt, Jr , Joseph Laubach, John Clark

Street Commissioners—Morgan Emanuel, Jonas Biery

High Constable—Charles Sigley

Auditor—John Williams

Judge—Isaac E Chandler.

Inspectors—David G Jones, Augustus H Gilbert

Assessor—Levi Haas

School Directors—James Ginder, Owen Rice, Charles Nolf, Charles G Schneller, George W Klotz, James Wilson

Justice of the Peace—John Hudders

Constable—Joseph Lazarus

STREETS

The opening and grading of streets began at the lower end of the town, on land owned by Frederick Biery Front Street was laid out by the Court of Quarter Sesions during 1841 For a long while it was called ''Cinder Street'' since it was graded with furnace slag The work was done in 1853 under the direction of Elias Mertz, surveyor

During 1848, Second Street, as far as Church Street, was laid out by the court After the incorporation of the Borough, Town Council opened one street after another until seven numbered streets and Howertown Avenue afforded passage north and south, and ten named streets cross the former at variant angles.

The break in the course of certain streets, e. g , Second at Church Street and Bridge at Third, was caused by the location of a building prior to the laying out of the street

WARDS

To facilitate municipal elections and in order to secure equitable representation for each section of the borough in Town Council and the School Board, forty-nine citizens petitioned the Court, April 11, 1876, for a division of the Borough into two wards. The Court appointed Eli J. Sieger, J. F Newhard and W. B. Powell as commissioners to examine the territory and report to the Court

Their recommendation to divide the Borough into two wards (First Ward and Second Ward), with Church Street as the boundary line between them, was confirmed by the Court, January 19, 1877

EXTENSION

Application to extend the Borough limits on the east was made in 1909. The object of the petition was to annex East Catasauqua, a territory comprising about 435 acres The decree of annexation was handed down October 3, 1909, and East Catasauqua was constituted the Third Ward. The commissioners were William Weisley, John R. Tait and James T Davies

The Second Ward was divided into two parts (Second Ward and Fourth Ward) with Third Street as the dividing line. The Fourth Ward comprises the eastern or Howertown Avenue section. The commissioners were H W Hankee, Harvey H Knerr and Samuel Heilman

Benedict Mark, William Wilkinson, Elvina N Fehr and John W. Koch, being a majority of freeholders adjacent to and along the north and the east boundary lines of the Borough and in the same county, petitioned the Court of Lehigh to be annexed to Catasauqua The case was laid before the Grand Jury sitting for the Quarter Session of June Term, 1895 The Grand Jury having reported favorably to the petition, the Court decreed, July 2, 1895, that the properties named and their contiguous lots be incorporated in the Borough of Catasauqua

BOUNDARY ADJUSTED

The northern limits of Catasauqua were fixed to coincide with the boundary between Hanover and Allen townships This boundary, however, was in dispute for many years so that certain tax-payers and voters were in doubt as to where they lived. A report by commissioners appointed by the Court of Quarter Sessions of Lehigh County, was set aside January 6, 1889. At a later date commissioners were appointed by joint action of the Lehigh and the Northampton County Courts (Allen Township being in the latter County). The gentlemen were Major Samuel D. Lehr of Allentown, Birge Pearson of Easton and Thomas S. McNair, of Hazleton.

They located a point on the east bank of the Lehigh River, twenty perches south of Faust's Ferry, and a spot in the Monocacy creek, where it crosses the road leading from Hanoverville to Bath, Pa., and drew a straight line between the two points. This now also constitutes the boundary between the boroughs of Catasauqua and North Catasauqua.

"It cuts diagonally through Mr. Faust's property at Catasauqua and cuts off a small corner of the Bryden Horse Shoe Works property, thence it passes north of Theodore Bachman's house and touches the bay-window of Daniel Milson's house (now the home of James M. Lennon), it crosses Adam Rau's premises so as to cut it into two equal triangles, and it also cuts off a foot and a half of a corner of the stand pipe."

BRIDGES

Western approaches to the town were made by ferry or the bridge. A ferry line was run across the Lehigh River for many years, at a short distance below the present Hokendauqua dam. This was known as Faust's ferry, and the last traces of its existence disappeared during the last decade of the past century.

At Biery's Port, now Race Street, a company was formed and a chain bridge was built according to an act of Assembly of the State Legislature, passed March 5, 1824. Stocks were sold at twenty-five dollars per share. At a stockholders' meeting, held July 24, 1824, the following officers were elected:

President—Owen Rice of Bethlehem

Managers—Frederick Biery, Philip Faust, Charles D. Bishop and George Helfridge

Treasurer—Joseph Biery

Secretary—On the 26th of July, Jacob Blumer was appointed

The west bank of the river was known as "Pennsylvania Shore;" and the east bank, the "Jersey Shore."

In consideration of a cash payment of ten dollars ($10), and free passage across the bridge for himself and wife during their natural lives, Peter Miller granted sufficient land to form a proper approach to the bridge on the "Pennsylvania Shore." Frederick Biery did the same on the "Jersey Shore" in consideration of free passage for himself, his family and his employees for a term of twenty years. The bridge was suspended on two chains and afforded a clear passage way of thirteen feet.

Toll rates were fixed as follows.

A four-horse pleasure conveyance, twenty-five cents

A two-horse conveyance, eighteen and three-fourths cents.

A two-horse wagon load, twenty-five cents

A single horse and rider, six and one-fourth cents.

A horse or mule, four cents

Horned cattle per head, two cents

Foot passers, one cent

Annual rates ranged from one to over four dollars per year. Special rates were charged for extra heavy loads. The Crane company paid as high as three dollars for a single team. The weight limit was fixed at fifteen thousand pounds.

This bridge was swept away by the freshet of 1841, but a new chain bridge was built immediately. When business had multiplied and traffic increased during the early fifties, the swinging chain bridge was regarded too frail for the burdens that were imposed upon it.

According to an act of Assembly, a new company, known as the Lehigh County Bridge Company at Biery's Mills, was formed, July 26, 1852. The new bridge was a covered, wooden construction supported by massive arches resting on a heavy stone pillar in the river and firm abutments on either bank. The total cost of this bridge was $14,954.

After the flood of 1862 had wrecked this bridge, it was re-constructed and strengthened at a cost of five thousand one hundred and sixty-one dollars. Dividends ran up to twelve per cent per annum.

In 1892, the County bought the bridge, tore it down and replaced it with an iron structure. The cost of nineteen thousand dollars was shared with the

Lehigh Valley Railroad Company, and the Rapid Transit Company, so that the former paid eight thousand dollars, the latter five hundred dollars and the County ten thousand five hundred dollars

THE CRANE COMPANY BRIDGE

The ore used in the furnaces was hauled by team from Whitehall and South Whitehall townships With the increase of the furnace capacity came the multiplication of ore teams and consequently an enlarged toll bill by the bridge company The haul via Biery's bridge also meant a hard mile to traverse, especially during certain seasons of the year

The Crane Iron Company resolved, about 1845, to build a bridge of their own immediately above their furnaces The statute laws of Pennsylvania, however, forbade the erection of a bridge so near an existing bridge

To circumvent this statute, the Iron Company purchased land on both sides of the river and thus were in a position to construct a private bridge The public was granted free use of this bridge until the Crane Iron Company acquired a majority of the stock of the Biery's bridge, when, according to statute privilege of the State, toll was collected

During 1857, the bridge was reinforced and strengthened in order to carry locomotive ("The Hercules") and ore-cars brought in over the newly-constructed Catasauqua and Fogelsville Railroad After destruction by the flood of 1862, a wooden arch bridge, similar to the Biery's bridge, was built During the nineties the company discontinued asking toll, and, when the railroads began to construct the large "gondola" cars, it was found that the bridge was incapable of bearing their weight and also afforded too narrow a space for their passage Orders for coke and other materials included the stipulation that the larger type of cars must not be used for these shipments.

During 1904, the company removed the old wooden structure and erected a modern railroad bridge, capable of supporting the weightiest and most massive rolling stock in use Thus the community was limited to the use of the Race Street bridge or the Hokendauqua bridge for passage across the river, much to the discomfort and inconvenience of the traveling public

Public-spirited citizens now started a movement looking toward an over-head bridge at the foot of Pine Street   The late, lamented Mr. T. F Frederick should receive special recognition in this connection on account of his indefatigable labors with Borough Councils, County Commissioners, the railroads, and the Lehigh Coal and Navigation Company, as well as the President Judge of the Courts of Lehigh, until the bridge became a reality   It was formally opened on Memorial Day, 1908

RAILROADS

The traveling and transportation facilities of Catasauqua have always been superb   Although it may never become a seaport, the Iron Borough now is and bids fair to greater developments as a railroad centre of no mean proportions   Six distinct lines form its arteries of commerce and its avenues of trade.

In the fall of 1855, rails were laid on the bed of the Lehigh Valley Railroad as far as Catasauqua   A locomotive, the "General Wall," borrowed from the Central R R of N J , with one car attached, conveyed coal barons, iron magnates, landlords and financial monarchs as far as the Crane bridge.   An impromptu parade was formed and the march made across the bridge to the Eagle Hotel   After a dinner at the Eagle, the party proceeded to Hokendauqua to view the furnaces just erected   A nonagenarian of Easton, Mr Thomas McKean, a recruiting army officer, accompanied the party

Ore for the furnaces was hauled by heavy teams from various mines throughout the County   A line of teams nearly a mile in length was a customary sight   During rainy seasons, the "ore roads" became well nigh impassable.   In order to reduce expenses and cease damaging the public roads, the Crane Company, assisted by the Thomas Iron Company of Hokendauqua, sought a charter from the State for a railroad from Catasauqua to Fogelsville, and to the Red Lion Hotel near Mertztown.

The application for this charter was presented to the Legislature by Mr. James W Fuller, Sr   His efforts met with intense opposition.   Indignation meetings were called and the efforts of the "Black Republicans" bitterly denounced.   It was claimed that a railroad would cut up and destroy the beautiful farming districts of the Jordan Valley, and be a source of terror to beasts and danger to man

By perseverance and tact, Mr Fuller succeeded at last in securing a charter for the construction of a plank road on the common highway of the ore-teams A short distance of the plank road was built Soon planks were forced out of place by the weight of the loads hauled, others broke and splintered until the road became very dangerous and, especially for pleasure carriages, nigh impassable

After prolonged efforts, the railroad charter was secured, and the construction of the "Catasauqua and Fogelsville R R " begun in the spring of 1856 The formal opening of the road as far as Rupp's station followed during the summer of 1857 The extension of the road to the mountain at Rittenhouse Gap, the field of magnetic ore-mines, was completed later

The Iron Bridge on the Catasauqua and Fogelsville R R has an extreme length of 1,165 feet The iron superstructure is 1,100 feet in length, consisting of eleven spans of 100 feet each, with a height of 104 feet above the bed of the Jordan creek This was doubtless one of the longest bridges in the country at that time The first locomotive crossed the bridge July 14, 1857

The Philadelphia and Reading R R Company secured 60 per cent of the stock of the Catasauqua and Fogelsville Railroad and thus the latter passed into the control of the former and is operated as an important feeder of the Lehigh Valley Railroad, whence it draws large trade for the Reading System, meeting its East Penn branch at Alburtis, Pa

With the multiplication of manufacturing establishments throughout the Lower Lehigh and Delaware Valleys, and especially, the metropolis of the Empire State, came the demand for enlarged coal transportation facilities The Lehigh canal was no longer equal to the task

The stockholders of the Lehigh Coal and Navigation Company resolved to petition the Legislature for a charter for the construction of a railroad from the rich coal fields of the Wyoming Valley to the junction of the Delaware and Lehigh Rivers The new road relieved the congested traffic of the canal, and also offered transportation facilities during the winter months It was called The Lehigh and Susquehanna Railroad, and, after being leased by the Central Railroad of New Jersey for nine hundred and ninety-nine years, it was styled The Lehigh and Susquehanna division of the Central Railroad of New Jersey. The road was opened for traffic in 1868.

In order to facilitate the development of the brown-hematite properties along its line, the Thomas Iron Company per contract with Mr Tinsley Jeter and his associates, built the Ironton Railroad from Hokendauqua and Coplay to Ironton and to certain limestone quarries and ore beds along the base of the Kittatinny Mountains This road was chartered March 4, 1859 The grading of the road-bed was commenced at Ironton August 2, 1859 In spite of a severe winter, the road was thoroughly ballasted by spring, and the first train of loaded cars passed over it on May 24, 1860. The entire capital stock of the Ironton Railroad was bought by the Thomas Iron Company, February 1, 1882, since that time it has continued to operate the road. There is probably no railroad in this country that, considering its mileage, handles so large a tonnage of shipments as the Ironton Besides carrying ore, limestone, coal and other traffic, it taps the heart of the cement body Ten cement mills are located along its lines

Passenger service was established November 1, 1898 It connects with the Lehigh Valley Railroad at Hokendauqua, Pa It exchanges shipments with other roads at Coplay and Catasauqua, the latter place being its junction point with the Reading Railroad, the Lehigh Valley Railroad, the Central Railroad of New Jersey, the Crane Railroad, and the Lehigh and New England Railroad

In order to facilitate shipping, to extend certain tracks, and incidentally save a very large outlay of cash for transfer and shifting of cars by and from other roads, the authorities of the Crane Company applied for a charter for The Crane Railroad Company, July 28, 1905 The coveted charter having been granted, the Crane Railroad tracks were extended eastward via a subway into the Kurtz Valley, where it connects with the new tracks of the Lehigh and New England Railroad

The tracks have also been extended northward along the course of the canal until they connect with the Central Railroad of New Jersey Its total mileage is 3 31 miles

During the summer of nineteen hundred thirteen another important branch of the great railway system of the country found growth in the direction of the "Iron Borough" The Lehigh and New England Railroad Company extended its lines westward from Bath, Pa When they reached Catasauqua they shrewdly found the Crane tunnel built as an outlet for the "Crane Railroad" to a much-needed cinder dump, and thus gained an entrance to Front and Wood Streets, a most desirable location for a terminus

This spur opens a short and direct route into New York and the New England States, and is bound to demand a large trade. It was formally opened on Monday, March 23, 1914, when officials of the Crane Company and the Lehigh and New England Railroad Company entered town in a special train

THE CANAL

Legislation affecting navigation on the Lehigh River was begun as early as 1771 and continued until about 1820, but conditions in the river proved unfavorable to such a prospect. A Lehigh Navigation Company was incorporated in March, 1818, and the Lehigh Coal Company was chartered in October of the same year. During 1820 the two companies were consolidated into the Lehigh Coal and Navigation Company

Steps were taken toward the construction of a canal from Easton to White Haven. The canal was completed from Easton to Mauch Chunk by the summer of 1828. The Commissioners of Inspection reported favorably to the Governor of Pennsylvania, July 3, 1829. The men most prominently identified with this important undertaking were Josiah White, Erskine Hazard and a Mr Hauto

On account of the heavy grade in the course of the river, Catasauqua had to be well locked, one being placed at the Hokendauqua dam, north of town, another at the Crane furnaces in the centre of town, and the third at Koehler's, about a mile south of the Crane lock. The dimensions of the Crane lock are 22 feet in width by 95 feet in length, with a drop of 8 feet

Originally grain and coal were floated down the Lehigh to the Delaware River, and thence to Philadelphia, on flat-bottom boats called "Arks." At their destination the "Arks" had to be sold, as well as their cargo, since they could not be floated against the rapid current of the river

The first excursion to Biery's Port was run on the canal from Allentown on Friday, June 26, 1829, and an "Ark" bore the merry crowd. The canal affords not only boating, especially coal shipping facilities, but also water power for many industries along its course

Hot blast for the initial furnaces of the Crane Company was blown from two cylinders driven by water power from the Canal. Whilst it became necessary to erect blast engines to run the enlarged plant, the old water power system as a motive force at the furnace is still in operation.

Working the mines for twenty years rewarded the Lehigh Coal and Navigation Company with a greatly enlarged output. Their shipments (via canal) during 1821 amounted to about 1,000 tons. The reports of 1837 show the tonnage to have been 224,000 tons. The Lehigh Coal and Navigation Company, therefore, sought every possible opportunity to encourage the establishment of industries along its water course. In 1838 they offered water privileges extending from Hokendauqua to Allentown to any person who would invest $30,000 in the erection of a furnace and run it successfully for three months by the exclusive use of anthracite coal.

From 1845 to 1865 two boat yards were maintained for building and repairing purposes. Bogh Brothers were located on the site of the present Fire Brick Works. Ginder and Rehrig conducted their business at a place opposite the Catasauqua Hotel.

MAIL SERVICE

The rural free delivery of mail matter is not as modern a system of distribution as some choose to consider it. For many years a stage line was run from Allentown to Mauch Chunk and by this medium mail matter was delivered at certain central points along the route. A coach line carrying mail via Catasauqua was also maintained between Bethlehem and Cherryville. Deliveries were made three times weekly.

A post office was established at Biery's Port in 1844 and placed in charge of Samuel Colver. A symposium of the recollections of various local authorities drive to the conclusion that the post office was domiciled in various quarters along Front Street. It is said that upon the appointment of Nathan Fegley as postmaster, 1846, the office was located at Front and Bridge Streets.

Another authority informs us that at certain times it was located in the third house above Union on Front Street, that it was then moved to a small house next door above the "Catasauqua House," then to Church Street near Front, where Mrs. S. E. Creveling was postmistress; next to Front Street into a building nearly midway between Church and Bridge Streets, where Capt. W. H. Bartholomew was postmaster. During 1889 it was moved into the Swartz building, farther up in the block.

After the erection of our beautiful three-story post office building on the corner of Bridge and Railroad Streets, by capitalists identified with the National Bank of Catasauqua, and at a cost of $25,000, the weary wanderings of the post office ceased. In 1907 it was moved into its new and comfortable quarters.

Since the close of 1909, the department has maintained the carrier system. Three daily deliveries are made throughout the business portion of the town and two in the residential sections. Four collections are made from thirty-five boxes located in various parts of the town.

Post Office.

The force comprises a postmaster and an assistant; three clerks, auxiliary clerk and a special delivery messenger; four carriers, a sub-carrier and a mail messenger. A recent statement indicates the volume of business done at this office.

Daily mail handled:

    Outgoing (pieces) .... .2800

    Incoming (pieces) 1600

Registered mail during 1913:

    Outgoing (pieces) 2247

    Incoming (pieces) 2233

Stamped paper sold during 1913 ....$13,340

Domestic orders paid during 1913 ... .$21,950

Domestic orders issued during 1913 .. ..$34,048

International orders paid during 1913 ....$ 1,318

International orders issued during 1913 ....$ 3,426

The postmasters and their tenure of office are the following

Samuel Colver, 1844-46	Isabella D Duff, 1865-71
Nathan Fegley, 1846-50	Adaline Creveling, 1871-77
Joseph Laubach, 1850-53	Wm H. Bartholomew, 1877-89
Nathan Frederick, 1853-54	Edmund Randall, 1889-94
Augustus H Gilbert, 1854-55	Jonas F Moyer, 1894-98
Solomon Biery, 1855-61	Henry Davis, 1898-1900
Arnold C Lewis, March-Nov, 1861	Charles Graffin, 1900-08
Frank B Martin, 1861-62	Samuel S Graffin, 1908-
Charles D Fuller, 1862-65	

EXPRESSAGE AND TELEGRAPHY

Express accommodations have been quite satisfactory ever since the advent of the railroads David Kline, a painter by trade, is said to have been the first station master and freight agent at the Lehigh Valley depot He hauled many shipments across the bridge on a wheelbarrow

During the sixties a certain Mr Giering had charge of the "Central Express" office John Black succeeded him and moved the office into his drug store next door below the Catasauqua House Allen T Reber followed Mr Black and conducted the business in an office in the rear of the Eagle Hotel

The Philadelphia and Reading Railroad Company maintained an office on Front Street near Bridge, which was in charge of William Craig for a season Mr George Fuller succeeded Mr Craig The Philadelphia and Reading Express Company delivered over the Catasauqua and Fogelsville and the Central Railroad of New Jersey

During the eighties the United States Express Company supplanted the Philadelphia and Reading Express Company at Catasauqua and transferred the office to the depot of the Central Railroad of New Jersey Of the agents we note Messrs Jason C Miller and J P Hartman

On March 15, 1878, the long and sucessful career of Mr S B Harte as express agent at Catasauqua began He was first employed by the Central Express Company When the Central and the Adams Companies combined under the title of the Adams Express Company, Mr Harte was continued in charge

February 1, 1892, the Adams Express Company withdrew from the Lehigh Valley Railroad and the United States Express Company succeeded. The office at the Central Railroad of New Jersey depot was discontinued and all the business was transferred to Front Street, opposite the Eagle Hotel, and Mr Harte was in full charge of all the Express business of town

Mr S. B Harte resigned his position February 14, 1914, after a continuous service of 36 years. His son, Henry S Harte, succeeded him and proves himself a competent and pleasing incumbent

During December of 1912 the Adams Express Company established an office on Bridge Street as a sub-station of their Allentown office. N P Hanson served as agent for three months. Charles Solt followed him and after a brief tenure was succeeded by A T Henderson, the present agent

Miss Maggie Duff, daughter of Isabella D Duff, the post-mistress from 1865-71, served as telegraph operator in an office connected with the post office. Maggie is still sounding the keys in a Philadelphia office

If the names of all the telegraph operators who clicked the keys for Catasauqua's hurry-up calls were collected, they would form quite a roll. Records show that Peter J Eberhard rendered a lengthy service

When the Western Union Telegraph Company had established an office here, Mr S B Harte was employed as operator, May 15, 1876, which was two years before he took up the express agency. Thus Mr Harte was telegraph operator for the Borough for thirty-eight years. During Mr Harte's tenure, he taught and sent out, practically all over the United States, more than fifty graduate operators

In May, 1913, the Western Union telegraph office was moved to the depot of the Central Railroad of New Jersey and placed in charge of the agent, Preston H Ackey

STREET CARS.

There is probably no town in the whole Lehigh Valley so favorably situated for traveling facilities as Catasauqua. Workmen living in the remotest section of the Borough can reach trains or cars for destinations in all directions within less time than a twenty-minutes' walk

Catasauqua is almost centrally located between the great cement mills to the north and the mammoth iron works to the south of her, and although she has a fair proportion of mills and works of various descriptions within her own limits, she rests beyond the reach of blighting cement clouds and blackening soft coal works.

When the opportunity came, the Borough Council promptly passed an ordinance, dated May 11, 1891, giving permission to the Allentown Passenger Railway Company to operate its railway within the limits of the Borough of Catasauqua, by electricity, and for that purpose to erect its poles, string its wires, etc

The ordinance stipulates that on improved streets the Company shall pave between the rails and two feet on the outer sides of the rails of their tracks in a manner as is directed by the Street Committee

It also restricts the Company to use the railway tracks within the Borough limits for no other purpose than to carry passengers On account of the inability of the old wooden bridge to carry the weight of tracks and trolley cars, the line was built from Allentown via Second, Chapel and Front Streets at Fullerton, to the west end of the bridge

So as to maintain charter-rights, tracks were laid from the canal bridge on Race Street to the Horse Shoe works on Front Street, and a little bounding horse car of the most ancient type constituted the equipment

When the iron bridge was completed, during 1893, the trolley cars ran through the town via Race and Front, Arch and Third Streets on a line dividing at the Hokendauqua bridge. One arm reaches out into Siegfried, Pa, and the other to Egypt, Pa Forty cars on their regular schedule run through the Borough to Siegfried, and thirty-nine to Egypt Besides these an extra service of seven cars daily between Allentown and Catasauqua during rush hours is maintained

The Allentown Passenger Railway Company metamorphosed into the Allentown and Lehigh Valley Traction Company, and, after another lapse of time, into the Lehigh Valley Transit Company The trackage of the complete system is 154 miles.

OF CATASAUQUA 19

On the 22nd day of December, 1903, the Borough Council passed an ordinance granting permission to the Hanover Central Electric Railway Company to lay and operate a double track trolley system, south on Howertown Avenue to Walnut, thence east on Walnut to American, south on American Street to Kurtz's Lane and east on Kurtz's Lane, now Wood Street, to the Borough limits The Hanover Electric was supposed to run via Schoenersville to Bethlehem—but there was no "Juice"

WATER

The first water works consisted of a well sunk by the Crane Company opposite the furnaces on Front Street, and a "Municipal pump," whence the whole community drew water The pump was made of a log-bored stock, octagonal in shape, and about fourteen inches in diameter, and a leather valve suction bucket, worked by an iron rod and a long iron handle balanced with a knob on the end

Around the old pump many an impromptu colloquy occurred by the chance meeting of friends and foes, men and maidens, the bearers of life's burdens and the carefree lovers of youth

The Lehigh Crane Iron Company more than fulfilled the conditions laid down in the proffers of the Lehigh Coal and Navigation Company and thus the water rights from the Hokendauqua to the Allentown dams were ceded to the former

In those days the crystal purity of the Lehigh River was not contaminated by sewer systems of various descriptions and, therefore, a pump was attached to the water wheel that drove the hot-blast for the furnaces, in order to draw water from the river for the town's use

David Thomas directed his son Samuel, who was then a student at Nazareth Hall, to stop off at Bethlehem and take measurements of the pump used there in order that he might have a model and some data to go by in the erection of Catasauqua's first water works The gentleman who generously supplied Mr Thomas with desired data was Richard W Leibert, who still resides in Bethlehem

The work of construction was begun before the charter grant was completed. A four-inch main was laid from the pump to Wood Street, to Second, up Second to Church, and up Church Street to a point above Limestone Street, where a basin or reservoir was built Water seeping through the walls of the basin softened the underlying strata of limestone and caused a number of caverns which were dangerous A large wooden tank was built beside the basin to serve its purpose

During 1854, a four-inch main was laid on Front Street to Bridge During 1856, a three-inch main was attached at Front and Bridge Streets, and continued up Bridge and Second Streets to the new residence of David Thomas, located at Second and Pine Streets The main on Front Street was extended to "Puddler's Row," above Chapel Street

During 1872, the Company expended over $25,000 on extensive improvements On some streets larger, and on others, new mains were laid

A new pumping station, twenty-three by twenty-five feet in dimensions, was built below furnace No 6 It was equipped with a steam pump in addition to the old water power system Its capacity was 185,000 gallons per day. To equalize the pressure on the mains and water pipes, a large stand pipe was erected in front of the pumping station

Toward the close of the nineteenth century, the Clear Springs Water Company was chartered and secured water rights on both sides of the river from Cementon to Allentown The Crane Company, through its receiver, returned the water rights in its name to the Lehigh Coal and Navigation Company, who, in turn, ceded the rights of the Catasauqua Water Works to the Clear Springs Water Company

Under date of August 28, 1903, an agreement was entered into by the Clear Springs Water Company and the Borough of Catasauqua, that the former supply the town according to the following schedule of net rates

One family, first spigot	$ 6 00
Bath tub	$ 3 00
Wash stand, first	$ 3 00
Closet, first	$ 3 00
Pave wash, each	$ 1 50

Stationary wash tub, first	$ 1 50
Steam or water heater	$ 1 50
Hotel	$50 00 to $100 00
Hydrants on streets	.$ 12 00
Beer pumps	$ 15 00
Fountains	.$ 7 50

A discount of twenty-five per cent. was allowed on all bills that were paid within twenty days from the first day of the month on which they were issued The above contract terminated December 31, 1907

Although the Clear Springs Water Company did all they could to furnish water desired by the consumer, there was constant complaint against the condition of the water furnished, and when the rates to consumers were announced in January, 1908, many discontinued the use of the water

The Fire and Water Committee was directed to inquire into conditions and ascertain the approximate cost of a municipal water plant

They inspected various plants, and invited engineers of experience to view the location selected for wells by a geologist sent by the State Board of Health.

A citizens' meeting was called in the Town Hall, Thursday, July 23, 1908, when it was proposed to ask the tax payers to agree to a loan of $80,000, to sink wells and proceed with the erection of a municipal plant The Council resolved unanimously to submit the matter to the tax-payers at the November election There were 776 votes in favor of a municipal plant, and 74 opposed to it

Two wells, ten inches in diameter, were sunk two hundred and forty feet into the earth at Walnut and St. John Streets, and were secured with a steel casement almost to their full depth Both wells were tested by air lifts for seven successive days and nights and proved to contain an inexhaustible supply The State Board certified to the absolute purity of the water

Drill-engineers were set to their task in March, 1910, and by October the pumps were in operation The men who deserve credit for this successful enterprise are Dr C J Keim, Burgess, and his councilmen, Henry W Stolz, Alfred J. Leh, Martin Graver, Thomas Jones, William McCandless, and Oscar Shugar

PUMPING STATION.

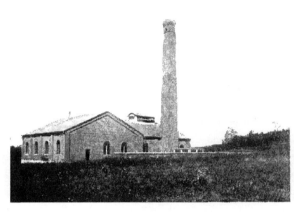

THE PUMPING STATION.

The pumping station is a one-story, fire-proof, brick building, large enough to double the capacity of its present equipment whenever needed. There are two 125 horse power high pressure tubular boilers, two one million gallon pumps, and two air compressors in operation.

The dimensions of the reservoir and aerator are seventy-two feet in diameter by fourteen feet, six inches in depth, and afford a capacity of 364,000 gallons. It is constructed of steel and concrete, and bears a roof of cement tiling, and screened ventilators, assuring protection against all impurities.

The Water Tower (stand-pipe) is located on Catasauqua's highest elevation, a spot near Sixth Street and half a block north of Walnut Street. It is of steel construction, fifteen feet in diameter and eighty feet high, with a capacity of 125,000 gallons.

The system of water mains consists of pipes, ranging from sixteen to six inches in diameter and totals an extension of seven miles. This system is divided into sixty-three districts, any and all of which may be closed off at will. Thus only the people of the square in which repairs are made need be inconvenienced for the time being. There are 790 taps from mains to houses and 75 hydrants.

Thirty-five Matthews-type hydrants with six-inch base connections, two two and one-half inch nozzles for hose, and one four-inch nozzle for steamer have been located at prominent street corners.

The average quantity of water pumped per week is 3,500,000 gallons, and the average consumption of coal is twenty tons weekly. The total receipts average $8,500 per annum.

DRINKING FOUNTAINS

Public spirited citizens attended a meeting in the fall of 1912 for the purpose of considering ways and means for the erection of drinking fountains for man and beast throughout the town. A committee charged with the matter was appointed. Captain Joseph Matchette, Chairman, Edmund Randall, H. H. Riegel, M D, William Weisley and Chester Frantz. The solicitors appointed by the committee were: John Moat, George T Boyer, Frank C Beck, Alvin A Houser, George O Houser, Reuben Weaver, and Cooper Weaver.

Four fountains (for man and beast), one for each Ward, and an extra one, on Front Street, were purchased for $380.00 from the J. L Mott Iron Works, New York, through the kind offices of Charles E Frederick.

The well known plumbing firm of Beck and Frey connected up the fountains at a cost of $120.00. Mrs. Kate Fuller generously paid for the fountain in the Fourth Ward.

FIRE PROTECTION.

At the suggestion of David Thomas, a meeting of the villagers was called, November 4, 1845, for the purpose of organizing a fire company. Thirty-seven men were in attendance.

Owen Rice	John Lees	David Thomas
John Kane	Noah Phillips	William J Aull
Edward Clark	Cochrane McLaughlin	John McIntyre
Henry E Kildare	Charles Dempsey	John Hunter
Isaac Miller	William Neligh	James Hunter
Thomas Dempsey	William Pollock	Alex. McCurdy
Alexander Miller	Jacob Smith	James Dempsey
Robert Campbell	Morgan Emanuel	Mark Dempsey
Richard Davis	Neil McKeever	Patrick Dempsey
George Jenkins	Thomas Miller	James McAllister
Arthur McQuade	Wm McClelland	John Clark
	John Thomas	
William Boyle	Samuel Thomas	William Davis

FIRST FIRE ENGINE.

They adopted the name, "The Humane Fire Company." The charter of incorporation was granted March 14, 1846. A hand force pump, attached to a large tank mounted on four wheels, was purchased from a Philadelphia Fire Company. The pump was operated by a pair of handles extending over the truck at either end. To give it full force the strength of twenty men was taxed. Under full pressure a strong stream could be thrown over the highest building in town. A bucket brigade from some neighboring well supplied the water in the tank.

The engine was housed in a frame building on Second Street, near Church Street, now the site of the Crane stables. There was also a hose carriage fully equipped to convey water from the plugs of the new water works to the engine tank, on streets where mains had been laid.

The destruction, by fire, of the machine shop of the Crane Company, in 1865, demonstrated the inefficiency of this primitive apparatus. Engine (handpump) and hose carriage were stripped of their brass mountings and taken to the ominous shades of an ancient tree near the round-house of the Catasauqua and Fogelsville Railroad, where their existence wasted like fadeth the aged couple that watcheth the last glimmer of light slowly dying away beyond the terraced heights of Fairview cemetery. It is a pity the old guard has not been sheltered and preserved for proud participation in the pageantry of Old Home Week.

THE PHOENIX FIRE COMPANY.

The Phoenix Steam Fire Company No. 1 was so named after a friendly company of this name in Easton, Pa., and was organized April 23, 1866, in the old Temperance Hall on Second Street, where the Crane stables now are.

The Crane Company had long since built the brick fire hall on Front Street, close by the old pump, for the Humane Company, which had disbanded prior to the organization of the Phoenix.

The first official board consisted of William Williams, president; W. H. Horn, secretary; David Davis, treasurer. The charter membership consisted of thirty men.

THE PHOENIX FIRE COMPANY.

From April to October, 1866, one hose carriage was the only apparatus the company had. This was purchased from a Philadelphia party by Thomas Jones and William McMonigal. There were also a few hand chemical fire extinguishers. The company was also granted the use of the old pump-engines still stored in the Fire House.

A steam engine was purchased from the Button Fire Engine Company, Waterford, N Y, and was delivered at Catasauqua, November, 1866 During the eighties another hose carriage, a gig and hook and ladder truck were purchased

When the Unicorn Silk Mill was destroyed by fire, the engine was so badly damaged that it was condemned At this fire two prominent members of the Phoenix Company perished John A. Good and Charles Frick

A new and larger fire engine was purchased from the Button Fire Engine Company, November, 1890 This engine is still in use. The present outfit of the Phoenix Company consists of the engine, two hose carriages, one gig, one hook and ladder truck and twelve hundred feet of hose.

Prior to the erection of the Town Hall, 1868, the Company was quartered in the Fire Engine House on Front Street In the Town Hall the members enjoy the comforts of a large parlor, and an assembly room containing pool tables and other devices for entertainment.

The present officials are President, Robert P Richter, Vice-President, Norman Steinhilber; Treasurer, Oliver Griffith, Secretary, Francis H Sheckler. The Company had an enrollment of two hundred and one members

THE SOUTHWARK HOSE COMPANY NO 9

The Crane Iron Company purchased from the Southwark Hose Company No 9, located at Third and Lombard Streets, Philadelphia, Pa., their steamer "A" This was a first class engine with a rotary style pump. The Philadelphia Company requested that the name Southwark and the No 9 be continued with the engine.

The Southwark Hose Company No 9 was therefore organized February 4, 1873, in Foy's Hall with John Williams as chairman and David T Williams as secretary pro tem All the charter members of the Southwark were employees of the Crane Iron Company

The initial officials were · President, Charles W. Chapman, Vice-President, Joseph Hunt, Secretary, David T Williams, Treasurer, Robert E. Williams.

The Southwark Hose Company No. 9 of Philadelphia, Pa, presented its namesake at Catasauqua with all the books, seal, charter hats, and belts owned by them. The books show that the Southwark of Philadelphia was organized May 6, 1806.

Having overhauled the engine, the Crane Company presented it to the Southwark people, with the proviso that they be granted the use of it whenever desired.

The original house of the company was the Crane pattern house on Front and Wood Streets. It not being desirable to continue housing this company in their pattern house, the Crane Company built the two-story fire engine house for the Southwark Company on the corner of Second and Church Streets.

SOUTHWARK ENGINE HOUSE.

The building is well equipped for the comfort and pleasure of its members. Steam heat is carried to it by pipes extending from the furnaces to the hall. In recent years a hose-tower has also been erected. The members of the Phoenix Fire Company have been noble minded and fraternal toward their new neighbors.

The first parade of the Southwark Hose Company No. 9 followed an invitation by the Phoenix, April 19, 1873; and on Thanksgiving Day of the same year, the former were ushered from the pattern shop to their new home by the latter. Joshua Hunt made the presentation speech for the Crane, and R. Clay Hemmersley responded for the Fire Department.

For a number of years the Crane Company aided the Southwark Hose Company No. 9 to the amount of ten dollars per month, until April 15, 1895, when the latter became a part of the Catasauqua Fire Department.

The Southwark people purchased from the Silsby Fire Engine Company, June 6, 1890, the engine still in use.

While in active service at the Unicorn Silk Mill fire, April 24, 1890, John Graffin was caught under a tottering wall and was so seriously injured, that death soon followed. The present officials are:

President, John McCandless; Vice-President, Wilson Scott; Secretary, C. E. Sheckler, Jr.; Treasurer, Edwin O. Oldt.

THE CHAROTIN HOSE CO. NO. 1.

The incorporation of North Catasauqua as a borough was effected during 1908. The growing sentiment for adequate fire protection found full expression at a citizens' meeting held November 15, 1909. Thomas Quinn, Justice of the Peace, presided.

"Charotin" is based on a tradition which says that the Indian Chief Charotin granted to white settlers the tract of land now comprehended in North Catasauqua. From this tradition springs the name, "The Charotin Hose Company No 1"

Burgess Fred W Hunter and Council prevailed upon the Clear Springs Water Company to lay additional water mains and install fire hydrants The same Council purchased a desirable plot of ground from the Lackawanna Land Company and began a movement favoring the erection of a municipal building and Fire Engine House.

By a special ballot of the citizens in July, 1910 it was decreed that the building should be erected Building operations began in April, and by October 14, 1911, its dedication took place The new building is located on the corner of Sixth and Arch Streets. It contains a large assembly room on the second floor, an apparatus and lounging room on the main floor and a banquet hall in the basement.

Its equipment consists of a combination Chemical Hose and Ladder Truck, purchased by popular subscription, and one thousand feet of rubber composition hose, provided by Council The company consists of one hundred sixty-three members, and has an enviable record for successful combats with devouring flames They belong to the State and Four County Firemen's Association with a standing of a high order, and therefore merit implicit confidence and liberal support Its present officers are President, William Thomas, Secretary, Clarence Kriebel; Treasurer, Clifford C Young

THE EAST END INDEPENDENT HOSE AND CHEMICAL COMPANY NO I

Individual opinions and desires of leading citizens of the new Third Ward gradually moulded men's minds into favoring the organization of a Fire Company An initial citizens' meeting was held at the Fairmount Hotel, June 7, 1911, at which prominent citizens of the Borough addressed their fellowmen On June 21st, another meeting was called, a company organized, and officers elected.

The title adopted was "The East End Chemical and Hose Company No 3" When the Borough Council could not see its way clear to grant recognition to this newly organized Fire Company, as was reported by their committee, July

8, 1911, it was resolved to change the name to "The East End Independent Hose and Chemical Company No. 1."

Meetings were held, by the courtesy of the School Board, in the vacated school house on North Fourteenth Street in the Third Ward. By popular subscriptions, festivals, etc., sufficient funds were accumulated to warrant the purchase of three hundred feet of hose, a hose cart, and a plot of ground on Race Street as a first step toward the erection of a Fire Hall.

EAST END FIRE COMPANY.

A resolution to proceed with building operations was adopted May 1, 1913. The building is a one-story brick structure, twenty by sixty feet in dimensions, and equipped with the latest conveniences and appliances. The charter membership consisted of eighty-five men, and the present enrollment is one hundred fifty. The present officers are: President, Harvey W. Snyder; Vice-President, Wayne Frantz; Secretary, Clarence C. Kurtz; Treasurer, F. R. A. Goldsmith.

LIGHT, HEAT AND POWER.

The first street lighting in the Borough and vicinity was by open flame gas burners on lamp posts. When, during very cold weather, the service leading to the lamps would freeze, the system became practically useless.

The Catasauqua Gas Company was chartered during 1856, and was one of the oldest gas companies in the Lehigh Valley.

Production by coal cost the consumer four dollars fifty cents per thousand feet. Water-gas, or the manufacture of gas from oil, was a later product. Although the generating set for this production of gas is still intact, it is not in operation

In 1900, the Catasauqua Gas Company was consolidated with the Consumers' and the People's Gas Companies into the Northampton Gas and Electric Company In November, 1907, a Bondholders' Committee reorganized the Lehigh-Northampton Gas and Electric Company into the Lehigh-Northampton Light, Heat and Power Company, which through a Bondholders' Committee disposed of the gas portion to the Allentown-Bethlehem Gas Company, Lessee, December 23, 1913

The production of gas for the year 1913 was 19,000,000 feet, which was consumed by 1153 patrons in Catasauqua, North Catasauqua, Coplay, Northampton, Hokendauqua, and West Catasauqua.

The approximate length of gas-mains is fifteen miles, and the value of the property is about one hundred fifty thousand dollars

The Allentown-Bethlehem Gas Company proposes to enlarge mains and service pipes, and to extend lines on streets not now supplied

The Catasauqua Electric Light and Power Company was organized in 1890, and on April 7th of the same year, Town Council granted the new company the right to occupy the streets of the Borough with poles and wires as was necessary for the conduct of its business

The generating system was of the old Edison, three wire direct current style, which is now practically obsolete in the Lehigh Valley In 1900, the Catasauqua Electric Light and Power Company, the Northampton Electric Company and the Lehigh County Electric Company were consolidated with the gas companies mentioned above, into the Lehigh-Northampton Gas and Electric Company

In November, 1907, a Bondholders' Committee reorganized the Lehigh-Northampton Gas and Electric Company into the Lehigh-Northampton Light, Heat and Power Company, which, through a Bondholders' Committee disposed of the electric portion to the Lehigh Valley Light and Power Company

From the beginning, progress was not very rapid until about 1900, when alternating current was distributed to what is now termed the Borough of

Northampton on the east, and the Borough of Coplay on the west side of the river.

During 1890, the gas street-lighting was discontinued and the ordinary thirty-two candle power lamps substituted, which was the system of street lighting in the Borough of Catasauqua until 1900, at which time a contract was made with the Borough to furnish arc lamps to aid deficient service.

LEHIGH—NORTHAMPTON POWER HOUSE.

At present, a new style system, termed series street-lighting, is used in connection with the arc lamps. This is a great improvement over the old style system used in 1890.

During the past few years, electricity for motive power has been introduced and is rapidly supplanting the smaller isolated installation; and, with the cost of manufacturing current being reduced yearly, it will become a matter of economy for some larger manufacturers to substitute electric current for motive power

The territory being served with electricity consists of the Boroughs of Catasauqua, North Catasauqua, Coplay, Northampton, and Fullerton and Egypt The number of consumers is one thousand, and the value of the plant is estimated at two hundred thousand dollars.

COMMUNICATION

Two telephone lines place Catasauqua in communication with the rest of the world, and the fact that two exchange stations are located here shows that this is a centre of the language commerce of the earth

Town Council passed an ordinance, April 7, 1890, granting the Bell Telephone Company of Pennsylvania the right to occupy highways and streets with poles and wires for the proper conduct of its business and satisfactory service of its patrons

The Company pays into the Borough treasury the sum of twenty-five cents per annum for each pole bearing not over four wires, and an additional five cents for each additional wire raised The service of the Bell is superb Six operators are in charge of Catasauqua's Exchange, and the number of patrons in the Borough at present is two hundred thirty-one

On Febuary 5, 1900, Council passed an ordinance granting privilege to the Lehigh Telephone Company to enter town and conduct business The Company paid the expenses incurred in draughting and publishing the ordinance, and agreed to supply the fire-engine houses, office of the Chief of Police and Council chamber with phones free of charge

The franchises granted by this ordinance shall not be assignable or transferrable without the consent of the Borough authorities on pain of forfeiture of said rights and franchises.

The services of the Lehigh have improved steadily until today they compare favorably with the best The Exchange is manipulated by five persons, and the number of patrons in town is one hundred seventy-six

A wise and proper provision with all parties, erecting poles and stringing wires in the Borough of Catasauqua, is that the Borough reserves the right to place fire alarm apparatus on poles, and string wires upon them, as may be expedient

POLICE FORCE

The first High Constable of whom we have found any record was Charles Sigley, who was appointed March 18, 1853 An ordinance prescribing certain rules for the government of the department was passed in 1870 Bartley Clark was then High Constable and William Koons his assistant

Charles E Sheckler was appointed June 7, 1875, and has served as public guardian ever since, save a brief intermission of four years, 1908-1912, when J Henry Leickel was chief of Police

Chief Sheckler is a familiar figure on our streets which he guards zealously against vagrants and the scions of evil and harm Our Lockup is not an institution which inspires much of aesthetics but it serves our Borough well as a terror to evil doers It is a dark background to the sublime picture of human being out of which the penitent errorist may the better behold the beauty of a righteous life and solemnly resolved to walk in the rays of its happy day, when freedom's air is breathed again

It is interesting to note the names of men who wore brass buttons and swung the Billy to the measured time of their gait

John Hinely	Joseph Schwab	Edward Allender
Charles Sigley	E F Huffort	George Shellard
John Wint	Osbin Laub	Chester Meitz
Peter Loux	William Bloss	Jerry Schoenenberger
Henry Sellers	Hopkin Hopkins	William Mason
Mr McKeifer	William Moat	Elias Bush
Joseph Lazarus	Edward Bickel	Andrew Smith
Bartley Clark	Joseph Mertz	Howard Benvenuti
W A Hilbert	Andrew Smith	Alvin Roth

HEALTH

On the fifth day of June, 1893, Town Council passed an ordinance whereby a Board of Health was created for Catasauqua In compliance with an Act of Assembly, the Borough was divided into five Districts The Secretary of the

Board and the Health Officer were placed under bond to the amount of one hundred dollars and three hundred dollars, respectively

An ordinance of thirty-two sections was adopted by the Board, June 13, 1893, giving directions for the removal of obnoxious or infectious matter, warning against wilful filthiness, and prescribing the best methods of preventing the spread of disease

The Health Officer is amenable to many rules, chief among which is the duty to inspect cellars and other apartments of the homes of the Borough with a view to cleanliness and the health and happiness of our people.

Austin A Glick, Esq, has served as secretary of the Board since its organization The Health Officers were William K Biery, January 6, 1893 to March 2, 1896, Stephen Frick, March 2, 1896 to May 31, 1909, James Dyatt, May 31, 1909 to August 3, 1913, C Frank Hunsicker, August 5, 1913—

The members of the Board besides Secretary Glick are. President, James M Le Milson, M D, Oscar J Stine, Clifford H Riegel, and Amandus Boyer

THE CATASAUQUA CHARITY SOCIETY

At a public meeting held Tuesday evening, January 24, 1911, in the Bridge Street Presbyterian Church, at which every congregation in town was represented, a unanimous vote was cast to organize a Charity Society Mrs Jennie A Griffith of Easton addressed the meeting and gave valuable information as to the manner and method of conducting such a society

Dr. Charles L Fry presented a constitution and by-laws, which were unanimously adopted The reasons for such an organization are the following

"To promote effective co-operation between Churches and private agencies that relief, when needed, shall be adequate and shall be obtained from proper sources, to prevent imposition and unwise duplication of relief, to investigate applications for relief, to keep permanent records of all cases investigated, to organize a body of friendly visitors who shall personally attend upon cases needing counsel and advice; to procure work for poor persons who are capable of being wholly or partially self-supporting, to repress mendicancy by the above means and by the prosecution of impostors "

The following officers were elected: H J Reinhard, President; A A Glick, Secretary, H R Hall, Treasurer, J. Arthur Williams, Joseph Matchette, P J Laubach, J. F. Moyer, E J Lawall and William Weisley, Board of Managers

The receipts for the three years of its existence are $800 07 and the expenditures $768.01.

The officers of the Society at present are: H. J. Reinhard, President; A A Glick, Secretary, J. Arthur Williams Treasurer, J. F Moyer, E J Lawall, J S Stillman, Arthur A. Greene, Edmund Randall, Joseph Matchette, Board of Managers.

CIVIC LEAGUE.

During the fall and early winter months of 1912, a number of the ladies of town attended a very wholesome Mission Study Class in the Chapel of the First Presbyterian Church Through the influence of their study, and the mutual conference it afforded, a temper for local betterment was awakened It therefore was resolved, January, 1913, to organize a Civic League of Catasauqua and to abet any and every measure that tends to improve and beautify the place of our abode

Women of other cities and towns were invited to address the League Much valuable information was attained and the ardor of the ladies enkindled not a little. Forty names were enrolled at its inception Through the courtesy of the School Board their meetings are held in the High School Building A concert by the Muhlenberg Glee Club in the High School Auditorium netted them some cash, which added to their small treasury, raised by means of dues from their members, enabled them to purchase waste-material receptacles which are located at certain vantage points in the town

Their officers are: Mrs Harry Barnhurst, President, Miss Dorothy Williams, Secretary, Miss Ella Schneller, Treasurer

CRANE IRON WORKS.

CHAPTER II—INDUSTRIES

CRANE IRON WORKS.

Before proceeding to the statement of certain historical facts regarding this Company, it will no doubt prove interesting to introduce such information as is available regarding the first use of Anthracite coal in the manufacture of pig iron in the United States

We are celebrating in Catasauqua in the year 1914, the seventy-fifth anniversary of the erection of blast furnaces from which pig iron was first produced on July 4, 1840, and at which plant Anthracite coal has continued to be used in the making of pig iron at Catasauqua almost continuously since the erection of the first furnace until the present year, and it might be of further interest to note here the fact that the year in which this celebration is being held marks the first year in the history of the furnace plant in which Anthracite coal has not to some extent been used as a fuel for the making of pig iron

It is not claimed by any one with a knowledge of the history of pig iron manufacture that the furnaces at Catasauqua produced the first pig iron made by the use of Anthracite coal in the United States, but it is true that the furnaces here, erected in 1839, were the first of all the early Anthracite furnaces which were completely successful from an engineering and commercial standpoint and which continued to manufacture pig iron successfully by using Anthracite coal, over a long period of time

We quote from several authentic articles on this subject as these contain the most carefully compiled information in existence with regard to this branch of the iron industry. The following extract is made from a report of the Pennsylvania Board of Centennial Managers to the Pennsylvania Legislature at the Session of 1878 and forms a part of a volume entitled "Introduction to a History of Pig Iron Making and Coal Mining in Pennsylvania" by James M Swank, who was the Secretary of the American Iron & Steel Association for forty years, his term of service beginning January 1, 1873

"Down to 1838 all the blast furnaces in the United States, with the exception of a few coke furnaces, used charcoal for fuel In that year pig iron was successfully made in Pennsylvania from anthracite coal We present below a complete account of the first steps that were taken to use the new fuel in blast furnaces.

In 1840 Jesse B Quinby testified, in the suit of Farr & Kunzi against the Schuylkill Navigation Company, that he used anthracite coal at Harford furnace, Maryland, mixed with one-half charcoal, in 1815. He believed himself to be the first person in the United States to use anthracite coal in smelting iron In 1826 The Lehigh Coal & Navigation Company erected near Mauch Chunk a small furnace intended to use anthracite in smelting iron The enterprise was not successful. In 1827 unsuccessful experiments in smelting iron with anthracite coal from Rhode Island were made at one of the small furnaces in Kingston, Plymouth County, Massachusetts These experiments failed because the blast used was cold About 1827 a similar failure in the use of anthracite took place at Vizille, in France Doubtless other unsuccessful attempts than those here recorded were made to smelt iron ore with anthracite coal, but these were probably the earliest

In 1828 James B Neilson, of Scotland, obtained a patent for the use of hot air in the smelting of iron ore in blast furnaces, and in 1837 the smelting of iron ore with anthracite coal by means of the Neilson hot-blast was successfully accomplished by George Crane, at his iron-works at Ynyscedwin, in Wales Mr Crane began the use of a blast furnace obtaining 36 tons a week In May of that year Solomon W Roberts of Philadelphia visited his works and witnessed the complete success of the experiment. Mr. Crane had taken out a patent on the 28th of September, 1836, for smelting iron ore with anthracite coal. Upon the recommendation of Mr Roberts, after his return from Wales, the Lehigh Crane Iron Company was organized in 1838 to manufacture pig iron from the anthracite coal of the Lehigh Valley In that year Erskine Hazard went to Wales for the company and there made himself acquainted with the process of making anthracite iron He ordered to be made such machinery as was necessary, under the direction of George Crane, the inventor, and engaged David Thomas, who was familiar with the process to take charge of the erection of the works, and the manufacture of the iron Mr Thomas arrived in the summer of 1839, and to his faithful and intelligent management much of the success of the enterprise is due The first furnace of this company was successfully blown in on the 4th of July, 1840 But it was not the first successful anthracite furnace in this country, as will presently appear

On the 19th of December, 1833, a patent was granted to Dr F W Geissenheimer, of New York, for smelting iron ore with anthracite coal, by the applica tion of heated air. Dr Geissenheimer made experiments in smelting iron ore with anthracite at the Valley furnace, northeast of Pottsville, but they were not successful, although the results achieved were highly encouraging ''

There are mentioned several experimental operations at Cressons, Schuylkill County, at South Easton, Northampton County, and at Mauch Chunk during the years from 1836 to 1839

He continues:—

"The next furnace to use anthracite was the Pioneer, built in 1837 and 1838 at Pottsville, by William Lyman, of Boston, under the auspices of Burd Patterson, and blast was unsuccessfully applied July 10, 1839 Benjamin Perry, who had blown in the coke furnace at Farrandsville, then took charge of it, and blew it in October 19, 1839, with complete success This furnace was blown by steam-power The blast was heated in ovens at the base of the furnace, with anthracite, to a temperature of 600 degrees, and supplied through three tuyeres at a pressure of 2 to 2½ lbs per square inch The product was about 28 tons a week of good foundry iron. The furnace continued in blast for some time A premium of $5,000 00 was paid by Nicholas Biddle and others to Mr Lyman, as the first person in the United States who had made anthracite pig iron continuously for one hundred days Danville furnace, in Montour County, was built by Biddle, Chambers & Co, and was successfully blown in with anthracite in April, 1840, producing 35 tons of iron weekly with steam-power Roaring Creek furnace, in Montour County, built by Burd Patterson & Co, was next blown in with anthracite, May 18,, 1840, and produced 40 tons of iron weekly with water-power A charcoal furnace at Phoenixville, built in 1837 by Reeves, Buck & Co, was blown in with anthracite, June 17, 1840, by William Firmstone, and produced from 28 to 30 tons of pig iron weekly with water-power The hot-blast stove which was planned and erected by Julius Guiteau of the Mauch Chunk furnace, was situated on one side of the tunnel head, and heated by the escaping flame of the furnace. This furnace continued in blast until 1841 Columbia furnace at Danville, was built in 1839 by George Patterson, and blown in with anthracite by Mr Perry on July 2, 1840, and made from 30 to 32 tons of iron weekly, using steam-power The next furnace to use anthracite, and the last one we shall mention was built at Catasauqua, for the Lehigh Crane Iron Co, in 1839, by David Thomas It was successfully blown in by him on the 4th of July, 1840, as we have stated, and produced 50 tons a week of good foundry iron, water-power being used.

It will be observed that while Mr Neilson invented the hot blast, Dr Geissenheimer was the first to propose the use of anthracite coal by means of heated air for the manufacture of pig iron, and that Mr Crane was the first to successfully apply the hot blast of Mr Neilson for this purpose Dr Geissenheimer experimented as early as 1833 with ovens for heating air before its introduction into the blast furnace in which anthracite was used as a fuel, and his patent bears date of that year, but his invention was not successfully applied until after Mr Crane had made iron at Ynyscedwin Dr Geissenheimer is entitled to the honor of having proposed what Mr. Crane was the first to accomplish His patent limited to the United States, was purchased by Mr Crane, who, in November, 1838, patented some addition to it in this country The patent was never enforced here, but Mr Crane compelled the ironmasters of Great Britain to pay him tribute Dr Geissenheimer died at Lebanon, Pa, where he had long resided

The discovery in 1839 and 1840, that anthracite coal could be successfully used in the manufacture of pig iron gave a great impetus to the iron industry in Maryland, New Jersey and New York, as well as in Pennsylvania The rich magnetic ores of New Jersey were first smelted with anthracite coal by Edwin Post, Esq, at Stanhope, in 1840 On the 1st of January, 1876, there were 225 anthracite furnaces in the country, 161 in Pennsylvania ''

Vol III of the Transactions of the American Institute of Mining Engineers contains a ''Sketch of the Early Anthracite Furnaces'' by William Firmstone, Glendon Iron Works, Easton, Pa, this paper having been submitted at a meeting of the Association held in Hazleton in October, 1874

He refers to the erection of the first furnace at Catasauqua and concludes

''With the erection of this furnace commenced the era of higher and larger furnaces and better blast machinery, with consequent improvements in yield and quality of iron produced

It was the commencement of an enterprise that, under the able management of Mr Thomas, resulted in building up one of the largest and most successful works in the Lehigh Valley, now consisting of six blast furnaces, some of them 60 feet high and 17 or 18 feet in the boshes, producing 250 tons of pig iron a week, and using the escaping gas to raise steam and heat the blast ''

In the year 1892 there was published a ''History of the Manufacture of Iron in all ages, and particularly in the United States from Colonial times to 1891.'' The author of this history was James M Swank, to whom reference is made above, and in his preface to this edition, Mr. Swank states

''In the collection of the materials for this volume I have been exceedingly fortunate in possessing a personal acquaintance with most of the leading actors in the wonderful development of our American iron industry during the present century, and in learning from their own lips and from their own letters many of the incidents of that development It is the exact truth to say that, if the preparation of this history had been delayed for a few years, it could not have been written, for many of these pioneers are now dead ''

This latter contribution may therefore be regarded as an authority with respect to the subject which it covers, and we quote from it a single paragraph

"David Thomas was born on November 3, 1794, at a place called, in English, Grey House, within two and a half miles of the town of Neath, in the County of Glamorgan, South Wales He landed in the United States on June 5, 1839, and on July 9th of that year commenced to build the furnace at Catasauqua He died at Catasauqua on June 20, 1882, in his 88th year At the time of his death he was the oldest ironmaster in the United States in length of service, and he was next to Peter Cooper, the oldest in years David Thomas's character and services to the American iron trade are held in high honor by all American iron and steel manufacturers He is affectionately styled the Father of the American anthracite iron industry, because the furnace built under his directions at Catasauqua and blown in by him was the first of all the early anthracite furnaces that was completely successful, both from an engineering and a commercial standpoint, and also because he subsequently became identified with the manufacture of anthracite pig iron on a more extensive scale than any of his contemporaries He was the founder of the Thomas Iron Company, at Hokendauqua, which has long been at the head of the producers of anthracite pig iron. The first two furnaces of this Company were built by Mr Thomas in 1855."

It will be observed that in this statement, Mr Swank gives us in a very few words the historical position of Catasauqua with relation to the use of anthracite coal in the manufacture of pig iron

CORPORATE EXISTENCE

A charter was granted to the Lehigh Crane Iron Company on May 16, 1839, for twenty-five years under an Act of the Legislature of Pennsylvania entitled "An Act to encourage the manufacture of iron with coke or mineral coal and for other purposes," passed June 16, 1836 The charter was renewed in 1864 for a further term of twenty-five years, expiring in 1889

In 1872, when an increase was being made in the Capital Stock, the corporate name of the Lehigh Crane Iron Company was changed to "The Crane Iron Company"

The property, rights, franchises and privileges were transferred on January 30, 1895, to the Crane Iron Works, the existing corporation, which was, upon application, granted a perpetual charter on October 8, 1908

ACQUISITION OF RIGHTS

The Lehigh Coal & Navigation Company, feeling that their interests would be promoted by securing the business of manufacturing iron from the use of anthracite coal to be extensively established along the line of their canal improvements and in order to encourage and induce the same, at a meeting of their Board of Directors held July 2, 1839, passed the following resolution —

"*Resolved,* That the Lehigh Coal & Navigation Company will give in fee simple all the water power of any one of the Dams between Allentown and Parryville except so much thereof as may in the opinion of the Managers be necessary for the Navigation and Two hundred inches of water under a Three feet head at each Lock for propelling Boats and other crafts on the said Navigation, to any Company or individuals or their assigns who shall actually expend or cause to be expended Thirty Thousand Dollars in improving the Site for Iron Works and in making the experiment of Manufacturing iron from the Ore with anthracite coal, should this amount be required to be expended before succeeding in the manufacture of iron The fee of the water power to become vested in the said Company or individuals or their assigns either upon their succeeding in making iron at the rate of twenty-seven tons a week, or in case of failure when they shall show to the satisfaction of the Lehigh Coal & Navigation Company that the sum of Thirty Thousand Dollars has been expended as above mentioned in making the attempt The land belonging to the Company suitable for using the said water power upon, and not necessary for the navigation, shall be included in the Deed Should they succeed in making iron with anthracite coal, then not more than one fourth of the water power thus granted shall be used for any other purpose than in the manufacture of iron from the Ore, or in the manufacture of articles from iron thus made The water in all cases to be so drawn as not to interfere with the navigation and subject to the regulations contained in the Company's printed deeds The dam must be specified and the work commenced by the first of September One Thousand Eight Hundred and Thirty Nine, and at least Fifteen Thousand Dollars expended in the work within two years from that date "

On July 8, 1839, the Lehigh Crane Iron Company signified their acceptance of the proposal of the Lehigh Coal & Navigation Company, which had subsequently been confirmed by action of its stockholders, and on December 15, 1840, the Lehigh Crane Iron Co , having fulfilled the conditions imposed, were granted a conveyance of the property and water rights by the Lehigh Coal & Navigation Co.

In a report submitted by the President to the stockholders of the Crane Iron Company on May 28, 1884, the following information with regard to the erection, dismantling and replacement of the furnaces is given —

"The first furnace, commonly designated as No 1, was constructed in the year 1840, and was 45 feet in height x 11 feet bosh

Furnace No 2 was built in 1842, and was 45 x 13 feet

Furnace No. 3, in 1846, was 55 x 16½ feet

All of these furnaces were fitted up with iron hot stoves, and the three had a total average weekly capacity of about 420 tons

In 1879, No. 3 fell down, and it was then determined to remove the three old stacks, and to erect new ones upon the sites of Nos 1 and 3, and to place fire-brick hot stoves upon the ground formerly occupied by stack No 2 Nos 1 and 2 were accordingly torn down in 1880, and the new No 3 was completed and blown in in November, 1880

The new No. 3 is 60 x 17, and the new No 1 was completed in 1881, and is 75 x 18 feet

The cost of new No 1 was $103,461 74, and of No 3, $96,211 10 The old boilers had been in use from the original erection of the plant and were no longer safe They were replaced with new steel boilers, which with the boiler house cost $84,410 23.

The increased capacity of the new furnaces required additional blowing engines, and two new engines were furnished by the I P Morris Company and put in operation in January, 1884, at a cost of $31,283 43

These expenditures have been fully justified by the result As compared with the old furnaces, which they have replaced, there has been a saving of ½ ton of fuel to a ton of iron, and an average saving of about 75 per cent per ton in labor

The new furnaces have not yet done as well as may reasonably be expected, but No 1 furnace made 22,281½ tons in the year 1883, of which 19,600 tons were foundry iron, and No 3 furnace made 19,507½ tons, of which 15,443 tons were foundry iron The largest weekly output of No 1 furnace was 510 tons The largest weekly output of No 3 was 450 tons

The dates of construction and sizes of remaining furnaces are as follows —

No 4, 1849	55 x 17½
No. 5, 1850	...60 x 17½
No 6, 1868	.60 x 17½

Of these, No 4 requires to be relined, No 5 (which has fire-brick hot stoves erected in the year 1877) is in blast, and No 6 is ready to be blown in when desired The capacity of the five furnaces is about 1800 tons weekly, or 90,000 tons a year."

It will be seen therefore that in 1884, five furnaces remained as follows:—

```
No. 1, 1880 .................................. 75 x 18
No. 3, 1881 .................................. 65 x 17
No. 4, 1849 .................................. 55 x 17½
No. 5, 1850 .................................. 60 x 17½
No. 6, 1868 .................................. 60 x 17½
```

In 1889 No. 3 furnace was raised to the height of 75 feet and continued standing until the latter part of 1913 when it was dismantled. No. 4 furnace was blown out in July, 1890, and several years later was dismantled. No. 5 furnace was torn down in 1908 and a furnace known as No. 2, size 80 x 17½, was erected on this site. No. 6 was torn down in 1904, and the plant therefore consists of only two furnaces at this time known as Nos. 1 and 2, the combined annual capacity of which is about 130,000 tons.

EMPIRE STEEL & IRON COMPANY.

The Empire Steel & Iron Company was incorporated under the laws of the State of New Jersey, March 13, 1899, acquiring and operating blast furnaces in Pennsylvania, New Jersey, Virginia and North Carolina. The Company has disposed of its holdings in the South and now operates furnaces at Topton and Macungie, Pennsylvania, and Oxford, New Jersey, and extensive magnetic ore mines at Oxford and Mount Hope, New Jersey.

EMPIRE OFFICE.

The Company also controls, through stock ownership, the Crane Iron Works, Catasauqua, Pa., the Crane Railroad Company, Catasauqua, Pa., Mount Hope Mineral Railroad Company in New Jersey, and the Victoria Coal & Coke Company in West Virginia

From its New Jersey Ore Mines is supplied a large proportion of the ore used in the operation of its furnaces, and the development of these mining properties has been carried forward along modern lines in the past few years, resulting in a largely increased output

The General Offices of the Company have been located at Catasauqua since June 1, 1900

THE THOMAS IRON COMPANY

Eighteen interested people attended an initial meeting called to discuss plans for the organization of an Iron Company This meeting was held February 14, 1854, at Mrs White's tavern on Centre Square, Easton, Pa The building is now used by the United States Government as the Post Office of the city of Easton A resolution was adopted calling the Company "The Thomas Iron Company" in honor of David Thomas who projected it, and in recognition of his work as pioneer in the successful manufacture of iron by the use of anthracite coal

The capital stock was fixed at two hundred thousand ($200,000) dollars, steps taken to procure a charter and a committee appointed to select and purchase a site for the works David Thomas was authorized to purchase the Thomas Butz farm situated on the west bank of the Lehigh River, about a mile above Catasauqua, as the most eligible site for the works The farm contained 185 acres 90 perches and the price paid for it was $37,,112 50 The deed passed July 7, 1854.

The Board of Managers resolved, March 14, 1854, to construct two blast furnaces, known as Nos 1 and 2 Contract for the mason work was given May 10th to Samuel McHose of Allentown, Pa Samuel Kinsey was employed as the first bookkeeper and his services continued for twenty-four years

A contract for the first two boilers was made April 7, 1854, at a cost of $9,353 on the wharf at Brooklyn; and for two beam blowing engines on boat

THE THOMAS IRON COMPANY PLANT.

at Cold Springs, N Y., at $42,600 The engines had steam cylinders of 56 inches diameter, and blowing cylinders of 84 inches diameter by nine feet stroke.

At a meeting of the Board of Directors, June 8, 1854, the name of the place of the furnaces was selected and adopted The suggestion had been made to call it Coplay—the town above it being called "Schriber's" at this time But after some discussion the suggestion of Hokendauqua, by David Thomas, was adopted

"Hokendauqua derives its name from a small creek which empties into the Lehigh on the eastern side, about half a mile above the village It is an Indian word, 'Hockin' in the Delaware Indian language signifying 'Landing ' The name, in fact, was not given to a stream of water, but was an exclamation used by the Indians at the time the first Irish settlers located there in 1730 It was probably made use of in speaking to the surveyors, a large portion of the streams were named in this manner by the surveyors " (See Henry's "History of the Lehigh Valley," page 300)

On November 9, 1854, the town was laid out, and the streets named Homes were built in 1868 for the General Superintendent, the Superintendent and other members of the staff. Rows of brick houses were also erected for the employees of the Company The town has been supplied with spring water, pumped from a spring on the river bank, since 1855 The Company also donated land for a school house and for the Presbyterian Church

The following list shows the date when each of the six furnaces at Hokendauqua first produced pig iron (list made in 1904)

Furnace	Date	Present Size
No 1	June 3, 1855	17 by 80 feet
No. 2	October 27, 1855	Abandoned
No 3	July 18, 1862	17 by 80 feet
No 4	April 29, 1863	Abandoned
No 5	September 15, 1873	17 by 60 feet
No 6	January 19, 1874	17 by 60 feet

The Thomas Iron Company owns furnace properties whose values run into millions. Besides Hokendauqua, plants are located at Alburtis, Pa, Island

Park, Pa., Hellertown, Pa., and their holdings in ore lands and lime stone beds are almost endless. They own properties in New Jersey, and in Pennsylvania near Hellertown, Rittenhouse Gap, Red Lion, Bingen, and in North and South Whitehall, Salisbury, Upper and Lower Macungie and Longswamp Townships. They own the Ironton Railroad which is noted in this volume. The Thomas Iron Company also subscribed 40 per cent of the original cost of the Catasauqua and Fogelsville Railroad.

At the opening of the current century, the iron market was good. Nine furnaces were in full blast, producing an output of 260,000 tons. At present but one furnace is in operation in Hokendauqua. The affairs of the Company have always been well managed. Thomas Iron Company stocks have been considered gilt-edged investments. During the first fifty years of its history, the Company paid dividends amounting to 560 91 per cent.

In Hokendauqua the Company established a Church, gave $3500 towards the erection of a building and donated the land. At Alburtis they donated property for a church and $1000 for a cemetery. They also gave $500 toward the Hokendauqua parsonage. In honor of five employees who gave their lives for their country during the Civil War, the Company made a generous gift of money toward the soldiers' monument erected in Fairview Cemetery. The war tax on pig iron alone paid to the United States Government from July, 1864, to July, 1866, was $200,423 83.

THE GRIST MILL

The original mill on the site of the present Mauser and Cressman mill property was established in 1752, five years before the ford across the Lehigh River was built.

It would be interesting to reproduce the harmonies of the splashing old millwheel, with the intermedes of the fulling mill that stood near by, and the obligato strains of the glittering saw that sliced the parent stem of many a denizon of the forest into building material for the new palaces of the burg.

The mill race, along whose brush grown edge the morning lays of a thousand throats of the harbingers of spring were the daily inspiration of men and maidens wending their way to toil, ran from the Catasauqua Creek close by the Race Street bridge at the Davies and Thomas foundry, through the site of the Dery silk mill and the front yard of the Mauser home.

Tradition affords us no information of the proprietorship of the old mill until the beginning of the nineteenth century, when Frederick and Henry Biery bought the place. Solomon Biery succeeded his father Frederick and continued

MAUSER & CRESSMAN FLOUR MILLS

in business until toward the close of the fifties, when Milton Berger and William Younger secured the property. Upon Mr. Berger's death, Mr. Younger carried on the trade until 1891 when it fell into the hands of the National Bank of Catasauqua.

Uriah Kurtz operated the mill for the Bank until 1895, when it was bought by George Mauser.

The old fulling mill was discontinued during the days of Solomon Biery and the saw mill cut its last slabs some time during the eighties.

Upon the death of George D Mauser, in 1898, the property naturally fell into the hands of Frank B Mauser and Allen H Cressman, who have operated the mill since As soon as Mr. Mauser took possession of the mill, he installed new machinery in every department and doubled her capacity He abandoned the use of water from the intermittent Catasauqua creek and secured all his power from the canal A railroad side track was also introduced along the rear of the mill, and a power shovel for unloading grain shipped in bulk

Fire destroyed the entire mill in 1898, after which it was rebuilt with another doubling of its capacity and the installation of the most improved and up-to-date machinery.

"The Mauser and Cressman" is a household motto for flour in countless homes in all our Eastern States

F W WINT COMPANY, LIMITED

The firm of F W Wint Company, Limited, is engaged in the sale of Lumber, Coal and Planing Mill Work A certain proportion of several grades of their lumber is sawed directly from the logs in their various tracts of timber The following is a short sketch of the history of the concern

After Nathan Fegley of Mauch Chunk abandoned his lumber-yard, where the Town Hall of Catasauqua is now located, and went back to Mauch Chunk, John Stoddard of White Haven leased a track of land from Owen Swartz at Front and Spring Streets He shipped lumber here from White Haven on boats, and had Owen Swartz as his agent to sell the lumber This was as early as 1853 Some years prior to the Civil War, he sold his interest to Owen Swartz, who carried on his business of selling lumber until 1863, when he took in Horatio D. Yeager as partner and carried on the business as Swartz and Yeager In 1870, Owen Swartz sold his interest to Ferdinand W Wint, who conducted the business as Yeager and Wint until 1872 Then Geo W Cyphers purchased an interest and the firm was conducted as Yeager, Wint and Cyphers Upon the death of Cyphers, about 1873, the interest was purchased by Yeager and Wint, and for a time the business was carried on as H D Yeager and Co In 1874, Yeager sold out to F. W. Wint, Owen F Fatzinger and James P. Wint, who conducted the business as F. W. Wint & Co. Upon the death of F. W. Wint in 1882, Rufus M

Wint became a member of the firm. These men traded under the same firm name until October, 1900, when the said partners organized a stock corporation under the Limited Partnership Laws, Frank J. Fatzinger and Owen A. Fatzinger becoming stock-holders. Since this time the business has been carried on as F. W. Wint Company, Limited.

In the early history of the firm, logs were purchased at Easton and rafted here where the logs were sawed into lumber by a steam saw mill. This lasted as

F. W. WINT CO.

long as it proved a commercial proposition. At present their saw mills are located on their various tracts. A planing-mill and coal-yard have been added to their business.

The plant has been enlarged at various times, particularly by the purchase in 1902, of the ground of the Catasauqua Rolling Mills.

The concern is capitalized at $60,000, carries a stock of about 2½ millions of feet of lumber, and is equipped to furnish anything made from wood. The sales cover a wide territory and their business has been gradually on the increase. They employ from 60 to 75 hands

PINE OLEIN MANUFACTURING COMPANY

A secret process for the manufacture of a sweeping compound and general disinfectant was bought in 1909, by F C Smith and Franklin Trumbauer of Allentown, which they named "Pine Olein"

After experimenting for about a year they perfected the product, and then admitted Frank J Fatzinger and Owen A Fatzinger into the project Shortly after this, F C Smith retired and in 1912 Rufus W G Wint succeeded Franklin Trumbauer in the venture

The manufacture of the product has been carried on with marked success and it bids fair to become an industry of importance P J McNally is the local representative The plant is located at the foot of Spring Street

DAVIES AND THOMAS COMPANY

In 1865 Daniel Davies bought an old planing mill in East Catasauqua and fitted it up as a foundry and machine shop He had as a partner William Thomas (no relation to the present Thomases), and they traded under the name of Davies and Thomas This partnership continued for two years, when William Thomas retired from the firm and returned to Wales, and Daniel Thomas & Son continued the business until 1876, when Daniel Thomas died

The works were then shut down until February, 1879, when James Thomas bought a half interest in the business and with George Davies, the son of Daniel Davies, formed the new firm of Davies & Thomas, and did business under a partnership agreement until the death of George Davies on October 1st, 1894

On December 21st, 1894, the firm of Davies & Thomas Company was organized into a charatered company, with a capital of $100,000 The stock was afterwards increased to $300,000

James Thomas was president of the last named company until his death on December 18th, 1906, and was succeeded as president of the company by his son Rowland D Thomas at the meeting of the company in January, 1907 who con-

DAVIES & THOMAS COMPANY PLANT

tinued as president of the company until November, 1911, when Leonard Peckitt was elected to the presidency and continues in that office to the present date

The following persons have served as directors of the company during its lifetime as a chartered company

JAMES THOMAS,	ROWLAND T DAVIES,
ROWLAND D THOMAS,	GEORGE DAVIES,
HOPKIN THOMAS,	JAMES T DAVIES,
D H THOMAS,	HARRY E GRAFFIN
C R HORN,	

The present Board of Directors is made up as follows

LEONARD PECKITT, *President,*

ROWLAND D THOMAS,	GEORGE DAVIES,
HOPKIN THOMAS,	HARRY E GRAFFIN

The officers of the company are as follows:

LEONARD PECKITT, *President,*   HARRY E GRAFFIN, *Treasurer,*
CHARLES R HORN, *Secretary*

The general agent of the company was A R McHenry until his death in 1898, when C R Horn was appointed to succeed him, and fills the position to the present time, operating from the company's general offices in New York City, the centre of all big work.

The Davies & Thomas Company has been a furnisher of material for all the large contracts for underground railway and tunnel work requiring cast iron material for their constuction in the cities of New York, Philadelphia, Washington, Baltimore, etc.

For the various tunnels under the harbors of New York City, this company furnished eighty per cent (80%) of the cast iron material used in their construction, and as these tunnels were of eight (8) different designs, it constantly necessitated changes in the patterns for the cast iron castings used in the various designs to meet the requirements

The Davies & Thomas Company is considered the pioneer in the above line of work and their ideas and plans have almost universally been adopted and accepted by engineers constructing the same

When you ride through the various tunnels connecting New York with Jersey City, Brooklyn and Long Island City, you will pass through tunnels whose construction material is almost entirely the product of this company

At the present time the company is engaged on a contract for the manufacture of the lining of a large sewer tunnel for the Borough of Queens, Long Island, which work will keep the foundry very busy for an entire year.

The future of the company has a very bright outlook, as other large projects for tunnel work are expected to materialize in the near future, of which a goodly share no doubt will be awarded this company

Another large activity of this company is the manufacturing of cast iron material used in the construction of Water Gas Plants, and since 1880, and up to the present time, they have manufactured all the castings used, first, by A O Granger in this work, and later by the United Gas Improvement Company of Philadelphia, Pa, in the equipment of their water and coal gas plants, and ninety per cent (90%) of the water gas plants operated in the United States show the product of the last named company. This work is continued, year in and year out, and keeps employed at the foundry from sixty to seventy-five men continually

The plant, in 1876, was but a small stone foundry, employing very few men, but its growth has been steady and continued from year to year, until at the present time the Davies & Thomas Company have a foundry occupying over 16,000 square feet of floor space, equipped with electric and boom cranes and four cupolas, three machine shops fully equipped, a large power plant with boiler and engine room for the manufacture of electricity for the running of the entire works The plant has a capacity of two hundred tons per day of finished castings They had employed over six hundred men at one time when the foundry was running full

The plant at the present time is under the management of Mr Hopkin Thomas as General Manager, who, with Leonard Peckitt, President, Harry E. Graffin, Treasurer, and C R Horn, General Agent, constitute the working force operating the plant

LEHIGH CAR, WHEEL & AXLE WORKS.

On or about March 13, 1866, a co-partnership was formed by James W. Fuller, Charles D. Fuller, James H. McKee, James Thomas and William A. Thomas under the name of McKee, Fuller and Company to engage in the manufacture of Car Wheels. A tract of land was selected on the line of the C & F. R. R., west of the Round House, but upon further investigation it was thought advisable to erect the plant on the main line of the L. V. R. R., and a tract of about eight acres of land was purchased from Jacob Lazarus, which is now a part of the operations of the present Company.

The plant originally had a capacity of fifteen wheels per day. The market for the output was limited and the railroad people were not anxious to try a new

LEHIGH CAR WHEEL AND AXLE WORKS

wheel which had not demonstrated a reputation, and Mr. Fuller in later years was heard to say that were he to live his life over, he would hesitate long before he would engage in an enterprise so fraught with danger to human life and destruction of property as a possible faulty wheel.

On account of the limited market and the panic of 1873-8, the returns were small, and it was also necessary to reinvest the net proceeds in the purchase of adjoining land and additional machinery. Some of the partners dropped out and ten years later James H. McKee and James W. Fuller only remained as partners.

They then struggled along with varying success and discouragements until 1880, when the Erie Railroad desired to purchase a large quantity of modern eight wheeled cars. Inasmuch as the successful contractor was obliged to finance the proposition by taking car trust debentures in payment, there were few proposals for the contract Mr. Fuller undertook this immense proposition, and finally succeeded, after long negotiations, by pledging the private fortunes of the partners. A favorable contract was made and the firm purchased the car plant of Frederick and Beck, which had been idle for some years, then owned by the National Bank of Catasauqua, and at once became busy At one time the lumber arrived so fast that every siding was blocked with laden cars between Allentown and Catasauqua, and for a time fifteen hundred men were employed and Fullerton became a thriving village

At this time Mr. Fuller telegraphed to his brother-in-law, James Thomas, then residing in Alabama, if he would come north and re-open the Davies Foundry, he would give him an order for the small castings, sufficient to keep the foundry busy for one year This offer was accepted and Mr Thomas came north at once

From this time on the success of the firm was assured and on February 13, 1883, William W. McKee and B Frank Swartz were admitted to the firm At about the same time a forge to forge the axles was added, and the business increased so fast that in the first six months of 1883 they built, complete, eighteen hundred forty-nine eight-wheeled cars This business amounted to $2,800,000 for the year. The capacity of the works in 1884 was sufficient to do a business of $4,000,000 per annum

During these years James W Fuller's application to his business was incessant, and for the first six years he was not only the Manager, but Traveling Salesman, working generally fifteen to eighteen hours in every twenty-four It was nothing unusual for him to arrive from the west at East Penn Junction, and walk home at midnight, stopping at the works to see if his watchman was on duty and all was right at the plant

It was this constant devotion to the business interests of the firm, and pluck and determination that wrested success from a failing enterprise

After the death of James H McKee, the interest of his several heirs was placed on sale and acquired by the remaining members of the firm It became a necessity, owing to the large interests involved, so as to prevent jeopardy to the interests of the others in case of the death of the remaining partner interested, to incorporate the plant A charter was obtained February 5, 1901, and the outstanding interests purchased, and the business continued under the name of "The Lehigh Car, Wheel & Axle Works."

For some years the business has changed. Wooden cars are no longer made and the railroads manufacture their own wheels. The plant is now principally engaged in manufacturing machinery for cement companies and has a large foreign trade.

The plant comprises sixty acres. The railroad tracks were removed to the eastern end of the plant, the old public road was vacated and new roads were opened so as to form a continuous acreage. The company maintains a reputation as up-to-date in the business world, and employs a large force of competent mechanics and workmen of high intelligence and character.

THE EAGLE BREWERY.

Herman Kostenbader and Conrad Schaffer began to brew Lager Beer at what they called the Eagle Brewery, in 1867. In 1872 John Krentzer of Philadelphia bought the interest of Conrad Schaffer after which the firm was known as

THE EAGLE BREWERY

Kostenbader and Krentzer. Mr. Krentzer died in 1876, since which time Mr. Kostenbader, having bought his partner's share from his estate, was in business for and by himself. During the summer of 1902, Mr. Kostenbader took his sons, August F and Herman A, into partnership with himself, and although the father died early in 1909, the sons continued under the firm title of H Kostenbader and Sons

The Eagle Brewery has undergone many renovations since it was founded A new ice house was built in 1886 After some failures of the ice crops due to mild winters Mr Kostenbader installed a ten ton ice machine in 1892 Artificial ice was a novelty in those days People almost went into ecstasy over beholding a bouquet of beautiful roses embedded in a fifty pound block of ice, clear as crystal The firm also erected a new and enlarged brew house and boiler department During 1900, Mr Kostenbader greatly enlarged his storage cellars and, in order to maintain an even temperature during all seasons of the year, supplanted the old ice machine with a machine of a capacity of fifty tons The storage cellars and facilities for cooling beers were again enlarged in March of 1914

On account of repeated agitations regarding the absolute purity of the water supplied this town, and because of the water rates which were almost prohibitive to a plant that uses as much water as a brewery, Mr Kostenbader determined to dig an artesian well It was completed in 1896 The well is two hundred five feet deep and is fitted up with an airlift pump whose capacity is three hundred gallons per minute The mean temperature of the water is fifty-two degrees Mr Kostenbader was fortunate in striking a vein out of which flows a soft clear and perfectly pure water

The firm established a bottling plant during 1905 This plant, like the brewery, is fitted up with the most improved machinery The thought of cleanliness and purity is written over every department They who know how to use and properly appreciate good beer say "Kostenbader" The sales of the firm during 1913 amounted to 13,370 barrels

THE CATASAUQUA BREWERY

The brewery known as the Catasauqua Brewery was established in 1867 by Matthew Millhaupt He had a successful but brief career He died in 1872 Mr Millhaupt's widow continued the business and Christian Stockberger served her as brewmaster This combination succeeded so well that after a while Mr Stockberger became proprietor of the brewery by winning Mrs Millhaupt as his bride. Mr. Stockberger died in 1885. The sons-in-law of the widow, Henry Geisel and Felix Keller, now took charge of the brewery; but their venture failed. A Frenchman, whose name tradition has forgotten, brewed ale for some months and failed.

Through endorsements the property fell into the hands of Wen Fatzinger and Frank Butz, who, however, did not run the brewery. In October, 1900, Henry Kirsch and H. H. Rice bought the property, made some improvements and

CATASAUQUA BREWERY

began to brew beer. The latter soon purchased his partner's share and continued alone until November, 1906, when the present proprietor, Charles L. Lehnert, bought the property. Mr. Lehnert is a practical brewer, who learnt his trade in Germany. He has made some wonderful improvements to the old Catasauqua Brewery. He enlarged the boiler-house and the engine room, and built a bottling house. During 1909 he erected a three story brew-house and equipped the same with the best machinery obtainable. He began the construction of new storage cellars in 1913. Into these he has placed enameled steel tanks. The present output of this brewery is eight thousand barrels of beer and porter. Mr. Lehnert also manufactures an excellent grade of soft drinks, and stamps his name with a worthy pride upon all his products.

THE LEHIGH FIRE BRICK WORKS.

The Lehigh Fire Brick Company was established 1868 by McHose and Ritter in a frame building on the present site, between Front St. and the Lehigh Coal & Navigation Co. canal, and lying between the F. W. Wint Co., Ltd., and Bryden Horseshoe Co.'s plants. This building was burned down in 1872, and the stone structure now standing was built in its place by Joshua Hunt, Samuel Thomas and John Thomas.

LEHIGH FIRE BRICK WORKS

In 1903 the concern was re-incorporated and is now known as the Lehigh Fire Brick Works. It is advantageously situated, having connections with the Lehigh Valley, Central Railroad of N. J., Phila. & Reading and Lehigh & New England Railroads.

The concern is successfully engaged in the manufacture of all standard and special shaped fire bricks for furnace, foundry, milling and general purposes.

L. H. McHose, son of one of the original members of the firm, Samuel McHose, and a pioneer in the fire brick business in this part of the country, is now president of the company.

THE CATASAUQUA DISPATCH

Edmund Randall opened a printing office on the first floor of the Esch Building on Front Street below Mulberry Street, on September 1, 1870 Feeling encouraged in his venture, Mr Randall issued a monthly advertising sheet which he distributed throughout Catasauqua and neighboring towns This gave rise to the suggestion of a local newspaper which Mr. Randall at once proceeded to publish. He called it the Catasauqua Dispatch and brought forth weekly issues

There never was a news sheet issued in the whole valley that was so homogeneous in all its publications as the Catasauqua Dispatch Its utterances were fearless and breathed a spirit absolutely true to itself. The Dispatch championed the cause of many public utilities, a few of which are the Pine Street Bridge, our Greater Schools, the Municipal Water Plant, and the Old Home Week Celebration

It has always preached a high standard of morals, and, indeed, was a potent force in moulding the thoughts and acts of young and old It was ever ready to shout for patriotism, and, during Memorial or Independence week, it bristled with spicy lines that told of the deeds and lives of the great and good men of the nation.

Mr Randall is one of the oldest and most widely known members of the State Editorial Association. The last number of the Dispatch from his pen is dated Friday, April 10, 1914 In this issue Mr Randall delivered a beautiful and long to be remembered valedictory.

He upon whom the old editorial mantle feel is one of our own townsmen A gentleman, a scholar, a Christian are the general terms that most briefly describe his character The public can expect to read with complacency all manner of good literature as well as spicy and up-to-date news articles in the columns of the Dispatch, and any worthy propaganda that aims toward uplift and prosperity will not only find support but manly leadership in the Dispatch The new editor is John S Matchette

BRYDEN HORSE SHOE CO

The Bryden Horse Shoe Company was organized in 1882 Joshua Hunt was its first president, Oliver Williams, secretary and treasurer Horse shoes originally were manufactured here under patents of George Bryden, of Hartford, Conn Finished shoes, with toe and heel caulks, were made under hammers for use principally on street car horses About thirty men were employed for several years and the daily product was from two and one-half to three tons With the passing of the street car horses, the company was obliged to seek other outlets for its product and to do this it became necessary to increase the plant accordingly In 1888, this was accomplished and the capital stock was increased to one hundred thousand dollars Jacob Roberts of Poughkeepsie, N Y, was engaged to equip the plant for the manufacture of the pattern shoes used by the general blacksmith trade and the output was trebled

After many years of effort and varying success, the company's product had made a name and place for itself in the markets of the country and to-day it is one of the largest plants of its kind in the world, producing a larger variety of horse shoes than any other one plant During the Boer War, 1899-1900, the company supplied the British War Department with about a car-load of horse and mule shoes weekly, and the authorities of that Department have continued to place orders with the company at intervals ever since

On the death of Oliver Williams in 1894 (who had been elected President and Treasurer in 1884), George E Holton, then Vice-President, was elected to the office of President and Treasurer, T F Frederick continuing as Secretary and so remaining until his death in 1909, when H Morley Holton succeeded him as Secretary

The plant has grown steadily and to-day it occupies about seven acres of ground Its daily production is from forty to fifty tons of horse shoes A complete line of racing plates is also manufactured The paid up capital stock has been increased from time to time and to-day it is six hundred twenty-five thousand dollars About three hundred men are given steady employment in manufacturing productions of the highest standard, which are sold not only in North America and Great Britain but also in New Zealand, Australia and South America. The officers of the company are: Mrs. George E. Holton, President, who succeeded Mr. Holton upon his death in 1913; H. Morley Holton, Secretary and Treasurer; Paul E. Miller, General Manager.

THE WAHNETAH SILK COMPANY.

This company was chartered "to manufacture silk fabrics" in 1890, when it began to run on a production of silk plush. The plush business, however,

WAHNETAH SILK MILL

proved unprofitable, so that during 1902 this machinery was substituted for broad silk looms.

Now the Wahnetah plant began to grow. Building was added to building until their present equipment comprises seven hundred looms and such other departments as are necessary to prepare the silk received in skein for use on the loom.

The Wahnetah Company buys its raw silk directly from the raw silk importers in New York City. From the importers the raw silk (Japan silk) is shipped to the throwsters (Spinning Mill). From the throwsters it is shipped to the dye-house from which it comes in skeins to the weaving mill.

The latest improved machinery is installed throughout the plant, and, being operated by competent help, produces a stock of the finest grade silks, which finds ready sale in any market.

Whilst the Wahnetah prospers our whole town feels the pulse-beat of its life. An average of five hundred persons earn their daily bread here.

The first president of the Company was James Thomas, who was succeeded at his death by William R. Thomas, Jr., the present incumbent, who is also general manager of the plant. Mr. Frank M. Horn has served as Secretary and Treasurer since the organization of the Company. Mr. William M. Alford and Sons, New York, are the managers of the sale's department.

THE DERY SILK MILL.

Ground was broken for a silk mill at Front and Race Streets in March, 1897, and building operations were undertaken forthwith. One hundred and fifty looms and all needed accessories were installed, and in August of the same year, the plant was in full operation. During the summer of 1899, the capacity of the mill was doubled by the erection of a large addition. The plant of D. G. Dery possesses not only excellent light, the best of sanitary and ventilation arrangements, but also modern improvements, looking to the health and safety of employees. The building is three hundred feet by fifty feet in dimensions, three stories high with auxiliary buildings attached—the whole equipped with the most modern machinery. Employment is furnished to three hundred people, whose production is mostly colored and black dress silks. The output reaches about twenty thousand pieces per annum, finding sale in all parts of the United States.

Mr. Dery understands fully the requirements for silk manufacture and the best methods of supplying them.

THE CATASAUQUA BOILER WORKS

This industry was established by Samuel McCloskey in April, 1901, in a small shop on Front and Willow Streets.

After a successful career of two years Mr. McCloskey's brothers, John, William and James, came from the far west in order to join their brother in this business.

Orders multiplied until the old shop became too small to do rapid and successful work. The company, therefore, bought the site of the old Rolling Mill property on Front Street, above Pine, where they had ample room and employed between thirty and forty men.

During 1907, the partnership was dissolved, and the place of business sold. Messrs. John and James McCloskey went west again.

The following year Samuel started his business again at his original place, and succeeds in doing a fine business. His shop is well equipped. Ten to fifteen men find constant employment there.

EMANUEL & COMPANY

Emanuel & Company with its main office at Catasauqua, Pa., organized as a corporation January, 1904, with the following officers:—Mr. David L. Emanuel,

Pres, and Mr George W Aubrey, Secretary and Treasurer The chief object of the company is to manufacture and crush blast furnace slag for roofing and manufacture concrete work

The first Plant was erected at Catasauqua, Pa, on the slag bank of the Crane Iron Works After this slag was exhausted, the Crushing Plant was removed to the bank of the Thomas Iron Company at Hokendauqua, Pa, at which place there is a Crusher located now The second Crushing Plant, which has been in operation since 1911, was located at a different bank of the Crane Iron Works at Catasauqua, Pa Various banks were leased, and Crushing Plants erected and operated from time to time at Poughkeepsie, N Y, and South Bethlehem, Pa

The use of slag for concrete work being an experiment, it required a number of years of hard work to introduce it to Architects, Contractors and Engineers, and it was not until the last few years that it was adopted by the Architects and Engineers for the leading manufacturing and contracting concerns in this section From that time on the growth of the slag business has been very remarkable, and to-day, the two Crushing Plants operated by Emanuel & Company turn out almost one thousand tons daily

The present officers of the company (1913-1914) are Paul E Miller of Catasauqua, Pa, President and Treasurer, and Miles T Bitting of Allentown, Pa, Secretary.

The Company sells its product all over the Middle Atlantic States, New England States, and Southern Canada It employs about seventy-five men the year round, most of whom reside in Catasauqua and near-by towns

GOLDSMITH'S PLANING MILL

Franklin Goldsmith is a native of Alburtis, Pa, where he served his apprenticeship as a carpenter Well qualified for the trade, he struck out into the world and soon found his way to Catasauqua Here he served for contractors until 1886, when he resolved to start in business for himself Mr Goldsmith has always had the reputation of doing first class work, which not only kept him very busy, but obliged him to increase his force of men repeatedly

In the spring of 1907, he began the erection of a large planing mill, boiler house and lumber sheds His equipment is complete and well nigh perfect The machine room alone measures ninety by one hundred thirty feet. There is nothing made of wood that this progressive firm is not prepared to produce.

During 1909, Mr. Goldsmith admitted his son, Franklin R. A., into partnership. "Young Frank" learned his trade under his father, which together with a course at college, has thoroughly qualified him for his position. The firm,

GOLDSMITH'S PLANING MILL

Franklin Goldsmith and Son, whose mill and offices are at 808-814 Race Street, now employ an average of forty men.

YOUNG'S BOILER COMPOUND COMPANY.

Mr. Harry R. Young has been interested for many years in boiler preservation, and in the protection of the lives and limbs of many men who fire boilers.

After many tests of waters and neutralizing acids by which solidifying substances in water are reduced to a minimum, Mr. Young succeeded in producing a boiler compound that rivals the best known product of its kind. He received his patent in 1908.

Nearly two hundred customers scattered throughout Pennsylvania, New York, New Jersey, Massachusetts, Colorado, Virginia and other States, testify to the positive effectiveness of the Young's Compound. A quality that shows this compound to be of superior value is that it is absolutely safe, as well as certain in action; and, if overfed to the boiler, it will not foam as is the case with so many similar products.

Mr. Young associated some gentlemen with himself so as to form the Young Boiler Compound Company, which does business at 1025 Third Street.

LEICESTER RUBBER COMPANY.

RUBBER WORKS

The Leicester Rubber Company was incorporated under the laws of the State of New Jersey, June 10, 1910, by A. De Piano, President; Joseph F. Maher, Vice President; and William M. Maher, Sec'y. and Treas. The Company conducted a rubber business in the City of Trenton for almost four (4) years, when the business developed to such an extent that it out-grew its location. In looking for a more modern plant, they came in contact with the mill formerly occupied by the O'Brien Rubber Thread & Webbing Company, Catasauqua.

In July of 1913, they purchased this mill with all its equipment and removed their present plant from Trenton to Catasauqua. Mr. I. Fineburg, a very prominent scrap-rubber dealer of Trenton, identified himself with the Company. After considerable expenditure in setting up new machinery, etc., they started business here in the month of September, 1913, and met with instant success.

They manufacture rubber mechanical goods, door mats, baby carriage tiring, fruit jar rings, heels and soles and also reclaimed rubber to a great extent.

At the present writing the outlook for business is very favorable, as they have orders ahead sufficient to run their works for three or four months. Their plant is very busy, employing about 25 people.

They ship goods to all parts of the United States, Alaska, Honolulu, Hawaii.

THERMOMETER WORKS

The firm of Kevs Bros. & Co., manufacturers of Clinical Thermometers, was organized in Catasauqua March 1st, 1911. Their present location is 115-117 Bridge St. The manufacture of these thermometers is a new industry in Catasauqua, and, therefore, a few remarks about the manufacture of them would not be amiss. The glass tubing is made in Corning, N. Y., and shipped to them in six foot lengths, and then they cut it up to any required length. The bulb is then blown on to this tubing and filled with mercury. This operation takes great skill, and can only be done by experienced mechanics. After this, the thermometers have to go through twenty different stages before they are completed.

They are sent to the large cities, and sold from there to all parts of the world. The members of the firm learned their trade in England, and since locating in Catasauqua, received a large government order for the manufacture of 12,000. The thermometers, which took two months to make, are now being used in all Government Hospitals in the United States. The firm at present is extremely busy, having contracts for the entire output each week.

THE CATASAUQUA SILK COMPANY

The youngest Silk Company is the Catasauqua, organized November, 1911. The original members of the firm were: James J. Seyfried, Wilson J. Smith, Edwin J. Smith and Frank J. Schleicher.

These gentlemen purchased the beautiful two-story office building on Race Street and the Central Railroad of New Jersey from its builder and owner, Preston H. Kratzer, and converted it into a mill.

Looms were running on broad silk by the end of December, 1911. During 1913, the plant was enlarged so that now they have floor space and auxiliary machinery sufficient to run fifty looms.

Under the capable management of Mr. H. O. Glase, their Superintendent, the firm produces a good quality of silk which finds ready sale.

THE CATASAUQUA GARAGE

Charles Wentz and Nicholas Dugan determined to establish an Automobile repair shop and supply house at the corner of Pine and Railroad Streets, on the eleventh of April, 1911.

During July of the same year, Philip R Lynch purchased the interest of Mr Wentz Since that time the co-partnership is known as "Lynch and Dugan " Both of these men are practical machinists

Their line of work embraces general repairing of machines and supplying parts and materials.

They store and groom cars, and also supply cars for hire

The business prospects for these young and reliable men are very bright

THE HERRINGTON FURNITURE COMPANY

The Herrington Furniture Company was organized in March, 1911, by F C Herrington and C H Edwards, Jr , and located its plant at 1126 Second Street. The business of this firm is to upholster furniture and sell to the trade Their sales territory is chiefly the States of New York, New Jersey and Pennsylvania They also do repair work.

THE PEERLESS AUTO SERVICE.

The Peerless Auto Service was instituted at Railroad and Almond Streets, North Catasauqua, in December, 1912, for the accommodation of the general public This service is equipped with Taxi-Cabs and Five and Seven Passenger Cars Careful drivers accompany each car Dr H J S Keim is the Proprietor, and his name stands a sufficient guarantee of security to any one who knows the Doctor

CATASAUQUA MOTOR CAR WORKS

Preston H Kratzer, son of R Frank Kratzer, served his apprenticeship while still quite a young man While in the employ of Mr. Goldsmith he conceived the idea that he might succeed as contractor, and so launched forth some seventeen years ago He enjoyed the confidence of men of affairs and secured some valuable contracts These he fulfilled most conscientiously He built a large planing mill known as the South End Planing Mill During the fall of 1913, Mr Kratzer associated with himself as partner Lewis M Jones The latter paid special attention to the contracting for and the erection of buildings, while the former launched out upon a new industry known as The Catasauqua Motor Car Works The floors of the planing mill were cleared and machinery, contributory to the construction and repairs of motor cars, introduced There were expert foremen in the paint and wood departments as well as in the machine shop. A large storage and exhibition building was erected. The plant had over twenty thousand square feet of floor space. All indications pointed toward great success, when during the night of March 4, 1914, all but the storage house burnt to the ground and five fine machines with it. This was a severe blow to a keen and enterprising business man. The ruins of that conflagration remain undisturbed at this time.

THE CRYSTAL ICE COMPANY.

ICE PLANT

In these modern days of wholesome and sanitary living, the refrigerator seems to play a larger part than the coal bin. The former is now in perennial use. Pure ice, much more than clear ice, is the great demand. Certain gentlemen with Henry G. Walker, President, William J. Montz, Vice President, C. O. Fuller, Secretary-Treasurer, and William H. Satelle, Chief Engineer, organized the Crystal Ice Company in 1913.

They purchased a property at Peach and American Streets and immediately began to dig an artesian well. They had a lucky find. The well is one hundred seven feet deep, has an eight inch bore, and a capacity of 200 gallons of water per minute. The temperature of the water is 52 degrees, Fahrenheit. Only well water is used in the manufacture of ice in this plant and all the water is distilled before it is frozen into ice. The capacity of the plant is forty tons of the very best ice in twenty-four hours. The average weight of the cakes of ice is three hundred pounds. The Company is capitalized for twenty-five thousand dollars. The first ice was produced on Thursday, April 30, 1914.

CHAPTER III.—CHURCHES.

THE FIRST PRESBYTERIAN CHURCH.

The institution of the First Presbyterian Church at Catasauqua was coincident with the establishment of the Crane Iron Works in 1839. The general manager of the Company, Mr. David Thomas, is the reputed founder of the Church. Through his kindly offices, the Company donated a triangular piece of ground—with a base of one hundred sixty-four feet, and each leg one hundred fifty-eight feet—at the extreme limits of its land, on a road leading from Allen Township on the north to the old town of Bethlehem on the southeast. The first building of the congregation, constructed of boards set upright and shingle covered, was located in a woods on the south side of the triangular plot. Its whitewashed walls, both inside and out, for which a generous supply of slacked lime in a hogshead was continually kept in a shed at the rear of the building;

First Church Building in Town—First Presbyterian Church

its rough hewn benches; its long iron rods passing through and through the building near the ceiling at symmetrical distances and fastened with nuts on the outside to enhance the stability of the wooden structure; its swinging camphene lamps suspended from the ceiling by slender rods passing through small holes in the ceiling enabling the lamps to be raised or lowered at will—the wonderment of curious children; all challenge the imagination.

Later, at the suggestion of Mr Thomas, the Crane Iron Company donated sufficient land at the rear of the old reservoir on Church Street to enlarge its triangular into a rectangular plot, with dimensions of three hundred fifty by two hundred feet

The history of this congregation was concisely given in an address by Samuel Thomas, son of the founder, upon the occasion of celebrating, on September 23, 1904, the "Semi-Centennial Jubilee" of laying the corner-stone of the present church on the north-east corner of Second and Pine Streets The address is as follows

"Just fifty years ago, in the peace and calm of the early twilight of a beautiful September evening, a group of Christian worshippers assembled to witness the ceremony of laying the corner stone of the First Presbyterian Church in whose shadow we are now standing, first in name only but not in point of erection

The first church was a little frame building 25 by 35 feet, built by David Minnich, in the woods between the reservoir and what is now Mrs John William's garden (now the property of Mr J W Fuller, Jr), at the upper end of Church Street, on land donated by the Crane Iron Co The time was the last Sunday of December 1839 cold and stormy, when the ground was covered with snow, and brother John and I had nailed planks together to use as a plough to open paths through the heavy fall of snow The storm was so severe that after the corner-stone had been laid by Rev Landis, pastor of the Allentown Presbyterian Church (the first English Church in Lehigh County), the little congregation were obliged to continue the services in the home of Father Thomas, which is still standing opposite the Crane Iron Works

Of that little band of Presbyterian pioneers, I can find only three survivors besides myself Mrs Bender (nee Peter), and Mrs Owen Swartz, her sister, and Mrs Rehrig (nee Lackey), all the others having passed on to the beyond towards which we also are hastening

As near as my memory serves me, those present on this interesting occasion were the following —'Father' and 'Mother' Thomas with their five children (Jane, Gwenny, Samuel, John and David), Mrs James Lackey and daughter Maggie, John Samuels and daughter Rachel, Mrs John Leibert, John Peter and family, Aaron Bast, Charles Breisch, Lawrence Landis, Mrs Jonathan Landis and Andrew Archer There were doubtless others, but these stand out clearest against the past

The little building has been demolished and the venerable black oak tree has been removed, in whose forked branchs I, as a boy, hung the bell which called the faithful to prayers This bell passed into the hands of the Crane Iron Works, by whom it was used once a month on pay-days to call the men together. It still hangs on a branch of the tree, close to the office, where the curious may each find it The tree and bell were natural means to a spiritual end and though they have passed out of use, the spirit abides for this church whose semi-centennial we celebrate to-day, and its great development into other churches, such as the Bridge Street Church, the Church at Hokendauqua, the Bethel-Welsh Congregational Church (known as 'Mother' Thomas's Church), the Churches at Lockridge, Ferndale and Richard's Mine in New Jersey, and the Presbyterian Church at Thomas in far-off Alabama

All these Churches are living branches of the tree which was planted in faith and hope fifty years ago on that inclement winter Sunday by a band of earnest Presbyterian men and women The women are worthy of special mention for they too carried their share of the burden cheerfully and nobly Well do I remember my sister Gwenny, Rachel Samuel, Maggie Lackey and Susanna Peter, brave and helpful young girls, who carried water in pails all the way from the canal to scrub and clean the church, and as the building was used for a day-school during the week, every Saturday morning it required their earnest attention

In a recent interview with Mrs Owen Swartz and Mrs Rehrig, whose personal recollections of the early times in the history of this Church are very clear, I was reminded that Church services were held in my father's house until the completion of the building on March 22, 1840.

This little white-washed church was used for worship until the present building was ready to·be occupied in 1856 Two years after the laying of the corner stone, the church was dedicated, free of debts My thoughts dwell with especial pleasure upon those far-off days, and the building of those early Walls of Zion in our adopted home

As I review those early years, I see the earnest figures of my father and mother, who were strangers in a strange land, zealous from the beginning to see a house of worship planted here When the Church was organized it numbered only three, father, mother and sister Jane, and father was then ordained as first Elder

About two years later, David Williams, Sr, located with his family at Catasauqua and he became a member of this Church, and soon afterwards he was inducted into the eldership He was a most excellent man, and though in poor health he was strenuous in all good works It was he who took up the collection and acted as treasurer of the Church He died August 14, 1845, and his remains were laid to rest in the church yard after services in the little church where he had served so well

As the population increased the church in the woods became too small A special meeting of the congregation was therefore held to discuss ways and means for securing a new building A committee was appointed consisting of the pastor, Rev Cornelius Earle, David Thomas, Morgan Emanuel, William McClelland and Joshua Hunt

By arrangement with David Thomas (who had donated some adjoining land to enlarge the church property on Church Street), an exchange was made of that land which secured to the congregation the site of 180 by 180 feet at the corner of Second and Pine Streets, upon which stands to-day the present Church, the parsonage and the Chapel Plans having been made and adopted, sufficient funds were raised to warrant the new enterprise

The corner stone of the old church was brought here and deposited just previous to the ceremony of laying the new corner stone It was fashioned by Charles Breisch and bears the date of 1839, which can be seen on examination It is a gray sandstone from near Kreidersville In the new stone a copper box was laid which, according to custom, contained a Bible, some coins, local papers, and whatever the copper box of the old corner stone had contained An address was delivered by Rev Richard Walker of Allentown, and Rev Leslie Irwin of Bath assisted in the services.

On Sunday, the 11th day of May, 1856, the church was solemnly dedicated to the worship of God. Rev. George Duffield, D. D., preached the dedicatory sermon, Rev. C. Earle and Rev. R. Walker taking part in the services. Rev. Jacob Becker preached German in the afternoon.

Only a few remain who were then from twenty to thirty years of age: Mrs. Thomas Bear, Charles Graffin, Daniel Milson, James Nevins, William Kildare, Charles W. Schneller, Mrs. Quigg, and those who were from ten to twenty years still among us are: Mrs. John Thomas, James Thomas, Mrs. James Thomas, Mrs. Emma C. Williams, Rebecca Siegley, Mrs. Kate Steward, William H. Glace, Joseph Matchette, Mrs. Herbert James, Samuel Davis, David Davis, Owen F. Leibert, Joseph McFetridge, John McFetridge, Mrs. John Knauss, Mrs. James Torrance, Martha Wilson, Thomas Jones, Mrs. William T. Snyder, Mrs. Edwin Mickley, Mrs. James W. Fuller, and Archibald Courtney."

FIRST PRESBYTERIAN CHURCH

The present Church edifice is built of brick, semi-Gothic in style. The main building is forty by sixty-three feet, exclusive of tower and pulpit recess. It has a transept on the south side twenty by thirty feet which forms part of the audience room, and also an organ transept on the north side, ten by twenty feet. The organ was the gift of David Thomas. The Church steeple is one hundred fifty feet high and has a fine-toned bell in it. The congregation was regularly incorporated in 1853.

As commemorative of the reunion of the Old School and the New School Assemblies of the Presbyterian Church, a memorial chapel was built on Pine Street, at the rear of the edifice, in 1871. The corner stone was laid May 13th, and the dedication took place on December 10th. This building is also of brick, semi-Gothic in style, thirty-five by eighty-two feet. It contains rooms for all Church purposes; and it is used regularly for mid-week services and by the Sabbath School.

Forty feet northwest of the church, fronting on Second Street, there is an attractive and well planned parsonage, built of brick, in style corresponding with the church.

Rev. Cornelius Earle served the congregation as pastor in a most satisfactory and efficient manner from October 14, 1852 to 1898, when he resigned, after a continuous service of forty-six years. During the year 1899, the regular services were conducted by other licensed Presbyterian clergymen.

Rev. Charles H. Miller was elected as the successor of Rev. Earle, and he has served the congregation in a most efficient manner since February, 1900. The membership of the Church on May 1, 1914, was two hundred thirty-five; of the Sunday School, three hundred.

A Sunday School has been conducted in connection with the Church from the beginning, and the superintendents have been prominently identified with the Church as Elders:

David Thomas, 1839 to 1847; Elder from 1839 to 1882.

Joshua Hunt, 1847 to 1882; Elder from 1847 to 1886.

John Williams, 1882 to 1892; Elder from 1874 to 1892.

Joseph Matchette, 1892 to——; Elder from 1892 to——.

REV. C. H. MILLER

IMMANUEL EVANGELICAL CHURCH.

George Eliot tells us how, with a single drop of ink for a mirror, the Egyptian sorcerer undertakes to reveal to any chance comer far reaching visions of the past. With similar drop of ink, the historian will endeavor to reveal some visions of the past—the beginnings of an institution which has been wielding much good in the Iron Borough and which to-day stands as one of its beloved monuments—the Immanuel Evangelical Church.

The story of its beginning, like the beginning of every Church, is interesting. Way back in the early forties, a few brave and devoted families, realizing the need of a Church in this community, formed themselves into a class and conducted religious services in the homes of Henry Enock, Abram Yundt, Silas Yundt, William Neighly and others, some of Catasauqua's early residents. The Reverends C. Hesser, J. C. Farnsworth, C. Hummel, J. Kramer, D. Wieand, E. Bast, Abraham Schultz, J. Hoffman and others nobly served as the first preachers. Under the preaching of these now sainted gentlemen, the class grew in religious fervor and zeal, as well as in numbers.

A church edifice was found necessary and yet the class was unable to undertake its erection alone. An appeal was made to the public generally for help. A subscription book, headed "Catasauqua, May 18, 1848, AN APPEAL TO THE FRIENDS OF RELIGION," and, among other things, setting forth, on its first page, that the Evangelical Association of Catasauqua is in great need of a house of worship and that the Society is small and unable to undertake the building alone, was circulated. From the subscriptions appearing in this book, there seems to have been a generous response to the appeal. The book contains the subscriptions of Joseph Yundt, Valentine Knoll, Matchis Knoll, Enoch Yundt, William Neighly, Charles G. Schneller, David Thomas, Mrs. David Thomas, Owen Rice, James Lacky, Nathan Fegly, Mariah McIntire, Jonathan Snyder, Henry Yundt, Charles Brish, Joseph Huber, W. Weaver, Charles Dyely, Samuel Romig, Lewis Bogge, Martin Simon, Jesse Brown, John Peter, David A. Protzman, Samuel Walters, Isaac Larash, Charles Seem, Daniel Seem, Jacob L. Miller, Julius A. Miller, Samuel Colver, William Gross, Jacob Gross, Andrew Kromer, Samuel Miller, Samuel Glace, Morgan Emanuel, William Phillips, William Heller, William Newhard, Reuben L. Seip, George W. Andre, John Williams, Henry Getz, Conrad Seig, Nathan Frederick, Fisher Hazard, Owen Swartz, Jonas Biery, Mrs. Matilda Andreas, William Swartz, Joshua Hunt, Jr., John Thomas, James

M Snyder, Joseph Laubach, Reuben Leisering, Owen Frederick, J W Fuller, Frederick Eberhard, Charles Sigley, Jacob Deily and many others

In the same year, namely 1848, the first church (or meeting house as it was then called) was built on the triangular lot or piece of ground situate on Howertown Road below Mulberry Street The building was a small, plain brick structure, with the Church cemetery adjoining In those days it required much courage to be an Evangelical But the few members were intensely in earnest They consecrated and devoted themselves to the work, and like the early Apostolic Church, "they found favor with God and the people," and from year to year members were added to the flock Reverends H Bucks and N McLehn served the new Church as senior and junior pastors, respectively They were lovable Christian gentlemen of ability and tact and under their pastorate the new born congregation began to develop into a mighty power.

The late Charles G Schneller, deceased, was the Secretary of the first Official Board and was actively identified with Immanuel Evangelical Church up to the time of his death, July 13, 1909 In 1854, Charles G. Schneller was elected class leader and was given his Class Book by Rev Christian Meyers, the preacher then in charge His Class Book shows the following to have been members of his class Charles G Schneller, Mary Schneller, William Velich, Sarah Velich, Refina Buchman, Julian Buchman, Aaron Bast, Catharine Bast, Elizabeth Weber, Jacob Rothman, Wilhelmina Mohry, Amos Bachman, George W Andrew, David Tombler, Fyetta Tombler, Charles Donecker, Aaron Fretz, Sarah Fretz, Jacob Frey, Caroline Tombler, Edward Gilbert, Anthony Kindt, Calvin Bleam, Jacob Fretz, Elizabeth Fretz, Elizabeth Velich, Hannah Velich, Caroline Boyer, Ellen Buchman, Joseph Fry, Levina Simon, Mary Ann Mohrey, Polly Hahn, William Neighly, Sarah Neighly, Julian Haines, Stephen Hahn, David Shafer, Matilda Shafer, George Hoxworth, Aaron Fatzinger, Amaline Fatzinger, William Bachman, Henry Sellers, Catharine Sellers, John Tombler, Jacob Keller, Sarah Keller, Joseph Hixon, Mary Hixon, Michael Rothrock, Elizabeth Rothrock, John Weibel, Mary Weibel, Sebilla Kester, Owen Wentz, E Swartz, Catharine Laub, Amanda Rothrock and Samuel Missimer

In twenty years the congregation had grown very large and the old church building was found entirely too small to accommodate properly the crowds of people who attended the services. In consequence the old church property was abandoned in 1868, and in that year the present commodious brick edifice was erected at Second and Walnut Streets, at a cost of twelve thousand dollars ($12,000), under the pastorate of Rev. J. C. Lehr, which, too, has been remodeled and beautified several times since then. The members of the building committee were Owen Swartz, President; Charles G. Schneller, Secretary; William Michael, Aaron Glick and David Tombler. Here, likewise, the work prospered under the signal blessing of God.

The famous Rev. Moses Dissinger was pastor here. The present senior bishop of the Evangelical Association, Bishop Thomas Bowman, Presiding Elders B. F. Bohner and T. L. Wentz also served as pastors of Immanuel Evangelical Church.

IMMANUEL EVANGELICAL

The regular Church attendance had reached upwards of eight hundred (800) and the work was growing beautifully when alas! factional disagreements arose within the Church and the unfortunate disruption took place in 1891, and many of the members withdrew their membership and joined the St. John's United Evangelical Church at Walnut and Limestone Streets, whereby Immanuel suffered and has not yet been able to regain its former power.

In 1904, the present modernly equipped parsonage was built at a cost of three thousand ($3,000) dollars. The building committee were: Rev. J. Willet Boyer, pastor, Charles G. Schneller, Christian Garbian, M. Thomas Heilman, Richard O. Heilman, Robert Demmrich and William F. Engler.

The Church has always been opposed to Church fairs, festivals and lotteries, and recommends the employment of other means for raising funds for its support.

On January 1, 1890, the Ladies Aid Society of Immanuel Evangelical Church was organized and it has since its organization been a great blessing to the Church.

On December 20, 1891, the members of the Church organized the Young People's Alliance and it has enjoyed a very busy and useful career.

On the evening of September 23, 1904, there assembled in the prayermeeting room of the church a number of its good women, who had become interested in missionary work, and organized themselves into the Women's Missionary Society for the purpose of systematically studying and handling the mission work, and much practical good has it been able to accomplish.

A Junior Young People's Alliance is also one of the active departments of the Church work.

J. G. SWENGEL

And last, but not least, the Sunday School, which has always been the live feed wire of the Church, is doing its great work continually ever since the organization of the Church.

The following is the roll of the preachers who served Immanuel Evangelical Church: Reverends H. Bucks, N. McLehn, J. Eckert, M. Sindlinger, C. Hummel, N. Goebel, Jacob Gross, Christian Meyers, Elias Miller, George Knerr, T. Seabold, W. Bachman, W. L. Reber, Moses Dissinger, G. T. Haines, A. Boetzel, Thomas Bowman, Isaac Hess, C. K. Fehr, R. Litzenberger, John Schell, John Koehl, J. O. Lehr, C. B. Flichr, George Knerr, Jacob Adams, Seneca Breyfogel, R. M. Lichtenwalner, B. F. Bohner, H. J. Glick, Thomas L. Wentz, J. K. Seyfried, W. A. Leopold, C. V. B. Aurand, Joseph Specht, C. K. Fehr, J. C. Bliem, A. S. Kresge, C. C. Moyer, J. Willet Boyer, A. H. Doerstler, Henry Wentz, and J. G. Swengel, the present pastor.

The present Board of Trustees and Stewards are William F. Engler, President; M Thomas Heilman, Secretary; Harrison E. Missmer, Treasurer, Charles George and Oliver Graver.

The Church has had on its roll the names of many of the most prominent business men of Catasauqua, and many of them have already crossed over into the Great Beyond To think of the many who have worshipped in Immanuel Evangelical Church in the past and are no more, to recollect their names and reflect upon their noble characters, and to recall their many Christian kindnesses, all cause one to cry out in tearful anguish,—

"Oh! where are the flowers of yesterday?
The winds have blown them all away."

BRIDGE STREET PRESBYTERIAN CHURCH

It is often found a difficult task to discern the very first points in important events that are of recent occurrence, but the difficulty is greatly increased when we attempt to learn the beginning of events that date back more than half a century On careful investigation it has been ascertained from trustworthy records, that the early history of what is now known as the Bridge Street Presbyterian Church is intimately associated with that of the venerable Presbyterian Church in the nearby Allen Township

The present location in earlier times constituted a part of Northampton County, to which place were attracted a large and excellent class of immigrants from Wales, and from the North of Ireland, by the then bright prospects of obtaining useful and remunerative employment at the furnaces of the Crane Iron Company.

The people who came from the last named country desired to be recognized and distinguished in the land of their adoption, as had been their ancestors for several generations, under the designation of Scotch-Irish Presbyterians By this particular name they, and the immense numbers who previously and subsequently came from the Province of Ulster, in the north of Ireland, with their numerous descendants, are to be known, while at the same time they constitute a valuable and component part of our great American nationality

They, therefore, naturally and properly desired to enjoy in their new Catasauqua home religious advantages of the same character and order with which they had been so happily familiar in their native Presbyterian Ulster. With such principles and feelings they welcomed the glad prospect of having Christian fellowship with their new and their near neighbors, the descendants of their countrymen, the thrifty and friendly farmers of the rich and prosperous "Scotch Irish Settlement," the nearest point of which was but four or five miles distant from the Company's furnaces. This strong feeling of affiliation was tenderly fostered by the then beloved pastor of the Mother Church, the Rev Leslie Irwin He, too, was a native of the north of Ireland He came to America in 1834, and in the following year visited the "Settlement," as it was usually called For a time he was the Stated Supply, and afterwards the settled pastor of the "Allen Township Church " Records show that previous to 1845 Mr Erwin had visited and preached to the New Scotch-Irish Settlement on the Lehigh These visits and religious services were kept up with regularity for several years, notwithstanding that a distance of eight or nine miles separated the residence of the faithful pastor from his new missionary field In time there arose a desire to have a regular and separate church organization in their midst In furtherance of this laudable object, a petition, numerously signed, was presented to the Presbytery of Newton, April 26, 1850, in compliance with which a committee was appointed to visit the place, and take such action as the circumstances might seem to require That committee met at the time and place appointed, and subsequently reported to Presbytery that on May 7, 1850, the First Old School Presbyterian Church of Catasauqua had been duly organized, on which occasion thirty-two members were enrolled James McClelland was elected and ordained to the office of Ruling Elder The Church continued under the above title until the reunion in 1870, when the Old School and the New School united under the name of The Presbyterian Church in the U S A, at which time the pastor, Rev. Wm Fulton, gave to the congregation the name Bridge Street Presbyterian Church The young Church increased rapidly in numbers and in spiritual strength In all those years there was no public hall or other building where the people could assemble for their accustomed worship The circumstances of their situation necessitated their meetings to be held in private houses in the winter season. In the summer time they resorted to the nearby woods, and there extemporized a temple in which they praised and prayed and preached and heard the word of God with gladness.

On Sabbaths, when no services were held in Catasauqua, or in the adjoining woods, many people walked out to the country Church, the other part of Mr. Irwin's pastoral charge, about six miles distant, to worship with the Christian brethren in the Settlement. These discomforts of distance and travel, together with the increasing numbers and resources and Christian zeal, suggested the necessity of making an earnest and united effort to provide suitable accommodations at home. In carrying out this good purpose, a plain Union Church building (there is no reason to believe that this was a Presbyterian Church) was erected and located on what for that reason was then and is now known as Church Street. That, however, did not seem to give the desired satisfaction

BRIDGE STREET PRESBYTERIAN CHURCH

and accommodation for any length of time. In the lapse of a few years the increase of population and of the Church, and other causes made it necessary that there should be a separate and independent Church edifice. Under these circumstances, the congregation contributed liberally for the erection of their own and first Church building, which in 1852 was erected upon the site which is still occupied for the purpose, on Bridge Street. In the same year, or very soon afterwards. Mr Irwin succeeded in having erected, on the adjoining lot, the present suitable and substantial parsonage, into which when completed, he moved his family After a residence of about six years in the Catasauqua parsonage, Mr Irwin removed to his farm near Bath, but continued to supply both Churches until the spring of 1865, when, at his own request, the pastoral relation of fifteen years' duration was dissolved The Catasauqua Church, in the last year of his ministry, reported to Presbytery one hundred five members on its roll Mr Irwin was held in highest esteem by all who knew him He died November 26, 1873, in the sixty-eighth year of his age

Mr Irwin was succeeded almost immediately after his resignation by the Rev James Tewers, who accepted the call of the Church and was installed in September, 1865 The ministerial services of Mr Tewers continued for but three years His successful pastorate was seen in the gratifying increase of Church members, and in the orderly and godly lives of those who had the privilege of hearing the gospel of the grace of God preached by a man who felt in his own heart the power of saving truth The necessity for a larger and a more substantial edifice now became apparent The new church on the old site was completed during the pastorate of Mr Tewers The burden of rebuilding lay heavily upon Mr Tewers' heart and affected his health to such an extent that he gradually sank to his death, August 24, 1868

In December, these people called their third pastor, Rev Wm Fulton, who was duly installed over a united and enthusiastic congregation The seven years of this pastorate were eventful times in the history of the Church Large and interested audiences attended on all the Church services, for Mr Fulton was a strong preacher and a successful pastor A heavy debt of over seven thousand dollars had remained on the Church property from the time of its erection The burden seemed to become heavier as the years rolled by, and at times it threatened the most disastrous results Notwithstanding many discouragements, Mr Fulton accomplished a good work in building up the character and stability of the Bridge Street Church, as well as in securing a reduction of well nigh five thousand dollars on the debt In June, 1893, Mr Fulton made a lecturing tour west and while crossing the prairie in a coach between Bur Oaks and Albim, Kansas, he received an electric shock during a severe storm, from the effects of which he died at Albim, July 9 His mortal remains were brought by his son to the cemetery at Catasauqua and laid to rest beside those of his beloved wife.

Rev David Harbison succeeded Mr Fulton and was installed pastor on May 2, 1876 This pastorate continued uninterruptedly, until the close of November, 1901—a period of twenty-five years—when Mr Harbison moved with his family to College Hill, Easton, having retired from the active ministry, "Willing and ready to retire to the calm repose of the coming hours of a long life and a long pastorate and there await the solemn and the joyful call 'enter into the joys of your Lord '"

Rev B Hammond was called to the pastorate at a congregational meeting held Friday evening, May 23, 1902, and was duly installed Thursday evening, July 17, 1902 Mr Hammond served the congregation seven years, when, after a short illness, he died February 11, 1909 During his pastorate over one hundred fifty persons were added to the membership of the Church The property was greatly improved and an Estey pipe organ was installed in the church At the time of his death the membership was two hundred thirty, and the total indebtedness, two hundred dollars

The present pastor, Rev H W Ewig, was called by the congregation on Friday evening, September 3, 1909, at which service Rev C H Miller of the First Presbyterian Church presided Rev. Dr A J Weisley of Trenton preached the sermon Rev Plato T Jones of

REV H W EWIG

Easton delivered the charge to the pastor and Rev L B Crane of Easton delivered the charge to the people During the present pastorate seventy-five persons have been received into the Church membership, and the benevolent contributions have increased about sixteen per cent. over the preceding five years The comfort of the congregation has been greatly added to by the installation of a steam heating plant, and the Church grounds and parsonage are in first class condition In secular education a good record has been made by the members Almost, if not altogether, twenty-five of them have taught school and the percentage of Normal School graduates is the highest in the Borough

ST PAUL'S EVANGELICAL LUTHERAN CHURCH.

During the winter of 1851 and '52, it became apparent that there was a sufficient number of Lutherans ready to found a congregation, whereupon, in union with their German Reformed brethren, they resolved to build a church The Lutheran members of the committee charged with the work consisted of Messrs George Breinig, Samuel Koehler and Charles Wolf

The site on which the Union Church was erected is the one still occupied by St Paul's Church It contains one acre of ground, purchased May 18, 1852, by Samuel Colver (Lutheran) and William Biery (Reformed) trustees, of St Paul's Union Church, from Mr Henry Kurtz and wife Lydia, for the sum of three hundred dollars The document was witnessed by George Frederick, Sr, and George Breinig.

The corner stone of the new Church was laid July 4, 1852, by the pastors, the Rev Jeremiah Schindel and the Rev Dr Jacob Becker and son Rev Cyrus Becker The mason in charge was Mr Charles Siegly

The new church was solemnly consecrated on Christmas Day, 1852 The first vestry was composed of Rev Jeremiah Schindel, President, Messrs George Breinig and George Frederick, Elders, and Messrs Jonathan Snyder and Reuben Patterson, Deacons.

In the fall of 1853 Pastor Schindel resigned this Church in order to devote more of his time to the other congregations of his large parish, and the Rev William Rath, his assistant, succeeded him.

The first communion record, made by Rev. Rath, contains sixty-eight names. Pastor Rath preached his farewell sermon, July 7, 1861. The Rev. Dr. F. J. F. Schantz was elected June 13, 1861, and began his labors on July 21, and now introduced services also in the English language. The congregation also observed all festival days of the Church year.

ST. PAUL'S EV. LUTHERAN OLD CHURCH

On August 13, 1865, a pipe organ, built by Mr. Hanzleman of Allentown, Pa., at a cost of eleven hundred dollars, was consecrated with appropriate services. Having received a unanimous call to Myerstown, Pa., Dr. Schantz resigned, August 11, 1866.

During the interim, the Rev Carl Schlenker supplied the congregation with German services, and Rev Prof E F Koons of Muhlenberg College, with English preaching.

The Rev Jacob D Schindel, D D , was elected March 10, 1867, and entered the service of the congregation, June 1st The new pastor was greeted by certain contentions at the very threshold of his pastorate Although there was a definite understanding between the two congregations as to the part ownership and use of the Union Church, services conflicting with each other's rights were frequently arranged for Sectarian elements also crept into the Union Sunday School This naturally caused contentions that ultimately led to a separation The Lutherans retained possession of the Church property, paid the Reformed three thousand six hundred dollars for their half-interest, and assumed the debt resting on the Church, amounting March 1, 1868, to four thousand dollars, not counting the interest

A constitution, placing the congregation on a proper doctrinal basis, and bringing the same into correct synodical relations, was adopted May 14, 1868 , and on January 1, 1871, a resolution to incorporate the Church was passed Legal proceedings were instituted against this, but objections were finally withdrawn in open court and the charter granted

In the spring of 1872, efforts were made to remove the dead buried on the lot adjoining the Church building No burials had been allowed there since the property came entirely into the possession of the Lutheran congregation The last bodies were exhumed in the fall of 1873 In view of the congregation having stopped burials on the church lot, Mr James W Fuller, Sr , and wife, Clarissa, presented the congregation with four full lots in Fairview cemetery for the burial of unclaimed bodies, and the remains of the deceased poor whom the congregation interred

According to a unanimous resolution, morning and evening services were required of the pastor on each Lord's Day, which interfered seriously with Pastor Schindel's services in his country congregations On this account, but chiefly because of a bitter factional strife between the German and certain English elements in the Church, the pastor presented his resignation to the Council. Nov 12, 1872

The language contention resulted in the withdrawal of about twenty-five persons from the Church. These people founded the Holy Trinity *English* Evangelical Lutheran Church in the spring of 1873.

ST. PAUL'S EV. LUTHERAN CHURCH

The people still remaining in St. Paul's Church now strongly urged Pastor Sehindel to withdraw his resignation, which he promptly did, with the promise, that he would remain until the congregation was able to support its own pastor.

In the spring of 1879 Mr. William Roesch, through the solicitude of Philip Storm, whose liberality to his Church was proverbial, purchased a bell to take the place of the broken one in the tower. After having been in use for about eighteen months, the new bell broke, whereupon Mr Roesch bought another which is still in use

For nearly a decade, the congregation had no debts nor any new enterprise to engage its energy and occupy its attention It was very clear however that for better Sunday School accommodations some building operations must be begun On May 24, 1887, a resolution to build a new church was adopted, and the following building committee appointed Messrs Simon Breinig, Frederick Eberhard, John L Witt, Cain Semmel, Samuel M Snyder, Uriah F Koehler and Tilghman F Frederick

The last service in the old church was held on June 12, the mason work of the new church was begun July 2, and on the 7th of August the corner stone laid The old corner stone, laid in the old church, July 4, 1852, was now planted into the north-eastern corner of the new building The pastor who laid the new stone was a son of the pastor who laid the first corner stone.

The cost of the new church was a trifle over fourteen thousand dollars

The Second Conference of the Ministerium of Pennsylvania, predecessor of the Allentown Conference, added to Mickley's and Coplay congregations of Pastor Schindel the Egypt and Laury's Churches, to form a parish The latter two congregations issued a unaimous call to Pastor Schindel February 7, 1888 Rev Schindel accepted this call, and so resigned St Paul's Church February 8 On April 1, 1888, his labors in St Paul's Church ceased

Through the zeal of Mr F F Frederick the flag-stone pavements along Howertown Avenue and around the church were laid, and the iron fence erected during 1888.

The Rev Joseph W Mayne was unanimously elected pastor on June 8, 1888 and having accepted the call, entered upon his labors here during July The new church having now been completed, consecration services were held August 5, 1888

Donations to the new church were made as follows The pulpit by Mrs C Breinig and son, four chancel chairs by Mrs Mary Alice Steward, a table by Mrs Jeanette Frederick; Baptismal Font by S S Class No 14, taught by Miss

Mary L Beitel and the Lecturn by Mrs Mary J Frederick in memory of her departed children, Edith L and George T

A special meeting of the congregation was held Sept 15, 1890, at which Pastor Mayne proposed, "That in order to secure a permanent home, the congregation borrow the necessary money and build a parsonage, and he will obligate himself to pay the interest until such time as the congregation shall see fit to pay for the building"

The proposition was adopted unanimously, and the price of the building limited to thirty-five hundred dollars The building committee consisted of Messrs. William A Heckenberger, James Dilcher and James C Beitel It was finished by the spring of 1891 at a cost of four thousand two hundred sixteen dollars Pastor Mayne resigned on March 27, 1892, and preached his farewell sermon May 8, 1892

Rev James F Lambert preached for the congregation on the 22nd of May, 1892, and was elected pastor on the 29th of May The call was extended on June 9 and installation services held July 10 After a thorough revision of the roll, 524 names were found in good standing

On November 13, 1894, the congregation received a bequest from the late Mrs Amelia Faust of two hundred fifty dollars which, minus the inheritance tax, netted two hundred thirty-eight dollars Mr. and Mrs Paul C Broadbeck presented the congregation December, 1895, with two beautiful white and gold hymn boards in memory of their deceased children, Ralph C and Minnie L, who followed each other closely in death by scarlet fever, June 24, and July 11, 1894. The boards were replaced later by marble tablets beautifully wrought

The Kirchen-Buch, published by authority of the General Council, was adopted Jan 1, 1896 The monthly system of envelopes, as a means of raising funds, was adopted Jan 1, 1901

At the congregational meeting Jan 1, 1902, it was resolved unanimously to observe the Golden Jubilee of the congregation with appropriate services during the week beginning June 29, 1902 An interesting history of the Church, Sunday School, and all of the Church Societies was written by the pastor as a memorial of the occasion

The congregation resolved, Aug 9, 1902, to remove the four turrets on the tower of the church and build a spire crowned with a gilt cross. January 1, 1903, the pastor's salary was increased and the request made that he discontinue his services in St. John's Church at Fullerton, Pa., where he preached for over nine years.

After extensive improvements reconsecration services were held February 7, 1904. The unveiling of an oilpainting portraying the Ascension of Christ, by the Misses Marie and Helen Kostenbader, in memory of Carl Immanuel, the youngest child of the family, was an impressive feature. The painting is the gift of Mr. H. Kostenbader and family. This picture was remounted in the enlarged church by Messrs. August F. and Herman A. Kostenbader. Other memorials and gifts are Altar Crossby Mrs. Sarah C. Steitz in memory of her husband Henry G. and her children, a Missel Stand and Bible by Dr. and Mrs. Joseph Heckenberger in memory of their sons Clarence Dech and Ralph Heller, Vases by Mr. and Mrs. F. Goldsmith's mother, Mrs. Elizabeth Dieter. A number of ladies furnished altar vestments, and the F. W. Wint Lumber Co. presented solid walnut pedestals.

In July, 1905, the congregation was declared free of debt and a mortgage of fifteen years' standing was burned. On Jan. 1, 1909, on motion of Mr. T. F. Frederick, the congregation resolved to provide larger accommodations for her fully graded Sunday School. Plans prepared by Mr. A. H. Leh of So. Bethlehem were adopted April 15, and a building committee consisted of Messrs. H. Kostenbader, W. J. Smith, F. Goldsmith, R. Frank Kratzer, J. J. Seyfried, J. H. Witt and C. S. Wonderly. The building committee served as contractor and Mr. F. Goldsmith as foreman in the work.

The corner stone was laid August 15, 1909, by the pastor, assisted by Rev. Jeremiah Schindel, the grandson of Pastor Schindel, the founder of the Church. A four thousand dollar pipe organ, built by Mr. C. F. Durner and Son at Quakertown, Pa., was placed into the added part of the church.

The dimensions of the original church were seventy-two by forty-five feet and of the addition seventy by thirty-eight feet, giving the edifice a cruciform shape. The total cost of the improvements amounted to twenty-five thousand dollars, nearly half of which is paid. The terazza floor and steps in the chancel were the munificent gift of the late Mr H Kostenbader An eagle lecturn, and a marble tablet properly inscribed are the gift of Mr William H Glace, Esq , in memory of his father, Mr. Samuel Glace, a devout elder of the Church Windows were presented "Clinging to the Cross" by Mr J C Beitel and family, "I am the Vine" by Mr and Mrs. P J Laubach in memory of Mrs Sarah Deily; "Knocking at the Door" by Mrs Flora A E Heckenberger, wife and children, "Gathering into the Fold" by Mrs Mary J Frederick and family in memory of Mr T F Frederick, "Virgin Mother and Child" by Mr H Seltmann and family, and "Christ in Gethsemane" by Mr Franklin Goldsmith and family The pastor's stalls are the gift of Mrs Mary A Steward and family in memory of Mr Henry A Steward. The baptismal font is the gift of the Misses Charlotte and Cecilia Kostenbader The Vestry resolved unanimously, April 27, 1910 "That the pastor be authorized to wear the Clerical Robe" and Mrs Sarah C Broadbeck and Mr. Charles T. Dilcher procured a beautiful garment

Consecration services were held July 17-22, 1910, in which a number of Lutheran pastors, and all the Clergy of town took part

Through the liberality of Mrs. Matilda Kostenbader and the handiwork of Mrs Ida S. Solt, choir vestments were procured during the summer of 1911 The Choir Stalls are the gift of the Choir

St Paul's congregation now numbers nine hundred forty-two members in good standing

SALEM REFORMED CHURCH

The Reformed people of Catasauqua, who lived at the time when the place was known as Biery's-Port, worshipped either at Schoenersville or Howertown Feeling that to attend divine service nearer home would afford much comfort and ease, yet loving the Church of their fathers, they were granted the use of the Presbyterian chapel, on such days or hours when the Presbyterians had no service, and thus they held periodic services here from 1848 to 1852, under the pastorate of Rev. Jacob C Becker, their pastor at Schoenersville and Howertown Churches. We must not omit to notice here that much credit is due Mr. Nicholas

Balliet for bringing the Church interest of the Reformed people into such definite shape. He was a zealous laborer in the cause of the Christian religion, and a devoted member of the Reformed Church.

After some time an organization was effected by the pastor, Rev. J. C. Becker, and a movement set on foot to build a church, but its membership being only about one hundred, he covenanted with the Lutheran people, who started about the same time under the pastoral charge of Rev. Jeremiah Schindel, and they agreed to buy a lot and built on it jointly; consequently, a committee was appointed by the two congregations, consisting of Messrs. George Breinig, Samuel Koehler, Charles Nolf (Lutheran), and Mr. Solomon Biery (Reformed). The site on which the union church was erected is the one still occupied by the St. Paul's Lutheran Church on Howertown Avenue. The corner stone of the new church was laid on the 4th of July, 1852, at ten A. M. by Rev. Jeremiah Schindel and Rev. J. C. Becker and son Cyrus J. Becker. Rev. Schindel preached the sermon. On Christmas Day, 1852, the new church was dedicated to the service of the Triune God. The ministers taking part in the services were Rev. Jeremiah Schindel, Rev. J. C. Becker, Dr. Hoffenditz, Rev. Apple, Rev. Jos. Yeager and Rev. William Rath.

SALEM REFORMED CHURCH

The union of the Reformed and the Lutheran congregations lasted till the year 1868, when the Reformed congregation made an overture to the Lutherans to buy or sell. The Lutherans accepted the offer and bought out the Reformed in March of the same year, the consideration having been thirty-six hundred dollars. The Reformed people then built a church for themselves on a lot donated by Mr. Joseph Laubach on the corner of Third and Walnut Streets. The corner-stone was laid in April, 1869, and the church was dedicated in the fall of the same year. This congregation was known as the First Reformed Church of Catasauqua Meanwhile the Reformed congregation, under the pastorate of Rev Cyrus J Becker, who had succeeded his father, the Rev J C Becker, worshipped in the Bridge Street Presbyterian Church and also conducted a Sunday School in the same place Dissensions arose very soon in the congregation, Rev Becker. who also was the pastor of the Schoenersville and Howertown congregations, having been requested to resign those congregations and become the pastor of the congregation in Catasauqua alone Rev Becker refused the proposition and resigned as pastor of the First Reformed Church in 1870 This resignation was confirmed by the East Pennsylvania Classis at their annual meeting at Kutztown, Pa, May 16, 1871, leaving the congregation without a pastor, which resulted in weakening the congregation and reducing it to a small membership The congregation, now being without a pastor, was occasionally supplied by Rev. T O. Stem of Hellertown, and other ministers sent here by the East Pennsylvania Classis During those unfortunate days the church building had been rented to three different denominations, each of which had received accessions to its membership through disintegration of this congregation, so that there was scarcely anything worthy of the name of a Reformed congregation existing at the time The Sunday School was entirely scattered and teachers and scholars had been absorbed by other denominations to which also a number of the Church members had gone over The organization (two elders, three deacons and three trustees) still existed, but the congregation, as it once was, was no more

In the fall of 1873. Rev. A B. Koplin was called by the East Pennsylvania Classis to look after the Reformed interests, and he succeeded in effecting a new organization under the former title During his pastorate the Sunday School was reorganized and the congregation again placed on a good foundation Its membership was over one hundred, but the property being burdened with a heavy debt, its growth was retarded After serving the congregation four years, he resigned in the spring of 1877 His resignation was accepted, and on May 7, 1877, East Pennsylvania Classis dismissed him to Tohickon Classis. After the resignation of Rev Koplin, a call was extended to Rev J J Crist, a graduate of the Theological Seminary at Lancaster, Pa , who became the pastor and was ordained and installed on May 31, 1877, by Revs S A Leinbach, A G Dubbs and J E Freeman

When Rev Christ began his pastorate, the debt was still a heavy burden on the congregation, and, to make matters still worse, the steeple of the church, which was one hundred and sixty feet high, was damaged by a heavy storm on the afternoon of October 23, 1878, when sixty feet of it was blown down, and lay a shapeless mass upon the ground The consistory met on the following evening and immediately took action on the repairing of the same A committee was appointed consisting of Owen Romich, Ellen Fehnel, Priscilla Fehnel, Cecilia Troxell and Amanda Johnson to collect funds to make temporary repairs On September 10, 1879, a Young Peoples' Association was organized The object was to promote a social, moral and intellectual improvement among its members, and aid in the liquidation of the church debt It has done good work during its thirty-three years of existence

The debt being still a heavy burden, the church was finally sold by the sheriff in 1880, and the organization under the title of the First Reformed Church disbanded, but in April of the same year, at a public meeting called for the purpose of organizing a Reformed Church, a new organization was effected under the title of Salem Reformed Church of Catasauqua, Pa The organization bought the property from the sheriff, and efforts were at once put forth to pay the debt on the property, which amounted to about thirty-three hundred dollars During all this time there was little progress in the increase of membership, so that in 1884 the membership was only about one hundred eighty But the debt, which had been the chief hindrance, now being reduced, there was a prospect for a more rapid increase of membership

On January 5, 1885, the Mite Society was organized This organization consisted of married women of the congregation, and the noble work and self sacrifice of these mothers during all these years can not be estimated The large sums of money placed in the Church treasury, and the beautiful Altar railing which bears the Society's inscription will stand as a lasting monument to their memory.

During the pastorate of the Rev. Mr. Crist, great progress was made in all the various branches of the Church. The Sunday School, Mite Society, Young People's Association, and congregation made strong efforts, and finally the debt was paid in 1886; but the saddest part of all this was that the health of the pastor, Rev. J. J. Crist, failed, and he was compelled to resign, after serving the congregation faithfully for nine years. His resignation was accepted in the spring of 1886.

Having been without a pastor for some time, the congregation was supplied by Revs. Jared Fritzinger and T. N. Reber of Allentown. On June 3, 1886, Rev. W. F. More, a graduate of Lehigh University and the Theological Seminary at Lancaster, Pa., was ordained and installed as pastor, and on Sunday, June 6, 1886, he preached his introductory sermons. From now on the congregation took a forward step. In 1887 it became self supporting and in 1888 the annex was built. In 1890 the church was painted and the steeple erected, which was blown down by a heavy storm on October 23, 1878.

REV. A. P. FRANTZ

The new Church hymnal was introduced in 1891, and in 1893 a centennial celebration took place, when the church was beautifully decorated with historic decorations. The year 1894 may be noted as the banner year for its Sunday School work, more of the older members of the congregation having attended during this than during any of the former years. There was a good supply of teachers and all took part in the work. Under the pastorate of Rev. More the congregation increased in membership. The Sunday School becoming in need of better accommodations, it was finally decided to erect a Sunday School building. The building was erected in 1902.

After Rev. More had served the congregation faithfully during eighteen years, he resigned to become the superintendent of Bethany Orphans Home at Womelsdorf, Pa. He preached his farewell sermon June 5, 1904.

The congregation extended a call to Rev A P Frantz, B D , of Springforge Pa He preached his first sermon on Sunday, August 21, 1904, and December 4, 1904, he was installed as pastor by Rev W H Wotring, D D , Rev H A Frantz and Rev J G Rupp

The debt which was incurred by remodeling the church and in rebuilding the Sunday School room during Rev More's pastorate was finally paid A steam heating plant was installed, and the duplex envelope system was introduced and proves successful The congregation at present has five hundred two members, and the Sunday School is the second largest in town

The officers of the consistory of the congregation are Rev. A P Frantz, B D , President, Dr A J Becker, Vice President , H W Hoffman, Secretary , W M Follweiler Treasurer

ANNUNCIATION B V M CHURCH
Second & Union Sts
Rev Jno A Seimetz Rector

The parish of the Annunciation B V M , briefly called St Mary's, traces its origin back to the year 1852 Father Tanzer, who was then stationed at Easton, gathered the few scattered German families, and regularly, at stated times, came from Easton and attended to their spiritual welfare

The Holy Sacrifice of the Mass was celebrated for the first time in the home of George Schneider, located on Church St , No 300 The house is still in existence Later, George Schneider removed to No 128 Second St and then to 105 Second St , where these services were continually held

In the year 1856, the small, struggling congregation had increased by emigration to eighteen families The house of George Schneider became too small to afford room for them all, and relying upon the help of God, they acquired a small plot of ground at the corner of Second & Union Sts In 1857 the small frame church was built, which was dedicated to the service of God on the 9th of Sept , 1857 Henceforth services were held regularly once a month, as the parish then formed a mission of St Joseph's, So Easton The Church then had a membership of about seventeen to nineteen families, whose names, as far as can be ascertained, follow Peter and Mary Freund, John Blum and Mary Blum, Frank Roth, Jacob and Mrs Geiss, Martin Englert, Caroline Englert, Ludwig and Pauline Englert,

ST. MARY'S ROMAN CATHOLIC CHURCH

Adam and Elizabeth Freund, Nicholas Schmidt and wife, John and Theresia Dillinger, George and Josephine Schneider, Conrad Schaeffer, Thomas and Mrs. Linder, John and Mrs. Gessner. In 1857, when the German Catholic Church, which was located at the corner of Ridge Road and Allen St., received its first permanent pastor, in the person of Rev. J. Tuboly, the Annunciation parish of Catasauqua was severed from So. Easton, and attended to as a mission from Allentown. Father Tuboly served until March, 1858. In April, 1858, he was succeeded by Rev. Charles J. Schroeder, who again in May, 1860, was followed by Rev. Rudolph Kuenzer. Father Kuenzer served until 1862. He was followed by Rev. Xavier Kaier, 1862-1863, and the Rev. Joseph Kaelin from 1863-1869.

Allentown requiring the services of its on pastor, the Annunciation B. V. M. of Catasauqua was attached to Bethlehem. The first to attend Catasauqua from Bethlehem was the Rev. John Alber who more frequently held services in Catasauqua. He bought a plot of ground in Hanover Township for a Cemetery in 1874; all burials previously were made in Fairview Cemetery, Catasauqua. Father Albert served the congregation until 1875; his successor was the Rev. Joseph Winter who attended to the then growing parish until May, 1877. Rev. Joseph Winter was succeeded by the Rev. J. H. Badde who came from Bethlehem and served from May, 1877 to 1884, when he was appointed as the first resident pastor of the parish.

REV. JOHN A. SEIMETZ

In 1882 Father Badde built the first Parochial School containing two rooms, obtained the Sisters of St. Francis as teachers, who resided in a house which he bought, near the corner of Second & Union Sts.

In 1878 Rev. Badde built the brick church, the small frame building proving too small. Its dimensions were 38 ft. by 70 ft., and it was dedicated Aug. 18th, 1878. Father Badde served until August, 1886, when he was succeeded by Rev. J. F. Fechtel on August 15th.

In Feb., 1888, Father Fechtel found a successor in Rev. F. J. Schlebbe who continued the work until April 27th, 1889, when Rev. John A. Seimetz, the present Rector, was appointed by the Most Rev. P. J. Ryan, D. D., Archbishop of Philadelphia, Dec. 26th, 1889. Father Seimetz bought a piece of ground from Mrs. Josephine Schneider and in 1890 began the erection of the present Rectory.

ST. MARY'S R. C. RECTORY

It was occupied on the following Oct., 1890. In 1891, the interior of the church was greatly beautified and instead of the old stoves standing in niches in the wall, a furnace was installed in the cellar.

The congregation grew continually and, in 1896, the old church proved entirely too small for the congregation.

In June, 1896, Father Seimetz began alterations and an enlargement of the church, 37 ft. by 47 ft. The whole interior was remodeled. The enlargement proved sufficient and the practically new church was dedicated by Archbishop Ryan on Thanksgiving Day, Nov. 26, 1896. Today it is one of the finest churches in the Lehigh Valley. Father Seimetz, requiring more teachers for his school, added two more class rooms to the old school erected in 1882. In April, 1899, he

ST. MARY'S R. C. SCHOOL

began the erection of a beautiful Sisters' House at the corner of Second & Union Sts. The Sisters took possession of their new home Nov. 2, 1899, and it is sufficiently large for all the Sisters added to the teaching staff until today. The number of pupils increased to such numbers that the school accommodations proved too small. Father Seimetz saw the necessity to build a new school, which building he soon undertook. In May, 1904, the old school was broken away and a new modern structure erected. The school is 70 by 71 ft., three stories high; it contains eight class rooms, cloak rooms and all modern equipments On the third story there is an assembly room 41 by 70 ft., equipped with a fine stage.

The School Building was dedicated on Thanksgiving Day, 1904, by the present Most Rev. Archbishop of Philadelphia, Edmund F. Prendergast, D. D. This school proved so satisfactory that several more Parochial Schools of the Archdiocese of Philadelphia were accordingly built. Yet the work of Father Seimetz was not finished. In Sept., 1905, he bought a plot of ground west of the school building, which was converted into a playground for the children.

In Feb., 1909, Father Seimetz bought the Kester property adjoining the Rectory. In May he began erecting a large addition to the Rectory built in 1890. He improved the Church surroundings by a beautiful lawn with shrubbery and roses, which in the spring and summer time is the admiration of all. In 1912, on the occasion of his "Silver Jubilee of Ordination," he erected a beautiful Gothic Altar in commemoration of his deceased parents, Mathias and Mary Seimetz. This Altar was supplemented later on by two others, one in honor of the Blessed Virgin Mary, the other in honor of St. Joseph, both harmonizing with the High Altar in all details.

On Christmas Day, 1912, the new Estey Organ which he had installed in Nov. and Dec. of the same year, was dedicated and used for the first time. On Dec. 31st, 1913, he bought over three acres of ground as an addition to "Gethsemani Cemetery" in Hanover Township.

On April 26, 1914, Father Seimetz celebrated the 25th Anniversary of his Pastorate in Catasauqua, being in point of service the oldest priest in the Lehigh Valley. The Parish of the Annunciation of Catasauqua is well organized and societies and pious congregation established for all, young and old.

The Church property of the Annunciation Church, Catasauqua, Pa., is one of the largest and most valuable in the Lehigh Valley.

ST. LAWRENCE ROMAN CATHOLIC CHURCH

Prior to the year 1858, the English speaking Catholics of Catasauqua and vicinity met in the homes of Bartholomew Murtaugh and Ed. Crampsey for worship. Father Rearidon of Easton, Pa., ministered to their spiritual needs by cele-

OF CATASAUQUA 107

brating Mass in these homes. In 1858 the congregation decided to erect a church edifice. Park Damsey and Bartholomew Murtaugh bought from the Faust Estate a lot on Second and Chapel Streets for this purpose.

Under the direction of Rev. Lawrence Brennan a beautiful and commodious church was erected and subsequently consecrated for divine worship. The first

ST. LAWRENCE R. C. CHURCH

resident pastor was the Rev. L. J. Miller who was succeeded by the Rev. Edw. McKee in 1862. Father McKee labored zealously for twenty-one years and under his ministrations the congregation enjoyed great prosperity. It was during his pastorate that additional land adjoining the church was bought and solemnly consecrated for a cemetery. Father McKee resigned in 1883 and was succeeded by the Rev. B. J. Conway, who was pastor of the Church until 1896.

REV. HENRY I. O'CONNOR

In 1896 Rev. Peter A. Quinn was appointed rector. It was during the pastorate of Father Quinn that the Parochial School Building and Convent was built, a perpetual monument to the loyalty and devotion of the members of the Church. Owing to poor health, Father Quinn resigned and the present incumbent, Rev. Henry I. Connor, was appointed by the Most Rev. P. J. Ryan, Archbishop, in June, 1907. The labors of Father Conner are greatly appreciated by his parishioners, comprising about nine hundred souls, and the Church is in a properous condition. There are one hundred eighty-three scholars in regular attendance in the Parochial School, which is in charge of the Sisters of St. Francis.

GRACE METHODIST EPISCOPAL CHURCH.

Methodism in Catasauqua did not have the early beginning that other denominations enjoyed. However, as early as 1843, there were those living here who desired Methodist services. By invitation, the Rev. Newton Heston, who was then stationed on Allentown Circuit, came to Catasauqua and preached to a small congregation assembled in the house of Mr. Isaac Lorash, who lived on Church Street, near the present Town Hall. The preaching services in Mr. Lorash's house were irregular, on account of the large territory traveled by the preachers on the Allentown Circuit.

The room in the Lorash house becoming too small to accommodate the congregation, Mrs. Jeannette Frederick and Mrs. Amelia Matchette secured from the School Board the use of the school house on lower Second Street for the services. These elect ladies collected the sum of twenty dollars annually to pay the preacher. Mr. Samuel Steele and Mrs. Margaret Rodgers were also among the first and most active workers in the organization of a Methodist Episcopal Church in this place. The old lamps used in early services in homes and school house, together with collection boxes, Bible, and Hymn books are still in the possession of the Frederick family.

It was not until 1855, under the leadership of Rev H A Hobbs, preacher in charge of Allentown Circuit, with Rev Isaac Thomas as junior preacher, that the work in Catasauqua showed signs of development. In 1858, Rev F D Egan conducted regular services in the Second Street school house His labors were blessed with a revival, during which more than twenty persons professed conversion and united with the Church These, with nine that had already been organized into a society, constituted the beginning of a better day

In 1859, the pressing need was a Church edifice The little band of Christians proved their devotion to the Church of their choice by assuming the responsibility of erecting a Church building They bought a lot on Front Street above Walnut from James W Fuller, Sr, and in June, 1857, the corner stone was laid Rev F D Egan officiated on this occasion On a cold winter's day, December 25, 1859, the basement of the church was dedicated

The first session of the Sunday School was held Feb 25, 1860, at 7 30 P M in the church Arthur Campbell was the first superintendent The Board of Trustees held their first meeting at the house of Joseph Reichard April 17 1860 The members present were Charles Graffin, Arthur Campbell and Joseph Reichard A charter of incorporation was granted by the Court of Lehigh County, November 17, 1860

During the year of incorporation, the organization became financially embarrassed on account of the cost of their church property exceeding the estimate, and probably other causes The financial obligation was so heavy for the little society, that they were obliged to appeal for out-side help The Philadelphia Conference took action to render assistance, but, since very little money was forthcoming, finally, on July 26, 1862, Charles B Hainty, Esq, High Sheriff of Lehigh County, sold the property at public sale to Tilghman H Meyers, who bought it for the creditors

The property, however, was saved to the Denomination by the faithful band of Christians, by the liberality of Mr James W Fuller. Sr, and Clarissa Fuller, his wife, and by the heroic assistance of the Presiding Elder of the

District, Rev Dr D W Bartine, who secured money from friends in Philadelphia and elsewhere on the District

Catasauqua M E Church was made a separate appointment by the Philadelphia Annual Conference in the year 1864, and Rev Charles W Bickley was sent as pastor Rev Bickley was eminently adapted to the needs of the Church and community He preached with great acceptability and he enjoyed large congregations A revival of great importance swept over the community, the loftiest and the humblest, rich and poor alike, gave themselves to God Some seventy persons professed conversion, most of whom identified themselves with the Church

Toward the close of Rev Best's pastorate, the Church edifice was completed Rev S B Best's service of three years from 1866-69 was highly satisfactory

From 1869 to 1881 the Church was served by some of the choice men of the Philadelphia Conference, some, however, succeeding better than others in this field In the year 1881, beginning with October, Rev O S Garrison became pastor, appointed by Bishop Harris to fill the unexpired term of Rev L B Hoffman Rev Garrison remained pastor in charge until March, 1884 His ministry on this Charge marks another era in the history of the Church A great revival of religion took place during his pastorate His discourses were logical, argumentative,, and clothed with power. He labored with men of the lowest walks of life, and because of his towering personality, was able to lead men by the score to the Master More than one hundred persons made an absolute surrender to God during his ministry

It was during the pastorate of Rev Garrison that the house and lot on the corner of Third and Walnut Streets were purchased from William H Laubach for seven thousand five hundred dollars This property was to be a permanent site for the church and parsonage

Under the administration of Rev A J Amthor, 1887-89, the property on the corner of Third and Walnut Streets as sold to the Crane Iron Company, and the lots on Fifth and Walnut Streets were purchased by the Congregation The commodious and modern parsonage now upon the lot was erected and first occupied by Rev Amthor

Perhaps the crowning event of Methodism in this town, aside from bringing men and women into the Kingdom of God, is the erection of the magnificent stone edifice during the pastorate of Rev. C. H. Rorer.

January 7, 1890, James Thomas, Dr. H. H. Riegel, John Morrison, and Rev. C. H. Rorer were appointed a Building Committee. On March 24, 1890, the contract to build a new Church edifice was awarded to J. S. Allen of South Bethlehem. The chief glory lies in the fact that by the self-denial and liberality of

GRACE METHODIST EPISCOPAL

the members, Grace Methodist Episcopal Church was dedicated, December 21, 1890, free from debt. The approximate cost of the property and equipment is thirty-five thousand dollars. This "Church Cathedral" will ever remain a monument to the love and liberality of the members of the congregation.

January 8, 1894, the Quarterly Conference appointed a committee composed of Thomas B. Glick, Austin A. Glick, James Thomas and H. J. Reinhard to prepare a set of new Records of the Church. The committee prepared a set of fine Records at a cost of sixty dollars. This fact is mentioned because District Superintendents and men of prominence, who have examined many Church Records, pronounce these the best on the North District of the Philadelphia Conference.

It is fitting to state that Rev. C. M. Simpson, who was pastor from 1892 to 1897, remained longer than any other preacher in the history of the Church.

During the pastorate of Rev. F. F. Bond, an Esty Pipe Organ was installed at a cost of three thousand dollars. Other improvements, amounting to thirteen hundred dollars, were made and all expenses met. "Money raising," about this time, was a comparatively easy matter, as men like James Thomas, B. F. Swartz, George Davies and Jacob Roberts were consecrated to the Lord.

The Sunday School room, Class rooms, and Parlor were frescoed and the wood work revarnished at a cost of six hundred and fifty dollars, during the pastorate of Rev. R. A. McIlwain, 1904 to 1907.

REV. A. L. SHALKOP, Ph. D.

The Church membership at this time is two hundred thirty-five. While numerically small, devotion to all the interests of the Church is manifest. The Church property, including parsonage, is clear of any indebtedness and is valued at a conservative estimate of forty thousand dollars. The Rev. A. L. Shalkop, Ph. D., is the present pastor.

The following is a complete list of pastors who served this Church

Rev Newton Heston, 1843-1845	Chas W Bickley, 1864-1865
George Quigley, 1845-1846	Henry F Isett, 1865-1866
George Quigley and T C Murphy, 1846-1847	Silas B Best, 1866-1869
	J J Jones, 1869-1871
W W McMichael, 1847-1848	William B Howell, 1871-1874
Joshua H Turner and W H Burrell, 1848-1849	J Pastorfield, 1874-1876
	G Oram, 1876-1878
D. R Thomas and N C Stockton, 1849-1850	D M Young, 1878-1881
	L B Hoffman, 1881-1881
S G Hare, 1850-1851	S O Garrison, 1881-1884
W H Brisbane, 1851-1853	John Stringer, 1884-1887
Samuel Irwin, 1853-1854	A J Amthor, 1887-1889
Samuel Irwin and J M Hinson, 1854-1855	Charles H Rorer, 1889-1892
	C M Simpson, 1892-1897
H A Hobbs and Jesse Thomas, 1855-1856	E C Yerkes, 1897-1899
	I M Foster, 1899-1901
H A Hobbs and J H Boyd, 1856-1857	F F Bond, 1901-1904
	R A McIlwain, 1904-1907
H H Hickman, 1857-1858	J E Grauley, 1907-1911
F D Eagan, 1858-1860	W Holden Pickop, 1911-1913
S G Hare, 1860-1862	A L Shalkop, 1913-
E T Kenny, 1862-1864	

HOKENDAUQUA PRESBYTERIAN CHURCH

It was in 1854 that the Thomas Iron Company's works were started in Hokendauqua Amongst those who came to reside in the new village were seven members of the First Presbyterian Church of Catasauqua Their names were Samuel Thomas, Mrs Rebecca Mickley Thomas, William W Walters, M D , John McIlhenny, Thomas McClintock, William James, Mrs Mary James

On July 15, 1855, these seven were organized into the Hokendauqua Church by the Rev. Cornelius Earle of Catasauqua, who preached for them Sunday afternoons until a few months before the coming—March 27, 1869—of the Rev. James A. Little, of New York City, who became the duly called and regularly installed pastor of the growing Hokendauqua congregation.

A sightly church edifice, with all spire and commanding location was nearly completed under Dr. Earle's ministrations; and on Sabbath, September 26, 1869,

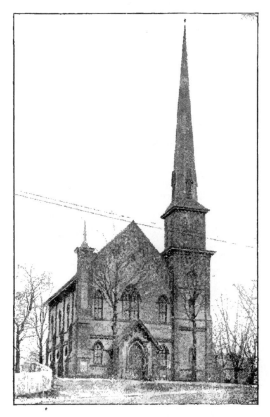

HOKENDAUQUA PRESBYTERIAN CHURCH

Dr. Little conducted long-to-be-remembered dedication services, assisted by distinguished Philadelphia divines.

From that time to the present the Hokendauqua Church has had remarkable prosperity, being free of all indebtedness, and having added to its membership, at every quarterly communion for forty-five years.

The Hokendauqua parsonage was built thirty years ago, has been and is still the handsome residence of Dr. Little and his family.

The Sunday School has enrolled at the present time two hundred and forty-four officers, teachers and scholars, and has always been a power for good in the community. It was also organized in 1855.

Both Church and Sunday School at Hokendauqua owe a lasting debt of gratitude to the splendid helpfulness of their benefactors, Mr. and Mrs. John Thomas. It was through their generosity that in 1892 an eighteen hundred dollar pipe organ was presented to the Hokendauqua Church, which still remains as a weekly reminder of their love and loyalty to their "Long-loved Zion."

REV. DR. LITTLE

In April, 1911, the much-beautified auditorium was re-dedicated, free of debt and with gratifying services, in which the neighboring pastors of Catasauqua and Coplay participated very fraternally and acceptably.

The present officers are as follows: Pastor, Dr. James A. Little; Elders, George Williams, Hokendauqua, Frank S. Hartman, Allentown, Gus. E. Oswald, Catasauqua; Trustees, Thomas Porter, Jr., Sec'y and Treas., Charles Campbell, William J. Faulkner, Edmund Hartman; Henry Hensinger, Organist; William Abernethy, Sexton. Sabbath School: George Williams, Superintendent; Miss May Porter, Organist; Miss Margaret Junkin, Sec'y; Miss Helen V. Little, Treas. Ladies' Aid Society: Mrs. James A. Little, Pres.; Mrs. Horace Boyd, V.-Pres.; Mrs. William J. Faulkner, Treas.

Counting only those who commune or contribute, the actual membership is one hundred twenty-six, a willing and faithful band, who do much for Christ and the Church.

THE ENGLISH LUTHERAN CHURCH OF THE HOLY TRINITY.

The majority of the members who entered into the organization of the Church of the Holy Trinity were members of St. Paul's Ev. Lutheran Church, Catasauqua. They withdrew from said Church because they could not secure in it, such provisions for services in the English language as they deemed de-

TRINITY EV. LUTHERAN CHURCH

sirable and necessary. This withdrawal occurred in connection with the annual congregational meeting of St. Paul's Church, January 1, 1873. On January 10, 1873, steps were taken for holding regular services in the English language. The Reformed Church was secured for this purpose. January 28, 1873, the name "English Evangelical Lutheran Church of the Holy Trinity" was adopted.

February 10, 1873, a constitution was adopted and signed by twenty-three persons A board of officers was elected at the same time The Holy Communion was administered by Rev Joseph A Seiss, D D , of Philadelphia, for the first time on May 4, 1873 Thirty-one persons participated May 27, 1873, Rev. Jno. K Plitt, of Greensburg, Pa , was unanimously elected Pastor and accepted the call on May 30, and took charge July 1 Ground was broken for the new Church edifice, corner of Third and Bridge Streets, October 14, 1873 The corner-stone was laid November 9, 1873 Rev Dr Muhlenberg, President of Muhlenberg College, delivered a discourse, Rev J D Schindel, pastor of St Paul's Church, took part in the services, Rev C Earle and Rev Mr Fulton were also present

The church was dedicated on Sunday, May 17, 1874 Dr Seiss had promised to preach the dedicatory sermon, but was unable to be present on account of sickness. Rev C P Krauth, D D , Vice-Provost of the University of Penna , and a professor in the Lutheran Theological Seminary in Philadelphia, kindly supplied the place of Dr Seiss in the morning and evening

Dr Muhlenberg spoke in the afternoon, and Rev E T Horn and Rev J D Schindel assisted in the liturgical services Rev Mr Earle, Rev Mr Fulton and Rev Mr Koplin also assisted Rev Prof M H. Richards succeeded Rev Mr Plitt in 1877 He was followed by Rev G W Sandt, who remained pastor until 1884, when Prof Richards acted as supply until Rev C S Kohler took charge in Dec , 1884 He continued as pastor until 1887, when he was succeeded by Rev Dr D M Henkel who cared for the congregation until 1889, when he was compelled by ill health to relinquish the charge Rev J D Roth was pastor from 1889 to May 1, 1893, his successor was Rev Paul G Klingler, who remained until called to St John's at Easton in 1896. Following Mr Klingler came Rev Wm. G DeAount Hudson, who was pastor until 1902 Rev Edwin F Keever began his pastorate in 1902 and remained until 1907, when he was called to Utica, N Y Rev Chas L Fry was his successor and remained with the congregation until Oct 1, 1913, when it became necessary for him to give all his time to the Church Extension work, with his headquarters at Philadelphia, Pa Since Rev Dr Fry's retirement,

Rev Prof J D M Brown has been supplying very satisfactorily as acting pastor. About two years ago the Congregation bought the Smith property adjoining the church and transformed it into a beautiful parsonage. The Church now numbers about one hundred sixty members, six of whom were among the thirty-one who communed on May 4, 1873. The Church recently celebrated its fortieth anniversary. The services were participated in by Rev Dr Edward T Horn, Rev Dr G W Sandt, Rev J F Lambert and Rev Dr Chas L Fry. The Sunday School of the Church has not changed its executive head as often as the Church, it having had three superintendents. The first was Col M H Horn who devoted so much of his time and thought to the school that it became popularly known by his name. The second superintendent was Oliver Williams, an ideal man for the office, who for sixteen years gave the school the very best of his care and concern, Sundays and weekdays, and it will long continue to bear the marks of his masterly direction. His successor, Supt J Arthur Williams, ably carries on the work and is never absent from his post summer or winter.

THE WELSH CONGREGATIONAL CHURCH

The iron works attracted a number of people from Wales. Among them were many pious souls who longed to worship God in their mother tongue. "Mother Thomas" (the title by which Mrs David Thomas was known) offered a lot at Fourth and Pine Streets for a Welsh Church.

The Rev David R Griffith was ordained a Congregational clergyman at Slatington, Pa., in the fall of 1881. He at once inspired zeal for the House of God among his countrymen and so led in the organization of the Bethel Welsh Congregational Church, which was effected with thirty charter members, November 26, 1882.

The corner stone of the new Church edifice was laid by Elizabeth ("Mother") Thomas assisted by her two sons, Samuel and John, while the pastor, Rev Griffith, spoke the appropriate words

The total cost of the property was $5,600, three thousand dollars of which was solicited by Rev Griffith and the balance was contributed by Mother Thomas. Thus the Church was begun free of debt, and has remained unencumbered ever since. It was consecrated to the service of God, December 2, 1883. Within a year of its organization the membership of this congregation grew to a hundred or more souls.

The first governing body, called Deacons, consisted of Edward Davies, David Griffith, John Williams, David Thomas, and Richard Thomas, Secretary.

The Rev. Griffith served the congregation as pastor for fourteen years. In 1897 the Rev. Tidwell Williams succeeded him, when this Church was united with the Slatington congregation to constitute a parish.

After a short time followed the Rev. T. C. Davies, another Mr. Davies, and the Rev. T. I. Williams. The present pastor is the Rev. Griffith, who was instrumental in founding the Church. He preaches a sermon in Welsh at the Sunday morning services and in English at vespers. There are still twenty names on the membership roll.

ST. STEPHEN'S EPISCOPAL CHURCH.

The first attempt to establish the Episcopal Church in Catasauqua was made by the Rev. F. W. Bartlett, rector of the Church of the Mediator, Allentown, who held services in the old school house on Willow Street, where for nearly two years the people worshipped regularly. On the removal of the Rev. Mr. Bartlett from Allentown, the services were held at intervals by the Rev. Cortlandt Whitehead, D.D., then rector of the Church of the Nativity at South Bethlehem, and now Bishop of the Diocese of Pittsburgh.

ST. STEPHEN'S EPISCOPAL CHURCH

In 1873 the Rev. C. E. D. Griffith of the Church of the Mediator, Allentown, took up the work, holding services in the Lehigh Valley station for nearly two years, when he removed from the diocese. After this time no efforts were made to continue the services for ten years, 1875 to 1885, when the present Bishop of Georgia, the Rt. Rev. C. K. Nelson, then rector of the Church of the Nativity, South Bethlehem, came occasionally and administered the Holy Communion.

On Sunday, the 23d day of April, in the afternoon, the Rev. R. H. Kline of Grace Church, Allentown, held a service in the Town Hall, with sixty people present. This service was the beginning of a permanent movement, from which the present Church and congregation have

INTERIOR ST. STEPHEN'S EPISCOPAL CHURCH

REV. J. B. MAY

come. Through the devotion of Mr. Kline, with the assistance of Layreaders Packer, Fichter and Meixwell, services were maintained in different places, until the coming of Bishop Talbot to the diocese, to whom the Rev. Mr. Kline committed the Mission. Bishop Talbot immediately appointed the Rev. Mr. H. Heigham, Ph. D., who remained for two years in charge of the work. Dr. Heigham was succeeded by the Rev. George A. Green in 1900. It was through the untiring energy of the Rev. Mr. Green and the loyalty of the people that the Church building came to be. The lot was the generous gift of Mr. and Mrs. Leonard Peckitt. Ground was broken for the foundation Sept. 25, 1900, and the corner stone laid Sunday, Oct. 28, and the church opened for the first service Easter Day, April 7, 1901. The church was consecrated on Sunday, May 21, 1905.

In June, 1905, the Rev. Mr. Green removed to Fishkill, New York, to become the rector of St. Andrew's Church at that place. In September, 1905, the present rector, the Rev. James B. May, came to Catasauqua. During this time the church has grown in numbers and influence, and many improvements and additions to the church property and its furniture, including a splendid pipe organ and large vested Choir, have been made. There is a large Sunday School and several other parish organizations.

The church is modeled after the most ancient of British churches, St. Martin's, situated just outside of the walls of Canterbury, and which was restored and used by Bertha, the first Christian Queen of England, about 580 A. D.

ST. JOHN'S UNITED EVANGELICAL CHURCH.

The Rev. D. S. Stauffer called a meeting of all persons who severed their connection from the Evangelical Association, October 5, 1894, for the purpose of organizing a new congregation.

A. E. Brown was elected chairman at the meeting, and James Missimer, Secretary.

After some discussion a congregation was organized and the following trustees elected: P. J. Heilman, John W. Souder, George Minnich, Sr., James Fahler and C. W. Weibel.

The Class Leaders were:

Class No. 1, P. J. Heilman and George Minnich, Sr.

Class No. 2, J. W. Souder and Frank Hepner.

Class No. 3, C. W. Weibel and Samuel Missimer.

ST. JOHN UNITED EVANGELICAL CHURCH

The Officers of the Sunday School were:

Superintendent, C. W. Weibel; Asst. Superintendent, J. W. Souder; Secretary, Henry Weibel; Treasurer, George Minnich, Sr.

REV. A. W. WARFEL

A meeting to consider the advisability of erecting a church was held October 30, 1894, and a resolution favoring a new building was adopted.

The building committee consisted of James Fahler, David Graffin, A. E. Brown, C. W. Weibel and P. J. Heilman.

The corner stone was laid with appropriate services by the Rev. D. S. Stauffer Dec. 2, 1894.

The building was completed and furnished for consecration on March 24, 1895. The present efficient pastor is the Rev. A. W. Warfel.

The following clergy have served St. John's Church:

Rev. D. S. Stauffer
Rev. R. M. Lichtenwalner
Rev. C. D. Huber
Rev. D. P. Longsdorf
Rev. J. Stermer
Rev. R. W. Hand

THE GREEK CATHOLIC CHURCH.

The Russian Greek Orthodox Catholic Church, called the Holy Trinity Church The First, is located on the corner of Fifth and Liberty Streets.

The congregation was organized in 1899 by a small band of Russian Emigrants from upper Hungary, where the oppression and greed of the United Greek clergy and the Magyar government is felt most keenly.

All the holy vessels, vestments, icons (images) and iconostasis (picture

GREEK CATHOLIC CHURCH

standing) which adorn the churchly brick edifice of the Greek Church were imported from Russia.

The congregation is composed of Russians mainly from Hungary and Russia, although there are also emigrants from Galitia, Servia and Roumania. Some Greeks and Syrians of Allentown and other towns also attend services on special occasions.

The congregation owns a commodious Parish House located beside the church, and a cemetery adjoining the Allen Union, near Dry Run.

Title to the property is in the name of Archbishop Platon, Archbishop of the Aleutian Islands and of North America.

The priest is under the jurisdiction of the Holy Synod of Russia whose headquarters are at St. Petersburg, and whose chief representative in this country is His Grace, the Most Reverend Archbishop Platon, seated at New York City.

Rev. Myron Volkay left the Orthodox Greek faith and became a Greek United Roman Catholic priest, which caused this small band of loyalists great concern until their first acknowledged pastor, Father Alexander Nemolovsky, came from southern Russia.

Father Nemolovsky organized the parish, instilled confidence into his people, and "governed and ruled the Church" most successfully for six years, after which he became the Right Reverend Bishop Alexander of Alaska with his residence in New York City.

Then followed: Rector John Kedrovsky, now at Coaldale, Pa., Rector Valdimir Znosko and Rector Gergins Belozorov, both in Russia. and since June, 1911, the Rev. John Ossipovitch Olshevsky is in charge. He was appointed as parish priest of Catasauqua and Slatington, with a preaching point at Williamstown, by His Grace, the Most Reverend Platon.

About sixty families, scattered throughout the large territory bounded by the Blue Ridge on the north and the South Mountains on the south, constitute this parish.

An adjunct of the Church consists in the Saint Cyrill and Method Russian Orthodox Society composed of over one hundred and twenty members. This brotherhood belongs to the Russian Orthodox Mutual Aid Society of North America.

The officers of the Church are:

President, Joseph Stehnach; Secretary, John Smajda; Treasurer, John Kresach.

These three men also serve as trustees of the Church.

ST. ANDREW'S SLOVAK CHURCH.

In the year 1902, the congregation represented by committee, consisting of Mr. John Fischer, Joseph Yurko, Joseph Pasco, Martin Benko, M. Burda, Andrew Posozo, Peter Parlo, W. Boroski, Joseph Farkash, M. Nedorostek and a few others, asked the late Rt. Rev. A. Msgr. Wm. Heiner, of East Mauch Chunk, Pa., to help them to get their own house of worship, in the most central location of the settlement of the Slovak nationality and Roman Catholic faith. This place was most properly selected at N. Catasauqua, Third St., near the Hokendauqua Bridge.

REV. JOSEPH KASPAREK

The new church under the name of "ST. ANDREW'S ROMAN CATHOLIC SLOVAK CHURCH" was started in October, 1902, and the people worshipped in the meantime in the John Small building, formally used as a school house of

N Catasauqua. The church was finished and dedicated in November, 1903 The church is built of best local brick and cost with contents and the lots adjoining it—the whole square—$25,000 00 The first rector of this Church was Rev Paul J Lisicky, from 1905 to 1912, who during his time built the rectory adjoining the said church for eight thousand dollars

This congregation comprises Slovak Catholic people from Catasauqua, Fullerton, Hokendauqua, Coplay, Northampton, Siegfried, Cementon, Egypt and Ormrod

The number of parishioners (souls) is seventeen hundred twenty-six

The present rector is Rev Joseph Kasparek

CHAPTER IV.—SCHOOLS.

SCHOOLS

Church and School are the two inseparable and irresistible forces by which a people are enlightened and a community is prospered in peace and happiness. The first school in Catasauqua was organized in the "Old School" Presbyterian Church with fifteen pupils at some time during the forties. A gentleman by the name of Landis was the teacher. A Mr. Evans succeeded Mr. Landis.

BUILDINGS

The first school building erected within the precincts of the town, according to the tradition of our oldest residents, was a frame structure built by the Crane Iron Company at the corner of Church Street and Limestone Alley. The second building was erected by Hanover township at the corner of Union Street and Railroad Alley. Upon its being declared a separate school district by the State Legislature in 1859, the Borough became the possessor of this property.

The third building was the Bridge Street school, located at Howertown Avenue and Bridge Street. A Mr. Alfred Cattemore solicited subscriptions for an Academy during 1848 and 1849. To the amount secured the Crane Company advanced a mortgage loan of twelve hundred dollars for the completion of the building, which was erected during 1849. This was the original Bridge Street building, and was regarded as a model school in those days. There were individual desks equipped with a book shelf and ink-well. The builing also had ceiling ventilators.

In 1856 the trustees resolved to discontinue this as a private school and sold the property to the Catasauqua School District for two thousand five hundred thirty dollars. After satisfying the mortgage to the Crane Company, the balance was divided in equal shares between the First and Old School Presbyterian Churches. The trustees were David Thomas, Robert McIntyre, Samuel Thomas, William Taylor, David Williams, Owen Rice, and John Peter. After a tenure of forty-seven years, when the Lincoln Building was completed, the Bridge Street property was disposed of at public sale to James W. Fuller for six thousand dollars. This sale was ratified by the Board, January 5, 1903.

The next school was located on Second and School Streets. It seems this was a substitution for the building on Union Street, but the date of its erection is nowhere traceable. On July 26, 1897, it was sold to Dr. H. Y. Horn for nineteen hundred dollars. This is now the property of the Lenox Manufacturing Company.

In 1858 the School Board leased the building at the corner of Front and School Streets (now the house of Mr. Frank Hunsicker) from Samuel Messimer

SECOND STREET BUILDING

for one hundred dollars per annum. February 26, 1859, the Board purchased a lot on the corner of Second and Walnut Streets from Adrian Barber for one thousand dollars. Contracts for the new building were awarded, June 9: carpenter work to William Biery, brick and plaster work to Knapp and Miller, brick to David A. Tombler, and lumber to T. H. Moyer. This is a substantial three story building containing six rooms, five of which are occupied at this time.

The Board purchased a lot on Front Street below Wood, April 14, 1868, from John T. Matchette for twenty-five hundred dollars; and erected thereon a two-story building which was sold, after a service of thirty-two years, September 10, 1900, to the St. Lawrence T. A. B. Society for five thousand dollars.

The Board resolved, December 5, 1894, to purchase from the Crane Iron Company the lot on Howertown Avenue and Peach Street for thirty-five hundred dollars. On the third of April, 1896, an additional lot, adjoining the former, was purchased for one thousand dollars. On the 8th of June, 1896, the Borough Council passed an ordinance vacating that portion of Peach Street between the

THE LINCOLN SCHOOL

two lots. It had previously been resolved, February 10, 1896, to erect a ten-room building on the original plot, but now it was decided to locate the building almost centrally on the enlarged grounds. The architect was Mr. P. Rudrauff, of Wilkes-Barre, Pa.; and the contractors were James Nagle and Son of Allentown, Pa. The total cost of this property was approximately $35,000.00. This building, called the "Lincoln School," was dedicated March 8, 1897. Dr. E. L. Kemp of the State Normal School at Stroudsburg, Pa., delivered the principal address A beautiful "marquee," which is a greatly valued shelter to the main entrance, was erected during 1909 at a cost of three hundred ninety-five dollars

The High School was quartered in different buildings at various times Upon the completion of the Lincoln Building, the problem of its location seemed solved, but a very few years revealed the need of additional room for the grades The Board resolved, September 1, 1909, to reconstruct and to equip the third floor of the building on Second and Walnut Streets and soon transferred the High School to that building This afforded no relief, it only transferred the congestion Already in October, 1909, efforts were made to secure a lot for High School purposes on the corner of Howertown Avenue and Walnut Street This endeavor failed During March, 1910, the Board essayed to buy the Koehler lot on Bridge Street and Limestone Alley, but this also defaulted The Board finally resolved, January 16, 1911, to erect the High School building on the large plot located on Howertown Avenue next to the Lincoln building

Since the debt on School properties still amounted to $17,377 12, the Board concluded to submit the question of a new High School building and the increase of indebtedness to a vote of the tax-payers The result of the election was four hundred twenty-five ballots in favor of progress and one hundred eighty opposed The election was held March 7, 1911 On the 25th of March, Ruhe and Lang, Architects, were engaged to draw plans, etc Plans having been adopted, the contract for the erection of the building was awarded to Franklin Goldsmith and Son for $35,905 Including plumbing (Schick and Hausman at $2095), ventilating system (The Monarch at $3582) and some extras, including equipment, the cost of the whole enterprise was about fifty-five thousand dollars

The building is a model, fire-proof structure The auditorium has a seating capacity of six hundred eight The stage measures twenty by forty-two feet and has dressing rooms on either side besides a centre door opening into a fire-proof stairway leading to the main floor and the school yard in the rear of the building There is school room capacity sufficient for two hundred fifty students Thirteen rooms are available for departmental work The Science department is fully equipped with an "Instructor's Table" and other appliances suitable for experiments in Chemistry and Physics There is also a fully equipped Chemical Labora-

HIGH SCHOOL

tory in the basement for students' use. The Commercial department is quartered on the second floor front, a large, well lighted room furnished with desks of the latest and most approved pattern and ten type-writers. The Gymnasium is placed in the basement and for the present is equipped for Basket-Ball. There are also a Museum, Alumni Hall, Directors' Room, Library, Superintendent's Office, cloak

TAYLOR BUILDING

rooms, drinking fountains, lavatories and all other accessories contributing to the comforts of teacher and pupil.

With the annexation of East Catasauqua, as the Third Ward of the Borough, came the accession of that portion of the schools of Hanover Township to the Borough; and incidentally also an indebtedness of $2277.12. The asset of the Third Ward is, however, a handsome recompense for all her liabilities. In order to enlarge the children's playground, a lot adjoining the Third Ward property was purchased October 6, 1910, from the Davies and Thomas Company for eight hundred ninety-two dollars and fifty cents. February 13, 1913, it was resolved to remodel and enlarge the Third Ward building. Jacoby and Weishample drew plans and F. Goldsmith and Son fulfilled the contract at nine thousand one hundred dollars.

VALUATION AND ASSESSMENTS

The first authentic records of the valuation placed upon Catasauqua's school properties is dated 1862, and the amount is thirteen thousand five hundred dollars In 1869 the amount was fixed at forty-eight thousand dollars The tax rate for 1868 was ten mills for the current, and eight mills for the building fund For 1871 the rate was thirteen and nine mills, for 1872, thirteen and six mills. The valuation for 1875 was sixty-four thousand dollars with an indebtedness of $14,555 In 1877 the rate of taxation was five and two mills, and in 1884 it shifted to six and one and one-fourth mills, in 1891, six and three mills, in 1901, eight mills, and in 1913 eleven mills The property valuation in 1911 was eighty thousand dollars with an indebtedness of $17,214 47, and in 1912, it rose to $130,000 and $62,000 respectively, and in 1913 the indebtedness stood at $76,801.34. The sinking fund held $4198 35.

CURRENT ACCOUNTS AND SALARIES

For the term of ten months, September 1, 1858, to July 1, 1859, the teachers' salaries ranged from twenty dollars to forty-five dollars per month In 1859 the Board elected Misses M A Davis, M. Duff, and J. Darling "to serve in case they are needed at fifteen dollars per month " In 1860 Mr Reuben Lichtenwalner was elected at twenty dollars per month The receipts for the year ending March 21, 1862, were $2,236 51 and the current expenditures were $1,969 20 In 1867 the salaries ranged from thirty-three to eighty dollars The average cost per pupil per annum for 1871 was $8 61 In 1875 the total receipts were $15,010 71 and expenditures $13 875 74 Salaries ranged from thirty dollars to one hundred dollars For 1895 the report shows receipts $15,838 74, expenditures $15,484.29. For 1913 the receipts were $27,295.09 and expenditures $23,215.17 The salaries range from forty-five to one hundred forty-five dollars per month

ORGANIZATION AND ENROLLMENT

From the records of County Superintendent, C. W Cooper, we note that in 1855 the enrollment numbered ninety-seven pupils. The teacher, Stephen Connaton, observed the following program

Open by hearing "A B C"

Reading English Text
Frost's United States History
Cobb's Third Reader
"Spelling in and out of the book"
Writing Copies
Arithmetic.
Clap's Geography
Grammar—occasionally
Close with definitions.

Superintendent Tilghman Good records for teacher H O Clark, 1856:

Enrollment 43
Pupils are well classed and instruction is given in writing, reading, grammar, geography, arithmetic, and spelling.
Geography and grammar are taught daily, except Saturday.
Tables as often as convenient
Progress is slow—attention to books not good—teacher, competent

The superintendent says of Miss Eliza McKee that her enrollment was 52 and that the attendance was regular, attention to study good, room clean, well lighted and heated   Teacher, competent.

Mr. C. H Russell enrolled 56 and Miss A. E Butcher, 56 Of both these teachers the records say that they were competent

The total enrollment in 1868 was High School, 35, and Grades, 527 scholars In 1869 the numbers were 40 and 674 The grand total of scholars in attendance during 1871 was 833.

The course of study adopted under Superintendent J O. Knauss, 1877, provided branches for Primary, Advanced Primary, Secondary, Grammar—First Class and Second Class, and High School (two sections, with two classes in second and three classes in first section).

The total enrollment for the term ending June 30, 1914, is: High School 115, Grades 664.

The percentage of young people attending higher grades a score and more years ago is much higher than at present on account of the many opportunities for the youth of the present day to find employment in stores, factories and offices not then in existence

HIGH SCHOOL

The first High School teachers, Mr W McFarland and Miss Kate M Smith, were elected July 5, 1866 In 1867 a full four years' course of studies was adopted The first commencement exercises were held in June, 1868, and the graduates were Alletta M Earle and Frank M Horn Both graduated with honors

In 1873 the High School course comprised studies for three years' work

First Year Written Arithmetic, Writing, Grammar, Natural Philosophy, Algebra, Geometry. Composition, Reading, Declamation, Drawing and Watts on the Mind

Second Year Spelling, Reading, Writing, Arithmetic, Grammar, Physiology, Algebra, Geometry, Composition, U S History Drawing, Declamation

Third Year Spelling Reading, Writing, Arithmetic, Grammar, U S History Algebra, and Map Drawing.

By way of comparison, in 1911, the following course of study was adopted by the School Board for the High School

Freshman Year

    1 English.
- (a) English Grammar
- (b) English Composition.
- (c) English Classics
    1. Irving's Sketch Book
    2 Longfellow's Evangeline
    3. Cooper's Last of the Mohicans
    4 Hawthorne's Twice Told Tales.

    2 Mathematics
- (a) Algebra
- (b) Concrete Geometry.

    3 Science:
Physical Geography

    4 United States History and Civics
    5 Latin and German
    6 Mechanical Drawing (Elective)

Sophomore Year
- 1 English
    - (a) English and American Literature.
    - (b) English Classics
        - 1 Shakespeare's Merchant of Venice.
        - 2 Eliot's Silas Marner
        - 3 Scott's Ivanhoe
        - 4 Coleridge's Ancient Mariner
- 2 Mathematics
    - (a) Plane Geometry
    - (b) Algebra
- 3 Science
    - Botany and Agriculture
- 4 History
    - Ancient and Mediaeval
- 5 Latin and German
- 6 Mechanical Drawing (Elective)

Junior Year
- 1 English
    - (a) Rhetoric
    - (b) English Classics
        - 1 Shakespeare's Julius Caesar
        - 2 Carlyle's Essay on Burns
        - 3 Webster's Reply to Hayne
        - 4 Tennyson's Idylls of the King
- 2 Mathematics
    - Solid Geometry (Elective)
- 3 Modern History (Elective)
- 4 Science
    - Physics
- 5 Latin and German.
- 6. Higher Algebra (Elective)
- 7. Mechanical Drawing (Elective)

Senior Year
- 1 English Classics.
    - 1 Burke's Conciliation with the Colonies
    - 2 Milton's Minor Poems
    - 3 Shakespeare's Macbeth
    - 4 Webster's First Bunker Hill Oration.

2 Mathematics:
   (a) Review of Plane and Solid Geometry
   (b) Trigonometry or Commercial Arithmetic
3. Science
   Chemistry or Commercial Geography
4 History of England
5 Latin and German
6 Reviews

COMMERCIAL COURSE

Junior Year:

1 Typewriting
2. Stenography.
3. Bookkeeping and Office Practice
4 English·
   (a) Rhetoric.
   (b) English Classics.
      1. Shakespeare's Julius Caesar
      2 Carlyle's Essay on Burns
      3 Webster's Reply to Hayne.
      4 Tennyson's Idylls of the King
5 Commercial Arithmetic
6 Commercial Spelling and Penmanship

Senior Year.

1 Typewriting.
2 Stenography and Court Dictation
3 Bookkeeping and Office Practice Work
4 Commercial Law and Commercial Geography
5 Business English and Business Forms
6 Commercial Spelling.
7 Penmanship and Rapid Calculation

This evolution did not come without struggle and difficulties

August 30, 1879, the following preambles and resolutions, presented by Drs C J Keim and H H Riegel, were adopted by the Board:

"Whereas it appears from the Public prints of the day that the People of the most intelligence and highest social position of the Borough of Catasauqua are opposed to making the school that is now called the High School, a High

School in reality, and Whereas this Board is opposed to continuing the application of the name of High School to a school that is not graded above a Grammar school, and Whereas this Board does not feel justified in appropriating the amount now appropriated for carrying on a Grammar school under the name of High School, and Whereas Mr Ulrich has signified his willingness to resign notwithstanding his election, therefore, Resolved that Mr Ulrich be requested to resign and that the school at present designated as the High School be abolished and that the pupils in said school be transferred to the school at present known as the Intermediate or second section of the High School and the name of the said school be called the Graded Grammar School and the school be put in charge of Mr Morris for the present, and thereby save Eight Hundred and Fifty Dollars ($850) to the tax payers of the Borough of Catasauqua "

Four members of the Board voted in favor of the resolution and two opposed it, however, afterward "it was agreed that further proceedings in the above preambles and resolutions be postponed," and the High School was saved to the community

Since the election of Mr T W Bevan in 1882 and our present H J Reinhard in 1899, the High School course has been developed more and more until to-day Catasauqua can be justly proud of a course which compares favorably with the best in the country Already, in 1886, Mr Bevan was charged with full supervision of all the schools, but since the completion of the High School building H J Reinhard fills the office of Supervising Principal. This combines the teaching forces of the Borough in such a way as to operate like one great pedagogic mind upon the community

Since 1912 the High School has added language, commercial, and scientific courses not hitherto taught, and expanded its benefits to a full four years' course

COLORED CHILDREN

The Board resolved, February 15, 1864, that Jacob Ross be authorized to give private lessons to all negro children in this district over five years of age that may apply for tuition In May it was resolved that the small room adjoining and opening into the large room on the first floor of the Bridge Street building be appropriated to the accommodation of negro children of the district applying for tuition, and that the teacher of said room also have the oversight and training of these children committed to him

THE BIBLE IN SCHOOL

When we behold the wisdom and far-sightedness of the fathers who laid the foundations upon which succeeding generations could contentedly build, we are often amazed They were not blind to their own good nor to the welfare of their sons and daughters. They knew man is not all meat, nor an exclusive bundle of brain cells, but that he is a living soul They had respect for personal peculiarities and doctrinal preferences and so provided for the reading of the Scriptures, leaving it to the Divine Spirit to impress the individual heart as is God's will

In 1858, December 16th, the Board took action as follows Whereas John Porter has neglected wilfully the reading of the Scriptures in his school, which is made imperative by the ruling of the Board, and whereas his conduct generally has not been of a character to inspire confidence therefore resolved that John Porter be dismissed from the office of teacher

The Board resolved, April 7, 1862, that the daily sessions of the schools shall be opened with the reading of the Scriptures and that the scholars assume a standing position during the reading The law of the Commonwealth of Pennsylvania requires —That at least ten verses from the Holy Bible shall be read, or caused to be read, without comment, at the opening of each and every public school, upon each and every school day by the teacher in charge, Provided, That where any teacher has other teachers under and subject to direction, then the teacher exercising this authority shall read the Holy Bible, or cause it to be read, as herein directed

That if any school teacher, whose duty it shall be to read the Holy Bible, or cause it to be read, as directed in this act, shall fail or omit so to do, said school teacher shall, upon charges preferred for such failure or omission, and proof of the same, before the governing board of the school district, be dischaged

PATRIOTISM

In 1864 the Board ordered the schools closed on the 18th of February in order to afford the teachers an opportunity to assist at the supper given to the soldiers of the 46th regiment. An invitation by the Grand Army to participate in the Memorial Day exercises in the spring of 1888 was accepted by all the schools. For many years the school children trooped after the "old soldiers" to Fairview cemetery. For the last six or eight years the High School classes sang patriotic airs during the exercises of the Fuller Post.

The Washington Camp No 301, P O S of A placed a U S flag in each school room in the Borough in the fall of 1888. On Thanksgiving Day, 1897, the Jr O U A M presented and unfurled a flag for the new Lincoln Building. The Hon W. C Weiss, of Bethlehem, was the orator of the day. The one hundredth anniversary of the birth of Abraham Lincoln was observed by a fitting celebration by all the schools gathered in the Lincoln Building, February 19, 1909.

TEACHERS' MEETING

A meeting of the teachers with the directors of the Borough was held August 30, 1869. The object of the meeting was to afford an opportunity for mutual exchange of opinion regarding subjects, subject matter and the best methods of impartation. August 4, 1873, the Board resolved: That instead of a teachers' institute in this district, the teachers shall form themselves into a class for the purpose of general improvement, that said class shall meet monthly in the H S Building and have exercises in Reading, Declamation, Grammar and such other studies as may be deemed proper—said exercises shall be open to the Board of Diretors.

The desirable elements of the past have grown into imperative demands for the willing minds of the present. For many years our teachers met once a month at three o'clock P M, for coloquies on school management and the study of professional themes. In 1911 the teachers resolved to convene bi-weekly at seven P M in order to study professional subjects, such as, Methods of Teaching, Mistakes in Teaching, The School and its Life, Thinking and Learning to Think, and many other kindred themes. Since the opening of the current term, bi-weekly meetings are held on Tuesdays at four-thirty P M. Kemp's "History of Education" was adopted for systematic study. Our painstaking Supervising Principal, who is in charge of the class, submits a series of searching questions upon the subject for each recitation. A general discussion is invited which constantly brings to light the most practical deductions

MONTHLY REPORTS

Since 1873 teachers have been required to furnish the Board with monthly reports giving the program of the school, the conduct and progress of each pupil and any other data that may be deemed important. Monthly grade cards of grades four to eight for the information of parents, and the enlistment of their interest in their children as well as in the schools have been issued by the teachers of those grades since 1868 The rubrics of the cards are arranged for a ten months' service and provide spaces for the monthly signatures of parents or guardians Since the introduction of the National System of Records, 1911, cards are issued for all the grades. Individual records of every pupil from his entrance to his graduation are preserved in a permanent filing case.

MUSIC

What was a matter of recreation, or an opportunity in days gone by, has now become a scientific branch of study in our schools Since 1893, when Mrs S K Brobst, of Allentown, was employed for the spring term at eight dollars per month, the rudiments of vocal music have been taught July 7, 1905, Miss M Adeline Davies was engaged as Supervisor and Instructor of Vocal Music Miss Davies is competent and diligent, and the beneficial results of her labors are felt in every church choir and all other musical organizations in the Borough.

PHYSICAL CULTURE

"Mens sana in sano corpore" is a motto that never grows old, and when children are at school all but two months in a year, and that in a town where the chores are light and indoors, there is all the more need of some form of physical culture In 1882 the Board directed that teachers give their pupils some form of calisthenics Our High School provides a room for some simple apparatus which the older scholars may use This department as well as that of domestic and other applied sciences will receive closer attention in coming years

THE MUSEUM

The Hon J F Moyer, a member of the State Legislature in 1901, procured from the Philadelphia Museum a number of specimens of minerals, fabrics, curios, photos, showing the production of articles from raw materials, and presented them to the schools as a nucleus of our Museum Botanical specimens, products of the taxidermist's art and other materials are being added constantly, which prove very profitable to the inquiring mind

CLOCK AND BELL

After the erection of the building on Front Street, a fine tower-clock and bell were placed into the steeple during the spring of 1869 When the building was sold to the St Lawrence T A B Society, the clock was placed into the steeple of the Town Hall The old master of time keepers has however yielded to the corroding elements and strikes the hours no more

TUNNEL.

On April 18, 1910, the Crane Railroad Company was granted the privilege of constructing a tunnel under a narrow strip of the school lot on Peach Street and Howertown Avenue In consideration of this favor the Railroad Company paid into the school treasury three hundred thirty dollars

CLASS DAYS.

Class Day exercises were authorized October 6, 1910 Caps and gowns for commencement occasions were authorized March 5, 1906

LECTURES.

On December 12, 1859, it was resolved: "That permission is hereby granted to the Catasauqua Senate and Lecture Association to use the third story room of the new building recently erected on Second Street, for their Lectures and meetings on Friday evenings of every week, the said Association to keep the said room and entry leading thereto in good order and condition Said lectures or meetings to commence with the lecture of Hon H D Maxwell on Friday evening, December 16; that such lecture be free to such scholars as are recommended by the School Board " Since the completion of the High School auditorium, the Alumni Association runs an annual entertainment and lecture course with signal success Six numbers constitute the course and only high class talent is employed The Alumni number 566 and are filling responsible positions all over the globe.

DEATHS IN THE BOARD

Col. M. H. Horn was a man of exceptional usefulness and prominence in the affairs of Catasauqua. In 1869 he was elected secretary of the School Board and "District Superintendent" of the Schools. Through him many progressive measures were promulgated. Upon his death in 1890 the Board authorized the following minute:

"Resolved, That in the death of Col. M. H. Horn we feel the loss of one who was foremost in the advancement of our Public Schools. To no man do we owe more for the present high standing of our schools than to him. For thirty years he was a member of the Board, was always to be relied on and an earnest advocate of every good measure for the advancement of the schools of the Borough, a generous companion, a good friend."

The demise of another valued member of the Board occurred when Mr. George Davies departed the scenes of this life. The action of the Board is appended:

"We, the remaining members of the Board, desire to put on record our conviction that in the death of Mr. Davies, the educational interests of Catasauqua have suffered a heavy loss. The public schools have lost a liberal minded and a liberal hearted patron, the teachers and pupils have lost a kind and considerate friend, who was ever ready to promote their interests. In the School Board we have always found in him a congenial associate, a wise and prudent counsellor, and an enthusiastic advocate of every thing that seemed necessary for the improvement of our schools."

NIGHT SCHOOL

In response to a petition signed by thirty-five patrons, the Board resolved, March 3, 1913, to open a Night School. Provisions were made for a three months' term, five nights per week and two hours for each session. The average attendance was sixty-three. Three teachers were employed. The branches of study included in the curriculum were Geometry, Commercial Arithmetic, Commercial Spelling, Typewriting, Stenography, Bookkeeping and Mechanical Drawing.

The report submitted to the School Board showed that there are in this town many persons of fine talents who crave advancement, but who are excised from educational advantages by the driving demands of a struggle for physical existence It was determined, December 8, 1913, to open a four months' term of Night School in charge of three teachers and a Supervisor, during the first quarter of 1914 The average attendance was thirty-four

The present School Board is composed of the following representative citizens.

J S Stillman, President
C H Riegel, Secretary
Edwin Chapman, Treasurer
J S Elverson
H B Weaver
R D Thomas
J J Williams

    The teaching staff is composed of the following·
    H J Reinhard, Supervising Principal
    Gus E Oswald, Principal of High School
    A C Lewis, Commercial Department
    C D Hummel, Science Department
    D F Gould, English Department
    Sarah J McIntyre, Intermediate
    Hannah Davis, A Grammar
    F H Sheckler, A and B Grammar
    Sarah McHenry, B Grammar
    Margaret Tolan, B Grammar and A Secondary
    Estella McKeever, A Secondary
    Ella Tait, A and B Secondary
    Mame Torrance, A and B Secondary
    Mabel Weisley, B Secondary
    Amanda Funk, B Secondary and A Primary
    Sophia Matchette, A Primary
    Mildred Heilman, A Primary
    Mildred Lawall, B Primary

Helen Buck, B Primary
Jennie Helman, B and C Primary
Elizabeth Scott, C Primary
Mary Leickel, C Primary
Mary McCandless, C Primary
M Adaline Davies, Supervisor Music

Complete list of teachers who taught in the Catasauqua Schools

App, Mary J , 1888-1890
Applegate, Anna D , 1906-1909
Butcher, Miss A E., 1855-1856
Barton, W. H., 1858-1859
Bear, Charlotte, 1869-1873
Bear, Sarah, 1870-1878
Breder, E H , 1870-1878
Bear, Eliza J , 1878-1884
Bear, Esther, 1873-1875
Beitel, C H , 1878-1880
Benner, George H , 1880-1882
Barr, J Frank, 1882-1884
Bevan, T. W , 1882-1899
Bates, C H , 1889-1890
Buck, A. H , 1902-1911
Buck, Helen K , 1911-
Brownell, C A , 1912-1913
Connaton, Steven 1854-1855
Clark, H O , 1855-1856
Clark, John, 1864-1865
Corwin, Jennie, 1864-1865
Craig, Mary M , 1880-1890
Clugston, Lizzie, 1884-1903
Corwin, Helen, 1905-1909
Duff, Mary, 1861-1863

Davis, Sarah, 1870-1883
DePue, Margaret, 1870-1875
Davis, Hannah, 1876-
DePue, John, 1879-1881
Downs, Hester, 1899-1911
Evans, Mary, 1861-1863
Ehl, J Morris, 1887-1888
Eberhart, Laura, 1888-1889
Funk, Amanda, 1872-
Frederick, T F., 1875-1878
George, M O 1864-1865
Glick, Jennie, 1865-1866
Garber, A P , 1865-1866
Gilbert, Hart, 1870-1871
Gould, D F , 1913-
Hammersley, R C , 1858-1864
Hammersley, Eliza, 1864-1871
Haldeman, W H , 1866-1869
Hill, John, 1872-1875
Hammersley, Alice, 1879-1880
Helman, Laura, 1884-1906
Helman, Jennie, 1889-
Hummel, C D , 1912-
Heilman, Mildred, 1913-
Kinsey, A. W , 1858-1873

OF CATASAUQUA 147

Kay, Sarah, 1876-1880
Kay, Alice M , 1879-1888
Kinyon, Jennie, 1889-1890
Knauss, J O , 1910-1912
Leibert, Margaret, 1858-1859
Lichtenwalner, Reuben, 1860-1861
Leibert, Gwennie, 1861-1868
Lyttle, Robert A , 1869-1875
Lambert, Alice M , 1890-1898
Leickel, Mary L , 1909-
Lawall, Mildred, 1910-
Lewis, A. C , 1912-
McKee, Eliza, 1856-1868
McFarland, W , 1866-1867
McKibbon, Annie M 1866-1868
Milson, Sallie, 1866-1871
McClean, Robert, 1868-1869
McMonegal, C , 1870-1873
Milson, Charlotte, 1872-1873
McIntyre, Sarah J , 1873-
McClelland, Jane, 1873-1875
McMonegal, Kate, 1873-1879
McMonegal, Rebecca, 1873-1905
Morris, W. T , 1873-1882
Muschlitz, J H , 1875-1902
McHenry, Sarah, 1880-
Moyer, J F , 1882-1885
Mealy, Delia, 1883-1889
McKeever, Estella, 1897-
McKeever, Emily, 1905-1910

McCandless, Mary, 1909-
Mitchell, Elizabeth, 1898-1906
Matchette, Sophia, 1909-
Oswald, Gus E , 1913-
Phillips, Anna, 1858-1860
Porter, John, 1858-1859
Phillips, Naomi 1859-1866
Pearson, Orantus, 1874-1876
Russell, C H , 1856-1858
Quigg, Margaret, 1870-1879
Reich, Irene, 1870-1873
Reinhard, H J , 1888-
Ulrich, A N , 1872-1880
Sigley, Rebecca, 1862-1877
Smith, Anna. 1865-1888
Smith, Kate M , 1866-1904
Snyder, B C , 1867-1871
Schrope, J H , 1902-1902
Sheckler, F H , 1906-
Scott, Elizabeth, 1909-
Snyder, Susan, 1912-1913
Tait, Ella, 1899-
Tolan, Margaret, 1902-
Torrance, Mame, 1893-
Wonderly, Lillie, 1866-1876
Wilson, Martha, 1869-1888
Williams, Cora D , 1890-1902
Williams, Lillian, 1890-1899
Witherow, Jean, 1893-1894
Weisley, Mable O , 1904-
Wentz, Herbert, 1906-1906

THE NORTH CATASAUQUA SCHOOLS.

NORTH CATASAUQUA SCHOOL.

Until recent years the Borough of North Catasauqua was a part of Allen Township, Northampton County. The children of this community attended the township school at Dry Run. The building which was a good model of the country school house stood near the southern approach to the trolley bridge that crosses Dry Run.

With the increase of population came the demand for larger school facilities. The Board of Directors of the township purchased a plot of ground on Second Street above Arch from the Faust estate and erected a two room frame building upon it. This was called the Faust school.

At a later date a lot was bought at Fourth and Arch Streets and a one room brick building was built thereon. Early in the nineties an extension of one room and a cross section of two rooms were added. The schools of the Second Street building were moved into these new and more commodious quarters. Some years later another two room cross section was added, making the building a double T shape. "And still they came."

North Catasauqua grew rapidly. Everyone knew that something definite had to be done. Public meetings were called. Addresses were delivered by County Superintendent Grim and others. A unanimous ballot of the citizens of the new Borough supported the resolution of the School Board to raze the old building and erect in its stead a modern structure, and equip the same with the most approved appliances. The Board purchased an additional hundred feet of ground from the Deily estate, by which addition the whole plot now covers one-fourth of a square, and is located in a most beautiful section of the Borough.

Paul C. Miller, superintendent of the Bryden Horse Shoe Works, drew the plans which provided for a ten room, two story brick building, strictly fire proof. There is also provision made for a library, a directors' room and a large auditorium. In the basement are play rooms, lavatories, boiler room, etc. The building has a large front entrance and two side entrances; and there are two stairways. It is heated by the Burt H. Harrison Aertube system whose fans also operate the perfect ventilation of the building. The contract was awarded to the Stine Brothers of Allentown for twenty-four thousand six hundred dollars ($24,600).

Dedication exercises were held on Thanksgiving Day, November 27, 1913. Nathan A. Bartholomew, Treasurer of the School Board, presided and delivered the historical address. The other three orators of the occasion were Joseph Kane, Pincipal of the North Catasauqua Schools, George Grim, Superintendent of Schools of Northampton County, and William H. Schneller, Esq., Solicitor of the North Catasauqua School District. The members of the Board were: Edwin C. A. Rockel, President; Harry Steyert, Secretary; Nathan A. Bartholomew, Treasurer; Henry P. Webber and Robert F. Rutman. The only changes in the Board since then is the substitution of the name of Charles H. Kosman for that of Mr. Rutman.

The teaching force consists of the following:

Joseph Kane, Principal, elected in 1907.
Elizabeth V. McNally, elected in 1901.
Martha Hammer, elected in 1913.
Mary F. Lichtenwalner, elected in 1913.
Edna G. Madtes, elected in 1907.
Agnes I. Souder, elected in 1910.
Minnie R. McCloskey, elected in 1902.

PROF. JOSEPH KANE

CHAPTER V.—FRATERNAL AND SOCIAL ORGANIZATIONS

CATASAUQUA LODGE, NO 269

I O O F

One of the oldest as well as the most influential fraternal organizations in the Borough is the Independent Order Odd Fellows. Odd Fellow Lodge No. 269, was instituted in the Eberhard Hall on Lower Front Street on Saturday evening, November 6, 1847 Robert E Wright, Sr., of Allentown, Pa , then D D G M of Lehigh County, under the jurisdiction of the Grand Lodge of Pennsylvania, had charge of the institution The charter for the institution of the Lodge was granted by the Grand Lodge on October 8, 1847 The Charter members were. David Tombler, Samuel Colver, Reuben L Seip, Daniel Siegfried, Aaron Bast, William Biery, Reuben Patterson, Thomas Frederick and Joseph Troxell

They were all initiated into Allen Lodge No 71 of Allentown, Pa , *for the purpose of instituting Catasauqua Lodge* The first officers of Catasauqua Lodge were N G , Reuben L Seip, V G , Aaron Bast, Secretary, Samuel Colver, Assistant Secretary, David Tombler Treasurer, Nathan Frederick , R S to V G , Joseph Troxell, R. S to N G , Thos Frederick, L S. to N G , Edw Zitman, L. S. to V. G , Reuben Grafty, Conductor, William Biery, S W , Daniel Siegfried , J W , Reuben Patterson , R S S , Charles Seem , L S S , Joel Sterner , I G , Absolem Stemer , O G , William Stillwagen , Trustees Wm Biery, Daniel Siegfried, Thos Frederick, David Tombler and Aaron Bast , Reuben L Seip, Rep to Grand Lodge These officers were elected July 29, 1848

The Odd Fellow Lodge first met in Eberhard Hall on Lower Front Street from the date of its institution until September 11, 1852, when it moved into Wm Gross' Hall, now the bottling place of August Hohl. It occupied this hall until the 4th of July, 1857, when it moved to the Lichtenwalner Hall On Christmas Day, 1857, the Lodge vacated Lichtenwalner Hall and rented Hunter's Hall on Lower Second Street, where they remained until October 31, 1868. It was on

October 31, 1868, that it was moved into Esch's Hall where the Lodge remained until November 8, 1890, when it purchased the large brick church building, situated on Front Street, from the Methodist Episcopal Congregation. The building with its many small rooms and commodious auditorium has proved to be the most pleasant place in which the Lodge has met. Recently the auditorium was renovated. The many beautiful paintings, symbolic of the Order, which adorn

I. O. O. F

the walls, together with new oak furniture, make the Lodge room one of the finest in the Lehigh Valley.

The present officers of the Lodge are: N. G., Russell Moyer; V. G., A. C. Lewis; Secretary, Wm. Samuels; Financial Secretary, Wm. F. Engler; Treasurer, Stuart H. Hauser; R. S. to N. G., R. C. Weaver; L. S. to N. G., B. Harrison

Porter; R. S. to V. G., John Gillespie; L. S. to V. G., Russell Wilkinson; Warden, John W. Keys; Conductor, Robert Bowen; R. S. S., Samuel Stolz; L. S. S., James Kendig; 1. G., Raymond Laubach; O. G., Daniel Gillespie; Chaplain, Wm. H. Smith; P. G., Chas. Frederick; Trustees: Wm. H. Scanlin, Wm. H. Hopkins and H. W. Stolz; Rep. to G. L., Jno. Williams; Rep. to O. H., Wm. H. Scanlin; Custodian, John Williams; Pianist, Wm. T. Scanlin.

Catasauqua Lodge meets every Saturday evening at 7 P M.

PORTER LODGE, NO. 284, F. AND A. M.

Porter Lodge, No. 284, F. and A. M., was instituted by D. D. G. M. James M. Porter, of Easton (after whom the Lodge was named), January 30, 1854, at 3.30 P. M. The corps of Grand Officers had constituted Bethlehem Lodge, No. 283, the day before, and Porter Lodge was the first Lodge they instituted in Lehigh County. The resident brethren were mostly members of Easton Lodge, No. 152, who always traveled to Easton by means of Brother Robert McIntyre's four horse team, whose enthusiasm in the Order induced him to furnish it at stated meetings The Charter members were Robert McIntyre, Levi Graft, James McCleary, August H Gilbert, Chas H. Nolf, Franklin B Martin, Charles Allen, William Goetz, William Biery, James Clugston and James W Fuller The first sessions of the Lodge were held in the Romich building, Front and Church Streets Then for thirty years the Lodge met in the Fuller Block, Front and Church Streets, and later in the Reis Building, No 513 Front Street, which building the Lodge purchased and especially fitted for Lodge, Chapter and club purposes, making it one of the most prominent society buildings in the Valley Five hundred sixty brethren have been initiated into the Lodge, from which number Barger Lodge, No 333 of Allentown, Slatington Lodge, No 440, Manoghasy Lodge, No 413 of Bath, Lehigh Lodge, No 326 of Trexlertown, and Allen Lodge, No 673 of Allentown drew charter members for organization

During the existence of the Lodge, Dr D Yoder served as Treasurer forty-seven years and Edmund Randall twenty-seven years as Secretary, which records for long and faithful services are quite unusual

The present membership is two hundred The following brethren are the present officers John W Walker, W M , Frederick K Constable, S W , Frederick I Walker, I W , Roland T Davies, Treasurer, David Davis, Secretary, Dr H H Riegel, H E Graffin and Allen T Heckman, Trustees Porter Lodge meets the first Friday in the month

FRATERNITY ENCAMPMENT, NO 156

I O O F

Fraternity Encampment, No 156, Independent Order Odd Fellows of Catasauqua, Pa , was instituted Thursday evening, June 6, 1867, in Hunter's Hall, on Second Street, by Franklin Smith, D D G P of Lehigh County under the jurisdiction of the Grand Encampment of Pennsylvania

The Charter for the institution of the Encampment was granted by the Grand Encampment on May 20, 1867 The Charter members were George Bowers, M H Horn, David Tombler, A F Koons, Frederick M Eagle, Daniel Gillespie, F F Giering, Henry Souders, Aaron Snyder, John Hunter, Henry

Eckensberger, Franklin Bower, Philip Storm, William Biery and James Hutchinson

The first officers of Fraternity Encampment, No 156, I O O F, were. C P, George Bower; H P, M H Horn, Senior Warden, David Tombler; Junior Warden, Daniel Gillespie, Scribe, A F. Koons, Treasurer, Frederick M Eagle, Guide. Henry Souders, First Watch, William Biery, Second Watch, John Hunter, Third Watch, F F. Giering, Fourth Watch, Henry Eckensberger, I S, Aaron Snyder; O S, Philip Storm; Guards of Tent, Franklin Bower and James Heberling, Trustees Henry Eckensberger, F F Giering, William Shoenberger

Fraternity Encampment meets in the Odd Fellows' Hall on Front Street, having a part ownership in the building While the membership of the Lodge is not so large, yet it does a great work in alleviating the sorrows and distresses among its members The present officers are C P, Joseph McKeever, H P, Samuel H Danner, S W, Robert McKeever, J. W, B Harrison Porter, Scribe, William Samuels, Treasurer, H W Stolz, O S, William J Evans, Sr ; I S, John W Keys, Guide, H W Stolz, First Watch, George Stettler, Second Watch, R F Moyer, Third Watch, Samuel Stolz; Fourth Watch, Harrison Smith, First Guard to Tent, Raymond Laubach, Second Guard to Tent, Staurt H Hauser, Trustees R. F Case, William J Evans, Sr, and M J Troxell

P O S OF A

P O S of A No 152 was organized in 1868 For a number of years the Camp was very prosperous, taking a large place in the social life of the town In 1872 the National Camp of the P O S of A was instituted in Allentown The local Camp took a prominent part in the ceremonies and the parade

Towards the end of the Panic of 1873, many men were unable to find work here and they sought employment in other places Very few of the members of the organization were left and, because of this, the Camp ceased to exist The records show that sixty dollars remained in the treasury The only other property was the hall furniture

On March 15, 1888, Washington Camp No. 301 was organized Interest in the reorganization was aroused by the members of the original Camp The old fraternal ties were strong and they felt that no other organization could take the place of the P. O. S. of A. Sixty-eight charter members were enrolled. That number has grown so that at the present time there are two hundred ten patriotic Sons of America in the Camp as earnestly following the flag during the days of peace as did the earlier patriots during the periods of national danger.

The prosperity of Washington Camp made it possible, in 1895, to purchase the Swartz property on Bridge Street. In 1902 the building was remodeled into

P. O. S. OF A. HALL

one of the most modern lodge edifices in this vicinity. The large meeting room is on the third floor and the banquet hall is on the second floor. Two stores occupy the first floor and the remaining rooms are used as offices. The property is valued at twenty thousand dollars. Washington Camp No. 301 is known as the richest in the county.

The membership is composed of the best of Catasauqua's citizens, all born on American soil. These men by their genuine interest in the organization and the principles for which it stands have been a powerful factor for good in the community. No body of men has done more towards arousing a love for the home community and the Nation, and in raising high the principles of good citizenship and loyalty to the land over which the Stars and Stripes float than Washington Camp of the P. O. S. of A.

IMPROVED ORDER OF REDMEN

On the 5th Sun of Hot moon G. S. D. 382, or the 5th day of June, 1873, G. C. of R., Andrew J. Baker, D. G. S., Bieber, P. S., Thomas K. Donnally of Tribe No. 18, and Jas. Gadds of No. 106, kindled a Council Fire in Catasauqua for the purpose of instituting a Tribe of The Improved Order of Redmen. There were twenty charter members. Having instituted and raised its members to the Chieftains' Council, an election was held with the following result: Thomas James, Prophet, William Wallace, Sachem, Teyschen Thomas, Senior Sachem, Frank Gorman Junior Sachem, John Evans, Chief of Records, and David A. Tombler, Jr., Keeper of Wampum. The first order for paraphernalia amounted to two hundred twenty-four dollars. The tribe continued for a period of eight years. According to the minute book of that time, Brein Mealy moved to discontinue business from March 12, 1881.

Seven years later, March 10, 1888, G. S., Thomas D. Tanner and P. S., John Manning of Tribe No. 84 and the members of Tribes Nos. 84 and 201 met in Schneller's Hall for the purpose of relighting the Council Fire of No. 204 Improved Order of Redmen, with the following members of the first tribe in waiting: Charles G. Morgan, John L. Jones, Frederick H. Richter, Edwin Jones, Alfred Jones, Wm. Howells, and Jacob V. Buskirk. At this meeting the following Palefaces were duly adopted and exalted to the Chieftains' Council: David Morrow, Alex Morrow, Robert McNabb, John Howells, Jacob Lewis, Harry Parrock, Albert Morris, Wm. Jones, Thomas C. Davis, Archie McFetridge, Thomas W. Williams, John McCandless, Wm. McCandless, Ashable Schirer, James Morrow, and Robert Clugston. The officers of this Tribe were: J. V. Buskirk, Prophet, Robert McNabb, Sachem, Wm. McCandless, S. Sachem, David Morrow, J. Sachem, Chas. D. Morgan, Chief of Records, and John McCandless,

Keeper of Wampum. The trustees were John L. Jones, Wm Howells, and J Van Buskirk. The appointed offices were filled by the Sachem as follows: First Sen., Jas Morrow, Second Sen., Robert Clugston, Guard of Wigwam, Albert Morris, Guard of Forest, Thos W Williams, First Warrior, John L Jones, Second Warrior, Alex Morrow, Third Warrior, Alfred Jones, Fourth Warrior, Harry Parrock, First Brave, Frederich H Richter, Second Brave, Edwin Jones, Third Brave, Wm Howells, Fourth Brave, Thomas C Davies.

The present membership has reached almost the four hundred twenty-five mark. The members at all times have taken an active part in the work, especially the degree work, which has attained a high standard in this tribe. The team has on many different occasions been called to sister Tribes to confer degrees on Palefaces, and it is said that the degree master could at any time call on enough members to form three teams to confer degrees.

There are thirty-nine Past Sachems in good standing. During the past twenty-six years, the Great Spirit has called twenty members to the Happy Hunting Ground.

During this last period of Council Fires, the receipts from all sources were $32,210.43 and the total expenditures $32,097.91. Investments in Water and School Bonds amount to $7,250.00, and in paraphernalia, $1400.00. The total paid out for relief was $12,993.00, sick benefits, $10,936.30, and death benefits $2,056.70. The current expenses for this period were $8,855.00.

The elective and appointive officers of the Tribe at the present time are Prophet, Jacob Moyer, Sachem Wm Gillespie, Junior S., James Gillespie, Senior S., James Troxell, Chief R., Calvin D Peters, Chief W., Wm S Dilcher, Keeper W., Harry R Young, First S., Jno Peters, Second S., Wm Heilman, Guard W., Samuel Wolfe, Guard F., Burton Piper, Warriors Chas King, H McFetridge, Jno Dougherty, Wm Eastman Braves Chas Miller, Wm Dougherty, Geo Mersch, Roland Elliott Pianist, Wm T Scanlin Trustees Daniel Gillespie, Wilson Scott, George Fehnel Representative to G C, Robert Montgomery, alternate, Wm T Scanlin Catasauqua Tribe meets every Thursday evening at seven-thirty o'clock.

REBEKAH LODGE.

Orpah Rebekah Lodge, No 159, was organized in the I O O F. Hall in June, 1887 At that time the hall was in the Esch Building On July 6, 1887, it was instituted by James B Nicholson P. G. Sire, the first officers having been: Alex. Morrow, N. G , Lizzie Clugston, V G ; William H Scanlin, Secretary, Charles R Horn, Treasurer

The Rebekah Lodge is a branch of the I O O F, and draws for its membership as follows: All Odd Fellows, their wives, mothers, sisters, and daughters, and all unmarried white women over eighteen years of age Its object is twofold. First, care for the widows and especially the orphans of Odd Fellows during sickness and distress, Second, the social welfare of its members and friends

The present membership in good standing is sixty-seven. The officers for 1914 are Rose Laubach, P G , Ella Hopkins, N G , Agnes Smith. V .G., William H. Scanlin, Secretary, Mary Struebing, Treasurer, Annie H Scanlin, Chaplain; Margaret Gillespie, Conductor, Eva Hopkins, Warden; Jennie Miller, R S. V G , Emma Williams, L S V G , Ann Jones, R A S , Lucy Bachman, L A S., William Ritter, I. G , Daniel Gillespie, O G ; Emma Weaver, Agnes Bennett, Emily Knoll, Trustees

The meetings are held the first and the third Tuesday evening of each month in the I O O F. Hall, on Front Street

CATASAUQUA CASTLE NO 241, KNIGHTS OF THE GOLDEN EAGLE

Catasauqua Castle No 241, K G E was instituted January 30, 1888

Through the efforts of the late Captain Edwin Gilbert, Jacob Van Buskirk, George Conrade and other citizens of Catasauqua, preliminary meetings were held at the Mansion House, of which Alfred Fry was proprietor, and afterwards in Applegate's Hall The castle was finally instituted in Knights of Friendship Hall by W. W Wetzel, District Grand Chief of Lehigh County, with a staff of Grand Officers selected from the castles of his jurisdiction, on January 30, 1888, with 43 charter members

The first officers of the castle were: Past Chief, Edwin Gilbert, Noble Chief, George Conrade, Vice Chief, J. S McFetridge, High Priest, Thomas McAllister; Venerable Hermit, Lewis Bloss, Master of Records, Jacob Van Buskirk; Clerk of Exchequer, Wilson J Smith, Keeper of Exchequer, Charles Phillips, Sir Herald, John Maguire.

The appointed officers were Worthy Bard, A H Newman, Worthy Chamberlain, William Scanlin, Ensign, Thomas Aubrey, Esquire, Frank H. Wilson; First Guardsman, Wilson F Ritter, Second Guardsman, Robert Rockel

The first two regular meetings of the castle were held in Applegate's Hall Finding the room too small for the rapid increase of its membership, efforts were made to lease the Knights of Friendship's Hall, where the castle was instituted They finally succeeded and the first regular meeting was held there February 20, 1888 The castle continued to meet here till Nov 17, 1890, when an offer was received from Washington Camp No 301, P O S of A, who occupied the hall in the old Bank Building on Front Street Having an opportunity to secure cheaper rent, the castle accepted, and the first meeting was held there Nov 24, 1890. The castle remained the tenants of the P O S of A until April 1, 1896, when Fuller Post No. 378, G A R, leased the hall The castle became their tenants and remained the same until January 13, 1902

Washington Camp No 301, P O S of A, bought the Swartz property on Bridge Street and made extensive improvements, including a large lodge room on the third story Finding the old quarters getting too small again for the rapid growth of the order, the castle finally leased the hall of the P O S of A, and became their tenants again January 13, 1902, and remained the same to this time

There were initiated into the mysteries of the order by Catasauqua Castle during its 26 years of existence 515 candidates, reinstated 27, admitted by card 1, suspended 269, and deceased 38, leaving a membership at present of 229

The receipts of the castle from January 30, 1888, to January 1, 1914, were $41 648 05 Of this amount $22,258 30 was paid for sick benefits and burial of the dead, $8,836 43 for working expenses, and $1 484 15 for paraphernalia and furniture.

The castle has invested in the Catasauqua, Lehigh and Home Building Associations, in the, Lehigh National Bank and in Bands and Mortgages $8,430 00; and a balance in the hands of the Keeper of Exchequer of $329 17

The total valuation of the castle is $10,243 32

The present officers of the castle are Past Chief, Clarence F Bartholomew; Noble Chief, Henry Kingcaid, Vice Chief, Edgar N Moyer, High Priest, George Smith, Venerable Hermit, Clayton Erdell, Master of Records, Nathan A Bartholomew, Clerk of Exchequer, John F Bartholomew, Keeper of Excheuqer, Rufus W S Wint, Sir Herald, Wayne Frantz; Worthy Bard, Charles Kurtz, Worthy Chamberlain, Edwin C Nagle, Ensign, Elwood Bartholomew, Esquire, Adam Freund, First Guardsman, Jacob Moyer, Second Guardsman, Alfred S Daniel, Trustees, Charles L Heckman, Jacob Moyer, Henry Bachman, Representative to the Grand Castle, Nathan A Bartholomew

The order of Knights of the Golden Eagle was founded by John E Burbage in Baltimore, Maryland, Feb 6, 1873, and was introduced into the State of Pennsylvania Oct 1, 1875

The primary objects of the Order are to promote the principles of true benevolence, by associating its members together for the trials and difficulties attending sickness, distress and death, so far as they may be mitigated by sympathy and pecuniary assistance, to care for and protect the widows and orphans of members, to assist those out of employment, to encourage each other in business, and by wholesome precepts, fraternal counsel, and social intercourse to elevate the membership and advance it to a higher and nobler life

ORDER KNIGHTS OF FRIENDSHIP

The Order Knights of Friendship is a benevolent, social and patriotic organization based upon the fundamental principles drawn from its motto Charity, Friendship, Companionship, and Knowledge

The Packer Chamber No 21 was instituted in Catasauqua, March 20 1888 Some of the most prominent and influential men of town and vicinity became charter members of the Order

On the 10th of May, 1910, a new Chamber was instituted under the honorable title of David Thomas Chamber No 72

This chamber is in a flourishing condition It meets on Tuesday evening of each week in the P O S of A Hall

THE ST LAWRENCE T A B SOCIETY.

The St Lawrence Total Abstinence and Beneficial Society was organized May 25, 1890 The first officers were: Spiritual Director, Rev B J Conway, President, Thomas Quinn, Vice President, John Crowley; Secretary, Robert J McIntyre, Treasurer, John O'Neil, Marshall, Edward Sweeney The Investigating Committee consisted of John O'Donnell, Thomas Small, and Edward Sweeney, the Stewards were James Fisher, Anthony Farrell, and Michael O'Laughlin The other charter members were. James Connell, Peter Quinn, Thomas Fisher, Dennis J Dougherty, Michael O'Mara, James T Cunningham, and Hugh Conahan

These men banded themselves together that their united efforts might advance the interests of total abstinence In addition to this primary object, they planned to carry out social and beneficial projects All three lines of effort have been largely realized

Until September 14, 1900, the Society met in different places Very often they gathered over the store of Thomas Quinn at the corner of Front and Walnut Streets At that time they purchased from the Catasauqua Public School District a two story brick school building on Front Street This has been used for the regular meetings, which are held the second Monday of each month, and for social gatherings During the winter months ,it has been the scene of many a basketball contest For a number of years the Society has supported a strong basketball team which has played games with the best amateur teams of this section

JR O. U A M

No Surrender Council, No. 103 of Jr O U A M, was organized December 18, 1881, with a charter membership of twenty-six The first meeting was held in Hunter's Hall on Second Street.

Paramount among its objects for existence are to encourage the reading of the Holy Bible in the public schools and to raise the American flag over the school buildings The local council has proven its sincerity by presenting flags to the schools of this and surrounding towns.

For the relief of the sick and distressed, the organization has a beneficial department which has paid out nearly twenty thousand dollars. The prosperity of No Surrender Council has been such that a magnificent hall has been erected on Front Street. This is a credit to the Order and the town.

The present membership is two hundred. Those holding official positions are: Councilor, Harrison Smith; Vice Councilor, George Williams; Recording

JR. O. U. A. M.

Secretary, Edwin Steyert; Assistant Secretary, Raymond Porter; Financial Secretary, Reuben Weaver; Treasurer, William H. Smith; Conductor, Roland Kurtz; Inside Sentinel, William M. Kane; Outside Sentinel, Charles A. Smith; Chaplain, James Beltz; Junior Past Councilor, Charles F. Eisle; Trustees, Samuel Gemmel, Harrison Porter and Elmer Kingcaid.

CATASAUQUA ROYAL ARCH CHAPTER, NO. 278

Royal Arch Chapter, No 278, was constituted April 11, 1894, by M E Grand High Priest Edgar A Tennis and Grand Officers, in Masonic Hall, with the following charter members John B Davis, M E High Priest, Abraham F Koons, King, Charles D W Bower, Scribe, Dr Daniel Yoder, Treasurer, Edmund Randall, Secretary, Dr Henry H Riegel, Owen F Fatzinger, Charles R. Horn, Charles W Chapman, Allen S Heckman, William W McKee, Edwin C Koons, Morgan Emanuel, John Matchette, and William R Thomas, Sr Seven of these brethren have since passed away Two Hundred twenty-three companions have been exalted, the Chapter furnishing charter members for Slatington R A. Chapter, No 292, and Siegfried R. A Chapter, No 295, and having a present enrollment of one hundred fourteen members

ST SYRIL RUSSIAN ORTHODOX SOCIETY.

Assembly No 16 of the St Syril Russian Society was organized February 10, 1895, with seventeen Charter members The cherished aim of kindred Orders that aid and protect their own was the fond ambition of the Russian Orthodox people in and around Catasauqua The specific purpose of Assembly No. 16 was the founding of a Church of their faith This they happily accomplished in 1899. The Society now numbers one hundred eighty members, and has one thousand ($1000) dollars in its treasury

The present officers are Andrew Wasco, President, John Smajda, Secretary, John M Kvesach, Treasurer

KNIGHTS OF MALTA

The Ancient and Illustrious Order of Knights of Malta instituted the Bruce Commandery, No 214, on December 21, 1896 From that time until the present, it has had a steady and healthful growth, the membership having reached one hundred sixteen

Both local and national organizations may look back with pride upon the past They are the direct descendants of one of the most knightly Orders They inherit all that made for good in the illustrious, religious and military Order of the Middle Ages Fraternal, military, religious and beneficial principles are the basis of their existence This heritage from the Crusades has been an invigorating and refreshing thought to its members, a shining and attractive influence in drawing the best type of men towards the Order.

Fraternally, it has been a very strong factor in the life of this community Finest and greatest of the services of this Order has been its beneficial work Here it has been a watchful guardian over its membership The benefits are five dollars for each week of disability, and one hundred dollars in case of death. Because of the income from invested funds of three thousand dollars, the dues are only twelve cents each week

The Bruce Commandery meets on each Wednesday evening in the P O S. of A Hall, Bridge Street

ORDER OF SHEPHERDS OF BETHLEHEM

The Order of Shepherds of Bethlehem of North America was founded and instituted at Trenton, N J , by Mrs Eva A Wychoff, November 9, 1896 Articles of Incorporation were taken out by Mrs Wychoff and her associates, who determined that this body shall afford the greatest protection and the most liberal benefits of any similar institution Their insurance feature means One Hundred Dollars per member.

The Star of Catasauqua Lodge, No 80, was organized nine years ago with thirty charter members Their present membership, in good standing, is ninety

CATASAUQUA CLUB

The Catasauqua Club was originally organized as a Wheelmen's Club on April 6, 1897, and had a very delightful season as a Bicycle Club When winter approached, it was deemed advisable to continue the pleasant social relations, and the present Catasauqua Club was chartered at the first meeting of the Club, held October 11, 1897

The following officers were elected Frank M Horn President, R S Weaver, Secretary, C R Horn, Treasurer, these gentlemen with Leonard Peckitt, James W Fuller, Jr , L H McHose, Herman Schneider, James M Lennon, R J McIntyre, and D T Williams forming the first Board of Governors

The Club has been in successful operation since The old Emanuel residence was bought and transformed into a cozy Club House, and a very well equipped bowling alley, which has been a source of much pleasure, was added Many interesting tournaments have been held with clubs from neighboring towns, and among the Club members The old round table in the cafe has been the center of many pleasant gatherings, when great questions were seriously discussed and the affairs of nations settled to the satisfaction of all present

The Club has always been very popular among the men of Catasauqua and pleasant memories of it are cherished by former members who are scattered far and wide

ST PETER AND ST PAUL SOCIETY

Assembly No 369 of the St Peter and St Paul Society of the Slavonic National Organization of the United States of America was instituted February 3, 1901. The prime movers in the organization of this local Chapter were Michael Mayernik, John Fisher and Walter Borowsky The St Peter and St Paul Society is the oldest of the Slavonic Orders in this country The officers of Assembly No 369 are. Joseph Yurko, President, Nicholas Graytzar, Secretary, John Smajda, Treasurer

AUQUASAT CLUB

In September, 1907, the Auquasat Club, a social organization of young men of Catasauqua and vicinity, was organized with quarters on the second floor of the building now occupied by Deemer & Litzenberger, electrical contractors

Shortly after, on account of a fire which destroyed all their possessions, they secured their present quarters which consist of two handsomely furnished club rooms, together with an elegant ball room on the second floor of the P O S of A Building, No 119 Bridge Street

The club enjoys a membership of thirty resident and twenty non-resident members, who are all prominent young men in this community and other communities

Frequent social affairs are held which afford a great deal of pleasure to the members and their friends

THE CHAROTIN CLUB

The Charotin Club was organized in 1907 with a membership of about eighty congenial people fond of social pleasures They leased the rooms in the third story of the Post Office Building, where every winter since, frequent gatherings have been held.

This club has been very successfully managed and has added materially to the attractive social life of the town. Visitors to Catasauqua have carried away very pleasant recollections of courtesies extended them by the members of this club, and the organization has become one of the institutions of the town The present officers of the club are James Sydney Stillman, President, Paul E Miller, Secretary, H J Weidinger, Treasurer

THE LYCEUM CLUB

In the spring of 1909, certain young men of town, desirous of organizing themselves into a body for the purpose of intellectual betterment, held a preliminary meeting April 13, 1909, the result of which was the formation of the Lyceum Club Through energetic co-operation thirty-three young men were induced to enroll as members and on May 1 of the same year the Lyceum was constituted, and secured as their quarters the two large rooms over the jewelry store of J C Beitel & Son, Front and Bridge Streets The first officers of the Club were John Frederick, President, John Edgar, Vice-President, Stuart Hauser, Secretary, and John S Matchette, Treasurer

It was on January 1, 1912, that the organization moved to more commodious quarters in the Edgar building, on Front Street, where they have remained up to this time Programs are rendered in the rooms and include debates, addresses, discussions in conjunction with musical numbers and social features.

The present officers are Robert E McKeever, President, Charles Hopkins, Vice-President, Edward Sandbrook, Secretary, and Ralph F Faust, Treasurer Of the original thirty-three members there remain six who are still active in the affairs of the Club, and the present membership is forty.

BRYDEN GUN CLUB.

The Bryden Gun Club was organized April 29th, 1909, for the purpose of providing recreation and enjoyment of the manly sport of Trap Shooting, a sport that has quality which must be experienced to be appreciated.

The Club has a membership of fifty-seven energetic men, all true sportsmen

THE CATASAUQUA GUN CLUB

Through their own efforts and labor they constructed and furnished their own Club-House, which is free from all encumbrance

The Bryden Gun Club has taken a place among the leaders of successful Gun Clubs in the East and their Annual Registered Tournaments are looked forward to with pleasure as they have the reputation for conducting their Tournaments in a most satisfactory and businesslike manner, and their hospitality and good fellowship is known and commented on far and wide

The grounds are situated in an ideal location for target shooting, having nothing but a clear sky for a back ground Several good records have been made there, among which might be mentioned a Pennsylvania State Record made by Neaf Apgar, who broke 422 Taregts out of 425, and had a straight run of 236 unfinished, J Mowell Hawkins, 216 straight unfinished, John Englert, 141 straight unfinished, Allen S Heil, 100 straight unfinished

The officers of the Club are as follows Granville Brown, President, George Silfies, Vice-President, Harry Steyert, Treasurer, Edgar C Jones, Secretary, Webster Hepner, Captain; J B McClister and John Haines, Trustees.

WOODMEN OF THE WORLD

The Catasauqua Camp No 250 Woodmen of the World was instituted June 30, 1910, by the district deputy, Frank E Leonard, assisted by the degree team of Alpha Camp No 232, Fullerton, Pa. The Charter membership numbered fifty-five

Besides striving for the mutual protection of their members in sickness or distress, and helpfulness to the bereaved in case of death, the Order covenants to erect monuments to the memory of their deceased brethren. Thus far two shafts have been erected by them in Fairview Cemetery

The Catasauqua Camp now numbers 202 members The Supreme Council throughout the United States and Canada now numbers 900,000 loyal devotees, and there is a surplus fund in the treasury of over $28,000,000

DEGREE OF POCAHONTAS

The Catasauqua Council No 212, Degree of Pocahontas, Improved Order of Red Men, was organized on the sleep of the 25th Sun, Plant Moon, G S D 422, or April 25th, 1913, by Past Sachem, William S Dilcher, with fifty-four charter members.

This Order has grown rapidly inasmuch as it has enjoyed fully the confidence of the community Its cherished principles are Freedom, Friendship and Charity

LOYAL ORDER OF MOOSE

Catasauqua Lodge, No 1362, Loyal Order of Moose, was instituted by M M Shea, National Director, on June 29, 1913 The charter was granted by the Court of Lehigh County on January 19, 1914 During the formation of the Lodge and up until May 1 1914, the place of meeting was in Odd Fellows' Hall on Front Street On the above date, the organization bought the Fatzinger property, No 754, Front Street, for seven thousand dollars and equipped it for Lodge purposes Since its formation it has had two deaths and paid $346 28 in benefits

On May 1, 1914, one hundred seventy-five members were installed by J J. Blackman This speaks well for so young an organization and surely indicates a bright future for it The present officers are Josiah Steckel, Past Dic , George Kemmerer, Dic , E A Hassler, Vice-Dic , E J Rodger, Tres , E J Lynch, Sec , Edward Fenstermaker, O G , Ed Bartz, S G , M Smith, Prelate, W F Kessler, Serg -at-Arms, R O. Heilman, Frank Fatzinger and P V Snyder, Trustees

TEMPERANCE SOCIETY

In his solicitude for the general welfare of the people, especially the uplift of the youth of the community. Father Thomas strongly urged and liberally supported a temperance movement during the early days of the Borough The temperance association was divided into the "George Crane Division" for adults, and the "Crystal Fount Section" for boys The original Fire Hall, located on Second Street, where the Crane stables are, was the place of meeting Men and boys of a certain age who did not belong to the association were obliged to give reason why they did not join It seems the general moral tone of the Borough was so elevated that it did not require the special censorship of the temperance society The association of pioneer days gradually disbanded

During the eighties Oliver Williams saw the need of a temperance sentiment. He organized quite a society which met for some time in the building on Front Street, opposite the Eagle Hotel and now used as an express office and as the Lehigh Valley freight station During the opening years of the new century, B F Hammond, Esq, father of the Rev. B. F Hammond, conducted a temperance movement in Schneller's Hall on Front Street above Bridge

Although these efforts proved sporadic, and gradually faded from view, the great cause of morals for which they stood and strove is growing as a nation-wide sentiment and is destined by divine direction to mould and hold the hearts and lives of men true to a clean, noble and prosperous citizenship

SOCIETIES CONNECTED WITH ST ANDREW'S CATHOLIC CHURCH

The oldest society under the direction of St Andrew's Roman Catholic Church is Society St Andrew's Branch No 157 of the First Catholic Slovak Union. It was organized November 25, 1894, and has a membership of ninety-eight

Society St Martoon's Branch No 470 of the First Catholic Slovak Union was organized November 6, 1904, at Cementon, Pa This branch has at the present time fifty-five members

The Pennsylvania Catholic Slovak Union Society, St Michael Branch No 132, was organized on September 25, 1905. There are thirty-one members at present in this organization

The Pennsylvania Catholic Slovak Union then established the Society St. Matthew's Branch No 52, at Northampton, Pa This Society has grown to fifty-six members

Society St Anthony's Branch No 72 of the First Catholic Slovak Union SOKOL was organized September 25, 1910. A powerful factor in the prosperity of this branch has been the military drill given the members So earnest have they been in basic principles of military tactics, that today they can present for exhibition a fine body of drilled men

The boys of St Andrew's banded themselves together under the guidance of the Junior of the First Catholic Slovak Union On June 11, 1911, they became the Society St Joseph Branch No 165 The growth has been very fine.

reaching one hundred sixty-five The strength and promise of the younger society augurs well for the future of the older societies of St Andrew's Roman Catholic Church

GEORGE W. FULLER POST, G A. R

The Lieutenant George W Fuller Post, G A R , was organized August 19, 1867, as Post 74, and disbanded June 30, 1871 It was reorganized April 15, 1872, and disbanded August 12, 1876 It was again reorganized as the present Post No 378 September 15, 1883, with twenty-three charter members as follows

Edwin Gilbert, Frank H Wilson, James Tait, Jr , Joseph Wray, Frank Scott, James Dyatt, John Matchette, Francis Erdell, Charles King, Joseph H Schwab Abram Miller, Conrad Klipple, John Patrick, Charles Laramy, Edmund Randall, Joseph Matchette, W H Bartholoemw, Charles E Sheckler, George Henry, Andrew Johnson, F M Eagle.

By Edwin S Osborne,

Dept Commander

Tho J Stewart,

Adjt General

The total number of names enrolled since its organization is two hundred sixty-five In the course of time the old soldier has been mustered out of the services of earth until the present enrollment totals only forty-six names The Post owns twenty Springfield rifles and some fifty-five pictures of battle scenes, and a case of army relics presented to the Post by the late Joseph Hunt. The Post also owns a small library composed of valuable volumes, besides an array of flags and standards The present Post commander is Francis Erdell, Senior Vice-Commander, Joseph Schwab, Junior Vice-Commander, George Henry; Adjutant, W R Houser, Sergeant Major, David Davis, Quartermaster, Martin Graver, Quartermaster Sergeant, Thomas Quinn, Officer of the Day, James R Henry, Chaplain, Joseph Matchette, Officer of the Guard, Henry Savitz, Trustees Joseph Matchette, David Davis and Thomas Quinn.

No organization, or body of men, in the country has ever stood out more prominently for patriotism, the love of home, life and liberty than "Our Boys in Blue " Their pageantry on Memorial Day, the thirtieth of May of each year rekindled the flame of love of liberty and "The Union forever" and fanned it into a brighter glow in the hearts of their countrymen than the rhetoric of the strongest orators the country ever produced. A grateful people marched to the strains of their martial bands to the silent mounds of their fallen comrades and aided with liberal hand to decorate the same with nature's spring offerings and the stars and stripes. And although the last man of that noble band shall soon countermarch to his final resting place, the patriotic impulse of the nation will continue the time honored custom so that the soldiers' graves shall be adorned with flowers and flags as long as the nation stands.

THE SOLDIERS' MONUMENT.

Patriotism is a poetic sentiment which touches the chords of that which is sacred and tender. Historic places, mementos of friendship and tokens of regard are clothed with this sentiment and invite contemplation. The world appreciates and glorifies the actions of those who have loved their country better than their homes, their families, than even their own lives. Their example inspires us with appreciation for the great inheritance that is ours because of their loyalty, devotion and self-sacrifice.

SOLDIERS' MONUMENT

At the close of the Great Civil War, the patriotic sentiments of this community and environs found an expression of appreciation of the services rendered by the volunteers of the town by the erection of a costly monument on the circular plot reserved in the cemetery. Upon this monument are inscribed the names, rank and regiment of each soldier who went forth to battle that the Union might be preserved, also the names of the prominent battles in which they were engaged. The names of one hundred fifty-seven men are inscribed, twenty-six of whom were killed or died in the service

With suitable and prophetic sacred inscriptions, capped by an overspreading American eagle and draping folds of the Union flag, the beautiful Italian marble shaft was dedicated with imposing ceremonies and a civil and military parade on October 3, 1866 Major A R Calhoun was the orator and delivered an inspiring address The Rev C Earle, D D, Secretary of the Monument Association, delivered the historical oration in which he declared that the nams of no civilian appeared any where on the shaft, due to the decision that "no man's name should be inscribed on the monument unless he had been sworn into the services of the United States, and had been under the enemy's fire" Hence it is what it purports to be, "A Soldiers' Monument" Space was reserved for the burial of veterans around the monument but the idea was abandoned subsequently The one aim of all concerned was that the graceful figure should stand out in bold relief against the azure blue o'er head without any thing around it to detract from its grace and glory

In 1871, General Charles Albright, a member of Congress introduced a special Act by which four siege guns and twenty-four cannon balls were donated to the Lieutenant George W Fuller Post, No 74, G A R, for the adornment of the first soldiers' monument erected in Pennsylvania After the reorganization of the Fuller Post, No 378 G A R, in 1884, the Secretary of War, Robert Lincoln, ordered the Commandant of the Watervliet Arsenal at West Troy, N Y, to issue to said Post four 64-pounder cannon, two of the English model of 1812, weighing 5,514 and 5,498 pounds, respectively and two U S guns of the 1819 and 1829 models, weighing 5,014 and 5,000 pounds, respectively These were placed at the four corners of the monument

The following names, with the rank and organization in which serving, and accredited to Catasauqua, are inscribed upon the shaft:

FORTY-SIXTH REGIMENT PENNSYLVANIA VOLUNTEERS

OFFICERS

Major Arnold C Lewis
Captain Joseph Matchette
Lieutenant William R Thomas
Lieutenant Robert Wilson
Lieutenant Edward Cramsie
Lieutenant James McQuillen
Orderly Sergeant Isaac Davis
Sergeant Daniel Davis

Sergeant Morgan Richards
Sergeant John J. Davis
Corporal Robert E Williams
Corporal William McMonegal
Corporal Hugh Lyons
Corporal John Patrick
Corporal John Moore
Corporal John H. Price

Musician Andrew Sinley

PRIVATES

Wallace Brown
John Blair
David Bachman
John Brown
John Cannon
Daniel Dwyer
Samuel Zellner
Hugh Dougherty
Philip Hill
George Hasson
Jeremiah Keefe
John Kilpatrick
John Leo
Thomas Mooney
John McMurtrie
James McCracken

James McLaughlin
John McQuillen
John McFadden
John Reed
Solomon J Rowe
David McCandless
Daniel Desmond
Alexander Doneghue
Michael Rohfritzs
John Richards
Patrick Reilly
John Son
Patrick Sullivan
William Thompson
Franklin Wards

FORTY-SEVENTH REGIMENT PENNSYLVANIA VOLUNTEERS

OFFICERS

Captain Henry S Harte
Captain Edwin Gilbert
Lieutenant George W. Fuller
Lieutenant Wm H Bartholomew
Lieutenant Augustus Eagle
Lieutenant Harry H. Bush
Lieutenant Thomas F Lambert
Lieutenant James W Fuller
Orderly Sergeant James Tait
Sergeant William H Glace

Sergeant W F Longenhagen
Sergeant John L Jones
Corporal Joseph H Schwab
Corporal G H Longenhagen
Corporal Martin O'Brien
Corporal Josiah H Walk
Corporal James E Patterson
Corporal Robert Cunningham
Corporal Augustus F Eberhart
Corporal Charles L Nolf, Jr

OF CATASAUQUA 175

Sergeant John W Heberling
Sergeant Richard H. Schwab
Sergeant Joseph J Lilly
Sergeant Albert H HcHose

Corporal Spencer Tettermer
Corporal James Ritter
Corporal W H VanDyke
Musician David A Tombler, Jr

PRIVATES.

David Andrews
Abram Bauder
Godfrey Betz
Stephen Beers
Hiram A Beitelman
William Christ
William Ehrich
Orlando Fuller
Frederick Fisher
Rainey Grader
Addison R Geho
Joseph Geiger
Joseph Gross
Joseph Hunsicker
William Herman
Isaac Jacoby
William Jordan
John Kane
George Kerchner
Nicholas Kuhn
William Kuntz
Reuben H Kern
Philip King
Charles King
Frank Leffler
J K. Longenhagen
Joel Laudenslager
John Lucky

Michael O'Brien
John Whorley
John P Weaver
F H Wilson
Gotheb Schrum
Nicholas Smith
Robert M Sheats
Griffith Reinhart
William Offhouse
John O'Brien
Daniel Newhart
Charles H Michel
Ambrose Dietrich
George Moll
W H Moll
Alfred Lynn
Jenkin Richards
Ed Matthew
Uriah Meyers
William Mensch
Benjamin Missimer
Charles Leffler
Aaron Laub
Emanuel Leffler
William Henry
G Assenheimer
John Weiss

OTHER VOLUNTEERS.

Charles Miller, 14th U S Infantry
Michael J Hooker, 1st Pa. Reserves
Joseph Shelly, 1st Pa Reserves
Stephen Shierer, 1st Pa Reserves
Samuel Roberts, 6th Pa Cavalry, Rush's Lancers
Charles Boyle, 6th Pa Cavalry, Rush's Lancers
Thomas Smith, 202d Pa Volunteers
William Paul, 188th Pa Volunteers
John Keefer, 16th Pa. Cavalry
John Graham, U S Navy

John Scholle, 3rd Pa Reserves
Peter Mack, 8th Pa Cavalry
James R. Henry, 8th Pa. Cavalry
W. H Berlin, 8th Pa Cavalry
John Case, 58th Pa Volunteers
John Saurwine, 58th Pa Volunteers
George Henry, 54th Pa Volunteers
Samuel Kiefer, 6th N J Cavalry

Abram Miller, 6th N J Cavalry
Robert Newhart, 6th N J. Cavalry
William Newhart, 14th U. S Infantry
John Bigley, 14th U S Infantry
Herbert James, 12th U. S Infantry
Joe Davies, 53 Pa Valunteers
James Hutchison, 53 Pa Volunteers
James McClelland, 53 Pa Volunteers

SPANISH AMERICAN WAR VOLUNTEERS

Roy Applegate
William Buckland
Frank Bartholomew
Edward Eagle
Stanley Fitzhugh
Edward Kane
Harry Lambert
David McMahon
William Paul
George Storm
William H Smith
John L Schick

John Scott
Henry Steinbecker
Paul Tildon
John W Thomas
John T Thomas
Ralph Weaver
Adrian Weaver
Charles Wetherhold
Henry Weible
Charles Williams
Philip Walters
David Yates

BATTLES OF THE 46TH REGIMENT

Winchester, Va, March 23, 1862
Middletown, Va, May 25, 1862
Winchester, Va, May 26, 1862
Cedar Mountain, Va, August 27, 1862
Sulphur Springs, Va, August 27, 1862
South Mountain, Md, September 14, 1862
Antietam, Md, September 17, 1862
Chancellorsville, Va, May 1, 2, 3, 1863.
Gettysburg, Pa, July 1, 2, 3, 1863
Resaca, Ga, May 15, 1864
Cassville, Ga, May 19, 1864
Dallas, Ga, May 25, 1864
Pine Knob, Ga, June 9, 1864
Kulp's Farm, Ga, June 22, 1864
Pine Tree Creek, Ga, July 26, 1864.
Atlanta, Ga, September 6, 1864
Cypress Swamp, Ga, December 8, 1864
Savannah, Ga, December 21, 1864
Chesterfield, C. H., S Car, March 2, 1865

Averysboro, N. Car., March 14, 1865.
Berryville, Va., September 5, 1864.
Coon Run, N. Car., April 10, 1865.
Raleigh, N. Car., April 26, 1865.

BATTLES OF THE 47TH REGIMENT.

St. John's Bluff, Fla., October 8, 1862.
Pocataligo, S. Car., October 22, 1862.
Sabine Cross Roads, La., April 8, 1864.
Pleasant Hill, La., April 9, 1864.
Cane River, La., April 25, 1864.
Manasses Plains, La., May 16, 1864.
Berryville, Va., September 5, 1864.
Opequan Creek, Va., September 19, 1864.
Fisher's Hill, Va., September 22, 1864.
Cedar Creek, Va., October 19, 1864.

THE PIONEER BAND.

A Brass Band was organized in Catasauqua during 1843. John Thomas was the leader; and the last surviving member of that band was the late Samuel Thomas. It would be interesting to see the shapes and sizes of the instruments used in those early days. After an existence of nine years the band was dis-

OLD PIONEER BAND

solved, mostly because its principal players moved out of town.

In 1865, the Catasauqua Band was organized, and taught by Prof. Vest Moyer. The leaders were Orange Fuller and Attilio Benvenuti; Secretary, Henry W. Ehrie. The members of this band were:

Henry C. Eckensberger, Fred W. Becker, James C. Beitel, William Koons, Frank Romig, Henry Rothrock, John Stuart, John Hill, Franklin Bower, Albert Breisch, Frank Seem, William Stuart, Hiram Beitelman, Frank Roth, John Thomas, Walter Biery, Robert A. Miller, Benjamin Bachman, Uriah Kurtz, Jacob Sigley, Charles Hill, David Tombler, Edward Seyfried, James Young, James Betz, Daniel Milson, Pres., Jonathan Price, Treasurer.

The Pioneer Band as organized July 11, 1873, in Laubach's Hall, now the upper floor of the Child's Grocery Store. Jacob Berkemeyer was conductor. Anthony. B. Buck served as conductor on various occasions. Conrad Horst conducted from 1890 to 1893, and C. F. Roth from 1893 to 1907. After Mr. Roth came John Walker, from 1907 to 1909; Clyde Walp 1909 to 1913; and the present conductor is Ignatz Suppan.

THE PRESENT PIONEER BAND

The band was chartered as the Pioneer Cornet Band of Catasauqua, Pa., September 2, 1881.

The Band played a whole week's engagement in Philadelphia during the great centennial of 1876. Probably their most important engagement was with the Americus Club of Allentown, when rigged like the Club members in gray overcoats and silk hats, they marched through the streets of Harrisburg on the occasion of the inauguration of Governor Pattison.

The present membership consists of twenty-eight men, who rehearse Monday and Thursday evenings of each week in Kostenbader's Hall. Their officials are: President, John Steitz, Vice-President, Elmer Newhard. Treasurer, James Miller, Leader, Clem Suppan, Assistant Leader, Clayton Steitz; Trustees, John Steitz, U. E. Snyder, and Isaac Sell.

The oldest Band musician in Catasauqua to-day is C. F. Roth, who was a member of the Band from July 11, 1873, to August 12, 1909.

THE CATASAUQUA CHORAL SOCIETY

When Mrs. Wells became organist in the First Presbyterian Church, in 1870, a Choral Society was formed and the first attempt to render classical music in Catasauqua was made. James Prescott succeeded Mrs. Wells in 1876 and developed the society to such a degree that people from all over the Lehigh Valley journeyed to Catasauqua to hear concerts that were worth while. The Borough still enjoys a lofty distinction for good taste and great skill in the rendition of high-class music. The only noticeable feature to-day is the fact that many places once proudly held by the Welsh and Irish are now meekly occupied by the Germans.

The late Clement A. Marks, Mus. D., of Allentown, trained a large chorus of men and women in the closing years of the last century and gave two fine concerts.

In connection with a series of public meetings held in different churches in town during the fall of 1912, Ralph C. Solt developed a large choir of musical people to a high degree of perfection. The rendition of a number of classical selections was pronounced fine and inspiring.

During the opening months of 1914 a large Catasauqua Choral Society was organized with Harry E. Graffin as president, Robert Ritter, vice-president, Robert E. McKeever, secretary, and Bertha Hopkins, treasurer. The director of the Society is Matthew F. Webber. One hundred sixty-one names are enrolled in the list of members. They rendered their maiden concerts in the High School Auditorium on the evenings of April 21st and 22nd. Their efforts were greatly appreciated by large audiences composed of people from all over the Lehigh Valley.

CHAPTER VI.—BANKS

THE NATIONAL BANK OF CATASAUQUA

The Bank of Catasauqua was incorporated by an act of the Pennsylvania Legislature, approved by Governor James Pollock on May 5, 1857. The incorporators mentioned in the act were: William Miller, David Thomas, John D. Stiles, Henry King, John Williams, Eli J. Saeger, Benjamin Rupp, Solomon Vogel, Owen Frederick, John Hudders, James S. Rees, Jonas Biery, Franklin B. Martin, Samuel Sieger, and David A. Tombler. The first meeting of the Board of Directors was held September 9, 1857. Those present were Eli J. Saeger, John L. Hoffman, Chas. Aug. Luckenbach, J. P. Scholl, David A. Tombler, David Thomas, Joshua Hunt, William Miller, Jonas Biery, James W. Fuller, 1st, Robert Oberly, Samuel Laubach, and Jacob Fatzinger. The Board was sworn in by Chauncey D. Fuller, Esq. Eli J. Saeger was elected President. At a meeting held on September 14 of the same year, a committee of two, Messrs. Saeger and Hunt, was appointed to "report a suitable person for Cashier." As the banking business of the Iron Company, the leading industry of Catasauqua at that time, was transacted at Easton, it was natural that the committee should look to that town for a cashier, and, on September 17, the committee reported in favor of M. H. Horn, Jr., of Easton, and he became the first cashier. He remained manager of the bank in the position of Cashier and President until his death in 1890.

The first place of business was in the Thomas Frederick residence on Front Street below Union, in the room now used as a barber shop. Probably few of the present residents remember the primitive surroundings of the time. On the customers' desk was a glass of shot into which the pens were stuck to take off the ink and keep them from rusting. A pan of blotting sand and a small scoop were provided to use in drying the endorsements on checks, as no blotting paper was in use at that time. An old fashioned fire-proof safe was the strongbox of the Bank. The management looked about for a permanent location for the Bank, and at a meeting held on January 12, 1858, among other offers of sites for the permanent location of the Bank, David Thomas offered "to present to the Bank a lot of ground at the corner of Bridge and Second Streets and five hundred dollars, if banking house is erected on said lot at any time during the years 1858-59." This offer was refused on a vote of six to five and the James Lackey property (now the Imperial Hotel) was purchased. Here the Bank was

THE NATIONAL BANK OF CATASAUQUA

located from 1858 to 1903, when it moved to its present location, which strange to say is the very property offered to it free in 1858 by David Thomas. It was not acquired under as favorable terms as those offered to it previously. The Lackey store building was remodeled and made suitable for banking purposes. In 1867 extensive alterations were made and the building then was considered very imposing. Business was carried on here until 1903, when the Bank was moved to the present modern structure at Second and Bridge Streets. The Bank was just fairly launched in business when the panic of 1857 occurred, and it was one of the very few banks that did not suspend specie payments during that trying time The panics of 1873-1878, 1893 and 1907 were also survived with credit to the strength of the institution

The Bank of Catasauqua was converted into a National Bank, June 20, 1865, and became a member of the Federal Reserve Association in March, 1914 This institution has always been closely identified with the manufacturing, mining, mechanical, mercantile and producing interests of the community; and has shared in its prosperity as indicated by the fact that the dividends paid to its stockholders since its organization, a period of fifty-seven years, average slightly over seven per cent. per annum. The bank has often sacrificed its own good for local interests but the general good of the town and vicinity has been benefited by its actions

The capital and surplus of the Bank at present is $740,000, with deposits averaging $1,300,000

The officers of the Bank since its organization have been as follows

PRESIDENT

Eli J Saeger, from 1857 to 1888
M. H Horn, from 1888 to 1890.
Frank M Horn, from 1890 to 1899
Owen F Fatzinger, from 1899 to 1903
Edwin Thomas, present incumbent, elected 1903

VICE-PRESIDENT.

John Williams, from 1884 to 1892
Owen F. Fatzinger, from 1892 to 1899
Dr H H Riegel, present incumbent, elected 1899

CASHIER

M H Horn, from 1857 to 1888
Frank M. Horn, from 1888 to 1890
Charles R Horn, from 1890 to 1899
Frank M Horn, present incumbent, re-elected 1899

ASSISTANT CASHIER.

Frank M Horn, from 1880 to 1888
Charles R Horn, from 1888 to 1890.
H V. Swartz, from 1904, present incumbent.

TELLERS.

John O Lichtenwalner
Tilghman H Moyer
Orange M Fuller
William H Horn
John J. Glick
Clifford H Riegel
Ralph C Boyer

CLERKS.

James W Mickley	John A Frederick
John J Glick	Charles G Heilman
David A Tombler, Jr	Ralph C Solt
Frank M Horn	Joseph J McKeever
Clifford H Riegel	Charles G Albert
Ralph S Weaver	Charles W Hopkins
Howard V Swartz	Ella V Schneller
Ralph C Boyer	Mame E Swartz

The present Board of Directors are:

Rowland T Davies	Lucius H McHose
G B F Deily	Leonard Peckitt
D George Dery	H H Riegel
J S Elverson	H. J. Seaman
Charles C. Keiser	Edwin Thomas
Charles E Lawall	Charles N Ulrich
George B Mauser	

At the breaking out of the Civil War, gold and silver immediately went to a premium, consequently fractional silver coin was withdrawn from circulation, and it was impossible to make change for amounts under one dollar Store keepers and landlords issued scrip in denominations from three cents up and much worthless paper was put into circulation To overcome this difficulty in Catasauqua, John Williams deposited an amount of money in the Bank of Catasauqua and issued certified checks against it in amounts of five, ten, twenty-five, and fifty cents, thus giving the people a currency that was absolutely safe and readily redeemed in legal tender at the Bank This substitute for currency was used until the government issued its "postal currency."

The notes of the Bank of Catasauqua were redeemable at its counter in gold or at its redemption agency in Philadelphia The five dollar bill in the center of the group is Number One—the first bill issued by the Bank and the first note of any kind paid out over its counter. The one dollar bill is the first note of that denomination issued by the Bank.

This Bank was one of the very few banks that did not suspend specie payments in 1857.

The first note paid out over the counter of the Bank when it opened in 1857 is a five dollar bill, numbered one, and was carried by General William

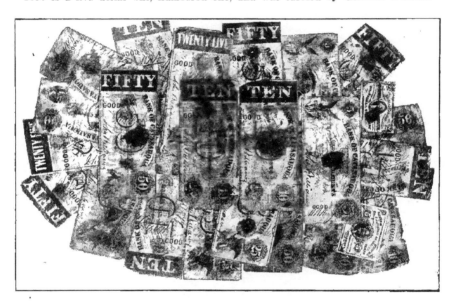

Lilly of Mauch Chunk for many years. This note is in the possession of the Bank and is framed with a full set of the notes of all denominations. This collection hangs in the Cashier's room at the Bank together with an interesting collection of small checks used as currency during the Civil War, when silver coin disappeared from circulation like magic. As soon as a premium was paid on gold and silver, for a short time, postage stamps were used to pay small sums; but as this was the only kind of money that would stick to you, it soon became unpopular. Merchants, hotel-keepers, etc., commenced to issue scrip to overcome the inconvenience of this substitute for money. John Williams issued checks for five, ten, twenty-five, and fifty cents which were certified as "good" by M. H. Horn, Cashier. These checks were used by the Iron Company in making pays, and passed current, as their payment was absolutely assured, until the Government issued the postal currency for amounts less than one dollar. This postal currency continued in use until long after the war and was so convenient that many regretted its disuse.

Since 1903 the Bank has occupied its magnificent stone structure at the corner of Second and Bridge Streets. This building necessitated an outlay of upwards of seventy-five thousand dollars and is as fine a building for banking purposes as can be found in any town of ten thousand people in America. The fire and burglar proof vaults, together with a safe deposit vault containing boxes to let, are of the latest design and mechanism

The popularity which it has attained is due in no small degree to the constancy with which its officials have kept in mind and lived up to their rule of courteous treatment to all, careful attention to details, anticipation of the needs of the banking public and progressive, yet conservative, management.

THE LEHIGH NATIONAL BANK.

On April 26, 1906, the Lehigh National Bank became a reality, when a number of the stock subscribers met and appointed a committee on organization, consisting of William H. Glace, Dr. Daniel Yoder, Herman Kostenbader, Sr., Owen Fatzinger, Charles W. Schneller, and Rufus M. Wint

The committee was instructed to decide on location, select a Board of Directors and look after other matters incident to organization

The Merchants' National Bank of Allentown was appointed the temporary depository of the new bank

On May 17, 1906, the directors met and elected William H Glace, President, James C Beitel, Vice-President, Hon Jonas F. Moyer, Cashier, John A Frederick, Teller, Burtis A Laub, Bookkeeper The directors were. James C Beitel, Dr A J. Becker, George H Dilcher, William H Glace, Herman Kostenbader, Sr, Frank B Mauser, B Frank Swartz, Charles W Schneller, Oscar J Stine, Rufus M Wint, and Dr Daniel Yoder, of Catasauqua, H. A Benner of Schoenersville, P J. Laubach of Northampton, James W Peters of Egypt, James J Seyfried, East Catasauqua, A H. Snyder of Weaversville; William H Fenstermacher and Thomas B Schadt of Coplay.

Temporary quarters for the new institution were secured in the Glace brick building, 423 Front Street, two doors above the Mansion House The bank opened for business on August 1, 1906, under the charter granted by William R Ridgely, Comptroller of Currency, on June 30, 1906 Over an hour before business began a crowd of people gathered, all eager to be the first depositor The honor went to Henry F Savitz, the Catasauqua coal oil dealer

During the day $104,173 11 were received in deposits The number of depositors was ninety-six, making an average of one thousand dollars deposited by each.

The new institution bought government bonds to the amount of thirty-five thousand dolars, for which it took out circulation. The bills were all in denominations of ten and twenty dollars, and were signed at the Merchants' National Bank by President William H. Glace and Cashier Jonas F. Moyer. The latter

LEHIGH NATIONAL BANK

signed bill No. 1 with a pen and holder presented by Hon. Fred. E. Lewis, President of the Merchants', and he preserved the pen and bill as a souvenir. The Bank prospered at once and the directors were set to work securing their own home. They engaged architect A. W. Leh of South Bethlehem to prepare the plans for a new building.

Where once stood the James W. Swartz dwelling and office building at Front and Bridge Streets is now located the handsome bank and office building of the Lehigh National Bank. The corporation purchased from the Swartz Estate the buildings located on the ground, forty-five feet on Front Street, one hundred eighty-seven feet on Bridge Street, and forty-five feet on Railroad Alley, for the sum of eighteen thousand dollars. The buildings on Front Street and on Bridge Street, as far as the Dispatch office, were torn down for the new bank, and building operations commenced May first, 1905, and throughout the year the work progressed variously The building contract was awarded to the well-known builder, W H Gangeware of Allentown.

The two-story building is forty-five feet on Front Street and seventy-seven feet on Bridge Street It is colonial in design, the materials being Corning terra cotta, with copper cornice and Wyoming blue stone trimmings. It is pronounced one of the finest and best equipped bank buildings in the Lehigh Valley

The Bank was the tenth in Lehigh County It has a capital of $125,000 It started out with deposits of $104,172.11 and now has deposits of $560,000. Loans and discounts are $366,161 78. The stock and bonds owned amount to $259,323 36 The earned surplus and profits are $61,000

The organization of the Bank at present is as follows James C Beitel, President, Rufus M Wint, Vice-President, Jonas F. Moyer, Cashier, Burtis A. Laub, Teller, John S Matchette, Bookkeeper, James Schreiber, Clerk The directors are James C Beitel, Dr A. J Becker, Frank B Mauser, August Kostenbader, Charles W Schneller, Oscar J Stine, Rufus M Wint, Dr Daniel Yoder, P J Laubach and James J Seyfried of this place, H A Benner of Schoenersville, James W Peters of Egypt, A H Snyder of Weaversville; William F Fenstermaker and George H Dilcher of Allentown, H W Bloss of Slatedale

HOME BUILDING AND LOAN ASSOCIATION

Besides our Banking Institutions of Town there are three other financial corporations They are the Home Building Association, Catasauqua Building and Loan Association, and The Lehigh Building and Loan Association.

The oldest of these three is the Home Building Association. A charter was granted by his Excellency, James A. Beaver. Governor of Pennsylvania, to the Association, and on March 4, 1887, it was incorporated under the laws governing these banking organizations The amount of the capital stock of the corporation was one million dollars divided into five thousand shares of the par value of two hundred dollars Only recently the Association voted to change the capital stock to five million dollars The present officers are Pres, Reuben F

Case, V Pres, John Fisher, Treas, Frank M Horn, Sec, Howard V Swartz, Solicitor, Chas N. Ulrich, Directors Owen A. Fatzinger, Plato W Troxell, Rufus M Wint, James M Lennon, Charles Kemp, P J McNally, Wm J Evans, Sr, Wm F Engler, George W Specht It meets the second Tuesday in each month

CATASAUQUA BUILDING AND LOAN ASSOCIATION

The second Building and Loan Association to be incorporated in the town is the Catasauqua Building and Loan Association It was incorporated under the laws of Pennsylvania on January 13, 1890 The amount of the capital stock of the Association is one million dollars, divided into five thousand shares of the par value of two hundred dollars The present officers are Pres, Edwin C Koons, V Pres, F J Fatzinger, Treas, H V Swartz, Sec, Roland Davies, Solicitor, Chas N Ulrich, Directors· Wm R Thomas, Jr, H B Weaver, Franklin Goldsmith, Allen S Heckman, Edwin Chapman, James Morrow, Jno Jordan It meets the first Tuesday in each month

THE LEHIGH BUILDING AND LOAN ASSOCIATION

The Lehigh Building and Loan Association was incorporated June 14, 1910 The amount of the capital stock of the Association is one million dollars divided into five thousand shares of par value of two hundred dollars each The officers are Pres, Dr A J Becker, V Pres, August Hohl, Jr, Treas, Jonas F Moyer, Sec, John Frederick, Solicitor, William H Schneller, Directors Joseph Troxell, Preston H Kratzer, William F Fenstermaker, Charles J Phifer, William J Montz, Frank C Beck, John Smajda, Rufus W G Wint, William A Follweiler, Preston L Beil, Evan B Guth

CHAPTER VII—TRADESMEN AND CRAFTSMEN

GEORGE B F DEILY George Deily, the father of George B F Deily, began the retail coal trade at Union and Canal Streets in 1849 and continued the business until 1862 In 1876 Edwin V Swartz reopened the yards and developed a lucrative trade which he felt constrained to release in 1882. Two years later George B F Deily stocked the yards with mountainous piles of all grades of coal and has conducted a mammoth trade ever since A yardman is in service during the entire year and three men with two teams are constantly devoted to making deliveries Mr Deily also opened a general store on Front and Union Streets in 1885 He carries a large stock of dry goods and notions together with a complete line of groceries

Mr Deily owns large and productive farms east of town and many valuable properties in and about Catasauqua He is considered a shrewd financier As a director of the National Bank of Catasauqua, his opinion and advice relative to investments and securities are constantly sought

J APPLEGATE AND SONS The store, known as Catasauqua's Department Store for a number of years, was established on the corner of Second and Bridge Streets by J Applegate and Sons, in 1882 In 1885 the place was enlarged The firm carried large lines of groceries, dry-goods, shoes and rubber goods, carpets and drapery, crockery, glass and china ware, wood and willow ware, etc September 1, 1909, they leased the grocery department to R A Clewell and Bro, who continued until January, 1912 Since the Clewell Bros retired, J Applegate and Sons are conducting the dry-goods trade only, devoting their whole building to dry-goods and notions

JOSEPH TAYLOR AND SONS This store on Second and Wood Streets was founded by John McKibben in 1868 During 1870 John Hunter turned it into a liquor store. Joseph Taylor began the general store business in 1868 at

234 Second Street Later he moved to 227 Second Street and in 1872 he bought out John Hunter. In due time Mr Taylor took his sons into partnership with himself so that the firm is known as Joseph Taylor and Sons The firm also carries some green goods, and for a while handled fresh meats

DAVID GILLESPIE, Jr The General Store on Second and Mulberry Streets was established by John Brown in 1849. He was succeeded by William Miller and Joseph Forest. David Gillespie, Sr , assumed the business in 1865; and his son David succeeded him in 1904 Additions to the store house were made in 1874, 1894 and in 1906 New lines of goods are constantly being added to the stock in order to meet the demands of the trade

JAMES E MISSMER With a capital of but fifty dollars, James E Missmer ventured into the mercantile life He began business in a small one-story frame building on the corner of Second and Arch Streets By close application he developed a trade of such proportions as to warrant the purchase of additional ground and the erection of a two and one-half story building The new structure occupies the site of the old one and is twenty by thirty feet in dimensions The stock consists of groceries, dry-goods and provisions In 1912 Mr Missmer also added the real estate and fire insurance business to his interests He sells lots of the Hunter farm and builds and sells houses

W B STEINHILBER William Steinhilber was a native of Minersville, Pa. After he attained to manhood, he was a mine foreman at Ashland for many years Later, he established a general store at Ashland and conducted it with success At the outbreak of the War, he enlisted in Company G of the 129th Regiment of the Pennsylvania Volunteers of Schuylkill County When he received his honorable discharge, he drifted into Catasauqua, and later built a grocery store during 1890 on Third and Almond Streets Success followed his enterprise to the day of his death, August 2, 1904 The business is continued by his son, W B Steinhilber

WILLIAM WEISLEY William Weisley established the General Store business at Front and Pine Streets in 1879, and has conducted a successful enterprise ever since. He carries a full line of groceries and dry goods besides a few special lines of china and glass ware By close application to business, by fair and square dealing, and by courteous treatment of his customers, Mr Weisley has built up a large patronage and a successful business

E J BOYER Reuben A Boyer established a general store on Second Street above Church in 1885 He sold out to Thomas Jacoby in 1864, and the latter conveyed the place to E J Boyer in 1871 Since this time Mr Boyer carries a stock of novelties, agate and queens-ware An addition was built to the store in 1891.

HARVEY F. HOFFMAN The general store on the corner of Walnut and Fourth Streets was opened by E A Troxell Until 1907 he was its owner and then Harvey F Hoffman bought the store. Four years later the present proprietor built an addition to the original building and increased his stock The line of merchandise now covers all that a community store should have for the convenience of the dwellers in the neighborhood The regular morning orders are carried to the homes by the delivery wagon and should any of the household necessities be required at short notice, it is but a step to Hoffman's

CATASAUQUA MERCANTILE COMPANY On August 17, 1906, a charter was granted to the Catasauqua Mercantile Company and the firm opened a business along the lines of the co-operative plan in a building at 758 Front Street, belonging to the Bryden Horse Shoe Company The originators of the plan were connected with the Horse Shoe Works and felt that the workers in the factory and all the residents of that section would be benefited by such a store They carry a large line of groceries and dry goods The second floor of the building is a ware room

The company at the present time is composed of the following officers President, Paul Miller, Secretary and Treasurer, John McAlister, Directors, W Foster Banks, Charles Frederick and John Moat

The present manager, Robert T. Rutman, took charge of the business in 1913. Under his efficient management, as well as under that of the six who preceded him, the Catasauqua Mercantile Company has built up one of the best local retail stores.

MATTHEW F WEBBER. The Matthew F Webber store, located on Second Street above Walnut, was opened originally by Preston Lindeman Reuben Lindeman succeeded the founder The present incumbent made his debut in the business in 1894 This store carries a full line of groceries, candy, notions and stationery

JAMES J SEYFRIED James J Seyfried is a native of Nazareth While still a child his father died, after which he became the charge of friends at Mt Bethel As a youth of eighteen summers, he drifted into Catasauqua, and worked for McKee & Fuller, at the Car, Wheel & Axle Works During the eighties Samuel Hock began the general store business on Eleventh and Race Streets In 1891 Mr Seyfried bought the Hock store and continued business on the corner until 1897, when he built the beautiful store and dwelling, the third door from the corner, where he continues his trade to the present time In 1899, Mr Seyfried admitted George C D Goldsmith into partnership, which continued until 1912 when Mr Goldsmith established and built a store for himself The Seyfried store has on sale groceries, dry-goods, notions, flour, feed, hard-ware, etc

H S WOTRING. The store building on the corner of Church and Limestone Streets was erected by Robert Miller in 1884, and devoted to the shoe trade William Steinhilber converted it into a general store Later Mrs John Downs conducted a store here Ammon H Bachman bought the property from Mrs Downs. H S Wotring purchased the place in 1907, and during 1910 he built an addition by which he more than doubled the capacity of his store He carries a full line of dry goods, notions, shoes, groceries, cured meats, etc

MILTON D WOTRING Three years ago Milton D Wotring, the largest stock holder in the Allentown Notion Company of Allentown, Pa, bought all the other shares This company had been conducting a large wholesale notion business throughout this section During the years of 1911 and 1912, he erected a large building at 1025 Fourth Street, Catasauqua The plans provided for a store and home into which Mr Wotring moved his business and family. He continued the wholesale business that had been started in Allentown and opened a fine general retail business

The large established wholesale business is conducted on the second and third floors. The agent employed by Mr Wotring travels throughout the cement regions and into the city of Allentown. On the first floor the retail department presents to the housewife of this section a very large variety of merchandise, groceries, dry-goods, hardware and notions In this day a necessity to a mercantile business seems to be a delivery wagon, but this store reverts to the older business method and sells all goods across the counter, thus saving the buyer the cost of transportation to the home

THE BOWEN GROCERY The ground upon which the P O S. of A building stands was purchased by Joseph Swartz in the beginning of the sixties During 1881 he erected a large store building in which he and his sons conducted the grocery business until 1887, when Isabella Swartz and her sister purchased the property David Walters leased the store and conducted a first-class grocery trade for many years In 1895 the property was bought by the P O S of A In January, 1903, John Bowen rented the store room for a branch of his large Allentown store The Bowen grocery contains any and every thing that is good to eat

THE CHILDS GROCERY COMPANY The store room in the Eagle Hotel Building on Front and Bridge Streets was occupied in 1856 by Joseph Swartz and Brother Their successors were R Beers & Company, D C Heberling and Martin Graver The last named took the general store business in 1893, and later added hardware to the stock During 1904 Mr. Graver retired and the F Hersh Hardware Company opened a branch store under the management of H H Aubrey. After the hardware store was moved to the Jr O U A. M Building in 1910, the Childs Grocery Company opened a store carrying a full line of groceries and meats

GEORGE C D GOLDSMITH. George C D Goldsmith was employed as clerk by Mr J J Seyfried in 1900 and at the end of six years was admitted by his employer into the business, thus forming a partnership. However, Mr Goldsmith was desirous of starting in business for himself. So in 1912 he suited action to his thoughts and opened a general store at 508 Race Street on November 1, 1912 His store offers to the Third Ward residents everything in groceries, dry-goods and notions

E. J ZIESER E J Zieser engaged in the grocery business in 1908 at the corner of Howertown Road and Locust Street During the spring of 1914 the store room was greatly enlarged Dry goods and groceries are the lines of goods Mr. Zieser handles

HENRY HARRIS Henry Harris, together with his son David, started a store in 1892 on Howertown Road The son continued with his father until seven years later, when, forced by sickness, he left for the west Mr Harris and his wife have conducted the store since that time Groceries, with Kolb's bread as a specialty, are sold in this place of business

GEORGE SMITH Orange Fuller erected a fine frame store and dwelling on the corner of First Avenue and Bridge Street, West Catasauqua, Pa , and let it out to Samuel Hoch, who, in 1884, began the mercantile trade here Two years later George Smith bought the stock and in due time the property, where he still conducts a general store Mr Smith remodeled the place a score of years ago. Dry goods, groceries and general merchandise constitute his stock

HARRY ONUSHAK Before William Steinhilber moved to Third and Almond Streets, he opened the grocery store at 1053 North Third Street On May 15, 1900, Harry Onushak came to Catasauqua from Mahanoy City, Pa , and purchased the Steinhilber store During 1907 he added to the height of the building until three stories were completed He also attached a meat market 65 feet in length He sells groceries, meats, dry goods, hardware, tinware, shoes, oil cloth, linoleums, etc

ANTHONY O'DONNELL Anthony O'Donnell opened a small grocery store at 1246 Third Street about 1902 Business increased to such an extent that it necessitated his doubling the capacity of the store in 1913. He carries all manner of groceries, green goods, and fruits

MARTIN BENKO   It is with surprising rapidity that the foreigner has taken hold of our American ways and customs even to the extent of building up-to-date and modern business places   Such has been the case with Martin Benko, who first established a small store at 1213 Third Street, but as business increased and store room was needed, he moved to 1209 Third Street   Here Mr Benko, together with his son, have a modern store, to say the least, carrying all kinds of groceries and dry goods

MRS WANDA KOZLOWSKI   The grocery store and meat market on Third Street above Arch was established by S M Kozlowski in 1900   In March, 1909, Mr Kozlowski retired. Mrs Wanda Kozlowski undertook the business in December of the same year and conducts a profitable trade   Groceries, smoked and fresh meats comprise her stock

PHILIP F KURTZ   The street-vender whose trumpet calls arouse the busy housewives of a community to thoughts of meals for the loved ones to whom they minister, gradually grows into the lives of the people and is quite as much an element in the comfort and happiness of the public as his daily rounds are profitable to his purse   *Fresh* fish, *prime* oysters, *ripe* fruit, and truck with the morning dew still sparkling in the leaves, is the staple "menu" of the huckster wagon of Philip F Kurtz. "Fritz" started in the business in the spring of 1872, and his tenor voice is still strong and clear

D M DOTTERER   D M Dotterer was busily engaged in manufacturing cigars in 1889, but owing to ill health was forced to give up the business in 1912   Then he turned his attention to the green grocery business and today Mr Dotterer can be heard from his team on the streets of our town announcing potatoes, cabbage, lettuce, oranges, etc   He also runs a small candy shop at his place of residence.

WILLIAM T HOLTZLEICER   Thirty years ago William T Holtzleicer began a huckster business   Since that time he has faithfully and happily served the people of Catasauqua with all kinds of vegetables   During a part of the time he conducted a store on Third Street, spending the morning on the wagon and the afternoon in the store. Of all food-stuff merchants the huckster is most heard. Unlike many others of his trade, Mr Holtzleicer's voice is music on the morning air as he calls out the kinds of vegetables on his wagon

PETER GEIGER. One of the old land marks on Front Street is the property owned by Peter J. Eberhard In the store room adjoining the residence occupied by Mr Eberhard and family, James Holly established a tailor shop early in the sixties After the "Holly" faded, the trade and proprietorship of this store changed repeatedly Now it was devoted to ice cream, then to notions; now to confectionery and bric-a-brac, then to green groceries The present incumbent, Peter Geiger, occupied it October 7, 1912, with green groceries, candy and notions. Mr. Geiger is determined to make a business place of No 203 Front Street, and he is succeeding.

WILLIAM S. WILLIAMS. The store at 623 Front Street has been occupied since May 30, 1912, by the retail business of William S. Williams His stock is mainly green groceries, carrying all varieties in season and the most called for kinds out of season He also has a line of regular groceries and canned goods. On the floor above he has an ice cream parlor The gradual growth of Mr Williams' business has necessitated an addition to his first floor room

MILKMEN Since this volume is dedicated to the posterity of Catasauqua as well as to the men of the past, it is not only fitting but most profoundly important that we announce the milkmen who do business in our town Most of the cows whose milk we imbibe are groomed on the "Dry-lands" which naturally guarantees that Catasauqua receives the yellowest and richest milk known in any town along the Lehigh.

Our Milkmen are Alfred J Sterner who began to distribute in November, 1887 Aaron Hess began before Mr Sterner and was succeeded by his son Albert, so that the Hess firm is the oldest milk distributor still in business Clinton U Miller began in about 1894. James Kearney began about sixteen years ago, Wilson Saylor, fifteen years ago, David F Mill, ten years, Smith and Son, ten years, Peter Roth, ten years, David Shoemaker, eight years, Palmer Koch, six three years.

Most of the dates, or years, given are simply approximations
years; Harvey Saylor, five years, Charles Balliet, four years, Reuben Lazarus,

KOCH AND YOUNGER. The flour and feed firm known as Koch and Younger was organized in 1897 and opened the store on Second Street above Wood at the same time. They carry a complete stock of flour, feed, grain, and poultry supplies Two men and one team are constantly employed to supply the large trade of this firm

THE FIVE AND TEN CENT STORE A J Etheredge and Company leased a commodious room in the Jr O U A M Building and fitted it up for the five and ten cent trade It would be futile to attempt to describe the stock of a Five and Ten Cent Store Even the peroration of the hand-bill of a public sale that speaks of "Articles too numerous to mention" fails to do justice to the description of a Five and Ten Cent Store Stock One thing is true, and that is: The stock is here.

ICE CREAM Charles Andreas, who for many years had charge of the large blowing engines at the furnaces, established the first confectionery and ice cream trade in town He located his store on Front Street above Bridge

Ambrose E Seyfried began to manufacture ice cream for the wholesale and retail trade at 613-615 Front Street in April, 1883 After the death of her husband, March 21, 1894, Mrs Seyfried continued the business in his name During 1891 she enlarged her place of business by adding twenty-five feet more to her building From 1892 to 1902 she also carried a large line of toys Her wholesale trade grew until her average output is estimated at 20,000 gallons per annum Her side lines are candy, cigars, and oysters

Stewart and Young began the manufacture of ice cream for the wholesale trade during the summer of 1903 They located on Third Street near Arch and erected a factory 13x16 feet in dimensions The increased demand for their product led them to rebuild their factory in 1909, and now they are quartered in a room 38x40 feet, equipped with the most modern machinery Their side line is confectionery and oysters.

A H. KIBLER During 1886 Samuel Hock built a general store at 468-470 Race Street James J Seyfried bought the place from Mr Hock in 1891 After Mr Seyfried moved to his new store, Mr. Hock conducted business for one year, when in 1889 John Brophy occupied the place. July 3, 1909, Amandus H. Kibler rented the establishment from Seyfried and Goldsmith and converted it into an up-to-date Ice Cream Parlor in connection with which he carries a

STORE OF A. H. KIBLER

stock of soft drinks, candy, tobacco, oysters, groceries and stationery. Being an exceptionally fine mechanic, especially along the line of small machinery, Mr. Kibler also conducts a jewelry and watch and clock repairing department. He bought the property from Seyfried and Goldsmith, November 15, 1911.

CLINTON FEHR. During the seventies William Sacks established a large cigar and tobacco trade at No. 144 Front Street and continued in prosperity until his death, April 7, 1912. Alvin Snyder bought the property which had been enlarged and beautified, and rented it to the present incumbent, Clinton Fehr. Mr. Fehr converted the store and the tobacco rooms into ice cream parlors. His stock consists of confectionery, cigars and tobacco, soft drinks and ice cream.

MRS. HEFFELFINGER. The small cozy candy and cigar store near the corner of Front and Race Streets was started in 1909 by Jeremiah Schoneberger. In 1911 Mr. Schoneberger died and then his widow kept the store until her death in 1913, when her daughter Mrs. Heffelfinger took hold of the store. Patrons of the trolley line are accommodated here by being able to purchase return tickets to the Queen City Candies, cigars, and tobacco are sold at this little store around the corner

MORRIS H. MOYER In September, 1911, Robert E Scheckler opened a restaurant and ice cream parlors on Front Street below Bridge He furnished meals at all hours, besides catering to the public through the sale of oysters, clams, crabs, etc , in bulk The Sheckler meals had a savory reputation throughout the town. In the spring of 1914 Morris H. Moyer acquired the stand and enlarged the parlors so as to provide accommodations for from eighty to one hundred guests at one time. Choice meals are served. Ice cream, candy, tobacco and cigars, and a full line of sea foods are offered A fine soda fountain has also been installed

MRS MARY EDGAR In 1902 Henry Zieser and William Edgar opened a lunch room at the corner of Front and Walnut Streets. They moved to 605 Front Street and two years later Mr Edgar became sole owner After his death in 1908, his widow Mrs Mary Edgar continued the business The patrons are served quick lunches upon the long counter.

THE EDGAR BROTHERS During 1911 the Edgar Brothers erected a 24 by 70 foot, two story, brick building on Front Street, below Pine The basement is leased to Roxberry, the barber The second floor is occupied by the Lyceum Club and the Dental rooms of Dr Chas Weinberg The main floor is devoted, by the Edgar Brothers, to a first-class restaurant. A fine soda fountain has been installed, and other equipment set so as to make the place attractive and comfortable The firm serves first-class meals, ice cream, cigars, candies, sea-foods, and all kinds of soft drinks.

MRS WINFIELD S DONKEL. The Confectionery store at 301 Peach Street was opened by Mrs. Winfield S Donkel during the spring of 1896 In 1913 the store was enlarged and beautified. Mrs Donkel's stock consists of candies, cigars and tobacco, and stationery.

FRANK A YOUNG An interesting place of business is the novelty, candy, cigar and soft drink store at 517 Front Street. The genial proprietor of the place, Frank A Young, purchased the stand from Edward Schlaugh in 1910 It serves the public a great convenience that Mr Young is magnanimous enough to sell trolley tickets to Allentown. There is no commission in this business. The recipient of fares would rejoice if tickets could scarcely be secured so that men would pay the coveted twenty cents per round trip instead of the benevolent rate of only fifteen

OWEN J SMITH   Owen J. Smith established a candy, tobacco, and cigar store on Pine Street in 1909, but moved to his present location, 1102 Second Street, in 1911   Here, Mr Smith enjoys as large a trade as his facilities allow He does carpenter work in his spare time as a means of adding to his income

OSCAR WEAVER   Oscar Weaver opened a small store in the front of his dwelling at 419 Race Street in 1909   Here he has continued to do business on a small scale selling groceries, candy, and cigars.

FRANK SNYDER   It was due to illness, not being strong enough physically to do manual labor, that caused Frank Snyder to open a small store on Race Street in 1903   At first he sold candy and cigars, but later he added groceries.

NICHOLAS RETZLER.   Nicholas Retzler conducts a cigar factory at 236 Second Street since March 28, 1909   He sells choice brands of smokes throughout both Lehigh and Northampton Counties   He carries a full line of smokers supplies, candies, ice cream, and soft drinks

JOHN G SACKS   John G Sacks opened a cigar factory on Church Street above Front in 1890   In 1897 he purchased the Quinn property No 701-705 Front Street and moved his factory into this building   This is the house of the Florimel   Mr Sacks employs several hands, who are kept busy throughout the year.

WILLIAM A SACKS   William A. Sacks opened a cigar store at 144 Front Street, and engaged in making cigars, in 1911   Two years later he moved to his present location, 223 Front Street, where he is busily occupied making the "Immense" and other cigars

JOHN J LAUBACH. One of the old tobacco stores in the Borough is the one at 603 Front Street. Prior to 1890 Fred Hunter was the owner of the store but in the above year he sold to the present proprietor, John J. Laubach. Up to 1911 he manufactured cigars. Mr Laubach has everything in the tobacco line.

C. D. W BOWER. Frederick Leickel began to slaughter animals and sell meats in 1850 and continued in business until 1857, when George Bower succeeded him. Mr Bower was succeeded by his son C. D. W. Bower in 1878. The latter developed the business to large proportions. He increased the slaughter house at Canal and Mulberry Streets, ran meat wagons and conducted a meat market on Bridge as well as on Front Street. In 1893 an overheated smoke house caused a fire which consumed the slaughter house. Mr Bower re-built and enlarged the place. He built a refrigerator large enough to store the carcasses of twenty cattle, thirty hogs, fifteen calves and fifteen sheep, besides all the by-products of this slaughter. During 1903 he installed a ten-ton Remington ice machine for cold storage. The scarcity of live stock and the great advantage that naturally accrues to the large packing houses induced Mr. Bower to discontinue the slaughter house and the Bridge Street market, concentrating all his business at his Front Street establishment.

PHILIP F WALKER. Early in the sixties John Eckert built a slaughter house on Howertown Avenue and School Street. He disposed of his products chiefly by means of delivery teams. During the eighties Philip F Walker learnt the trade in his shop and served as salesman until 1891, when he became Mr. Eckert's successor. Mr. Walker slaughtered an average of eight cattle, twenty-five hogs, eight calves and eight lambs per week. During 1893 he opened the meat market at number 228 Second Street, where he still enjoys an extensive trade. The old slaughter house has been abandoned long since. The stock consists of home dressed meats sold by Arbogast and Bastian at Allentown, Pa. The market contains a large refrigerator cooled by a three-ton ice machine, and is equipped with cutter, slicer, mixer, and scales of the most improved type. Thomas Walker serves his father in the business since the opening of the century. Deliveries are made by means of a team and auto-truck.

A A HAUSER   Wilson S Hauser began to slaughter on the premises of Andrew A Hauser, in the Third Ward, in 1890   He ran two meat wagons on a route covering Catasauqua, East Allentown and Rittersville   In 1896 he retired from the business   In 1901 Alvin A. Hauser took the old stand, remodeled the slaughter house, and on the 16th of August of the same year made his first delivery trip through Catasauqua and Northampton, Pa   In 1911 he bought the property from Andrew A Hauser, razed the old building, and erected an up-to-date and absolutely sanitary market

ACME BEEF COMPANY   The Acme Beef Company at 313 Walnut Street furnishes the tables of the neighborhood with meat of tenderness and quality   The largest stockholder and manager, Clayton Ziegler, built the market in 1911   The building is a red structure   The words, "Beef, Veal, Lamb, Pork, and Poultry," underneath the firm's name stands out prominently in the mind of a person after walking up Walnut Street

The Company, with a full line of meats and common groceries, by up-to-date business methods, has given the residents of this section prompt and efficient service

WILLIAM F KUEHNER   The first bakery in town was established late in the fifties by a Mr Hiskey on the property beside the Eagle Hotel on Front Street   The property was then owned by a Mr Laubach   Mr Hiskey delivered his products in baskets

In 1861 a Mr Albright started a bakery at 205 Front Street, the Frederick Eberhard Building, now occupied by baker Klingler. His baker was Charles King who now resides at Coplay, Pa   O M Fuller and Ferdinand Eberhard succeeded Mr Albright. It is said that this firm had a man named John Tombler on their delivery team   John had a constant run on cakes, so that the stock was never sufficient to reach around   He would return and say, "Heut' sin' sie awer gfloga"   Upon investigation it developed that the cause of his great run on cakes was that he sold fifteen for a dozen   John got his passport

August G. Eagle succeeded Fuller and Eberhard   In 1874 James Dilcher occupied the place, and in 1882 Mr Dilcher moved to 217-219 Front Street, where he built a new oven   The capacity of this oven is 400 loaves at one time

Mr Dilcher disposed of about 4700 loaves a week In 1893 his son George H. entered into the business with his father, and ran one of the delivery teams. After his father's death, June 2, 1897, George H. Dilcher purchased the property from his father's estate September 1 of the same year Mr Dilcher kept up the reputation of the firm for excellent bread and super-fine cakes

William F Kuehner acquired the property from George H Dilcher October 10, 1907. Mr Kuehner employs four bakers He runs three delivery teams over routes covering Catasauqua, West Catasauqua, Hokendauqua, Coplay and Fullerton His average output per week is 5700 loaves, and about 2700 dozen cakes. Mr Kuehner's head baker is Morris Moyer, a gentleman who has fired those ovens for over nineteen years The Kuehner baked stuffs need no special recommendation, their taste for more speaks for itself

H O HAUSER On June 22, 1914, it will be just twenty-five years since H O Hauser started in the baker business by buying out Wm. Storm, who was located at 762 Front Street Here he was busily engaged in changing flour into bread, cakes and other cookies for a period of thirteen years, when he moved to 740 Third Street. He equipped the building necessary to carry on the bakery business In 1904, 1910 and 1912 improvements and additions to the establishment were made, and to-day Mr Hauser can boast of having one of the latest bread mixers on the market. He enjoys a large trade and is always busily engaged in baking bread, cakes, pies, and other toothsome dainties to satisfy the wants of his customers.

ELVIN KEENER Daniel Keener, together with his son Elvin Keener, conducted a bakery at the corner of Second and Lehigh Streets, Hokendauqua, for two years Desirous of better facilities and a larger field, Keener and Son built a large residence and bakery at 1125 Third Street, North Catasauqua, in 1902 The partnership continued until 1912, when the father retired from the business, leaving the son as sole proprietor An ever-increasing demand for the Keener output taxes the capacity of the plant, although additions and improvements have been made since it was first occupied. Two teams are constantly employed, early and late, in dispensing its products

FRANK KLINGLER For a period of fifty-three years a bakery has been located at 235 Front Street. It was in 1861 that a Mr Albright from Philadelphia built the house and erected one of the first bakeries in this locality. The establishment has changed hands many times. The present proprietor is Frank Klingler.

THE W J SMITH COMPANY. During the summer of 1895, Mr Wilson J Smith began to distribute confectionery to candy shops by means of one horse and a small spring wagon.

When the season of muddy roads began, Mr Smith purchased a second horse so as to divide the draught burden between a double span.

After hard labor for a period of seven years, Mr Smith succeeded in building up so large a trade as to require the services of three two-horse teams and five men to handle all the goods.

In 1898, he purchased a brick stable on Race Street and converted it into a factory, storage, and office rooms.

Finding the work too onerous for himself alone to handle, he associated Edwin J Smith, his nephew, in 1904, with the business so as to form the W J Smith Company on the basis of a limited partnership.

In 1912 the firm purchased an auto-truck which is used on solid roads, while the horse teams are still in use on mud roads.

The territory of their route extends throughout the Lehigh and upper Delaware valleys and towns, and a narrow strip along the western border of New Jersey.

Their output during 1913 was about eight hundred fifty tons of candy.

THE FULLER OIL & SUPPLY COMPANY. Mr C H Fuller began to sell lubricating and burning oils, fish, cottonseed and lard oils, tallow, cup and gear greases, and mill supplies some time during 1898.

After his death Mr E H Donecker purchased the business from the estate, in March, 1912.

Mr Donecker also carries a line of pulleys, shafting and belting, the "Viola" anti-friction Babbitt metals, packings, hose and general supplies.

By careful attention to the trade and the use of sound business methods, the business has increased fifty per cent.

DEEMER & LITZENBERGER The progressive firm of Electricians, T J. Deemer and W J Litzenberger, established an office in Catasauqua, August 1st, 1903 They added another room to their display parlors on Bridge Street, in 1907, and now carry a complete line of electrical chandeliers, domes, motors, lamps, switch boards, and all manner of supplies They have wired and installed fixtures in many houses, factories, stores, churches and other public buildings in Catasauqua, Fullerton, Allentown, Kutztown, Palmerton, Lehighton, Walnutport and other neighboring towns and villages

AMMON H BACHMAN The Star Electric Company was established by Ammon H Bachman at Front and Cherry Streets, in August, 1908 Mr Bachman contracts for all manner of electrical work He is a competent mechanic and has many installations to his credit Repaid work is his specialty With him it means light on the subject at all times

JOSEPH MATCHETTE AND SON Joseph Matchette became connected with the Judson Powder Company of New York, in 1882 In time the E I Du Pont de Nemours Powder Company assumed control

He was the first demonstrator and user of high explosives in this section, as well as the first selling agent in the twelve counties of southeastern Pennsylvania, which constitute an agent's territory

Mr Matchette also sold the products of the Ingersoll Rock Drill Company of New York—later the Ingersoll Rand Company He did pioneer work also in this line, furnishing drilling machines and machinery for quarry and railroad construction work which was a means of greatly advancing operations in limestone, slate and cement industries

The Captain associated his son, Joseph D. Matchette, with himself in the business in 1891

Long experience in handling high explosives and drilling machines has placed Messrs Matchette and Son into a position to give expert advice and information to a great number of customers

GRAFFIN BROTHERS Harry E Graffin started in business as Manufacturers' Agent, November 1, 1897 He admitted his brother, George W , as partner on the 7th of April, 1898, and the firm title became "Graffin Brothers "

On December 31, 1911, George W withdrew from the firm and the business was taken over by Harry E Graffin who has continued under the old name

Graffin Brothers are Manufacturers' Agents for Mine, Mill and Quarry Supplies, Engines, Boilers, Pumps, Belting, Rubber Goods, Oil, Waste and a great many sundries

Established in the old National Bank Building on Front Street, its longest tenure has been at 125 Bridge Street, from which place it has been moved recently into the Lehigh National Bank Building

DANIEL MILSON, Jr   Daniel Milson, Jr , began the Coal business on Canal Street, below Race, in August, 1897

Three years later he opened a limestone quarry on the Frank Deily Estate in order to furnish fluxing stone to the Crane furnaces   A crusher was erected on the premises in 1902

During 1911 Mr Milson entered the old quarry of the former Kurtz Estate and installed a five hundred ton per day crusher   From this quarry much stone and crushed material has been furnished for the macadamizing of our important streets

JAMES FAHLER   The blacksmith adds much to the music of a busy community   When the wagon breaks, or the nut is lost no artist is so fine as he whose brawny arms give a graceful swing to the glittering hammer   Before the days of the patent calk, horseshoeing was much more of an art than it is now, and even yet no novice can trim a hoof or drive a nail where it will hold and not bring pain to the patient animal   John Koons opened the shop on Pine Street in 1855   James Fahler succeeded him in 1867, and, assisted by his son Francis, still continues in business

JOHN W HOCH   George Hoch pounded the anvil in the Rehrig blacksmith shop on Railroad Street, near Race, in 1891   In 1897 he built the shop on Race Street near the Davies and Thomas foundry   After his death, August, 1898, John W Hoch, his brother, bought the shop from his estate   John learned the trade from his brother George in the Rehrig shop, and his work proves him master of his art.

WILLIAM B MARK. Aaron Lambert was proprietor of the blacksmith shop on Peach Street above Howertown Avenue for many years. During the spring of 1880, Benjamin Mark who formerly lived in Phillipsburg, N. J., acquired the stand and conducted a successful trade until 1896, when he retired His son, William B Mark, began to learn the trade from his father at the age of thirteen years, and served his father with fidelity until the latter retired Since 1896 William does a large business in his line, and his services are in demand.

CHARLES W FRY. An early saddler in Catasauqua was Charles Rau, who opened a shop on Front Street below Bridge in 1861 Lewis M Fry worked for Mr Rau until 1863, when he bought and conducted the business for himself During 1875 Mr Fry was stricken blind, but he kept on with his work, cutting, fitting and sewing harnesses and collars as though his eyesight had not been impaired After his death, February 27, 1902, his widow, assisted by her son, Charles W Fry, continued the business, which ultimately fell into the hands of the latter. Mr Fry has his place of business on Second Street below Church, and carries a full line of saddlery with such accessory stock as is incident to the trade

WILLIAM J BUSS Since 1879 William J Buss has been making new and repairing old harnesses His shop is at 207 Second Street, where he has a line of all the furnishings that the horseman may need Machinery has taken, for the most part, the place of a harness maker, but, when a new part is needed in haste or the old is broken, the puller of waxed thread has his place, as of yore

HENRY J. WERTMAN In 1908 Henry J Wertman bought the estate of George F Wertman, the livery on Bridge Street back of the Penn Hotel In the days when the national game was conducted on a large scale in this and neighboring communities, Mr. Wertman was an enthusiastic rooter and supporter of Lehighton teams It was then that such men as Hugh Jennings were brouhgt out Now the *team* interest shows itself in the livery Eight horses are constantly ready for cab service The livery man has little use for the lighter driving horse, so he prepares almost solely for the heavier service.

WILLIAM B CLARK In the early forties the Old Eagle Livery was established and has furnished teams for the public from that day to this During the past forty years the business has been carried on under the following names Reber & Laubach, Reber & Clark, and Clark & Evans Today William B Clark is the sole owner. He built the large stable which his business now occupies on Second Street

Before the day of the trolley car and the automobile, a livery was the Mecca for pleasure seekers In those days this place had forty horses while now only eight are in the stable. The empty stalls stand a lonesome memorial of better days Then the night service was large, for the last train to Catasauqua left Allentown at ten-sixteen

On the second floor stands the large eighteen passenger tally-ho, almost a stranger to the dust of the road The omnibus is never hitched to In the place of these heavy vehicles, Mr Clark has a large touring car ready for hire

Light driving teams are seldom sent out. The horses are used for the most part in cab and funeral service.

SAMUEL P. GEMMEL On April 1, 1891, Samuel P Gemmel opened a grocery, five-and-ten-cent and tin store on Second Street above Wood Mr Gemmel is one of Catasauqua's modern tin-smiths, a craftsman of whom Schiller's words are appropriate "The work shall praise the master" During January, 1903, the store was enlarged and a full line of stoves, hardware (limited), variety goods, metal work, kitchen utensils and enameled ware was installed

CHARLES W SCHNELLER. The name of longest standing in a given business in Catasauqua is that of Schneller, associated with stoves, tinware and house furnishing goods Charles G. Schneller established a tin store on the corner of Second and Mulberry Streets in 1848 During 1854 he moved the business to Front and Strawberry Streets He continued in business until 1881 when he admitted his youngest son, Charles W , into partnership under the title of Charles G. Schneller and Son. In 1887 the senior member of the firm retired, leaving the avocation to his son. During 1868 the store was doubled in size In 1892 a line of hardware, paints, sporting goods, wall plaster, etc , was added to the stock The shop for metal work is connected with the store, and a number of employees are constantly turning out first class work

JOHN P SCHNELLER The patenter of the most scientific Hot Air Radiator known to the trade, John P. Schneller, started in business as a tinsmith in Catasauqua in the spring of 1880 After a lapse of five years he determined to make his fortune in Kansas While in the far west, Mr Schneller learnt of the death of John Lair of Lambertville, N J , whose stock he bought in November, 1886, and moved eastward The following summer he sold out at a handsome profit and returned to Catasauqua He opened his shop at Limestone and Raspberry Streets Afterwards a luring proposition attracted him to Emaus, where he bought the establishment of Charles Zellner In June, 1888, Mr Schneller again returned to Catasauqua with the full conviction that the morning sun first shines here, and her lingering rays last longest when they glow upon Catasauqua's twilight He built his store at number 120 Front Street He sells stoves, tin and agate ware, and does all manner of jobbing in his line as a first-class tin-smith

F HERSH HARDWARE COMPANY Martin Graver began to deal in hardware at No 505 Front St April 1, 1888, and developed a fine trade until 1904, April 1st, when he retired, and the business was assumed by the F Hersh Hardware Co This is a branch of the large stores of the Hershes in Allentown, Pa , and is in charge of Harry H Aubrey, as manager, and R A Savitz as clerk On May 1, 1910, the store was moved to larger quarters in the Jr O U A M Building The store carries a stock of everything that an up-to-date hardware store should contain

CHARLES SCHNEIDER Nearly fifty years ago Charles Schneider opened a store where the Ehle saloon is now located It was through Mr Schneider that many of the early settlers of this Borough furnished their homes, as he sold stoves, and all kinds of house furniture He kept his store here for thirty years, when, in 1902, he built his present store at 108 Second Street. Mr Schneider offers stoves, ranges, and many other articles in the house furnishing line

THE WALP SHOE   Some men are "to the manor borne," and this is quite appropriate when applied to Benjamin Walp, the shoemaker   He has never done any other work nor engaged in any other kind of business   Mr Walp was born and raised at Rockdale, Pa   During his younger years he worked at his trade in Scranton, Carbondale, and places in Lehigh County

In January, 1862, he came to Catasauqua and, for seven years, worked for Robert Streham   He set up his own bench in the Romig Building, Front Street near Race   Mr Walp was not merely a cobbler   The making of a shoe was a scientific effort for him   He measured and studied his subject s feet and constructed a last that was practically equal to a plaster cast of a man's foot and over that model he built his shoe

When his health failed and he went out of business in the fall of 1911, he had a regular lumber yard of lasts in his shop on Second Street near Bridge   Many of his patrons bought their lasts for use by some other shoe maker

So well pleased were men with his work that orders for as high as three pairs of shoes to one customer was not infrequent   He shipped shoes all over the United States.

Since his retirement from the business, his son, Edwin W , has taken charge of the shop , but the production of new work has been discontinued

JOHN STREHAM   Robert Streham worked upon the bench as a cobbler for John Wilson at Front and Bridge Streets from 1851 to 1856, when he started in business for himself   A number of young men learned the trade in his shop   He re-located his business several times ; but finally settled for good at 220 Second Street. His son John learned the trade from his father and, when the father retired in 1908, he continued to build and repair boots and shoes at the old place. Since 1910 Mr Streham devotes all his time to repair work

A OSTHEIMER   The Ostheimer shoe store, on Front Street above Pine, was established by John Blum in 1867   John Blum succeeded the elder Blum in 1894 and continued in business until 1904, when the present incumbent, A Ostheimer, took charge of the place   The younger Blum enlarged the store to twice its original size and in 1911 Mr Ostheimer added a modern repair department   The stock consists of everything in the boot and shoe line

SCHICK & HAUSMAN   The firm of Schick & Hausman was started at No 121 Front Street, August, 1890   Since that time, the business has grown to such an extent that at times more than twenty men are employed

They have done some of the largest and most important plumbing and heating jobs in this section

Their shop is equipped with machines and tools which permits this firm to perform all work entrusted to them in a satisfactory manner.

Their display room contains samples of plumbing and heating material from which customers are enabled to make their own selections.

Their present location, No 621 Front Street, permits the handling and storing of material which enables them, at short notice, to take care of a job of any size.

BECK AND FREY   David J Beck founded a plumbing establishment at 109 Front Street in 1910   After his removal to New York City, Frank C Beck succeeded his brother in 1904 and moved the business to 528 Pine Street   In the spring of 1911 Mr Beck associated Messrs John A and Monroe W. Frey with himself to form a partnership   The firm contracts for all manner of plumbing and has a number of fine jobs to its credit   The Webster system of vapor and vacuum heating is their specialty.

CHARLES KEMP   Simon Kemp began the gents clothing business on lower Front Street during 1866. In July, 1869, his brother Charles arrived from Germany and entered into partnership with him   During 1880 the firm moved into the fine store on Front below Bridge Street, where they developed a large custom trade   When his brother, Simon, died in 1908, Charles Kemp assumed the business   A shoe department was added in 1907   Mr Kemp is a merchant tailor of large experience and is well prepared to please the most fastidious

JACOB W LIPSKY. In 1889 Jacob W Lipsky opened a men's furnishing store at 515 Front Street   The business grew steadily and so encouraged the proprietor that he added a women's furnishing stock to his line of masculine attire   Mr Lipsky is now in a position to "fig-leaf" the whole household

SOLOMON SCHIFREEN During the seventies Fuller and Schlauch conducted a book and stationery store in Fuller's Block on Front Street above Church. The firm also ran a news stand and carried school supplies They were succeeded by Rev. Christ and later by Edward Sheckler When Mr Sheckler moved the stationery store to his new building on Church Street, John Clugston converted the place into a meat market In 1912 Solomon Schifreen turned it into a ladies' and gents' furnishing store It is indeed a miniature department store In the stock of furnishings may be found wearing apparel, head gear, shoes, jewelry, watches, clocks, musical instruments, etc

F. J CAMPBELL Here is a gentleman who is in love with his business and succeeds remarkably well This tale can be told of any man who is in earnest F J Campbell purchased the tailoring outfit of H L Miller at 129 Bridge Street, September 1, 1911 The increased number of customers demanded larger quarters On July 1, 1913, Mr Campbell moved to 215 Bridge Street, where he is well equipped to satisfy the most fastidious tastes

ALFRED L MILLER. Alfred L Miller has been in the tailoring business for eighteen years For ten years his shop was at the corner of Second and Church Streets and the past eight years it has been on the second floor of the Applegate building at 131 Bridge Street During the past few years he has done only part of his new work, sending the orders to the Royal Tailors of New York City The largest part of his work is cleaning, pressing and repairing Skilled and up-to-date tailoring, such as Mr Miller has given Catasauqua for eighteen years, is of much value to the men of a community

A. E SCHIELER COMPANY This paragraph must necessarily be brief and promptly written lest the styles change before it is finished Millinery means the largest field of art in the country It is confined to no genus in any kingdom, be it vegetable, animal, mineral, or the all-comprehensive chemical laboratory Mrs Charles Snyder opened the millinery store on Front Street below Mulberry in 1870 and conducted a thriving business until 1899, when Miss Annie E Schieler and Company, the company being Mrs Dr C J Keim, purchased the business In January, 1911, the firm name was changed to A E Schieler Company There is nothing in the line of ladies' and children's headgear this progressive firm does not have in stock or cannot promptly produce

C F ROTH   In 1874 Cornelius F Roth opened his Photograph Gallery at Second and Bridge Streets After an absence of one year, from 1877 to 1878, he returned to town and opened his gallery on the third floor of Schneller's Block After a season of successful operations he concluded to return to his old stand at Second and Bridge Streets, where he is still touching up the negatives of positive looks Mr Roth makes the unmistakable boast of having been by far the best photographer in town for many years He bases the confidence of his assertion upon the fact that he was the only photographer in the place Mr Roth is a clear headed and genial fellow He was elected Justice of the Peace in 1906, and re-elected in 1912.

IRA H MILLER   The photographer in Fuller's Block, on Front Street above Church, Ira H Miller, has had experience in his line for twenty years. He moved into his present bi-roomed quarters in July, 1913. His lenses are clear and strong, and for dark days or evening exposures he is equipped with mercury lights He offers first class work on photos, enlargements, and post card finishes

THE LAWALL BROTHERS   Jacob S Lawall served his apprenticeship as a student of pharmacy with his older brother, Cyrus Lawall, at Easton, Pa After he was pronounced qualified for the drug business he came to Catasauqua and opened a store, March 4, 1856, on Front Street in the building now occupied by the meat market of C D W Bower After two years he had built the present Lawall store at 409 Front Street, where the firm has conducted the business ever since An interesting feature in the building is a pane of glass in the show window It measures fifty by eighty inches and was set in 1858 At that time it was the largest pane of glass in Lehigh County Men looked upon it as a curiosity Blasts and explosions shattered other windows but the large glass in Lawall's show window is still intact

During Mr Lawall's time there was a transition from primitive to modern methods of illumination In his day the poor people lit up their homes with candlelight, while the rich used tallow oil—in fact different kinds of oils. Mr. Lawall manufactured an illuminant composed of a mixture of alcohol and turpentine. This afforded a much cleaner light than the neat's foot oil, although it was highly explosive. It was used in pewter or leaden lamps of various designs and was called burning fluid. When he died, March 4, 1889, his sons, Edgar J. and Charles E., succeeded him. The former was graduated from the Catasauqua schools, and the college of Pharmacy in 1882. The latter attended the town schools until he was almost through his senior year in High School, when his father needed him in the store, and he dropped out of his class. Subsequently he went to the College of Pharmacy at Philadelphia and graduated in 1884. Since the store was built it has been enlarged and altered several times. The firm carries a full line of drugs and medicines and such side lines as are incident to their trade and are needed to equip a first class drug store. They have a soda fountain in operation during the summer months.

HECKENBERGER DRUG STORE. The building occupied by the Heckenberger Drug Store and the Miss A. E. Schieler Millinery Company was erected

HECKENBERGER DRUG STORE

by Frederick Eberhard in 1859. The store room on the corner of Front and Mulberry Streets was occupied first by Daniel Davis and Company of Easton, who conducted a general store. Then followed Mr. Baird After him came A. F and John W. Koons, as the Koons Brothers, and then William Miller. Finally, a Mr. Menaugh of Newark, N. J , conducted a Dry Goods and Notions store here In 1874, William Heckenberger purchased the property, remodeled the store, and opened a Drug Store (Die Deutsche Apotheke) Mr. Heckenberger was the oldest son of the well known veterinary, William A Heckenberger While a member of the senior class in our High School, he was offered an apprenticeship in the drug store owned by John Black on Front Street above Bridge. He accepted the position and served his time. Then he attended the College of Pharmacy at Philadelphia, from which institution he was graduated March 10, 1874 From the fall of 1874 until his death, January 16, 1914, Mr. Heckenberger conducted his store His son, William W. Heckenberger, succeeded his father in business immediately after his graduation from the College of Pharmacy, in June, 1914. William W is a graduate of the Catasauqua High School He has made good use of his time and, being a young man of strong traits of character, he will hold the confidence of his father's patronage besides gaining new friends. During the time intervening Wm. Heckenberger's death and the occupancy of the store by his son, Mrs Cora Heckenberger secured the services of Dr. Lockman of Allentown, a registered druggist, as the manager of the store She also renovated the store and installed an up-to-date Walrus Soda Fountain.

JOHN FISHER After devoting some time to the mercantile business in Mahanoy City, Pa John Fisher came to Catasauqua, February 5, 1897 He served as proprietor of the Farmer's Hotel for one year In March, 1898, he directed all his attention to private banking and the foreign exchange business He also runs a steamship agency It is easy to secure passage and passenger accommodation to any port of the globe through Mr. Fisher, who makes himself personally responsible for accuracy and correctness of tickets and transports

TIME PIECES A sun-dial was set up near the gate leading to the David Thomas home on Front Street, by the Crane Company in 1840

In those days watches and clocks were expensive and not in genral use, therefore, a sun-dial in a public place was a valued convenience

Whoever was fortunate enough to possess a watch had to go to Massey's at Allentown in case of an accident until James C. Beitel established a Jewelry Store at 215 Front Street in 1863.

Beitel always spelt guarantee and still stands for full value to the purchaser.

In 1900 Mr. Beitel admitted his son, Robert J., into the business, hence the name "J. C. Beitel & Son."

In April, 1909, the store was moved into its new quarters in the Lehigh National Bank Building, where the firm maintains the most beautiful and the most modern jewelry store in the Lehigh Valley.

Mr. Robert Beitel took a course in optics, and now holds a diploma showing him fully qualified to examine eyes and fit lenses. An optical department has since been added.

The firm carries lines of Piammas, Silverware, Cut-glass, China, Diamonds, Watches, Clocks, Umbrellas, Fountain Pens, and all manner of Jewelry.

BOB SHARPE

ROBERT SHARPE. In Robert Sharpe, Catasauqua enjoys an asset that cannot be counted by cash nor valued in figures. Bob has been our auctioneer since 1872. When the air swells with Oh, Yes! Oh, Yes! to the accompaniment of a butcher's bell, every one knows there will be a vendue that night and that Bob will preside. Prices will soar in proportion to the number of jokes and jolly squibs he dispenses. Mr. Sharpe was born in Glascow, Scotland, on Christmas Day sixty-five years ago. At the age of six years he was brought to Mt. Hope, Lancaster County, Pa., where he grew up as a farmer boy. He came to Catasauqua in 1867 and wrought at the furnaces for many years. Since 1894 he runs a Corner Shop at Front and Church Streets. His stock consists of tobacco, candy, nuts, fruits, soft drinks, pretzels, etc. During his spare moments he delights to attract the young roosters in his neighborhood. He coaxes them to his knee when he feeds them peanuts and entertains his friends by encouraging them to crow. Mr. Sharpe built himself a beautiful home at Third and Union Streets, Fullerton, Pa., in 1905.

FREDERICK AND SCHERER. Owen Frederick began the Undertaking business on Front Street, June 3, 1848, and continued in business until his death in 1878. At that time the beautiful and stately appearing hearse was not in use but was introduced later by Mr. Frederick. Undertakers, and even Churches, owned a bier on which bodies were borne to their graves. The bier was a frame made of walnut, mahogany or cherry wood, resting on four legs, about eighteen inches in length. In the cross pieces of the frame were grooves bearing sliding clamp screws. Where the coffin was placed on the bier the sliding clamp screws were pushed hard against it and screwed down tight so as to prevent any slipping while being carried by the pallbearers. At each corner was an arm, or long handle, fastened by a strong hinge. Having placed the coffin on the bier and fastened it by means of the four clamp screws, four strong men, pallbearers, would straighten out

WILLIAM H. SCHERER

the handles by lifting them up on their hinges and then, at a signal given by the undertaker, elevate the bier to their shoulders, and thus bear the body to its grave. When a body was heavy extra men would change off those who had grown tired on the march When distances were too long for bodies to be borne to their graves, the casket (coffin) was pushed into the body of a farm wagon on which some or perhaps all of the surviving members of the deceased's family rode The children, or some light weight persons, usually sat on the coffin on the journey

Mr Frederick was also a cabinet maker, i e , a furniture builder The old fashioned rocking chairs were shaped to fit the persons for whom they were made This explains why we never see two such chairs exactly alike in height, width or tilt

Upon the death of Owen Frederick in 1875, his son-in-law, Henry A Steward, took charge of the business and continued therein until his death, April 3, 1897 During Mr Steward's nineteen years in the business he buried 2114 bodies, of which 553 were men, 474 women and 1087 children After the death of St Steward, his brother-in-law, Ogden E Frederick, and his "right hand man," William H Scherer, took the business and are running it in the name of "Frederick and Scherer" ever since

Mr Frederick is in charge of the furniture and upholstering department and Mr Scherer attends to the undertaking The latter is a practical embalmer and is extremely skillful in this art He has "held" bodies as long as nine days in a state of perfect preservation Since February 14, 1887, he was in the employ of Mr Steward, and rendered constant service with the Trocar Mr Scherer has also served his time at the bench as a cabinet maker A few years ago he re-built the beautiful hearse which they have in use and also designed and built their "first call wagon "

Frederick and Scherer added upholstery since their co-partnership

Since May 13, 1897, Mr Scherer buried 2349 bodies. Mr Scherer's records of persons, deaths and burials, are well nigh perfect Even the hour of death, the service and place of burial are given

ELMER E ERDMAN Charles Snyder opened an undertaker's establishment at 203 Front Street in the spring of 1882 and continued in business until his death in May, 1902 His widow, Mrs Ellen Snyder, waited upon calls until August of the same year, when Elmer E Erdman bought the establishment from the estate The first license granted to a woman undertaker in the State of Pennsylvania was issued to Mrs Snyder on September 26, 1898 She died September 26, 1906 Mr Erdman is a graduate of Prof H. S Eckees' Philadelphia School of Embalming and Sanitation since July 26, 1902 He is licensed by the State Board since June 26, 1905, and is a member of the State Funeral Directors' Association. During his business career to May 11, 1914, he interred nine hundred twenty-eight bodies.

HARRY F. ECKENSBERGER Henry J Eckensberger began house painting and paper hanging in town late in the fifties He was the first to introduce Lewis' whitelead to the town While painting at a window in the house of Solomon Biery, now the property of Miss Carrie Miller on Front and Union Streets, a squad of newly mustered soldiers marched by on their way to the front in obedience to President Lincoln's call. Mr Eckensberger was so stirred by the sight below him that he promptly climbed down from his scaffold and joined the ranks of the "Boys in Blue " After his return from the war Mr. Eckensberger resumed his chosen trade His son, Harry F Eckensberger, learned the trade from his father and struck out for himself in 1885 He employs six men.

TITUS R CASE Reuben Case is one of the old style painters He started in business in 1873, and three years later he added paper hanging to his trade There are very few men who know how to grain a panel so as to rival the natural cross cut of the wood This is an art which Mr Case can practice with astonishing accuracy His son, Titus R , learned the trade with his father, commencing at the tender age of ten years In 1901 the latter succeeded his father in the business

FRANK H D NEWHARD In 1875 Frank H D Newhard began work as a painter and paper hanger During all these years he has been beautifying the homes in this section He is a man of genial temperament, who has gathered throughout these years much of pleasantness to pass on to those whom he meets

CHARLES E SHECKLER, JR The fore-runner of the Sheckler stationery store was established at No 409 Front Street, by O. M Fuller and Edward Schlaugh, some forty years ago   Later O M Fuller purchased his partner's share in the business and conducted it as O M Fuller and Company   During 1891 Charles E Sheckler, Jr , bought the business, and, after conducting it at the old place for eleven years, he moved to his new establishment on Church Street, opposite the Town Hall   During the days when pupils furnished their own books and supplies, this store carried a heavy stock and was well equipped to cater to every want.   Since School Boards furnish books, this department has been closed out by Mr Sheckler   He carries a full line of stationery and wall paper, and contracts for house and sign painting and house decorating

JOHN K FEENSTRA A great deal of the beautifying of the homes and residences in the Borough and surrounding territory has been done by John K. Feenstra   On January 10, 1906, Mr Feenstra began work as a paper hanger and painter, and has his place of business located on Howertown Road near Walnut   The demands of his customers require the constant employment of two men

EDWIN OLDT   John T Williams and W. W McKeever combined to contract for hauling, moving, etc   In 1893 Edwin O Oldt bought the interest of Mr Williams and the firm name, Oldt and Company, was adopted   In 1895 Mr Oldt purchased Mr McKeever's share and continued in business for himself   Contracting, general hauling, and moving comprise Mr Oldt's business   So extensive is this enterprise that Mr Oldt employs the services of ten horses, four moving vans, three coal wagons, two extra heavy trucks and six carts   The Oldt barn burnt to the ground on the night of February 16, 1914. His horses and wagons, however, were saved   The barn was immediately rebuilt according to improved plans   Besides the new barn there is an office building and a wagon house

HOFFMAN AND FOLLWEILER   The contracting firm, composed of Alvin J Hoffman and W A Follweiler, established themselves on Church Street in 1902. By the end of five years their patronage had developed to such proportions as to require larger stables, sheds and storage facilities. They moved to Sixth Street below Chapel, where they erected a brick structure large enough to accommodate their various requirements. They have a large ice storage whence they supply their wholesale and retail trade with Bear Creek and Min-

HOFFMAN AND FOLLWEILER STABLES

eral Springs ice. They carry a stock of sand, cement, and vitrified bricks. They contract for hauling and cement construction. They also run a blacksmith shop. The firm uses eighteen horses in their business and also run four ice wagons and five hauling wagons. Their equipment is valued at about fifteen thousand dollars.

CALVIN D. PETERS. In 1912 Calvin D. Peters began taking contracts for cement work. His skill in the use of this kind of building material and his ability in handling the business side of contracts, both large and small, has brought to him much of this kind of construction work. The number of men that he employs varies from twelve to eighteen. The capacity of his mixer is large enough to handle the biggest local contracts. He has done a large part of the reenforced concrete building in this section.

CATASAUQUA GRANITE WORKS. Opposite the entrance to Fairview Cemetery on Lehigh Avenue, stands the stone cutting establishment of the Catasauqua Granite Works. Elmer M. Bernd, the proprietor, started the business in 1899 and since that date has set a large number of the monuments and headstones in Fairview. He buys the finished stone and with the assistance of one stone cutter does the lettering Mr Bernd is a skilled and careful workman, a reliable and successful business man

ZELLERS The native barber, Franz Zellers, now almost an octogenarian, is a native of Bavaria He learnt his trade in Vienna, to which city he came in 1848 Barbers, in those days, were expected to take a course in surgery so that they might be able to attend to many wants of the afflicted The barber who took the prescribed course was granted a diploma under which he was permitted to operate The law of the country also required the shops of surgical barbers to be kept open by night as well as by day Franz Zellers took the prescribed course in Vienna and was graduated at the age of eighteen years

He served his country for eight years in the Austrian Army, having been draughted in 1859 In 1866 he migrated to this country, and located as a barber, at Steubenville, Ohio He came to Catasauqua in 1871 and opened the shop at 507 Front Street

His son, Alvin R. Zellers, assisted his father, when a lad of but ten summers When he reached his manhood he entered into partnership with him , and when the father retired in 1898. the son succeeded him

A genial tonsor who knows how to administer a smooth shave is a source of great comfort and delight to his crinated victim that may be possessed of an effeminate skin

GEORGE W FITZHUGH Undoubtedly, one of the oldest residents as well as the oldest barber in point of service is none other than the colored gentleman, George W. Fitzhugh It was on June 30, 1873 (forty-one year ago), that Mr Fitzhugh came to Catasauqua and became an assistant barber to Wm Welch Mr Welch died on July 4, 1874, when the present proprietor launched into business for himself by purchasing the good will and barber shop from his former employer's heirs

The building in which the shop is located was originally the town fire-engine house built by a company of young men who were desirous of organizing a fire company Here for many years the old fashioned hand pump engine was housed and five charter members of that first company still survive The building is eighteen by twenty-one feet and is a one story structure.

Mr. Fitzhugh has the enviable distinction of having shaved every burgess except three, viz., Uriah Bruner, William Goetz, and A. C. Lewis; and furthermore, he has never missed one day in forty-one years in not being able to attend to his business.

QUINTUS H. SMITH. Quintus H. Smith never has any difficulty in remembering the time when he became an apprentice to Joe Norton, who had a barber shop at 223 Front Street. It was in the year of the great blizzard, 1888, that he started out with the ambition of becoming a barber. For four years he

INTERIOR OF SMITH'S BARBER SHOP

worked zealously with Mr. Norton when he went to Hokendauqua and set up a shop of his own on the corner of Second and Lehigh Streets. Remaining here three years, he located a new shop on the corner of Second and Mulberry Streets of town in 1896.

Peculiar to relate, Mr. Smith finally drifted back to the building where he had started out as an apprentice. A Mr. Moats had had a barber shop here in the meantime, but had left some time previous. Mr. Smith endeavored to build up the trade that Mr. Moats had abandoned. He succeeded very well and eight years later sold out to Kurtz Brothers of Bethlehem. Kurtz Brothers, in 1909, moved the shop to 215 Front Street, in the building formerly occupied by the Beitel Jewelry Store. Mr. Smith was retained by these people as their manager. It was here that the Kurtz proprietors furnished one of the finest tonsorial parlors in the Borough. They completely designed and made the furnishings themselves at a cost of $2400. However, Mr. Smith's dreams were to become proprietor of this up-to-date and first class barber shop, and accordingly two years later, he bought back the business from Kurtz Brothers, and ever since has continued as proprietor. During the past years his business has grown to such an extent that it requires the assistance of his two sons to attend to the trade.

WILLIAM ROXBERRY.

A number of years ago, when Catasauqua had one of the best semi-professional baseball teams in Eastern Pennsylvania, no less a personage than William R. Roxberry, the congenial and up-to-date barber, was the umpire. At the same time, Mr. Roxberry conducted his barber shop at Front and Walnut Streets where anyone desiring to have any tonsorial work done could also receive information as to the doings in the baseball world.

INTERIOR OF ROXBERRY'S SHAVING PARLOR

When the room occupied by Mr. Roxberry was converted into a motion picture theatre, it necessitated his moving into the Edgar building upon its completion, December 18, 1912. Here he invested one thousand dollars in equipment and to-day can boast of one of the most modern and sanitary tonsorial parlors in the Lehigh Valley.

OLIVER H. GIERING. Prior to Oliver H. Giering's assuming the proprietorship of the barber shop at 509 Second Street, he worked as an assistant to Mr Edwin Weiss In 1902 Mr Giering purchased the business from Mr. Weiss and has had charge of the shop since. About two years ago he remodeled his parlor and now can boast of an up-to-date barber shop Mr Giering has a long line of shaving mugs on his shelves which is indicative of a large patronage

ROBERT BAUMER. It seems that Robert Baumer, the barber at 1112 Third Street, has not had the usual experience of most barbers, in that he has not moved from the above place since he started in business Mr Baumer also has the distinction of having been the first barber in North Catasauqua Equipped with all the latest and up-to-date appliances and being a genial proprietor, he enjoys a lucrative trade.

EDWIN WEISS. Edwin Weiss located as a barber at 509 Second Street in 1887 and retained the proprietorship until 1902, when he sold out to O H Giering. From here he moved to 1143 Third Street, where he remained until 1905. Desirous of having a residence of his own, he built a dwelling at 1205 Third Street, with the barber shop in the front part of the building Here Mr. Weiss enjoys a large trade and helps to keep the gentlemen of North Catasauqua smooth of mien

JOHN H MISSMER In 1908 Samuel Roth established a barber-shop at 424 Second Street Two years later, April 2, 1910, the present proprietor bought out Mr Roth Within two months after starting, Mr Missmer added another chair and completely renovated the shop It is understood among the male members of his community that to have a good shave is to go to Missmer's

SAMUEL A ROTH Samuel A Roth started in business as a barber on February 15, 1909, at 424 Second Street. Here he remained a little over a year when he moved to 429 Front Street During 1912 the second-hand furniture store located at 611 Front Street was vacated and Mr Roth thought this place very desirable for a barber shop He changed the store room into a first class shop and now is able to satisfy all those desiring a hair cut or shave

WILLIAM E. JOHNSTON. William E. Johnston started in business on Race Street and remained there for a period of fifteen years. Upon the death of Joe Wehrley, who had his barber shop at 33 Front Street, Mr. Johnson purchased his present place of business. Shortly after, he installed all the latest sanitary appliances and completely renovated the shop. Here he has been located for the past one and a half years and attends to all the tonsorial needs of the gentlemen of the lower end of town.

THE MAJESTIC THEATRE. The pioneer moving picture man in town is W. H. Wentz. Mr. Wentz has had a feeling that much good can be done a community by affording it clean and instructive amusement; and, therefore, proceeded to build the Majestic Theatre on the corner of Front and Pine Streets in August, 1909. The building was twenty-four by sixty feet with a capacity

THE MAJESTIC THEATRE

of two hundred seats. Mr. Wentz has been concerned constantly with the comforts of his patrons so that not a season passed without his having made some kind of improvements; and during the spring of 1914, he built an addition to the Majestic so as to increase its size to fifty-five by ninety-eight feet and its capacity to seven hundred and five seats. The theatre is heated by steam, ventilated by a special ceiling apparatus, and has a fire-proof boiler-house. This is probably the first theatre of its kind in the state that is constructed according to legal requirements. Association films are used. Mr. Wentz is an extremely public spirited man. For recreation, as well as pleasure, he has been fitting his ground beside the theatre for skating in winter; for baseball in summer; for basket-ball in fall and for quoit pitching for all during the warm weather.

THE PALACE THEATRE. The Palace Theatre is the creation of William H. Manley and W. R. Roxberry, and is located on the corner of Front and Walnut Streets. Besides a moving picture show house, the Palace also offers vaudeville attractions. The building was completed October 12, 1912, and is most beautifully adorned.. Its size is thirty by one hundred feet and its capacity offers three hundred and fifty seats These people censor and select their films with caution so as to offer the public elevating and clean entertainment.

PALACE THEATRE

CHAPTER VIII—HOTELS

HOTELS

During the days of stage-coach travel the public house in a given community was the place around which the whole surrounding country centered Cities and towns then were situated far apart. A trip to Allentown and return meant a day's journey. No one thought of taking a "run" to the city after supper and returning for bed before the second watch of the night The nights, too, were dark, as God intended they should be, that men might all the better sleep The traveler could not know he approached a city by the reflection of her arc-lights in the heavens Only robbers haunted the dark waysides during the small hours of the night or perchance a belated wanderer who had lost his course To such a one the glimmering light that shone out of the distant maze of dropping dews was a welcome beacon Having reached its standard, lifting high the name of its location and genial host, the weary wanderer speaks a gentle Ho! to his willing beast, and implores the versatile landlord to tell him, "How far to my destination?", "May I lodge here for the night?" and countless other queries He now puts up at the Ho-tell.

BIERY'S HOTEL

The hostelry of Biery's-Port was Biery's Hotel, located on Race Street This is the beautiful, cut stone structure at the rear of the American Hotel. It was built in 1826 and its foundation and walls are still in a perfect condition The property now belongs to George B F. Deily.

AMERICAN HOTEL

The first large hotel which a traveler beholds when entering Catasauqua by trolley is the American It is one of the oldest hotels in the Borough, having been built in 1852. Later, in 1889, it was entirely rebuilt and made up-to-date in every respect. Today the hotel has thirty-two rooms and is capable of accommodating

AMERICAN HOTEL

about fifty guests. There were no less than fifteen proprietors since the time of its erection, the present one being George Monshein.

THE EAGLE HOTEL.

Joseph Laubach built the Eagle Hotel in 1850. Located on Front and Bridge Streets within easy access of the Catasauqua stations, the Eagle was a popular hostelry from the beginning. In 1861 his son, William H. Laubach, bought the business and continued until 1865, when his brother, Franklin P., succeeded him. In 1876 the father again took charge and continued until 1886, when Oscar H. Harte purchased the property. After Mr. Harte's death in 1891 his widow, Floranda, became proprietress. Mrs. Harte sold out to Captain W. H. Bartholomew who sold the property November 6, 1906, to the present proprietor, Edward L. Walker. The hotel contains thirty-six rooms and is modern in all its appointments and equipment. Many improvements have been made to the

EAGLE HOTEL

property at various times so as to keep the Eagle in pace with the times. The bar-room is especially well fitted out with modern and sanitary appliances. There is also a commodious stable connected with the hotel.

THE PENNSYLVANIA HOTEL.

The Pennsylvania Hotel was built by Harrison Hower in 1855. Two additions were made to the original structure at certain times, and in 1909, Mr. John W. Geiger, the present proprietor, remodeled the adjoining tobacco store and attached it to his hotel as a beautiful and inviting Rathskeller. The names of certain proprietors are still to be found but the tenure of their respective proprietorships are not known. Mr. Hower was followed by Edward Overspeck, and his brother Oliver, Adam Bellesfield, Aaron Vogel, Ed. Golding, Mr. Von Steuben, Moses Guth, Charles N. Alberts, and his brother George, Fitchie and Geiger, and the present proprietor. The hotel has thirty rooms and is equipped with hot and cold water and steam heat.

PENNSYLVANIA HOTEL

THE CATASAUQUA HOUSE

In 1849 Catasauqua had two hotels, the American house on the corner of Front and Race Streets, at that time the centre of the town, and the Temperance House, which was in the building now occupied by the Fuller Oil Company at the corner of Front and Church Streets. In that year Jessie Knauss came here from Cedar Creek and built the Catasauqua House. Because of the strong temperance sentiment it was very difficult to obtain a license. After a protracted contest the court at Allentown granted a license to the Catasauqua House and also to the Eagle Hotel, which was opened at the same time. To celebrate the license victory in both hotels a parade was arranged. With all the pomp of a Roman Triumph, bands playing and flags flying, the jubilant victors marched up Front Street.

With this spectacular origin the Catasauqua House has quietly lived on. At the end of a long list of proprietors is that of Frederick Schwegler, the present owner. He bought the hotel in March, 1906, and since that date has been its capable manager. The house has twenty-two rooms, heated by steam and lighted by both electricity and illuminating gas.

THE FARMER'S HOTEL.

This hotel, located on Front Street, but a short distance below the northern Borough limits, was styled originally, The Crystal Palace. It was built by Charles Clausen early in the sixties. When Owen McCarty got possession of it, he improved the property and called it The Farmer's Hotel. Mr McCarty was considered an exceptionally well qualified hotel man. The Farmer's Hotel was the center of many a political storm. Many a luminary of the County and State blazed from McCarty's piazza, and illumined the gaping crowd upon the perplexing issues of the day. In 1895 John Fisher acquired control of the property and managed the affairs of the hotel for seven years. About twelve years ago Frank McCarty took possession of the Farmer's and is still its proprietor. The building accommodates fourteen guests, is heated by steam, illuminated by gas and electricity, and supplied with hot and cold water. There is also stabling for seven horses.

THE ST GEORGE HOTEL

The St George Hotel was established at No 607 Front Street in 1859 by George Koop, a Veteran who served under Captain Harte in the Catasauqua Militia In 1872 the Hon Ernest Nagle acquired it and continued to be its scholarly proprietor until 1894 Mr Nagle had quite a reputation as a Latin scholar. Since 1894 Leopold Ehle conducts the place He now calls it Ehle's Cafe.

THE NORTHAMPTON HOUSE

This hotel dates back sufficiently to be considered one of the oldest hotels in North Catasauqua, although the exact date of its establishment has been lost David Jones was proprietor at the close of the eighties In 1890 the proprietorship passed into the hands of Alfred Hahn whose tenure lasted but two years Mr Hahn, however, accomplished a marvelous feat. Without a dollar to his credit, he erected the beautiful three story frame structure still standing on the eastern approach to the Hokendauqua Bridge, and furnished it in first class style Mr Hahn possessed a keen mind and bore a convincing personality.

Joseph Gorman acquired the property through a forced sale and after seven months passed the property over to Daniel H. Harris whose tenure is twenty-one years The house accommodates thirty-four people, is heated by steam, illuminated by gas and electricity, and furnished with hot and cold water There is also a commodious stable

THE IMPERIAL

After the National Bank of Catasauqua had finished her triumphal procession into her new home at Second and Bridge Streets, in 1903, her old habitation on Front Street below Mulberry was converted into a hotel, called the Imperial. This originally was James Lackey's general store, a building two and one-half stories high. During 1858, it was converted into a banking house, as the article on the National Bank relates In 1867 the building was enlarged and modernized so as to meet the growing demands of a progressive institution The first proprietors of the Imperial were Lovine Miller and John G Sacks Having bought the interests of these gentlemen, Adam Langkammer took possession in May, 1906, and is still the monarch of the Imperial The house is a three and one-half story brick building, heated by hot water and has a hot and cold water service Its capacity offers comforts to seventy-five guests.

THE CATASAUQUA BREWERY SALOON.

This place, No. 110 Second Street, is named the Catasauqua Brewery Saloon since it serves the public like a stream flowing directly from the spring. It was founded in 1869 by Matthew Millhaupt. In 1872 it passed into the control of Christian Stockberger; 1884, Mr. Hill; 1888, Felix Keller. There were a number

IMPERIAL HOTEL

of proprietors during the nineties: John Dold, Simon Butler, Charles Albert, Mr. Werkheiser, William McKeever, Ernest Ritter, Mr. Freeman, Jacob Lutz, Christian Walker, Harvey Gilbert. The present proprietor is Joseph Wirth. His house has accommodations for twelve guests. It is heated by steam and illuminated by electricity.

THE UNION HOTEL.

August Richter built the Union Hotel at the five points of Second and Union Streets and Howertown Avenue during 1871. After a long tenure Mr. Richter sold out to Samuel Wint who was succeeded by Benjamin Whitehall. M. Markward followed Mr Whitehall and in 1903 transferred the business to William Walker On October 9, 1911, Mr Walker sold out to Paul J Ambrose, the present proprietor The house affords quarters for eight guests

THE ORIENTAL HOTEL

The building on the south east corner of Mulberry Street and Howertown Avenue was erected by Samuel J Koehler as a general store and dwelling During 1898 Mr. Koehler converted the store into a bar-room and arranged the building generally for hotel accommodations After holding license for four years, Mr. Koehler sold out to M. Markward, the present proprietor. The house contains twelve rooms and is well illuminated and heated

THE MANSION HOUSE.

The Mansion House on Front Street below Bridge was erected by Captain Henry Harte during the sixties After a tenure of some years his son, Lewis K, popularly known as "Kos," succeeded him Other landlords were Albert Fry, Frank Medlar and Hopkins and Harteg Harteg sold out to Hopkins, who, January 24, 1889, conveyed the property to H R Blocker, the present incumbent The house contains twenty rooms and is equipped with hot and cold water, steam heat, electric light and telephone service

THE HOTEL FAIRMOUNT

License for this hotel, located at Race and Eleventh Streets, was first lifted by Theodore Geiger in 1897 After one year, Conrad A Steitz acquired it and continued as its genial proprietor until his death July 1, 1907. Since then, Mrs Frances Steitz and her son, Frank C Steitz, as manager, are conducting the business The house is a three story frame building, well lighted by electricity and heated by steam There are two rooms devoted to the accommodations of the public The hotel stable has stalls for ten horses

THE HORSE SHOE HOUSE

It is said that Mrs Malone started in business on North Front Street some years ago and continued until Stephen Czapp secured the place in 1900 In 1905 John Smajda bought it and is still its genial proprietor The house contains fifteen rooms heated by steam

THE HOTEL WALKER

Gottlieb Schramm reconstructed and equipped a building as a saloon on Race Street in the Third ward, some time during the eighties. In 1896 Edward L Walker took the property and improved it a great deal He also erected a stable large enough to accommodate eight horses He called the place THE HOTEL WALKER In 1905, Arthur Walker acquired the stand and continued until C H. Bellner relieved him by purchasing it in 1913 The hotel accommodates twelve guests

LIQUOR STORE

Messrs R Frank Stine and A C. Kramlich established the wholesale liquor business on Church Street, above Front, in 1872

In 1900, Mr Oscar J Stine came to Catasauqua and was employed by Stine and Kramlich as salesman

In 1898 he bought the copartnership share of Mr. Kramlich and the firm name was changed to Stine & Bro.

When Mr R Frank Stine's health failed, his brother bought the entire business, September, 1912, and now the sign reads, "Oscar J Stine, Wholesale Liquor Dealer"

By his genial personality and clean business principles, Mr Stine has developed a very fine trade

BOTTLING PLANT

August Hohl purchased the old Biery homestead on the north-west corner of Second and Race Streets in the spring of 1888, and converted the basement of the stately stone mansion into a bottling plant In the spring of 1901, Mr Hohl also began the wholesale liquor trade The business increased to such proportions as to warrant the search for new quarters In 1906, he bought from Mr McKeever the large three story building on Front and Race Streets The old store was converted into a well equipped and most sanitary bottling house, and wholesale liquor store During 1907, a cold storage plant was built at Race Street and the tracks of the C R. R of N J , where a large supply of beers, ales and porter is constantly laid up. Mr Hohl also manufactures all kinds of carbonated beverages His trade radiates around Catasauqua to the extent of fully twenty miles

CHAPTER IX—PROFESSIONAL MEN

DR FREDERICK W QUIG Dr Frederick W Quig came to this country in 1847 and for a time worked about the furnaces An accident occurring at the works brought about the discovery that Dr Quig had been educated at the University of Edinburgh, Scotland, for a physician He did no more manual labor, but opened an office in the McAllister home and continued to hold a very successful practice while he lived

When the "black cholera" was epidemic in the town, Dr Quig proved himself a hero He was never known to neglect a patient and lived an exemplary life In 1849 he married Ann Elizabeth Leslie of Mauch Chunk, whose death is of recent occurrence

DR GEORGE McINTYRE Dr George McIntyre, son of John McIntyre, was born in Philadelphia, Pa , in 1842 He went through our Borough schools, entered Claverack Institute on the Hudson, and two years later, was admitted to Lafayette College He graduated from this institution with honor in 1866, and three years later was granted a diploma from the medical department of the University of Pennsylvania.

Returning to Catasauqua, he opened an office and for a time practiced his profession, but in 1870 he left for Quincy, Illinois, where he died about three years later His was the first college diploma brought to the Borough by one who had gone through its common schools Dr George McIntyre was of handsome, dignified appearance, a general favorite, and his manners were the perfection of courtesy. His early death was much deplored.

DR H. H RIEGEL Henry Harrison Riegel, M D , the son of former sheriff of Northampton County, Daniel Riegel and his wife Hannah, nee Weaver, was born in Allentown, Pa., November 12, 1836.

While his father was proprietor of the Nazareth Inn from 1840, Henry attended the Moravian school at Nazareth Hall. At the age of eighteen years, he began the study of medicine under Dr. W. E. Barnes of Bath, Pa., and in the fall of 1855 he entered the medical department of the University of Pennsylvania, where he remained for one year. In the fall of 1856, he entered the Jefferson Medical College from which he was graduated the following spring.

Dr. H. H. Riegel opened his office at Cherryville, May 5, 1857, where he continued until June, 1861, when the "Westward Ho!" fever lured him to Saegerstown in Crawford County, six miles beyond Meadville. He remained until the following February, when, upon the importunity of his father, he returned and located at Weaversville, Pa., where he succeeded the late Dr. Walter F. Martin.

In the fall of 1869, he located at No. 27 Front Street, Catasauqua, where he enjoys the implicit confidence of a large constituency.

Dr. Riegel is the only survivor of eight of Dr. Barnes' students. In May, 1889, President Harrison appointed him a Pension Examiner to serve with Dr. P. L. Reichert, and Dr. H. H. Herbst. His commission ran out during Grover Cleveland's term. The doctor is a director of the National Bank of Catasauqua since 1879 and serves as Vice President of the Board. He participated in the organization of the Slatington Bank in 1875. He served three terms as school director, and was President of the Board during the time the Lincoln Building was erected.

DR. H. H. RIEGEL

He is a member of Grace Methodist Episcopal Church since 1870. As Burgess, he served the Borough from 1909 to 1914.

Socially, he belongs to the Masonic Fraternity—the Porter Lodge at Catasauqua, the Knights Templar at Allentown and the Rajah Temple at Reading.

The Doctor was married to Ellen J., daughter of Abraham and Elizabeth (nee Hummel) Gish, July 3, 1858. Their children are: Clifford H., Dr. William A., Emma L., the wife of S. B. Harte, and Mattie G., the wife of Thomas W. Keen, all of Catasauqua.

He is a member of the Lehigh County Medical Society (an Ex-President), the Lehigh Valley Medical Society, the Pennsylvania State Medical Association and the American Medical Association.

Although past seventy-seven years of age, the doctor follows up his daily practice with the zeal and buoyancy of a man in the prime of life.

William A. Riegel, M. D., son of Dr. H. H. Riegel and his wife Ellen J., nee Gish, was born at Weaversville, Pa., May 17, 1864.

He was graduated from the Catasauqua Schools in the Spring of 1880, and, after attending the Weaversville Academy for two years, he entered the tutelage of G. J. Benner in the preparation for college. He entered Pennsylvania College in the fall of 1881, from which institution he was graduated in June, 1885.

In the fall of the same year, he entered the Medical department of the University of Pennsylvania from which he was graduated in 1889.

On the 15th of May in the year of his graduation, he began the general practice of medicine with his father, and shares his noble reputation for conscientious attention to duty and laudable success in the treatment of his cases.

DR. WILLIAM A. RIEGEL

The Doctor married Miss Cora, daughter of Mr. and Mrs. William Steinhilber, July 20, 1892. There were born to them three children: Henry H., Dorothy I., and William A., Jr.

He is a member of the Blue Lodge, Chapter and Council of the Masonic Order. He has also affiliated with the Elks, Moose, Buffalo, and Woodmen of the World. Like his father he is medical examiner for a number of Life Insurance companies.

DR. DANIEL YODER. Dr. Daniel Yoder was born in Maxatawny Township, Berks County, September 30, 1833. He was the oldest of eleven children and is now the only surviving member of his family. He was educated at Bethlehem and the Vandeveer Academy of Easton. At the age of twenty he directed his attention to teaching and for a time had charge of the Levan school at Siegfried's. In 1855 he began the study of medicine under Drs. Edward Martin and son Walter of Weaversville, and the following year entered the medical department of the University of Pennsylvania, where he took a course of lectures.

Later he conducted his studies in the Pennsylvania Medical College at Philadelphia, from which he was graduated in June, 1858. He then entered into partnership at Catasauqua with Dr. F. B. Martin, after whose death he continued for himself. He opened an office on Front Street above Bridge and carried on a very successful practice for fifty years. He is the oldest surviving Homeopathic physician in the Lehigh Valley.

DR. DANIEL YODER

As a loyal member of the Masonic Fraternity, the Doctor served as treasurer of the Porter Lodge for forty-four years. He is also distinguished for holding the longest continuous membership of any Brother of the local I. O. O. F.

Dr. Yoder is a member of the following Medical societies: The American Institute of Homeopathy, the Medical Society of Pennsylvania, and the Lehigh Valley Medical Society. Of the last named he is a charter member and was elected its first President.

In 1863, when Lee invaded Pennsylvania, Dr. Yoder volunteered as a surgeon in the 38th Emergency Militia and served as Hospital Steward until the war was ended.

In 1861 he was married to Amanda E. Glace, daughter of Samuel Glace, who was prominently identified for a number of years with the Lehigh Canal and the Crane Iron Works in their early history. They recently celebrated their fifty-third anniversary. In 1873 he purchased a desirable lot at Third and Bridge Streets, Catasauqua, and erected a large brick residence and office where he still resides. Since his retirement, the Doctor has devoted much of his time in helping to organize and promote the Lehigh National Bank and in directing the erection of a fine Bank Building. He acted as chairman of the building committee. He is a director of the bank since its organization.

DOCTOR M. E. HORNBECK. The late Doctor Molton Edward Hornbeck was born at Allentown, January 27, 1842. His father was John Westbrook Hornbeck, a successful lawyer who practiced before the Lehigh County Bar. He was elected to the House of Representatives as a member of the 13th Congress, and was a cotemporary of Abraham Lincoln of Illinois, J. Q. Adams of Massachusetts, H. Cobb of Georgia, and A. Johnson of Tennessee. His mother was Maria Martin Hornbeck, and was the first post mistress appointed in Allentown. She held this position for sixteen years. On his maternal side Dr. Hornbeck traces a long line of medical men. He was the 35th in a direct line of the Martins to graduate from the Medical department of the University of Pennsylvania.

DR. M. E. HORNBECK

He received his early education in the public schools of Allentown. Later he attended the private school of Gregory in Allentown, after which he entered the Philadelphia School of Pharmacy from which he was graduated in 1862. After having served as druggist in the Martin Pharmacy at Hall and Hamilton Streets for a few months, he was mustered into the 128th Regiment of the Pennsylvania Volunteer Infantry, September 4, 1862, as a Hospital Steward. He passed through the battle of Antietam, Burnside's Second Campaign, the battle of Chancellorsville, besides some minor engagements. He was honorably discharged and mustered out of service May 19, 1863

He now took up the study of medicine with his uncle, the late Dr. Tilghman Martin of Allentown. After a course in the University of Pennsylvania, he was graduated in 1865. He came to Catasauqua to assist his uncle, Dr. F. B. Martin, who departed this life but three years later. He assumed full control of his uncle's practice and continued a most successful physician until he retired in the fall of 1901. He was surgeon for the Lehigh Valley R. R. Company for ten years.

Dr. Hornbeck was married to Miss Mary Laubach, daughter of Judge Joseph Laubach and his wife, a member of the Swartz family, in 1868. The Judge held office in Northampton County for twelve years and was a member of the U. S. Senate in 1855. Three children were born to them. Dr. J. L. Hornbeck, Catasauqua, Westbrook Hornbeck, deceased, and Helen, Mrs. R. A. Carter of Audenried, Pa.

Dr. Hornbeck died October 5, 1905, in the sixty-fourth year of his age. His body lies buried in the Fairview Cemetery.

DR. JAMES L. HORNBECK. Our present Doctor Hornbeck has an eminent right to his degree and station as a physician, being the thirty-sixth lineal descendant of the house of the Martins, the clan of doctors. He was born May 10, 1873, and received his preliminary education in the public schools of Town, from which he was graduated, in June 1889. He then matriculated in the Williston Seminary, East Hampton, Mass., where he graduated in the Biological Course in 1891. Until the fall of 1892 he assisted his father, Dr. M. E. Hornbeck, in his office work. At this time he entered the Medical Department of the University of Pennsylvania and graduated in 1895. Since his graduation he practiced medicine in Catasauqua, first as assistant to his father, and since 1901 as his father's successor.

Dr. Hornbeck entered into matrimony with Miss Helen Thomas, daughter of the late James Thomas and his wife, Mary Davies Thomas, in 1901. Their children are: Thomas Molton, James Laubach, Jr., and Dorothy Hornbeck.

The Doctor is a member of the State, County, Lehigh Valley and American Medical Associations. He belongs to the Philadelphia Medical Club, the Elks Club, and is a Chapter Mason. He is also a member of the Williston College Fraternity founded in 1844 and bearing the initials "F. C."

DR. C. J. KEIM. Charles J. Keim, M. D., the son of Leopold Keim and his wife Mary, nee Stahr, was born near Bethlehem, Pa., March 19, 1843. The land of the Keim family was purchased by an ancestor of this clan from the Proprietary of this State, William Penn. At the age of thirteen the subject of this sketch left the old farm for a career at school. He attended the Wyoming Seminary for a season, after which he took a course in Lasher's School, Easton, Pa. School days having ended, he became a clerk in a general store at Butztown, Pa. Later he drifted into a store in Allentown. In 1862 he was mustered in as a member of Company F., of the Fifth Penna. Home Guards, of Bethlehem. Upon his honorable discharge he opened a general store at Eighth and Hamilton Streets, Allentown, Pa.

After several years of business experience he sold out, came to Catasauqua and began to read medicine with Dr. M. E. Hornbeck. In the fall of 1873, he entered the Medical Department of the University of Pennsylvania from which he was graduated in March, 1873. Dr. Keim immediately opened his office in Catasauqua and developed a large practice at Number 742 Front Street, which he bestowed upon his son, Dr. H. J. S. Keim after his graduation from the Medico-Chirurgical College in Philadelphia.

DR. C. J. KEIM

Dr. C. J. Keim has always taken an active and intelligent interest in municipal affairs. In 1878 he was elected a member of the School Board in which he served the community for three years. He served three terms in Town Council of which he was president for some years. He was elected Burgess in the fall of 1905, and, when the election of 1913 came on, the memory of his able and faithful services during his former term polled sufficient votes to elect him again to this high office.

Dr. Keim is a member of the Lehigh County Medical Society, of which he served as president for one year. He also belongs to the Lehigh Valley Medical Society, and the State and American Medical Associations. The Doctor is a Democrat in politics. In religion he is a consistent member of Trinity Ev. Lutheran Church.

DR. H. J. S. KEIM. Dr. Harry J. S. Keim of Catasauqua, Pa., was born in the City of Allentown, and reared in Catasauqua, he being the son of Dr. Charles J. Keim, and his wife Eliza C., nee Seider. His father has been a medical practitioner in this Borough since 1875, and at present Burgess of this Borough, having served the Borough in this same capacity from 1906 to 1909.

Dr. Keim attended the public schools of this Borough until the year 1887, when he entered Muhlenberg College, attending there for two years. He then entered the Agthe Pharmacy in this Borough. In the year 1890, he entered the University of Pennsylvania for the study of Medicine, at which institution he studied for three years, after which he completed his medical course in 1894 at the Medico-Chirurgical College, Philadelphia.

In this same year (1894) he entered the practice of Medicine in this borough, affiliating with his father until 1905, when his father relinquished the practice of medicine entirely, Dr. H. Keim assuming the entire practice.

DR. H. J. S. KEIM

In 1895 he was married to Fannie H Heller of Allentown, unto them were born two daughters, Emma E and A. Florence In 1906, his wife died after a short illness of typhoid fever

In 1910 Dr H. Keim was again married to Mabel A Richardson of Allentown, and unto them was born a son, Charles R

THOMAS A SCHERER, M D   Dr. Thomas A Scherer was a physician of exceptional ability, especially along pathological lines His grandfather was Samuel Scherer, a native of Lehigh County. His father was born in Upper Milford Township, Lehigh County, Pa , and in early life learnt the trade of carpenter He was a boss carpenter at the Hokendauqua furnaces for twenty years, and, when he came to Catasauqua, he held a similar position at the Crane furnaces He retired in 1887 The Doctor's mother, Maria, a daughter of Mr. and Mrs. Peter Steinberger, also was a native of Lehigh County His older brother, William H Scherer, is a member of the firm of Frederick and Scherer, the Undertakers

Dr Scherer was born at Petersville, Pa , October 23, 1856, and at the age of twelve years entered the Franklin High School in Bethlehem Upon his graduation he became an apprentice with Barber and Company at Allentown as a machinist. Subsequently he found employment in the Davies and Thomas shops Not satisfied with his present station, he began to read medicine in 1880 under the direction of Dr. H H Riegel, who still is a gifted teacher as well as an able physician He entered the Jefferson Medical College in Philadelphia, and was graduated in the spring of 1883 He opened an office in Slatington in May of the same year The following year he returned to Catasauqua, the West Side, and enjoyed a large and growing practice until his death, March 9, 1912

He entered into Matrimony with Emma J , a daughter of Ferdinand and Dorothy E (nee Frederick) Briser, June 21, 1888 He took great delight in agriculture and the nursery His truck farm was a model of beauty and productiveness

DR. CHARLES E MILSON   Dr. Charles E Milson, the second son of Daniel and Elizabeth (Davis) Milson, was born in Catasauqua August 10, 1863 His general education was acquired in the public schools of Catasauqua and the

Weaversville Academy. After spending a short time in the office of Dr. Aaron Becker of Bethlehem, Pa., he entered the Hahneman Medical College, Philadelphia, Pa. On March 10, 1884, he was graduated from that institution with the degree of Doctor of Medicine.

On October 21, 1884, he was married to Camilla Eleanor Deily, the daughter of Francis S. and Sarah A. (Dich) Deily. To them four children were born: Gertrude, Helen, Ruth and Marie (deceased).

Dr. Milson's fraternal affiliations are: Past Master of Porter Lodge No. 284, F. and A. M.; Past High Priest of Royal Arch Chapter, No. 278; Allen Commandary No. 20, Knight Templar, Allentown, Pa.; Allen Council No. 23, R. and S. M., Allentown, Pa. He is a member of the Catasauqua Board of Health

He is an earnest member of the First Presbyterian Church and politically he is a staunch Republican.

DR. CHARLES E. MILSON

In the early days of Catasauqua many of her best citizens came from Wales, among whom was Daniel Milson. Dr. Charles Milson is endowed with many of the characteristics of those pioneer Catasauquans. He is an honored member of the medical profession, a loyal member of his fraternal organizations, and a highly respected citizen of his native town.

DR. ALFRED J. BECKER. Dr. Alfred J. Becker, the son of the Rev. Jacob and Mary Becker, was born at Siegfried, Northampton County, March 18, 1861. His father was a minister of the German Reformed Church, serving as pastor of the congregation at Towamensing ten years, and Shoenersville and Howertown forty-three years, where he preached with great acceptance to the people. The paternal great grandfather of this subject, Rev. Christian Ludwig, D. D., one of the fathers of the Reformed Church, was born in Germany Nov. 17, 1756. He resided in Bremen till 1793, when he embarked for America, arriving safely at Baltimore in August, 1793, and bearing with him the most flattering testimonials of his learning and piety.

The grandfather, Rev. Jacob Becker, was born in Baltimore and became a minister in the Reformed Church, preaching in Northampton and Lehigh Counties. He was also a Homeopathic physician, being one of the first graduates of the Homeopathic Medical College of Allentown, Pa.

Dr. Becker was reared in Catasauqua, his education being obtained in the common schools in Weaversville Academy under Professor Kuma's instruction.

DR. ALFRED BECKER

He commenced the study of medicine with his uncle, Dr. Aaron Becker, a graduate of the University of Pennsylvania and Assistant Surgeon of the One Hundred Ninety-eighth Pennsylvania Infantry during the Civil War. After leaving his uncle's office he went to Philadelphia and entered the Hahneman Medical College of Physicians and Surgeons, where he attended the clinics and lectures of the three year course, graduating in 1885.

Dr. Becker began the practice of medicine in Catasauqua, where he has practiced for twenty-nine years. During this time he has built up an excellent business and made for himself a host of friends. In the practice of medicine he has given evidence of the possession of professional qualifications and ability such as are won only through close application, earnest study and diligent research; and, is therefore accounted one of the leading Homeopathic physicians of Lehigh County.

Dr. Becker married on November 28, 1888, Ella, the daughter of Daniel Schreiber of Coplay, Lehigh County.

He is a member of the Lehigh Valley Homeopathic Medical Society and of the Alumni Association of the Hahneman Medical College of Philadelphia.

Fraternally he is connected with the Independent Order of Odd Fellows and the P O S of A, being a past officer of both bodies He is president of the Lehigh Building and Loan Association, and a director of the Lehigh National Bank He is Reformed in religious faith, and a Republican in political belief

DR JOHN S SCHNELLER   John S Schneller, M D, the son of Charles W Schneller and his wife Mamie (nee Schaeffer), was born in 1885   He attended the town schools for a number of years after which he was enrolled in the Allentown Preparatory School from which he was graduated in 1902   He received his degree of Bachelor of Science from Muhlenberg College in 1906   His medical training he acquired at the University of Pennsylvania and received his diploma in 1910   He followed this up with a special course in diseases of children and obstetrics interna at the Allentown Hospital   He opened his office at 532 Second Street in July, 1911, and has developed a very flattering practice

DR HECKENBERGER   The Veterinary Surgeon, William A Heckenberger opened his office in Catasauqua in 1850   He was born February 26, 1825, in Saulgau Wurtemberg, Germany   His father, Joseph Heckenberger, was sheriff and jailer in his native city and for fourteen years he sojourned in Russia   His mother was Louisa Pocarius also a native of Germany   The subject of our sketch sailed from Antwerp in 1848, and after a voyage of sixty days landed in New York   He sought this section of the country on account of his inability to converse freely in the English language   He was the first veterinary surgeon in these parts   His scholarship (he was a graduate of the German Gymnasium) and his great skill as a Veterinary soon gained for him a wide-spread reputation   He was engaged by the Bethlehem Iron Company, the Crane Company and a number of Coal-mining Companies to look after and treat their horses and mules   He was a member of the Veterinary Medical Association of Pennsylvania, and St Paul s Ev Lutheran Church   He died April 5, 1910, at the age of eighty-five years

Drs Joseph and Henry Heckenberger were graduated from the Ontario Veterinary College, Toronto, Canada   The former entered into partnership with his father in 1880 and continued with signal success until his death, March 17, 1908   The latter set up a practice in Pittston, Pa, where he continued until his brother's decease, when he moved to Catasauqua to become the successor to the firm of Dr W. A Heckenberger and Son. Dr Henry Heckenberger and family occupy the old homestead on Front Street above Union The Doctor is a genial and capable man having had an experience of more than thirty-six years in the profession.

DENTISTRY

Dr J P Barnes, late of Allentown, was the first dentist who operated in Catasauqua While a student under Dr Scholl at Bath, Pa , Mr Barnes made periodic visits to our town He carried his tools in a satchel and did a great deal of his work in people's houses His room was on Church Street In those days no narcotics, or pain killing drugs, were administered. Patients tried to sit still until a tooth was filed down to the gums and an artificial tooth inserted by a wooden pivot forced into the centre of the root People were not so ready then to believe that pain is only a delusion

During the forties Thomas Butz, who farmed the land now covered by the Hokendauqua Furnace, was an expert teeth extractor People for miles around would implore his services If men's agonies drove them to him during working hours, they would stop at the Butz farm house, secure "the hook" and carry it to the field where Mr Butz was at work Here the latter would plant his patient upon a stump, force the prong of the hook under the root of the tooth, hold his victim down with his knee upon the thigh, and by a mighty twist pry out the aching offender Exclamation ! !

WESLEY WILLOUGHBY, D D. S. Although he is a pain producer, he is a convincing demonstration of a Homeopathic principle which says, that like cures like To find the root of the matter causes pain , but when the pain is scientifically disturbed it ceases to ache Doctor Wesley Willoughby is the son of Captain John Willoughby and his wife Margaret Ann, nee Armstrong, and was born in Charleston, Canada, September 29, 1871 The Doctor passed through the grades of the schools of his native town After this he was matriculated in the Orangeville Boys' School, Orangeville High School, the Ontario College, and the Orangeville Collegiate Institute from which he was graduated in 1893. In the fall of the same year he entered the Dental department of the University of

Pennsylvania from which he graduated in 1896 While taking his course in Dental Surgery, he attended lectures in the Jefferson Medical College for two years.

On the 26th of August he opened his Dental parlors in the old National Bank Building on Front Street, where he built up a large patronage He opened a branch office in Siegfried, Pa , in 1897, but his home practice grew to such proportions that he was constrained to close the Siegfried office after but a few years tenure When the National Bank sold its old property and moved to Second and Bridge Streets in 1903, Doctor Willoughby built his comfortable quarters at number 125 Bridge Street and moved his equipment His place is home-like to his patients and his practice more than sufficient to tax his robust strength

Dr Willoughby was married to Miss Tillie C Frederick, daughter of Ogden R and Clara A , nee Fuller, Frederick, September 7, 1898 To this union was born a son named Wesley F

DR J EDWARD REHRIG That Dentist is most sympathetic with his patients who possesses the requisite skill to know where and how to cut, and has manly courage sufficient to make a finished excavation with the smallest number of strokes possible. These qualifications may be justly predicated of Dr J. Edward Rehrig.

The Doctor is a son of John C and Hannah M (nee Schock) Rehrig, and was born in Mauch Chunk, Pa., August 20, 1884 He attended the public schools of East Mauch Chunk until he was graduated in June, 1900 He was employed as bookkeeper by the New Jersey Zinc Company at Palmerton, where he served for less than a year, when he entered the Baldwin Locomotive Works, Philadelphia, Pa , and labored as a steam-fitter In 1903 he returned to Mauch Chunk to engaged in business with his father, who was the proprietor of the American Hotel

Mr. Rehrig entered the Dental department of the University of Pennsylvania in 1905 and was graduated in 1908 He now received the appointment of Resident Dental Surgeon in the Philadelphia General Hospital, where he remained one year He was honored with office of vice-president of the Kirk Dental Society during his senior year. He was the editor-in-chief of the class record of 1908, and was a member of Psi Omega Dental Fraternity

Dr Rehrig opened his Dental rooms in the Lehigh National Bank building in Catasauqua, April 1, 1909 On June 1, 1911, he was married to Miss Nellie J Miller of Bangor, Pa They are now the proud parents of a little Miss named Dorothy Miller Rehrig

Socially the Doctor holds membership in the Catasauqua Porter Lodge, No. 284, F. and A M., and the Royal Arch Chapter, No 278

WILLIAM H GLACE   William H Glace, lawyer at Catasauqua for 40 years, and a public official here for a time, was born Feb 12, 1839, on the farm of his grandfather, John Swartz, situated along the Lehigh River, one mile north of Catasauqua, at Dry Run He received his education in the public schools of the vicinity, and in Wyoming Seminary, at Kingston, Penna.

One year prior to the Civil War, he went to Charleston, S. C , and secured employment as entry clerk in the wholesale house of Thayer Dewing & Co While engaged here, he saw the weekly sales of slaves in an enclosed yard adjoining Broad Street, the thoroughfare of the city, and he observed the secret preparations which were made there for the "Conflict " A U S Arsenal was located in this prominent place, which was being filled with munitions of war by the then Secretary of War under President Buchanan Great numbers of open boxes with rifles were carried there and this performance at the national depository attracted much public attention.

Realizing that a conflict between the North and South was apparently imminent, Mr Glace determined to return home while he could do so without embarrassment, and shortly afterward he enlisted as a sergeant in Co F , 47th Penna Volunteers. He continued in active service for three years, having participated with his Regiment in all the battles of the Red River Expedition, and also in the numerous engagements of a part of the Northern Army in defending the outposts of Washington against the exciting raids by Confederates under General Early.

Upon his discharge from the military service, he became the bookkeeper and paymaster of the C & F R R Co at Catasauqua and he filled this position for two years. Then he studied law in the offices of John H Oliver, Esq , at Allentown, and was admitted to practice in the several courts of Lehigh County, April 13, 1868. Soon after his admission to the Bar, the Auditor General of Penna. (Gen. John F. Hartranft) selected him to be the Assessor of the National Banks in Lehigh, Northampton, and Monroe Counties, and he filled this position for two years from 1868 to 1870. During this time he had begun a preliminary

WILLIAM H. GLACE

practice of the law at Allentown. While there, in the fall of 1868, he was nominated for the Legislature by the Republican Party, and his popularity was shown by receiving the highest vote of his party.

In the Fall of 1869, he was nominated for Justice of the Peace at Catasauqua, and of the four candidates on the ticket he received the highest vote. He was commissioned for five years, and at the end of his term, this time was extended to the spring of 1875 by the new State Constitution of 1874, and he was commissioned accordingly He was elected Chief Burgess of the Borough and officiated for the year 1876 He subsequently served as Auditor for six years, as Borough Solicitor for seven years, and as School Solicitor for three years, and he also acted as a Notary Public for 28 consecutive years

In the practice of the law he directed his attention chiefly to the settlement of estates in Catasauqua and the surrounding townships, the examination and transmission of title to real estate in these districts, and the investment on reliable security, in all of which he became a safe adviser and recognized authority During the past twenty-five years he prepared the last wills of nearly all the prominent men of the community His practice in the respects mentioned became very extensive, which evidences the large volume of business transacted by him After a continuous practice of forty years, he retired from the active duties of professional life

While a student at law at Allentown, Mr Glace became a member of the first post of the G A R in Lehigh County, which was organized shortly after the close of the Civil War He has been a member for many years of the Historical Society of Pennsylvania at Philadelphia

In 1870, Mr Glace organized the Catasauqua Loan and Building Association, and notwithstanding the financial panic which extended from 1873 to 1877 and seriously affected this community, he directed its affairs in such a successful manner that it was dissolved in eleven years and all the shareholders received their money

In 1906, Mr Glace with other persons at Catasauqua, organized the "Lehigh National Bank," which embarked in the banking business and it has since been conducted in a successful manner He was selected as its first president and officiated two years

Mr Glace, having been prominently identified with the history and development of the community, published, in February, 1914, a compilation entitled "Early History and Reminiscences of Catasauqua" as a historical contribution towards the proper observance of "Old Home Week" which the citizens determined to celebrate

In 1874, Mr Glace was married to Mary Jennie Stark, a great granddaughter of Aaron Stark, who fell as a sacrifice in the awful "Massacre of Wyoming" in 1778, and whose remains repose under the historic Wyoming Monument

Mr Glace's father, Samuel Glace, was a native of Reamstown, in Lancaster County He was born in 1805 and when two years old his parents removed to Conyngham, Luzerne County He was educated in the English schools of the village, and when he became of age he located at Mauch Chunk, where he entered the employ of the Lehigh Coal and Navigation Co Shortly afterwards he went to Lehigh Gap and was the first person to manufacture hydraulic cement in the Lehigh Valley, a special paper on this subject having been prepared by his son (the subject of this sketch) for the Historical Society of Pennsylvania In 1830, he took up his residence at Biery's-Port upon receiving the appointment of division superintendent of the canal from the "Slate Dam," at Laury's, to the "Allentown Dam," and he filled this position for ten years, and afterward he served the Crane Iron Co as mining agent for many years. He lived in retirement nearly twenty years at his residence, No 307 Bridge Street, and he died in 1892, at the advanced age of 86 years He was married to Isabella Swartz, daughter of John Swartz, and they had two children William II (the subject of this sketch), and Amanda E . married to Dr Daniel Yoder

His mother's great-grandfather on the maternal side was John Jacob Mickley, a Huguenot Upon the revocation of the Edict of Nantes, his parents, with numerous other countrymen, were obliged to flee from France and locate in the Palatinate where he was born, and in 1733, he emigrated to Pennsylvania After landing at Philadelphia, he immediately proceeded up the Delaware and Lehigh rivers and settled in the vicinity of Egypt on a tract of land four miles north-west of Catasuaqua In 1763, while three of his little children were hunting chestnuts near their home, two of them were murdered by the Indians Other persons were also murdered during the Indian invasion. The Historical Society of Lehigh County in the Fall of 1913, set up a stone "marker" in Whitehall Township, about a mile from Egypt, to indicate the locality of the massacre, and the names inscribed on this "marker" include those of the two Mickley children. Three sons of this early settler were enlisted in the Revolution, and one of them brought the "Liberty Bell" from Philadelphia to Allentown, where it was secreted for a time in the cellar of Zion's Reformed Church.

Her great-grandfather, on the paternal side, was Nicholas Swartz, who settled in Longswamp Township, Berks County, in 1750, and in 1787 his son Christian migrated to the Irish Settlement in Northampton County, where he then built a large stone dwelling house along the Lehigh River near the outlet of Dry Run; and it was here that Mr. Glace's mother, as well as he himself, was born.

The residence of Mr. Glace is at 307 Bridge Street, Catasauqua, Pa., where he has resided almost continuously since 1855.

R. CLAY HAMMERSLY. R. Clay Hammersly was born in Dillsburg, York County, Pa., January 29, 1834, and died in Catasauqua, Pa., November 20, 1898. In his youth his father moved to Gettysburg, Pa., where he obtained his education in the public schools and in Gettysburg College from which he was graduated. After teaching for several years in his native county, he came to Allentown, Pa., where he taught school. While teaching in this city, he registered as a law student and entered the office of James S. Reese, being subsequently admitted to the bar with Capt. A. B. Swartz.

R. CLAY HAMMERSLY

He did not engaged in the practice of law at once, but came to Catasauqua where he taught several terms in a Grammar school. In 1863 he was elected Principal of the High School and continued in this position for two years. He was Borough Solicitor and was elected Justice of the Peace for the Second Ward, which office he held for many years During these years he became prominent and took a leading part in the affairs of Catasauqua He was one of the original members of the Fairview Cemetery Association, and was elected a member of the School Board in 1866, continuing in this office for a period of seven years He was also a Notary Public and did an extensive business in life and fire insurance He was a member of the Episcopal Church

Mr Hammersly was married to Miss Annie M Welty of Gettysburg and from this union issued the following children Dr William Hammersly of Philadelphia, Miss Alice, a trained nurse, and Miss Annie, who at the time of his death, lived at home

OSCAR J STINE Oscar J. Stine, Esq, was graduated from Muhlenberg College in June, 1882, and three years later received the degree of M A

Mr Stine read law with E H Stine, Esq, at Allentown, Pa, and was admitted to the Lehigh County Bar, June 7, 1886

He practiced law with David R Horne, Esq, then located at Wichita, Kansas, for one year

He returned to Lehigh County in the fall of 1887 and became the junior member of the law firm of Stine and Stine, the senior member being E H Stine, Esq.

In 1900 Mr Stine came to Catasauqua and entered the employ of Stine and Kramlich, the wholesale liquor dealers, whose successor he has become

ALEXANDER N ULRICH The patriarch of this branch of the Ulrich family in this country was a native of Alsace, France, and emigrated to America in 1708 He settled at Annville, Lebanon County, Pa A grandson of this pioneer was a prominent lawyer of Lebanon County, and, during the Revolutionary War, served as adjutant of a Pennsylvania regiment

The grandfather of our subject, the Rev. Daniel Ulrich, D D, was a prominent Lutheran clergyman who served the Ulrich's Church of Lebanon County as pastor for many years His son, Daniel Ulrich, was a man of fine qualities After graduation from Princeton he went to Jefferson Medical College, Philadelphia, Pa. Having received his degree as a doctor, he opened an office in Reading, Pa He was an able physician and above all a clean and courteous gentleman, which developed for him a tremendous practice not only in the city but also in the country surrounding Reading

The mother of our subject was of Scottish origin She was born in Fairfax County, Virginia, and was a daughter of Alexander Nesbitt, a native of Pennsylvania, a graduate of Dickinson College and a successful lawyer of the Old Dominion Her grandfather, Charles Nesbitt, was Provost of the University of Edinburg, Scotland, and is reputed to have been the most learned Greek scholar of all Europe in his day When Dickinson College was founded, Charles Nesbitt was urged to become its first President He accepted the proffer, and his fame assured the success of the institution

Charles N Ulrich, the son of Dr. Daniel Ulrich and Henrietta. nee Nesbitt, was born at Gettysburg, Pa, February 10, 1853 He was educated in Reading After graduation from the High School he was sent to some school in New England In 1871 he came to Catasauqua, where he became a teacher in the public schools In 1873 he was elected principal of the schools, which office he held for six years

He devoted much of his spare time to the study of law so that by 1885 he was admitted to the Bar at Allentown From that time until his death he devoted himself entirely to his chosen profession He was elected Justice of the Peace on the Republican ticket in 1883 and re-elected in 1888 and 1893 He was a member of the Lehigh County Bar Association Miss Irene Fuller became his bride July 11 1878 He departed this life December 29, 1910 His wife preceded him in death

Charles F Ulrich, the only child of this union, was educated in the Catasauqua schools, and Lafayette College, Easton, Pa, from which institution he was graduated in June, 1905 He studied law at different places and was finally admitted to the Lehigh County Bar in 1908 He fell heir to the beautiful and commodious law offices of his father on Bridge Street and enjoys the advantages of a remarkably well chosen library

AUSTIN A GLICK, ESQ, is the son of the late Mr and Mrs. Aaron Glick, who owned and cultivated a fine farm in the vicinage of Howertown, Northampton County, Pa. Later they moved to Catasauqua and took up their residence on Front Street, now the home of Thomas B. Glick, a brother to the subject of this sketch. Mr. Glick was graduated from the Catasauqua High School in the spring of 1876. After a course of preparation, he entered Muhlenberg College from which he was graduated in June, 1882.

He read law with John Rupp, Esq., and was admitted to the Lehigh County Bar on March 3, 1886. He immediately opened his office in the old building of the National Bank of Catasauqua, on Front Street, and later he moved into the P. O. S. of A. building on Bridge Street. Besides the general practice of law, Mr. Glick was Borough solicitor from 1893 to 1895 inclusive, and is Secretary of the Board of Health since its organization.

He is also engaged in the fire insurance business. His genial and encouraging helpmate is a daughter of the late Jacob Roberts and his wife, a Miss Relyea.

WILLIAM H. SCHNELLER. William H. Schneller graduated from the Catasauqua High School in 1898, and for a period of three years thereafter was engaged in the laundry business with the Empire Steam Laundry of Catasauqua, Pa. In September, 1901, he entered the Sophomore Class at Schuylkill Seminary, Reading, Pa., taking up the Classical Course and graduated and received an A. B. degree in 1905. In October of 1905 he entered the Law Department of the University of Pennsylvania and graduated and received his L. L. B. degree therefrom in June, 1908. Mr. Schneller registered as a Student-at-Law with the Honorable James L. Schaadt, of Allentown, Pa., and on motion of the Honorable James L. Schaadt on March 15th, 1909, he was admitted by the Honorable Frank M. Trexler, President Judge, to practice in the several Courts of Lehigh County. On the 18th day of October, 1909, on motion of E. J. Fox, Esquire, of Easton, Pa., he was admitted by the Honorable Henry J. Scott, President Judge, to practice in the several Courts of Northampton County. On April 1st, 1909, he opened his law

WILLIAM H. SCHNELLER

office in The Lehigh National Bank Building, Catasauqua, Pa, and has continued there ever since On March 18th, 1912, on motion of Ulysses S. Koons, of Philadelphia, he was admitted by the Honorable D Newlin Fell, Chief Justice of the Supreme Court of Pennsylvania, to practice as an Attorney and Counsellor of the said Supreme Court of Pennsylvania On the 15th day of March, 1909, immediately after his admission, he tried his first case in the Lehigh County court, at Allentown, Pa, and a month thereafter tried his first case in the United States District Court at Philadelphia, and has been actively engaged in the general practice of law in the various District and Appellate Courts of Pennsylvania and of the United States continuously since At present he is the solicitor for the North Catasauqua School District, of the Recorder of Deeds of Lehigh County, and of the Lehigh National Bank of Catasauqua, as well as of various other corporations and business firms

KOONS AND SON Abraham F Koons was born at Berlinsville, Pa, August, 1863 When but eight years of age he was left an orphan and as such enjoyed the most meager schooling possible He had a good mind which, coupled with a willingness to serve, soon brought him into demand for clerkship in country stores

When a young man, he drifted into Coplay where he managed a general store for Levi Haas, then Superintendent of the Coplay furnaces In 1856 he came to Catasauqua and entered into a partnership with Clinton Breinig at the corner of Front and Race Streets, later the property of Owen Romig and now in the hands of August Hohl.

After the Civil War this partnership was dissolved and Mr Koons established his business at Front and Mulberry Streets, now the Heckenberger Drug store Here he took up insurance and the real estate business In 1868 he quit the mercantile business In February, 1875, he was elected Justice of the Peace for the Borough of Catasauqua, to which office he was elected for five consecutive terms, and in which he served with an enviable record until his death, February 15, 1898

Edwin C Koons was educated in the Catasauqua schools and made good use of his time and opportunities When a young man, he learned the machinist trade at the Davies and Thomas foundry, where he served for seven years After a service of two years at the old Bryden Horse Shoe plant, he entered his father's office as clerk. Upon the death of his father, Governor Hastings appointed him Justice of the Peace, February 25, 1898, to fill the unexpired term. His commission ran out May 1, 1899 Since then he has been elected to his office for three consecutive terms, which bespeaks the value of his services and the esteem in which he is held by his fellow citizens His commission runs out December 31, 1915. Mr Koons possesses an exceptionally large and well chosen law library for the office of a justice Most of this was the accumulation of his father

THOMAS QUINN The subject of this sketch is a native of Ireland, who was brought to America by his parents when he was but a tender infant They located at Laubachsville, now the borough of Northampton After he had attained to young manhood and finished the course of studies prescribed for a country school district, he was sent to the Pierce Business College in Philadelphia With his diploma under his arm, he returned to Laubachsville in order to enter into partnership with the Associate Judge Joseph Laubach While the Judge presided over the Northampton County Courts at Easton, Mr Quinn ran the Laubach general store

In 1879 he came to Catasauqua where he opened a general store at the corner of Front and Walnut Streets After enjoying a fine trade for twenty years, Mr. Quinn retired and located at 1124 Second Street Since that time he was elected Justice of the Peace of the Borough of North Catasauqua for three successive terms This is a fine compliment to a worthy man Mr Quinn enlisted from Northampton in Company B of the 153rd Regiment of the Pennsylvania Volunteers He was wounded at Chancellorsville and taken prisoner For six weeks he lay in Libby Prison, until an exchange of prisoners was made He immediately rejoined his regiment but was wounded again in the battle of Gettysburg.

CORNELIUS F. ROTH, ESQ., was born at the Iron Bridge, Lehigh County, Pa., March 13, 1856, and is the son of Owen T. and Feyetta (Minnich) Roth. He came to Catasauqua in 1864 and learnt the art of photography from G. D. Lentz. His former wife to whom he was married February 7, 1878, was Miss Josephine Minnich of Walnutport, Pa. Their only surviving daughter is Matilda Feyetta Roth. Mrs. Roth having died December 18, 1893, Mr. Roth entered into matrimony with Cora E. Drumheller of Conyngham, Pa., February 28, 1901.

He was elected Justice of the Peace in 1906 and opened his office in his photograph parlors on Bridge Street. The community expressed its appreciation of his good judgment and sense of equity by re-electing him to his office in 1912.

CORNELIUS F. ROTH

CHAPTER X—BIOGRAPHICAL SKETCHES

BIERY. The farm land now covered by the lower portion of the town was the property of Frederick Biery at the beginning of the nineteenth century The Crane Company purchased the site of the furnaces from him He had five sons Daniel, Jonas, Solomon, David and William, and three daughters, Mrs Nicholas Snyder, Mrs Samuel Koehler, and Mrs. Jacob Buehler Three fine, two-story, cut-stone dwellings erected by him in 1826, 1830 and 1835, respectively, still stand on Race Street and are in a remarkably good state of preservation Frederick Biery died in 1845.

SOLOMON BIERY converted the dwelling erected in 1826 into an Inn and was its noble proprietor for many years He served as post master of the Burg from 1855 to 1861, and had a valuable interest in the firm of Frederick and Company, carbuilders at Fullerton His wife was Mary Magdalene, daughter of Mr and Mrs George and Hannah (nee Haas) Frederick She was born January 17, 1811, and died at the age of eighty-two years, August 29, 1893 Solomon and Magdalene Biery were the parents of Catharine, wife of the late Charles F Beck, father of our townsmen, Frank C. and George Beck Solomon Biery was born August 17, 1808, and died January 20, 1874. His mother's maiden name was Salome Knauss

JONAS BIERY was a thrifty farmer and lived in the old farmhouse on Race Street, east of Front, now the possession of August Hohl He owned all the land now covered by the Third Ward and the Howertown Avenue section of the First Ward Lime stone was quarried on his farm for the furnaces, and although his royalty was but three cents per ton it netted him over $40,000 He was born January 28, 1804. April 8, 1827, he was married to Salome Kiechel He died November 28, 1874

DANIEL BIERY tilled his farm near Weaversville, now owned by Peter

J Laubach, for many years David Biery owned a farm near Mickley's and William Biery died while young

FAUST Although there were two brothers, Bastian and John Faust, who, with their families, and upon invitation of William Penn, came from the Palatinate early in the eighteenth century and settled in Albany Township, Berks County, Pa It is surmised that Henry was the son of Mr and Mrs. Bastian Faust This son, Henry, who was the great-grandfather of Paul Faust, purchased the farm of 193½ acres of Robert Gibson He died April 14, 1795

His son, John Philip Faust, one of eight children, gained possession of the homestead and erected the beautiful stone mansion razed but a few years ago by the Bryden Horse Shoe Company in order to make room for the extension of their works

After John's death, about 1831, his son, Jonas Faust, who was one of four surviving children, took the farm at the appraisement of $55 per acre. Jonas Faust was married to Susannah Paul with whom he reared seven children Paul, of Catasauqua, Joseph, of South Whitehall, Reuben, of Catasauqua, David, president of the Union National Bank of Philadelphia, William. of Allentown, Elizabeth (Mrs Laub of Kreidersville), and Maria (Mrs Koch of Allentown) The picture inserted in Chapter XII shows the house and the brothers and sisters at an Old Home gathering some time during the seventies

Upon the death of Jonas Faust, in the fall of 1833, his son Paul took the farm at the appraisement of $50 per acre, January 24, 1834 His grandfather, John, bought five acres of land from George (Yarrick) Rockel, being the ground now bounded by Third Street on the West, Howertown Avenue on the East Pine Street on the South and Walnut Street on the North, and he sold eleven acres along the river-front to the Lehigh Coal and Navigation Company It was necessary for Paul to make himself responsible for three dowers, viz, to his great-grandmother, Catharine, who still lived and occupied a small house at the lower spring, now the site of the F W Wint and Company planing mill, to his grandmother, Barbara, who died October 4, 1842, at the residence of her daughter, the stone house at the Northampton (Stemton) entrance to the bridge across the Lehigh, and to his mother Susannah, who by a second marriage became Mrs Henry Breisch and lived at Third and Bridge Streets on an eleven acre farm, purchased from a Mr Gross

For a man only twenty-four years of age, and at a time when there was a stringency in the money market, to undertake such a proposition was no small matter Mr Faust however was a large-hearted, kind, and, at the same time, a fearless man He was a man of strong physical and mental characteristics. And, although designing and unscrupulous men often imposed upon him, he managed to pay off all his debts and hold a property valued at the close of the War at $75,000. In 1860 he began to sell building lots, the first of which went to the Catholic Church at Second and Chapel Streets

Mr Faust was born September 30, 1809 He married Amelia daughter of George and Polly (nee Wetzell) Breinig, January 6, 1835, and died November 12, 1883, aged 74 years His wife, Amelia, was born in Long Swamp Township, Berks County, Pa, September 7, 1816, and died March 14, 1894, at the age of 77 years There were five children Amy (Mrs Borger) of Peru Ill ; Walter, Jane (Mrs Koehler) of Easton, M Alice, and Clara B (Mrs Nicholas)

BREINIG The remotest ancestor of George Breinig is traced to Longswamp Township, Berks County, Pa The great-grandfather of George was a member of the building committee that erected the original Lehigh Church, near Alburtis, Pa, during 1745 His father's name was George; and his mother's, Elizabeth, a born Egner During his youth he was sent to school in the "Irish Settlement," now the defunct Weaversville Academy, and on his way to and fro he passed the beautiful farm irrigated by the Catasauqua Creek Some years later he purchased this fertile farm of two hundred forty-five acres, in Allen Township, from the estate of Peter Beisel, and took possession of it in 1832 His wife was a Miss Maria Wetsel Their son Simon Breinig, who was born at Mertztown, Pa. October 29, 1827, married Elizabeth Catharine, daughter of Joseph and Elizabeth, nee Ehret, Dech, February 13, 1862, and succeeded his father on the farm George Breinig died June 2, 1871, at the age of eighty years. He served as a member of the Building Committee of St Paul's Lutheran Church He was a strong, intelligent and self-reliant man. His son Simon farmed the old place for many years After his son Joseph entered into matrimony, Simon retired, leaving the farm in his son's care Simon Breinig died January 7, 1906, seventy-eight years of age

JOHN GEORGE KURTZ The pioneer of the Kurtz family in this section was John George Kurtz He settled in Hanover Township on the east bank of the Catasauqua Creek, in 1760 The wooded expanse of country extending to and far beyond Schoenersville was styled "Dry-lands" since this whole territory has no springs or rills, and during drought seasons of the year cattle had to be driven to the Lehigh River for water After Mr Kurtz had erected his house (now the stone house near the Rubber Works), he brought his family from the Fatherland In 1839 the large farm was divided into two sections One son, Henry, took the western, another, George, the eastern portion For many years these gentlemen refused to sell land for building lots, which shows why the Third Ward extends off toward the east like a thumb on a hand (the fingers being Catasauqua proper) While negotiations were going on for the purchase of the plot of ground on which St Paul's Lutheran Church now stands, Lydia, the wife of Henry Kurtz, threatened to scald with boiling water the gentlemen who came to bargain for the same.

JACOB DEILY wooed and won Miss Mary Geissinger, daughter of George and Christian (nee Hartman) Geissinger of Upper Saucon, Lehigh County, Pa., and was married March 17, 1813 Mr Deily was born September 15, 1789, and his wife, October 9, 1794. The newly married couple began housekeeping on Lehigh Hill, Allentown where Mr Deily worked as a cobbler Mrs Deily's father bought the George Taylor farm from John Beisel, June 13, 1821, after which Mr and Mrs Deily moved to the farm with their family George Taylor was one of the signers of the Declaration of Independence, and very probably built the stone farm house still standing above the southeastern corner of the Wahnetah Silk Mill The farm consisted of one hundred fifty acres of land which was very productive and soon placed Mr Deily upon his feet. The children whom they brought to maturity were George, Sarah, Mrs Rudolph Kent, of Philadelphia, Eliza, Mrs Daniel Levan, of Siegfrieds, Maria, Mrs Samuel Colver, of Allentown, Francis J ; Matilda, Mrs Robert Jaeger of Allentown, Solomon, and Clara, Mrs Edward Brown, of Bethlehem, Pa David Thomas and his family ate their first dinner at Catasauqua at the guests of Mr and Mrs Jacob Deily Mr Deily died May 14, 1881, at the age of ninety-one years, and his wife died March 26, 1883, at the age of eighty-eight years

GEORGE DEILY was born in Allentown, September 2, 1815, and worked on the farm for his father for fifteen years after he had reached his majority. In 1851 his father, Jacob Deily, "set him up in business" as merchant in a general store in the beautifully cut stone building now owned by George B F Deily on Race Street at the Canal Bridge His predecessors were James Lackey and Joseph Laubach The Deily store was a popular trading place and its shrewd proprietor rapidly accumulated wealth. The freshet of 1862 filled the first floor of the building with water to within but a few inches of the ceiling, and destroyed the whole stock Mr Deily disposed of his stock and converted the store room into the parlor of his home, and devoted all his time to overseeing his farms lying east of Catasauqua At the time of his death he owned five large farms He entered into matrimony with Elizabeth, daughter of Gen Benjamin Fogel and his wife Anna (nee Trexler) of Fogelsville, June 2, 1857, Their children are. Mary C , who was born July 14, 1858, and since July 3, 1889, is the wife of Peter J Laubach, who is her senior by six months from January 20 of the year of her birth, and George B F , who was born August 14, 1865 George Deily died at the age of eighty-seven years, November 17, 1902, and his widow died at the age of seventy-three years, October 4, 1831

FRANCIS J. DEILY was born July 31, 1824 Like his brothers, he worked on the farm, and after his father's decease bought it March 17, 1884 His brother, Solomon, who remained a bachelor all his life, stayed with Francis and his family and worked on the farm Later Solomon became a drover, and Francis and he butchered and peddled meat in and around Catasauqua Thus the brothers accumulated considerable property

Francis was married to Sarah A , daughter of Rudolph and Salome (nee Best) Dech of the vicinage of Bath, Pa , October 19, 1858 Their only child was Camilla E , who was born in the old Taylor house, September 5, 1863 She became the wife of Dr Charles E Milson, October 21, 1884, and became the mother of four daughters: Gertrude A., Helen C , Ruth D , and Marie.

Mr Deily built the beautiful brick home opposite the old farm house and retired early in the seventies Here he died October 9, 1897, at the age of seventy-seven years

JOHN PETER John Peter came from Heidelberg where he was born in 1799 His house stood in the Crane yards at a point west of the Express office He purchased his farm from Andrew Hower, the heirs of John Philip Faust, and others, and took possession of the same in 1823 His original dwelling was erected by John Youndt. Later he erected a stone mansion on Front Street above Walnut, now a part of the stables of F W Wint and Company He devoted nine years to weaving After the canal was completed he served the Company as lock-tender for some years That portion of his farm which had not been acquired by the Lehigh Coal and Navigation Company or sold into building lots he sold to David Thomas in 1851 He lived in Bethlehem until the death of his wife, when he made his home with his daughter, Mrs Owen Swartz, at Allentown, where he died at an advanced age Their children were· Franklin, Joseph, Susannah, and Mersena

JONATHAN SNYDER Another contemporary of the originals of Catasauqua was Jonathan Snyder, who came from Schoenersville, Pa. Mr Snyder was a bright man and an exceptionally fine penman He was given charge of the locks opposite the Crane Iron Works in 1839, and commissioned to collect all tolls for this section of the canal When the town became a Borough, he was elected and served as assessor for many years His only survivors are his grandchildren, the members of the Williams family at Second and Bridge Streets

DAVID THOMAS He whom a grateful people delight to call the Father of Catasauqua is David Thomas "Father Thomas" was a pioneer in founding many institutions in our town He was brought to this country to make iron with anthracite ("Stone-coal") coal, and although not the first in this country to use this material in the manufacture of iron, he was the first to make a successful use of it in a commercial way, wherefore he is affectionately styled the "Father of the American Anthracite Iron Industry " His mind and soul were not entirely absorbed in and welded into pigs of iron, but he enjoyed a broad and lofty outlook into divine and eternal things. Simultaneously with the furnaces, came the erection of a church (House of prayer) under his direction. Through the furnaces his men merited bread for the body and through the Church the Father of Lights gave Bread and all good gifts to His believing people. Father Thomas began the erection of homes for working people. He laid the first water mains that served a municipality with a necessary commodity. He erected the first public time piece, the sun-dial. His pen draughted many

DAVID THOMAS

ordinances for Borough regulation and legislation, which are still potent.

"Father Thomas" was the only son of his parents, David and Jane Thomas of Tyllwyd (Gray House), in the parish of Cadoxtan, Glamorganshire, South Wales, and was born November 3, 1794. When he was a youth of seventeen summers, he found employment in the machine shop of the Neath Abbey Iron Works. Six years later, 1817, Richard Parsons, the owner of the Yniscedwyn Iron Works, invited young Thomas to the superintendency of his works, including also the coal and iron mines. He held this position for twenty-two years.

Efforts were made in America to manufacture iron with anthracite coal in a number of places, but success had not thus far crowned the work. Mr Thomas experimented with hot blast stoves invented by James Neilson, in 1828, at the Yniscedwyn furnace. He obtained plans and a license from Mr Neilson to erect hot blast ovens by means of which, February 7, 1838, he declared the problem of the production of iron with hard coal practically solved. The Yniscedwyn furnace produced from thirty-four to thirty-six tons a week.

News of this success soon reached America, where able and enterprising men stood ready to utilize this valuable discovery. The Lehigh Coal and Navigation Company promptly arranged to send its representative, Erskine Hazard, to Wales, where he arrived, November, 1838, to investigate and study the operation of the new hot blast. After satisfying himself that Mr Thomas had solved the important problem, Mr Hazard entered into an agreement with him on behalf of the Lehigh Crane Iron Company to come to America and to erect and to operate blast furnaces, suitable for anthracite coal, on the Lehigh River.

Early in May the young iron master with his family consisting of his wife, Elizabeth, nee Hopkins, three sons—Samuel, John, and David Jr., and two daughters—Jane and Gwenllian (the latter, the wife of Joshua Hunt) set sail from Swansea bound for Liverpool, where they embarked on the clipper ship "Roscuis" for America. They arrived at Allentown, July 9, 1839. On July 11, with his son Samuel, he came on foot to Craneville (Catasauqua) then a primeval forest. By July 3, 1840, the first furnace was completed and in blast. The Crane Iron Company erected a home for him on Front Street directly opposite the furnaces. Mr Thomas occupied this dwelling with his family until 1856, when he moved into his new home erected by him on Second and Pine Streets.

The influence of Mr Thomas as an iron master extended far and wide. He was a promoter of the large iron works at Hokendauqua. He bore a large share of the enterprise that opened railroads, ore and coal mines, and stone quarries. He took a great interest in the political, financial, religious, and charitable institutions of the town. He was a consistent member of the Presbyterian Church and an ardent supporter of the local Total Abstinence Society. He died June 20, 1882, in the eighty-eighth year of his age, and his body rests in the Thomas vault in Fairview Cemetery.

SAMUEL THOMAS. Inspired by the example of a noble father, the "Father of the Anthracite Iron Industry in America," Samuel Thomas never departed from the sphere of an iron merchant. Although engaged in many and various enterprises he devoted most of his time and strength to the welfare of the Thomas Iron Company.

Samuel Thomas, son of David and Elizabeth (nee Hopkins) Thomas was born in Yniscedwyn, Brecknockshire, South Wales, March 13, 1827, and at the age of thirteen years his parents brought him to this country. He had studied English in Wales, and when the family was settled in Catasauqua, he was sent to school for two years at Nazareth Hall, Nazareth, Pa. Upon his return from school he entered the blacksmith and machine shops of the Crane Iron Works and learnt his trade. At the age of but nineteen years, he already took an active part in the management of the works. In 1848 he superintended the erection of a furnace for the Boonton Iron Company in Morristown, N. J. By October of that year the furnace was in blast. At the close of the year he returned to erect furnaces No. 4 and 5 at home. When the Thomas Iron Company was chartered during the winter of 1853 and 1854, and two hundred acres of land purchased at Hokendauqua for the erection of furnaces, Mr. Thomas was appointed superintendent, March 1, 1854. He erected two furnaces forthwith, and served the Company as superintendent for ten years. He was chosen a director of the Company and elected its president August 31, 1864. He organized the Lock Ridge Iron Company at Alburtis, Pa., and erected the first furnace in 1867. In company with his father he visited a section now known as Thomas in Alabama, in May, 1868, for the purpose of exploiting. In August of this year he went again and purchased large tracts of mineral lands. Mr. Thomas resigned the presidency of the Thomas Iron Company September 22, 1887, in order to devote himself to the erection of an iron plant in the South. His long cherished desire was brought to a successful issue under the management of his son Edwin as vice-president. The first furnace was built at Thomas, near

SAMUEL THOMAS

Birmingham, Alabama, under the name of the Pioneer Mining and Manufacturing Company. There were two furnaces, coke ovens, and coal and iron mines. The property was sold in 1899 to the Republic Iron and Steel Company.

Mr. Thomas was a keen student, a close observer and an able writer. His masterpiece was written on "Reminiscences of the Early Anthracite Iron Industry" and read by him before the American Institute of Mining Engineers at the California meeting in September, 1899. Like his father, Mr. Thomas took an active and effective interest in community affairs in Hokendauqua as well as in Catasauqua. He contributed liberally toward the erection of the Soldiers' Monument in Fairview Cemetery, made from designs approved by him, in memory of the brave men from Catasauqua and environs, who fought for the preservation of the Union, and this was the first erected soldiers' monument after the Civil War. Although he took a live interest in political affairs and voted with the Republican party, he never aspired for office. For many years he was an Elder in the First Presbyterian Church which he supported with a liberal hand. Mr. Thomas found his pleasing recreation in travel. He visited the scenes of his childhood on various occasions. A study of the architectural ruins of Syria and Egypt impressed him most profoundly.

He wedded Miss Rebecca Mickley, daughter of Mr. and Mrs. Jacob Mickley of Mickley's, Pa., in March, 1848. To this union two children were born: Gertrude, wife of Dr. Joseph C. Guernsey of Philadelphia, and Edwin of Catasauqua. Mrs. Thomas departed this life in the fall of 1891. In the spring of 1894 Mr. Thomas married Miss Julia M. Beerstecher, a native of Neuveville, Switzerland. He died February 21, 1906, and his remains rest in the Thomas vault in Fairview Cemetery.

EDWIN THOMAS

EDWIN THOMAS. Edwin Thomas, grandson of David, was born in Catasauqua April 9, 1853. He attended the public schools of town, prepared for college at Swarthmore, and entered Lafayette College with the class of 1873.

Upon leaving college he entered the employ of the Thomas Iron Company at Hokendauqua as machinist. After a service of three years he was placed in charge of the Company's plant at Lock Ridge, Pa., as superintendent. He retained this position for three years, when he accepted the superintendency of the furnaces of the Chestnut Hill Iron Ore Company, at Columbia, Pa. After two years he returned to the Hokendauqua plant of the Thomas Iron Company to serve for four years as purchasing agent and manager of the mechanical department.

In the Spring of 1886, he went South when the industrial spirit was just awakening, to assist the President of the Pioneer Mining and Manufacturing Company at Thomas, Ala., to design and to erect the plant. He served this company as President from 1892 to 1899, when the plant was sold. Under the new ownership he served as manager for one year, when he resigned and returned to Catasauqua.

Mr. Thomas is President of the Catasauqua National Bank; the Nescopec Coal Company; Director of the Upper Lehigh Coal Company; the Wahnetah Silk Company; the Thomas Iron Company; and a number of other industrial enterprises. He takes an active part in all municipal affairs and aids with a liberal hand any and every movement that tends to develop the Borough.

WILLIAM R. THOMAS. William R. Thomas, son of Hopkin Thomas, was born in Glamorganshire, Wales, May 30, 1829, and is at this writing one of the oldest residents and one of the finest mechanics in Catasauqua. When a boy his parents came to America and located for a time in Philadelphia. Afterward they moved to Beaver Meadows, where William R. received his education in the district schools. When he was sixteen years of age, he learned the machinist's trade in the shops located there. He remained at home until he was twenty years of age, when, having a strong desire to perfect himself in his line of work, he went to New York City where he received special instruction in the navy yards. After working here for two years, he went to La Salle County, Ill., and then to Amboy, where he engaged as an engineer on the Illinois Central Railroad, his run being between that city and Centralia.

WILLIAM R. THOMAS

On account of failing health, Mr Thomas returned east and joined his family, who had in the meantime moved to Catasauqua, Pa After he regained his health, he entered the employ of the Crane Iron Co as master mechanic, remaining with them until 1868, when he became a partner in the McKee, Fuller Company He was superintendent of the plant for two years, when he became connected with the Coleraine Iron Works in the erection of furnaces, managing their workshop until 1875. From this time until March, 1887, he was in the South, building furnaces and superintending mines in Georgia and Alabama, was superintendent of the Coleraine Iron Co, and later of the Thomas Iron Co, with whom he remained for seven years He was superintendent of the Crane Iron Works from 1887 to 1891, when in company with A and C H Fuller, he started the Globe Metal Works, remaining with them for one year Since that time he has been connected with the Davies and Thomas Company

William R Thomas was united in marriage in Janesville, Pa, in 1856, to Miss Martha Mayhew, a native of England Nine children were born to them as follows Frank H (deceased), James J, who lives at home, Kate (Thomas) Agthe (deceased); John W, of Littlestown, Pa, Helen, who also resides at home, William R, Jr, of Catasauqua, Ira (Thomas) Hawkins of Kingston, Pa, Mary (Thomas) Corsa of Amherst, Mass, and Fritz W, of Chester Pa

Mr Thomas is a Free and Accepted Mason, a Royal Arch Mason and Knight Templar Politically he is a Republican, and, although he does not take any active interest in political affairs, he maintains a deep interest in everything which promotes the best interests of the municipality Mr Thomas has a large circle of acquaintances whose friendship he has won through his integrity and genial social characteristics

JAMES THOMAS James Thomas was born in Philadelphia, September 22, 1836, and was the youngest son of Hopkin Thomas and his wife Catherine (Richards) Thomas, both of South Wales In 1853 he came with his parents to Catasauqua from Philadelphia He went to Parryville in 1859 to take the superintendency of the Carbon Iron Works In 1871 Mr Thomas left Parryville and

JAMES THOMAS

went to Jefferson County, Alabama, and while there became the general manager of the Irondale and Eureka Iron Company. He enjoys the distinction of having made the first coke iron in Alabama. In 1879 he returned to Catasauqua and formed a partnership with George Davies, under the name of Davies and Thomas, which continued until the death of George Davies in 1894. The following year the heirs of George Davies and the surviving member of the firm, James Thomas, took out articles of incorporation under the laws of the State of Pennsylvania with the corporate name of Davies and Thomas Company.

With every enterprise calculated to promote the prosperity of Catasauqua, Mr. Thomas was prominently identified and received the heartiest support. Through his efforts the Borough secured the Electric Light and Power Company of which he was one of the principal owners. He was president of the Wahnetah Silk Company and a director of the Catasauqua National Bank. Though he took no active part in politics, he was frequently chosen to occupy positions of trust and responsibility, and represented the Republican Party as delegate to the National Convention in Minneapolis in 1892. For six years he was a member of the School Board, taking an active interest in the welfare of our schools.

Mr. Thomas was married to Miss Mary Ann Davies, June 11, 1861. They are the parents of the following children: Blanche T., wife of Charles R. Horn; Mary C. Thomas (deceased); Rowland D. Thomas; Mrs. Ruth (Thomas) McKee; Helen T., wife of Dr. James L. Hornbeck; Catherine R. Thomas (deceased); Hopkin Thomas.

In religious belief, Mr. Thomas was a member of Grace Methodist Episcopal Church and was instrumental in securing the erection of the edifice adorning the corner of Fifth and Walnut Streets. Mr. Thomas was one of the best informed men, reading broadly upon all matters of general interest and carrying his investigations into the best of literature He was public-spirited, which, together with his high social standing and courteous manners, made him a very popular and honored citizen

FREDERICK George Frederick, the first, lived in lower Saucon Township, Northampton County, Pa His wife was Magdalena Ebert Their son George, the second, was born September 26, 1788. On July 29, 1810, he was married to Hannah Haas with whom he reared seven children. Mary Magdalena, wife of Solomon Biery, George, Nathan, who died at Allentown, Thomas, Owen, the undertaker, Hannah, Mrs Robert Steckle, who is still living at Allentown, and Pauline, Mrs Owen Diefenderfer, who died at Fullerton

George Frederick moved to Catasauqua with his family in 1828, and occupied the newly acquired farm, and the stone house that stood on the West Side, below the Hercules Metal Works, close by the L. V. R R tracks Mr Frederick was a man of some literary ability, and gifted with sound sense and a good judgment He was elected Justice of the Peace for North and South Whitehall Township, May 21, 1834 In October, 1836, he was elected a member of the House of Representatives of the State of Pennsylvania. Upon his return from the Legislature he retired from the farm and moved to Biery's-Port, now Front Street, below Union, and his son George took charge of the farm From 1853 to 1855 and from 1858 to 1863 he served as Justice of the Peace in town He died January 20, 1871 His wife, Hannah, died March 8, 1853, and hers was the first grave dug in the grave-yard at St Paul's Ev Lutheran Church The old grave-yard has long since been converted into a beautiful lawn

His son Owen, born January 27, 1822, was educated in the district schools, and, in 1839, he went to Easton to learn the trade of a cabinet and coffin maker After having served his full time of four years, he went to New York City where he spent five years working at his trade While in New York he met and married Miss Jeanette Bogardus, July 29, 1847 In 1847 he moved to Catasauqua and occupied the house still standing in the rear of the establishment of Frederick and Scherer, the Undertakers, and began the business which the present firm is carrying on successfully Mr Frederick was funeral director at a time during which there came a rapid transition from quaint old customs to many new fashions He was the first undertaker in this community to use a hearse. In his day bodies were preserved until funeral day by means of an ice-box as is described in the chapter of Reminiscences Besides conducting the undertaking business, Mr Frederick also established the furniture business, which in those days meant cabinet making. Hand made bed-steads, bureaus, chairs, grandfather clock cases, etc , beautifully inlaid, gracefully designed and substantially built, are scarce articles today because everybody wants them and is willing to pay fabulous prices for them

Owen Frederick died February 11, 1878, at the age of fifty-six years, and left his bereaved widow with the following children George, Mary Alice, Mrs Henry A Steward (who succeeded her father in business), Ogden E , who with William H Scherer succeeded Mr Steward, and Hannah L

George Frederick is father of three children. Mary (Mrs Gardner), Floyd and Ralph Mary Alice Steward has a son, Frederick A , and a daughter, Mrs Emma J Davis

Ogden E Frederick was born June 21, 1852 After his school days he worked with his father at the trade. In 1878 he was placed in charge of Fuller's book store, which he ran for seven years Since Henry A Steward's death, he is the senior partner in the firm of Frederick and Scherer

Mr Frederick married Miss Clara C Fuller, February 2, 1875 Their daughter, Tillie C , is the wife of Dr Wesley Willoughby.

T F FREDERICK While memory lingers upon a character like Tilghman F Frederick, one is constrained to say He sought not his own glory and yet was ceaselessly active for the delights and comforts of his home, the prosperity of his community and the upbuilding and maintenance of his Church

Mr Frederick was born in the old farm house below the Hercules Metal Works on the West Side, January 29, 1849. His parents were George Frederick and his wife Elizabeth, a born Reichard Father and Mother having died while he was a lad, Tilghman was reared by his uncle and aunt, Mr. and Mrs Solomon Biery. The district school provided him with his education, which he greatly prized and on account of which he was a staunch advocate of the system of public instruction. In 1862 and '63 he acted as drummer in the 176th Regiment Pennsylvania Drafted Militia.

After his return from the Army he became chief clerk for Frederick and Beck in the Car Construction Shops at Fullerton. When he had saved some money he took a course in the Eastman Business College at Poughkeepsie, N. Y., where he perfected himself as one of the finest penmen and accountants in the Lehigh Valley. He taught school two terms in Catasauqua, and one term on the West Side; and then learnt the trade of a machinist at the Crane Works.

T. F. FREDERICK

Having finished his apprenticeship he entered the employ of the Catasauqua Manufacturing Company, where he remained until the Bryden Horse Shoe Works were started. At first he assisted Peter F. Greenwood, the superintendent of the new works. After the latter's retirement, in 1882, Mr. Frederick was placed in charge of the same and remained in the employ of the company until his death.

Mr. Frederick was a member of Town Council for many years, and took an active interest in municipal affairs. He was a prime mover in securing the Pine Street bridge. Active as a fireman, he was a member of the Phoenix Steam Fire Company, No. 1, and president of that Association for many years. He was one of the originators and officers of the building associations of our town.

He was active not only in material affairs, but also in those things which abide forever. He was a member of the Council of St. Paul's Lutheran Church for many years, and served the congregation in an official way in all the departments of her work. What is true of the Church is emphatically so as regards the Sunday School of which he was Superintendent, clerk and teacher for over forty-five years.

He was married to Mary J , daughter of Mr and Mrs. Charles Andreas of Allentown, January 27, 1869 To this union were born and survive Charles E , Mary E., Mrs Frank J Reeves of Philadelphia, Harry, Alice C , Mrs Adam W Pflieger of York, Pa , and Agnes A Mr Frederick died March 31, 1909, at the age of sixty years

ROBERT McINTYRE Robert McIntyre was born in Glack, Ireland, May 10, 1814 His father, George McIntyre, a descendant of a long line of "Covenanters," was a man of note in the community Older step-brothers were in America and hearing much of the water-works for New York, then in course of construction, young Robert at the age of seventeen ran away from school to the nearby town of Moville, sneaked on board the "Progress" (a boat which made the Atlantic trip in eight weeks) and landed in New York without money or friends He got to George Clark, who with other young men had been aided by the elder McIntyre to come to America, and was cared for and allowed to handle the reins of a four-horse team This team conveyed the workmen from the "shanties" to the Water Works. When the news of the boy's arrival reached his father, there was much rejoicing but Robert could not be induced to return to his home and school He remained several years with Mr Clark of Holmesburg, who was already a wealthy man and contractor of the Water Works

The boy saved his earnings, which his father had promised to duplicate, and when the output of coal in and about Mauch Chunk began to attract attention, Robert McIntyre went there and began business for himself Here he met Marie Enbody, who, in later years, became his wife and the mother of eleven children Prior to the opening of the Crane Works, Mr McIntyre came to Catasauqua and his oldest son was born in the stone house at the Whitehall entrance to the bridge He built the big red barn on that property, sold the original Fairview Cemetery to James W Fuller, Sr , erected the first Jordan Bridge of the C & F R R , and sections of the "Lehigh Valley "

When the first Crane Bridge was thrown across the Lehigh, its piers abutted on his property. Litigation followed and in the Court House Records is the chronicle of an unusual and unique agreement signed by Crane officials of that day and on which Judge Trexler gave a forceful opinion in recent years

Robert McIntyre founded Porter Lodge, called it and his second son after James Madison Porter of Easton, was its first "Worshipful Master" and remained a strong advocate of the Order during his life When John Peter sold the original tract of land for Church and School purposes, Mr McIntyre paid one-half the cost and David Thomas one-half When the "Old School" separated from the "New School" Presbyterians, he saw to it that an equal division was made both of land and moneys, notwithstanding some strenuous objections thereto

He built the stone bridge over the Conemaugh, the only one to withstand the "Johnstown Flood" and when the Washington Aqueduct was planned by Montgomery C Meigs, he was its foremost contractor The immense bond required by the government was furnished by brethren of outside Masonic Orders Cabin John Bridge, a section of the supply aqueduct, is one hundred feet above the roadway and has a length of four hundred fifty feet Of it, in a recent issue, the "Philadelphia Times" says, "It is one of the sights of Washington, it is still the longest single span stone arch in the world, is one of the most daring feats of engineering skill in this country and stands to-day a magnificent monument to its builders"

A strong friendship for Stephen A Douglas led Mr McIntyre to purchase much land in Illinois and in 1865, he began the erection of a fine residence now in the city limits of Quincy In 1866, he removed from Catasauqua and several years later disposed of his farms in this section When he died in 1875, he was said to be the "richest man in Adams County" Reserved to a marked degree, a master in his judgment of men, loyal to his kin and countrymen, caustic in wit, he won a confidence and financial standing second to none of all the "early timers" in the town of Catasauqua

JOHN McINTYRE John McIntyre left Ireland in 1832, came to Philadelphia and for a number of years served as bookkeeper for Richard Clarke, contractor He married Jane Noblett of that city and some time after came to Catasauqua Here he entered the employ of the Crane Iron Company as shipper on its wharves and was prominent in all town affairs

He was a charter member of its first Church and when the village became a borough was elected to the Board of School Directors A number of houses on Church Street were owned by him, and when too old for active work, the Crane Company granted him a pension which he enjoyed while he lived His death occurred in 1887 when he had reached the age of eighty-seven

JOHN HUNTER. John Hunter was another Scotch Irishman who rose to prominence in this community He came direct from Ireland to Catasauqua in 1844, invested in canal boats and towed coal from Mauch Chunk to the Crane Works He attracted the attention of Superintendent Thomas and, therefore, did much contract work around the furnaces In 1852 he married the sister of Dr F W. Quig who was the regular physician employed by the Crane Company. He acquired considerable property and was noted for his ever-ready, helping hand to poorer people

WILLIAM McCLELLAN In December, 1851, William McClellan was chosen elder of the First Presbyterian Church His wife was Margaret Smiley and they raised a large family, each of whom was given a college degree The wife of John Houston was sister to McClellan and both names were prominent in the early days of the town There were several families of McClellans in those days and because they attended First Church, this branch was known as the "Welsh McClellans" Some of the sons are still living and each has attained prominence in his profession. With a number of other Scotch-Irish people, they were among the first to remove to Adams County, Illinois

WILLIAM PHILLIPS William Phillips was born in Wales, January 10, 1797. He emigrated to America in 1838 and settled in Tamaqua, Pa When David Thomas, Superintendent of the Crane Iron Company, heard of him and learned of his ability, he asked Mr Phillips to come to Catasauqua He arrived in 1840 and was employed as a keeper of the furnace He and Evan Jones were the keepers of the furnace when the first cast of iron was made, July 4, 1840

Mr Phillips was married to an estimable lady in Wales and their union was blessed with seven children, one daughter (afterwards Mrs Charles W. Chapman) was the only one born in America He continued a faithful and trusted employee of the Crane Company to the time of his death, May 19, 1867.

JOHN HUDDERS. John Hudders, a direct descendant of Michael Clyde, one of the original Irish Settlement leaders, who, coming from Ulster in 1728, bought rich land in Northampton County. He was brought to Catasauqua as bookkeeper for Robert McIntyre and for many years had charge of the Lehigh Valley Railroad depot. He taught school, was leader of the choir and elder of the Presbyterian Church, and lived to a good old age, honored and respected.

FREDERICK EBERHARD was born in Stuttgard, Wurtemberg, Germany, March 5, 1809. He learnt the trade of a copper smith in his native land. At the age of twenty-one he arrived in Philadelphia, where he found employment with the construction gang that built the first railroad between Philadelphia and Baltimore. Later he came to Mauch Chunk from which place he went out to work in the coal mines at Summit Hill.

FREDERICK EBERHARD

Coal and other produce was floated down the Lehigh and Delaware rivers to Philadelphia on barges or "Arks" as some people called them, and seeing profit in the business, Mr. Eberhard and a companion secured two mules and started in to float barges. This was done before the canal was constructed. The barge was loaded, and then two mules placed on the front end of it, and the trip was begun. When the water was high the movement was rapid, but when the water was low and the current sluggish the trip was tedious. After Philadelphia was reached both cargo and barge were sold and the boatmen started to ride back astride the mules, anxious to begin another trip. Mr. Eberhard however, purchased jewelry of all descriptions in the city and employed his time on the return trip by peddling his wares.

In about 1831 he went to work in the copper mines at Flemington, N. J. Here he met and married Miss Catherine, daughter of Peter Tillman and wife (nee Miller), in 1832, whereupon he moved into a small house at Dry Run close to where the trolley bridge now stands. For a while he made trips to Mauch Chunk where he labored as a blacksmith, twenty-six days for a month, at $18. When the erection of the furnaces began, Mr. Eberhard was employed to open and quarry stone at the pit above the Hokendauqua bridge. This is now the St. Lawrence quarry. Practically all of the stone used to build the first five furnaces at Front Street was quarried here by Mr. Eberhard, and the stone floated down the canal on barges. Mr. Eberhard contracted with the Crane Company for lime stone to be used in smelting iron, this he quarried out of the pit on Jonas Biery's farm, which now is the property of the Davies & Thomas Company. It was at this time that Mr. Eberhard erected his home on the corner of Front and Mulberry Streets, into which he moved his family. He also opened a quarry and, by so doing, prepared the site of the Lehigh Valley depot. This stone was hauled in small narrow-gauge cars drawn by mules over a bridge to the furnaces.

In 1864 Mr. Eberhard retired and moved to Second and Turner Streets, Allentown. In 1880 he bought the Peter Miller farm of 76 acres in Whitehall Township beyond the Round-house of the C. & F. R. R., and opened stone quarries. He also moved his family to this beautiful spot. Mr. Eberhard accumulated a great deal of property. He held stocks in the Lehigh Valley R. R., the Lehigh Coal Company, the Allentown National Bank, the Thomas Iron Company, the Wahnetah Silk Mill, and was a charter member of the Catasauqua Gas Company. He was a shrewd business man, a staunch Republican, and a firm confessor of his faith as set forth in the Augsburg Confession. He died June 24, 1893, at the age of eighty-four years. Mrs. Eberhard died August 7, 1881, at the age of sixty-seven years. The children whom they brought to maturity were: Eliza, Mrs. William Easterday, John, who was burnt with powder in the quarry in 1857, Ferdinand, William, who was killed in the quarry at the Iron Bridge, May 13, 1898, Ellen C., Mrs. Charles Snyder, Franklin, and Peter J.

FERDINAND EBERHARD was born September 25, 1837, at Dry Run. After his school days at Dry Run and Deily's School House, he entered into the quarry business with his father at the age of fifteen years. His particular duty was to superintend the drilling of holes into rocks, loading and setting off the blast. At the age of twenty-six years he succeeded his father in the business. The Jonas Biery quarry was abandoned because the town authorities objected to the blasting. In 1867 he contracted with the Thomas Iron Company for operations in the quarry at the Iron Bridge. The Eberhards quarried the stone for the Hokendauqua as well as for the Catasauqua furnaces. The stone for the two furnaces erected at Hokendauqua in 1871 was shipped from the Jordan Bridge quarry. Mr. Eberhard bought the first case of dynamite used in this locality. It was called "dualin" and sold at $1.25 per pound. His sons are still running the quarry on the farm in Whitehall Township.

FERDINAND EBERHARD

Mr. Eberhard was married to Miss Sarah A. Kean in 1864, who died in February, 1891; and late in 1892, he married Miss Mary R. Lambert. The children whom they brought to maturity are Carrie M., Mrs. Kemmerer; William F.; Franklin J.; George W.; and Edward H. Mr. Eberhard is a member of Porter Lodge, No. 284, since 1871, and of Grace M. E. Church.

PETER J. EBERHARD was born, April 25, 1850. School days being ended, January 1, 1869, he began to learn the art of telegraphy at the Lehigh Valley depot. In May of the same year he became assistant to John Hudders whom he succeeded in later years. After six years of service he was given the position of yard master at the Valley depot. When more help was employed at the station, Mr. Eberhard was entrusted with the ticket office wherein he served for many years. In all he served the Company for over forty years.

He entered into matrimony with Josephine, daughter of Mr. and Mrs. Aaron Bast, June 7, 1873. Their children are: Ellen J.; Frederick A.; Estella I.; Charles A.; Katie E.; Robert J.; and Emma J.

JAMES W. FULLER. The subject of this sketch was prominently known as the promoter of many business enterprises that have contributed in a large measure to the commercial and industrial activity and consequent prosperity of Catasauqua and the Lehigh Valley. The ancestry of the family can be traced back in a direct line to Robert Fuller, whose oldest child, Edward Fuller, was the patriarch of the family in America. He was a native of Norfolk, England. About 1607 he went to Holland with his brother, who was a physician. The name of Edward Fuller appears as the twenty-first signer of the compact drawn up on board the "Mayflower" previous to the landing of her passengers at Plymouth Rock.

JAMES W. FULLER

Chauncy Dorrance Fuller, the grandfather of James W. Fuller, was the son of Jehile Fuller of Connecticut. The former was born in western Pennsylvania, and his son, James W. Fuller, 1st, and father of the subject of this sketch, was born in Luzerne County, Pa., August 22, 1821. He married Clarissa, daughter of Henry and Catharine (nee Sterner) Miller, November 8, 1840. Abiel Abbott secured him as an employee of the Lehigh Canal Company. From 1855 to 1865 he served as Justice of the Peace. While a member of the State Legislature in the beginning of the fifties, David Thomas prevailed upon him to pray for a charter for the construction of the C. and F. R. R. During the Civil War Mr. Fuller became prominently identified with the political and military affairs of Pennsylvania and his influence with the Republican administration was generally recognized. He died November 22, 1872, at the age of fifty-one years and three months.

JAMES W. FULLER, 2nd, was born of these parents, March 16, 1843. He attended the public schools of town and private schools at Weaversville, Norristown and Kingston, Pa. At the age of eighteen he enlisted with the Boys in Blue, and became a member of Company I, 47th Regiment, Pennsylvania Infantry, under the command of Captain Henry S. Harte. He was promoted and mustered in as sergeant August 30, 1861. On October 30 of the same year he was elevated to the rank of adjutant. After a protracted illness, which overtook him during the first winter of the Civil War in Virginia, he was honorably discharged from the army and returned to his home.

JAMES W. FULLER, 2nd

For the next three years Mr. Fuller was salesman of queensware for a Philadelphia house. In 1868 he returned to Catasauqua, where he organized the firm of McKee, Fuller and Company, proprietors of the Car, Wheel and Axle Works. Beginnings of the plant had been made during the year preceding by Charles D. Fuller, an uncle, and William R. Thomas. The capacity of the shop at this time was fifteen wheels per day. The new firm at once commenced to enlarge the plant. They bought the defunct concern of Frederick and Company, built a forge and added an axle department. Since then the firm was known as the Lehigh Car, Wheel and Axle Works, and developed an enterprise of extensive benefit to the business prosperity of the community.

The town of Fullerton was laid out by Mr. Fuller in 1870 and was named in his honor. So devoted was he to his charge that he made his daily trips to the works, personally superintended the mixing of irons for the casting of the wheels, and made the rounds among his men in whose individual welfare he was vitally concerned. His advice was sought in many spheres and his opinions were valued. He was President of the Catasauqua Manufacturing Company; a director in the Thomas Iron Company, the Wahnetah Silk Company, and the Ironton Railroad. At the time of his death he was Vice-President of the Empire Steel and Iron Company and a director in the Lehigh Foundry Company.

He was married to Miss Kate M., daughter of Mr. and Mrs. Hopkin Thomas in 1864. Five children came to grace their happy home: George Llewellyn, who died at the age of twenty-one, Maud, the wife of J S Elverson, Blanche, Mrs Dr L A Salade, Mary Louise, Mrs H D McCaskey; and Lieut. Colonel James W. Fuller, 3rd He died, January 15, 1910, at the age of sixty-seven years, and his body lies buried in Fairview Cemetery.

A PERSONAL TRIBUTE

After Mr Fuller's death William H Glace, Esq., his friend for fifty years and his companion in sickness in the garret of a Virginia farm shack during the winter of 1863-1864, paid him a beautiful tribute. Mr Glace wrote:

> . "Owing to the forethought of his uncle, Lieut Geo W Fuller, a victim of the same war, two young girls, daughters of the owner, Mr Wren, attended us through that long siege of sickness where we lay nigh to death many weeks After a tedious convalescence, he recovered only in a measure, and was honorably discharged, whilst I recovered to serve the full period of three years
> In 1891 he said to me, 'I wonder what became of the Wren girls, let us go down and see.' We went to Washington and drove up along the Potomac to the Chain Bridge, thence over into Fairfax County, Virginia, and as we came near the place we could not fix our surroundings, as large trees had grown where there had been farm land, and we stopped at a farm house, when a man over thirty-five years of age, a Mr Catlin, came out, and we inquired if that house on the hill was the Wren house, and whether the 47th Pennsylvania Regiment and 7th Maine Regiment had encamped on yonder slope the first winter of the war. 'Oh, yes,' he replied, 'I heard my father say that the regiments lay there and lost 200 men that first winter, anyhow the Wrens live there' I shall never forget as he turned to me and said, 'How strange, did you hear him say, 'my father told me,' we forget a generation had grown up since that time' As we entered the house, the first object that attracted his attention was Lieu Geo W. Fuller's photograph in full uniform on the mantel
> We had dinner, after which he gave each of the two women a bank bag of gold. A young son of one of them, when he heard the clink of gold, exclaimed 'Now I can go to Washington and learn to be an Architect'
> Mr Fuller inherited from his father personal magnetism and an alert mind, grasping a subject quickly, almost intuitively; had an excellent knowledge of men and had that peculiar ability in a great degree possessed by men of large affairs in selecting men for positions of responsibility and trust and attach them to him by strands of steel From his mother he inherited a wiry constitution, free from taint, love of rural scenes, of animals and a rapid manner of speech . In all my life I never heard from his lips an unclean or unchaste word; never an oath, and under great provocation as a rule kept himself master of the situation. An aged mother had but to express a wish and it was granted, whilst he stood sponsor for his sister and brothers always ready to grant any reasonable desire. Fortunate indeed was the son and daughters who had the benefit of his advice and guidance, and it would be impossible in this short sketch to even enter the

door in describing the good deeds done by him, and fortunate is the town or community that can number a citizen like Mr. Fuller, whose life work lies within its boundaries."

WILLIAM T. SNYDER. No name is justly entitled to a higher place in the history of Catasauqua than that of the subject of this sketch, for it was borne by a man who most honorably discharged every obligation of life. He achieved success for himself and at the same time benefited the community in which he resided. He was recognized as a man of executive ability and clear judgment and efficiently discharged his duties thus commanding the respect and esteem of his fellow-townsmen.

William T. Snyder was born in Whitehall Township, May 30, 1839, and died July 26, 1902. He was the son of Felix and Lydia (Moyer) Snyder. His educational advantages were few. At an early age he was apprenticed to learn the machinist trade with an Allentown establishment. After serving his time he worked at Coopersburg and in the Crane Iron machine shops. Upon the erection of the Car Wheel Works at Fullerton, in 1867, by William R. Thomas, Mr. Snyder secured employment at these works. For thirty-five successive years he was superintendent of the wheel department. He was a mechanic of well known ability, having patented a wheel centering machine, two self-oiling wheels, a hydraulic gauge, and, in conjunction with James W. Fuller, a steel tire wheel. He was perfectly acquainted with every detail about the large establishment and was devoted to his employers. Fidelity was personified in every walk of life. Between Mr. James W. Fuller, 2nd, and Mr. Snyder there existed the closest fellowship and most implicit confidence.
the closest fellowship and most implicit confidence.

WILLIAM T. SNYDER

He was married July 31, 1862, to Miss Eliza R. Yoder. There were born to this union four children, one of whom died in childhood. Those living are William J., a prominent business man of Brazil, Indiana, Annie, wife of William B. Clark, Lizzie Y., wife of James Davies.

When President Lincoln issued a call for 75,000 volunteers, Mr. Snyder promptly responded and served an enlistment of three months in Company D, 9th Pennsylvania Volunteers, and accompanied General Patterson's army into Virginia as far as Martinsburg. When the time of his enlistment expired, he returned to Catasauqua and resumed his work as machinist. He became a comrade of the Lieutenant George W. Fuller Post, No 378, G. A. R.

Mr. Snyder was a man of a firm religious belief and held his membership in Grace Methodist Episcopal Church in which he filled the office of trustee, of steward, and of class-leader for many years. He was a liberal contributor to the support of the Church of his choice.

CHARLES G. SCHNELLER. Charles G. Schneller, one of Catasauqua's early settlers and prominent businessmen, was born in Bethlehem, Northampton County, Pa., on November 10th, 1821. His parents were George C. Schneller and Mary Brown Schneller. His father was born in the West Indies, his grandfather having come from Saxony, Germany, as a Moravian Missionary. He attended the Bethlehem public schools in the thirties and at the age of fourteen years began a seven year's apprenticeship in tinsmithing. In 1842, he opened a tinstore in Springtown, Bucks County, Pa., afterwards removing to Pleasant Valley, Bucks County, Pa., and in 1848 came to Catasauqua and opened the first tinshop in Catasauqua in the one and a half story frame building still standing on the northeast corner of Second and Mulberry Streets.

On the 15th day of February, 1849, he was married in Allentown, Pa., to Mary A. Heavner, an estimable Christian lady of Haycock, Bucks County, Pa. The happy union was blessed with the following children: Laura Schneller (deceased), Henry D. Schneller (deceased), John P. Schneller, Emma E. Schneller, Charles W. Schneller, and Mary M. Heilman (deceased).

Mr. Schneller immediately took active interest in the religious, political and business affairs of the town. He was one of the organizers of Immanuel

Evangelical Church, Catasauqua, and served that congregation in various capacities. For ten years he was Superintendent of its Sunday School and he served as a trustee from its organization until his death. For a number of years he served as treasurer and was Class Leader for many years. In 1894 he represented the congregation at the sessions of the General Conference held at Indianapolis, Indiana. Mr. Schneller was elected in 1853 as a member of the first School Board of the Borough of Catasauqua, and was Secretary of the Board for 16 years, and afterwards served as Borough Treasurer. He was a staunch Republican up to the time of his death.

In 1854 he built the three story brick business block, known as THE SCHNELLER BLOCK, at Front and Strawberry Streets, to which place he removed his business, occupying same until he retired from business in 1887, after 39 years of successful work. He did much of the water-main work performed in the Borough in the fifties and sixties. He was a volunteer during the Civil War and was already on his way to Harrisburg. However, Joshua Hunt needed him so sorely here in the installation of the water system that when he reached Harrisburg he was ordered discharged and returned home. He became connected with the National Bank of Catasauqua as a stockholder in 1857, and served as a director from 1878 to the time of his death. He was also one of the Board of Managers of the Fairview Cemetery Association. He was always interested in the growth and welfare of Catasauqua and at one time owned three acres of land on Walnut Street, between Fourth and Howertown Road, which is now built up and includes the site of Grace M. E. Church.

Mr. Schneller was an upright citizen, active in all which would elevate the moral and business standing of our town, and lived to be a grand old man. On July 13th, 1909, at the age of 87 years, 8 months and 3 days, he laid his head upon the bosom of the Universal Mother and, with her loving arms about him, sank into the sweet slumber which we call death.

THOMAS JONES. The subject of this sketch was born at Merthyr Tydvil, South Wales, April 26, 1838. He was the son of John and Rachel Jones who emigrated to America in 1842 and located at Minersville, Schuylkill County, Pa. On account of hip-disease he was unable to attend the public schools. Both his parents died while he was a lad of twelve years. He made his home with friends and supported himself by picking slate in a coal breaker.

THOMAS JONES

In 1852 he came to Catasauqua and was employed by the Crane Company as the carrier of the mails to and from the Allentown post office. After the opening of the Lehigh Valley R. R., when mail trains brought deliveries to town, Mr. Jones was set to drive a mule in a cart to haul ore from the canal to the furnaces. His habits of observation and eagerness to study, wherever he could, soon qualified him sufficiently to become an engineer and a machinist. He was chief engineer at the furnaces for eight years, and master mechanic of the C. and F. R. R. for twenty-five years. In 1861 he graduated from the Eastman's Business College at Allentown.

He was married to Miss Sarah Morgan, a native of Wales, in January, 1865. Of their four children but one, Mrs. Miriam L. Brown, survives. Mr. Jones served three terms in Town Council and two terms as Burgess. He was Superintendent of the Catasauqua Gas Company for five years and served as Secretary, Treasurer, and General Manager for a long period of time. He was Justice of the Peace for ten years, and a Charter member of the Phoenix Fire Company, which he served seventeen years as Engineer and eight years as President.

Mr. Jones is now living in retirement, enjoying "The company of my good wife, my daughter and family, and the many kind and estimable friends of my youth and later life."

The family are members of the First Presbyterian Church, where he sang in the Choir for many years. He is also a consistent member of the I. O. O. F.

DAVID GILLESPIE. Among the representative citizens of Catasauqua who have taken a commendable interest in every thing pertaining to the welfare of the community and who have contributed their quota to its progress, was David Gillespie. He was a well known and prosperous business man. By his upright manner and honest dealing he gained the confidence and respect of his fellow citizens. The best interests of the town found in him a friend and his support was never withheld from any worthy enterprise calculated to promote the general welfare.

Mr. Gillespie was born April 25, 1832, in the north of Ireland, County of Derby, and died in Catasauqua April 2, 1901. He came to America in 1852, at the age of twenty, and obtained employment with the Crane Iron Company as boss of ore bins. He opened a general store at 143 Second Street in August, 1865. His integrity, energy and frugality contributed to the success which he enjoyed, and he was justly numbered among the successful business men of town.

In June, 1854, Mr. Gillespie was married to Miss Sarah Hazelett by the Rev. Leslie Irwin, and they became the parents of the following children: Mary, the wife of Henry J. Leikel, Catasauqua; Mrs. Sarah Weisley, Catasauqua; Robert, of Coplay, Pa.; Margaret, wife of Charles E. Lawall, Catasauqua; Elizabeth, Martha, David, and John, at home.

DAVID GILLESPIE

In his religious affiliations, Mr. Gillespie was a consistent member of the Bridge Street Presbyterian Church, which he faithfully served as an Elder for many years. For forty years he was a member of the Independent Order of Odd Fellows, No. 269. In politics he was a staunch Republican and a most ardent advocate of the principles of his chosen party. For three terms he served on the

Borough Council. He served on the School Board for six years, and gave his support to all measures which were calculated to advance the educational interest of the community.

FRANK M. HORN. He who labors hard for his daily earnings and strives still harder to save and lay up a pittance of his cash knows, as no one else, the value of safety in a bank. One of the most conservative bankers in the Lehigh Valley is the Cashier of the National Bank of Catasauqua. Frank M. Horn is the third son of Colonel Melchior M. Horn and his wife Matilda M., nee Heller, and was born at Catasauqua, October 16, 1852. He was educated in the Borough

FRANK M. HORN

schools and was a member of the first class that received diplomas at the hands of the Catasauqua School authorities. Mr. Horn began his banking experience as a clerk immediately after he left school. He was soon promoted to the position of book-keeper, then assistant cashier and finally cashier. For a few years he was President of the bank, but his services were found much more valuable as a cashier and for this reason he consented to return to his desk. He was a member of Company I. of the Fourth Regiment of the Pennsylvania Volunteers, who passed through the riots in the Reading Cut in 1877.

On January 18, 1882, he married Miss Lizzie F. Williams, daughter of John and Emma Caroline, nee Heilig, Williams. Their children are Melchior Hay

Horn, Emma Williams, now Mrs Cornelius Van Inwegen of New York City, and the Misses Susan and Eleanor Traill Horn

Socially, Mr Horn is a member of the Porter Lodge F and A M, the Catasauqua and Charotin Clubs of Catasauqua, the Livingston of Allentown, and the Lehigh Country Club He belongs to the Allen Commandery of Allentown and is a Noble of Rajah Temple of Reading, Pa

JAMES LACKEY came to Catasauqua from Reading about the time when the first furnaces were erected He opened a store in a small frame building somewhere near the Lower Catasauqua depot of the C R R of N J, and later he occupied the new building erected by Mr. Biery in 1835 Subsequently he leased an acre of ground between the canal and the river about a square above the furnaces, and erected a store and dwelling, where he conducted business until 1850, when the Crane Company bought the property in order to extend its plant Then Mr Lackey moved his store to Front Street below Mulberry where he erected another building

In the fall of 1857 he was elected to the office of prothonotary of Lehigh County when he moved to Allentown His store building on Front Street was transformed into the Bank of Catasauqua Mr Lackey served as prothonotary until 1863, and as assistant in the office for many years thereafter He died in Allentown at an advanced age, and left the memory of a highly respected man

COLONEL MELCHIOR H. HORN One of the live spirits during the formative period of our public schools, and a potent factor in the making of the National Bank of Catasauqua, Colonel Melchior Hay Horn, was born in Easton, April 9, 1822 The occasion is rare when a man's ancestors can be traced back with definiteness to the second or third generation The Colonel's grandfather was Abraham Horn, who was appointed sergeant in Captain Thomas Craig's Company, Second Penna Battalion, January 5, 1776 He also served under Colonel Arthur St Clair in his Canadian Campaign during the Revolution During the war of 1812 he served as Lieut Colonel of the First R P V R under Colonel Thomas Humphrey. His grandmother, the wife of Abraham Horn, was Miss Susan Hay, a daughter of Melchior Hay, who came to Easton in 1738 Mr

Hay was of Scotch origin. He was a member of the Committee of Safety during the Revolutionary days and during the war served as a Captain in the army.

The Colonel's father was named Melchior Hay after his grandfather on his mother's side. He served with his father in the war of 1812. His wife was Isabella Traill, a daughter of Robert Traill, who hailed from Sanda, the Orkney Islands, and was born April 29, 1744. Robert Traill arrived at Philadelphia in October, 1763, after a stormy voyage of ten weeks. He came to Easton where he taught school and studied law. He was admitted to the Northampton County Bar in 1777, and was the third lawyer to locate in Easton. He was the clerk of the Committee of Safety and was commissioned a Major during the Revolution.

COLONEL MELCHIOR H. HORN

Thus we have before us Melchior Hay Horn and his wife Isabella, nee Traill, as the Colonel's parents. Melchior Hay Horn, Jr., spent his boyhood days in Easton, where he attended the Van de Veer school. As a young man he was employed as clerk in the general store of Winter and Yohe; and later served in the store of Mr. Burk. He tried the store business for himself but soon determined to relinquish the trade and take up his new profession as a surveyor. His talents as an accountant and financier having been recognized, he was offered the position of teller in Farmer's and Mechanic's Bank, now the First National Bank of Easton, Pa.

In 1857 he was offered the position of Cashier in the newly organized Bank of Catasauqua, which he accepted, and served with signal success until he retired in 1888. From now on he served as President of the Bank until his death in 1890. During the Civil War he served on the staff of Governor Curtin and aided in forwarding troops to the front. In 1862 he was elected Major of the Fifth Penna Militia, and in 1863 he was chosen Colonel of the Thirty-eighth Penna. Militia, which Regiment was sworn into the United States service

The Colonel took a lasting interest in the affairs of his home town A year after his arrival in Catasauqua he was elected a member of the School Board, where he was kept by repeated re-elections for eighteen years, when he declined another re-election He was peculiarly well qualified for this position through his early training in Easton, where school matters had been well advanced He served his town as Burgess for one term His opinions were heeded and many of his propositions still uphold and enhance life and property in Catasauqua He was largely instrumental in the establishment of the English Evangelical Lutheran Church of the Holy Trinity, and served as Superintendent of her Sunday School for many years

His life's partner was Miss Matilda L Heller, whom he wedded October, 1845 Their children were Susan Butz, now Mrs Martin L Dreisbach, of Easton, Pa., William Heller Horn, living in the City of Mexico, the Rev Edward Traill Horn, D D , L L D , Professor at the Ev Luth Seminary at Mt Airy, Phila , Pa , Frank Melchior Horn, Cashier of the National Bank of Catasauqua, Pa , Harry Yohe Horn, M D , of Coplay, Pa , Isabella Traill Horn, deceased, and Charles Robert Horn, salesman of the Davies and Thomas Foundry Company and residing in Catasauqua

Mr Horn passed from the scenes of this present life, February 28, 1890, in his sixty-eighth year, and his body lies buried in the family plot on Fairview Cemetery

LEIBERT John Leibert, 1st, built the house below Koehler's lock, known for many years as the Edward Seider home, early in the 19th century His son, John, married Catherine, daughter of John and Marian, nee Hackett, Tice, and located on the "Lowlands" now the cinder tip opposite Koehler's lock When the first furnaces were erected the authorities needed some one to take charge of the water power machinery, and, since all the Leiberts were mill-wrights by trade, John was importuned to come and operate the water wheels at the furnaces He moved his family to Wood Street, in 1841, where he died, April 1, 1845 His widow, Mrs. Catherine Leibert, erected the brick dwelling on Front Street, the third door below Willow Alley, where she reared the following children Mary Ann, wife of James Nevins, William Henry, master mechanic of the Bethlehem Iron works for many years, having been considered one of the brightest men in his line in the Lehigh Valley, Owen, superintendent of the Bethlehem Iron Works for many years, Sarah Jane, of Catasauqua, and Gwennie, wife of Jonathan Price, deceased Catherine Leibert was born in New York City, March 22, 1808, and died in her home on Front Street, February 25, 1898, at the age of 90 years

JAMES NEVINS "My father was a linen-weaver He read his Bible regularly and guided his family in daily devotions My wife was a Pennsylvania German woman She was a good woman, the best housekeeper I ever knew It is because of her that I own my fine, comfortable home " These were the plaudits of James Nevins, who never tired of repeating the same beautiful and inspiring lines When his steps grew short, his frame weak and his voice husky, and when he forgot many passing incidents, our aged neighbor never forgot his gratitude for the blessings vouchsafed him in those gone before

James was the son of Hugh and Jane, nee Brown, Nevins and was born in Londonderry, Ireland, June 13, 1826 He came to America in 1845 and wrought at Mauch Chunk for two years Then he came to Catasauqua, where he served at the furnaces for forty-two years He married Mary Ann Leibert, November 18, 1852, and died at the ripe old age of eighty-six years, January 26, 1912 His descendants who reached maturity are John, Owen, Emma, wife of James Morrow, and Margaret, wife of John Leibert The last named enjoys a wonderful gift of song

DANIEL MILSON DANIEL MILSON was born in Neath Glamorganshire, South Wales, February 28th, 1830, a son of Charles and Rachel (Thomas) Milson, the former born in England in 1783, and the latter a native of South Wales

He was reared in his native country and educated in the common schools of his native town

At the age of sixteen he started the boiler making trade with his uncle, Joseph Thomas, at Neath. He worked at the Neath shipyards up to the year 1852, then came to this country, landing in New York after a long and dangerous voyage of more than three months.

Shortly after his arrival he removed to Philadelphia, where he entered the employ of Merrick & Son, and later entered the service of the United States navy yard as a boiler maker, being one of the men who worked on the vessel that captured Mason and Slidel during the Civil War.

In 1854 he came to Catasauqua and for two years was employed by the Crane Iron Company, and after dissolving this connection he was employed by the Thomas Iron Company in the erection of their furnaces at Hokendauqua. In the latter part of the year

DANIEL MILSON

1863, in company with David Thomas, Jr., he went to Ohio, where they erected a furnace of which he was assistant superintendent until 1865.

In the latter part of 1865 he returned to Catasauqua, and opened a boiler shop on his own account, employing fifty men.

He retired from business in 1890 and took a trip to the scenes of his childhood, which proved a source of much profit and enjoyment. He was a member of the Presbyterian Church of Catasauqua, and in his political affiliations was a staunch Republican.

In 1861 he was united in marriage to Elizabeth Davies, a native of Wales, who bore him eleven children as follows:

Thomas H., Charles E., Annie, Elizabeth, David (deceased), Minnie, Joseph, Daniel, Henry (deceased), Mabel, and Eleanor. He died November 9th, 1905.

JACOB S. LAWALL. A glance at the lives of the representative men whose names appear in this little volume will reveal many sketches of respected and influential citizens, but among them none are more worthy or more deserving of mention than Jacob S. Lawall, who was a prominent business man of this Borough for a great many years.

JACOB S. LAWALL

A native of Northampton County, the subject of this sketch was born at Hecktown, October 13, 1832, and died in Catasauqua, March 4, 1889. As a youth he attended the public school at Farmersville of the same county. He learned to be a druggist with his brother, Cyrus, of Easton. Having bought the drug business of a Mr. Brunner, who kept his store in the building now occupied by Mr. Bower's meat market on Front Street, he came to Catasauqua. In 1859 he erected a brick building on Front Street above Church, and located his drug store in this structure. In 1869 he built a large dwelling on Bridge Street where he and his family resided to the time of his demise.

On October 13, 1857, Mr. Lawall was married to Catherine Buss, a daughter of Jacob Buss. This union was blessed with seven children: Harry E. (deceased); Edgar J., of Catasauqua; Charles E., of Catasauqua; Idella, wife of Dr. Dumm, of Mackeyville, Pa.; Emily, wife of Dr. Gable, of Lancaster; Marion L., wife of Rev. W. W. Wilcox, of Walden, N. Y.; Thomas W. (deceased).

In his religious affiliations, Mr. Lawall was a member of Trinity Ev. Lutheran Church, which he helped organize and, to the support of which he was a liberal contributor. He was a member of Porter Lodge No. 284, F. and A. M. In politics he was a staunch Republican. As a citizen he was public spirited and progressive, and contributed his full quota for the upbuilding and development of the best interests of the community. He justly merited the esteem in which he was held.

CHARLES W. CHAPMAN. Charles W. Chapman came of sturdy parentage, his father, Joseph H. Chapman, being a native of New London, Conn., and his mother, Martha Wooley, being from Philadelphia, and of English descent.

CHARLES W. CHAPMAN

He was born at Mauch Chunk June 29, 1836, and died in Catasauqua March 13, 1904. He was in his 68th year at the time of his death. His family were raised and educated in Mauch Chunk.

In 1853-54, when the Lehigh Valley Railroad was being constructed through this valley, he associated himself with his brother, Lansford F., as a civil engineer and gained a practical knowledge of railroad construction. When the Catasauqua and Fogelsville Railroad was projected in 1856, he and his elder brother laid out the route, the terminus at that time being Chapman, a station named after the family.

In 1858, he was engaged to run the lines for the North Penn and Delaware Railroad from Freemansburg to Delaware Water Gap. In 1859, he accompanied contractor Robert McIntyre to Washington, D. C., and did the engineering work of the Cabin John Viaduct, which carries the Capital water supply over the Potomac. This stone-arch structure is said to be the largest of its kind in the world. In 1860, he returned to Mauch Chunk and entered the employ of the Lehigh Coal and Navigation Company. Soon after, the Civil War broke out and Mr. Chapman was mustered into the service as a Second Lieutenant of Co. E., 28th Regiment Pennsylvania Volunteers. This regiment won a great name in the Armies of the Potomac and Cumberland. He was promoted to First Lieutenant February 1, 1863, and was mustered out July 30, 1864. His brother

Lansford, promoted to Major in January, 1863, was killed in front of Chancellorsville Hotel during that bloody engagement, May 3, 1863 Charles W Chapman was engaged in the desperate battles of Antietam and Gettysburg

In 1865, he returned to Mauch Chunk and reentered the service of the Lehigh Coal and Navigation Company, and in the fall he went with an engineering corps to Broad Top as superintendent of the Broad Top Coal and Iron Company and opened up several coal mines

In July, 1867, he was made superintendent of the Catasauqua and Fogelsville Railroad and continued in that capacity until the time of his death. In November, 1890, the Reading Railway Company purchased of the Crane Railway Company a controlling interest in the C & F R R , and Mr Chapman was retained as supervisor of the road

On November 13, 1860, he was married to Miss Annie, daughter of the late William Phillips She preceded him in death by four years They were blessed with two sons, Lansford F , a civil engineer of New York City, and Edwin, a machinist in the employ of the Atlas Cement Company

In the life of Catasauqua, Charles W Chapman has borne a prominent part For many years he served as Borough Engineer For twenty-four years he was a prominent member and president of the School Board Fairview Cemetery was laid out by him and for many years he was superintendent of the same and president of the association, never accepting any pay for his efficient services

He took an active interest in the several building associations and was an influential member of the Masonic Order, being a Past Master of Porter Lodge, No 284, F and A M , and a Companion of Catasauqua Royal Arch Chapter, No 278, and a member of Beacon Council, No 422, Royal Arcanum of Allentown In politics, he was a conservative Republican As a citizen he was always foremost in promoting the advancement of the community , in morality and temperance he was outspoken , as a friend he was steadfast and true

ARNOLD C LEWIS Arnold Colt Lewis, son of Sharp D Lewis and Deborah Fell (Slocum) Lewis, was born in Wilkes-Barre, March 2, 1826 The pioneers of his family were members of the Society of Friends, who came from Glamorganshire, Wales, about the year 1863 Arnold C was the sixth in the lineal descent from Ralph Lewis, who settled in Haverford Township, Chester County, Pennsylvania. He served throughout the Mexican War as a Second Lieutenant of the Wyoming Artillerists. After the war he turned his attention to law and was admitted to the bar of Luzerne County, August 5, 1850. Nine years later he came to Catasauqua and with his brother, Sharp D., Jr., bought the Catasauqua Herald from Peter Kelchner.

In answer to Lincoln's call for volunteers, he began to organize a company for the war. With forty-three men he went to Harrisburg, where they united with others from Bethlehem, Pa., forming Company C. 46th Pennsylvania Infantry. The company, with Mr. Lewis as Major, was mustered in, September, 1861, and was given its colors by Gov. Andrew G. Curtin.

On September 22, 1861, they were marching toward Frederick City, Maryland. Sergeant Sanaghan of Company C., who had been reduced to the ranks for breach of discipline, threatened the life of his Captain. To prevent him from doing harm, the Major ordered Sanaghan tied behind one of the wagons. Freeing himself, some one gave him a cartridge and as the Major rode past, the disgraced officer shot him from his horse. He died soon after and his body was sent in a metallic coffin to his home. The interment was in Fairview Cemetery and afterward the body was removed to a cemetery in Allentown. In the death of Major Lewis, at the hand of one who pretended to have the welfare of his country at heart, the nation lost a brave officer when she needed him most.

Only a few months before he left on his fatal march to the south, he married Amanda M. Rohn, daughter of William and Sarah (Weaver) Rohn. To them was born one son, Arnold R., who is now one of the firm of F. Hersh and Sons, proprietors of the largest hardware stores in the Lehigh Valley.

He was a Republican and an ardent supporter of Abraham Lincoln, with command of the "Wide Awake" organization that did so much towards the Martyr President's election. With his commanding presence he could do much for his country for which he gave up his life.

WM. G. LEWIS. The subject of this sketch, Mr. William G. Lewis, was undoubtedly one of the best known Welshmen in the State. He believed that life is a school and in consequence stored his extraordinarily retentive memory with valuable information which he utilized in his social intercourse with men. He was genial and kind, and possessed an attractive personality by which he was able to make and retain a large circle of friends. He was no less esteemed and loved by the Welsh people in this country than he was honored and respected by his own fellow citizens. He was affable and well informed on all subjects and for this reason his company was eagerly sought and his opinions valued. He was prominent in the Welsh musical, educational and literary circles. The Allentown Eisteddfod, in which Mr. Lewis always took an active interest, at their session in Allentown, Pa., Nov. 25, 1897, in a preamble and a series of resolutions, paid him a worthy tribute.

WILLIAM G. LEWIS

Mr., William G. Lewis was born December 20, 1841, at Briton Ferry, South Wales, and died in Catasauqua, November 27, 1897. He was a son of Griffith Lewis and spent his youth and early manhood in his native town. In 1864 he came to America and located in Catasauqua, where he entered the employ of his uncle, Morgan Emanuel. After he had demonstrated to his uncle that he had more than ordinary business ability, he was given an interest in the business, that of selling powder and other explosives, under the firm name of Emanuel, Lewis & Co. It was owing largely to his enterprise and square business dealings that the trade of the company grew to immense proportions. In his trade relations he came in contact with men prominent in mining and quarrying interests and by these he was justly esteemed.

In June, 1863, he was married to Miss Margaret Allen. Twelve children were born to them, two sons and three daughters surviving: Griffith R., a prominent druggist and business man of Cripple Creek, Col.; William M., Manager of the Grand Rapids Muskegon Power Company, Muskegon, Mich.; Margaret E., wife of Mr. Frank M. Tait, Dayton, Ohio; Ellen J., a teacher in a private school, Baltimore, Maryland; and Lydia, who resides with her mother on Pine Street, Catasauqua, Pa. As husband and father, Mr. Lewis was loving and devoted. His home was his chief joy and the welfare of his family was the object of his zealous care.

Mr. Lewis was a member of the First Presbyterian Church and, in 1872, was chosen a ruling elder, which office he held at the time of his death. He was well versed in the Bible and his attendance upon all Church meetings was prompt and unfailing. He was a Past Grand of Catasauqua Lodge, No. 269, I. O. O. F., and a member of Iron Lodge, No. 1964. K. of H. In his political belief he was a staunch Republican. Among his townsmen no one was more highly respected and the confidence reposed in him was never misplaced. As a citizen he measured up to the highest standard and all projects having the general good in view found in him a generous and active supporter.

PHILIP STORM. Philip Storm was a native of Bavaria, Germany, and was born on the Rhine, September 12, 1829, being a son of John and Elizabeth Storm, both of whom were natives of Bavaria. He attended the common schools until he was fourteen, when he began an apprenticeship at the trade of tailor. At the age of nineteen he embarked at Antwerp on a sailing vessel and after a voyage of fifty days landed in New York. He first located at Eliazbethtown, N. J., but later walked the entire distance to Catasauqua. For nine years he was employed loading coal on canal boats at Mauch Chunk. In 1858 he returned to Catasauqua. During the war he enlisted in Company D., 176th Pennsylvania Drafted Militia and served nine months. Upon his return he was employed by the Catasauqua Manufacturing Company until 1889, when he started buying and selling scrap iron.

PHILIP STORM

He was a member of the Borough Council for three years, was elected burgess in 1881 and re-elected three successive years. He also served as health officer for twelve years. At the county convention in 1875 he was honored by the Republican party with the nomination for sheriff, but was defeated at the polls.

Mr. Storm was a member of St Paul's Lutheran Church, a member of Porter Lodge, No 284, F and A M ; Allen R. A Chapter, No 203, Allen Commandery, No 20, K T , and Fuller Post, No 378, G. A R.

In 1851 Mr Storm was united in marriage to Gertrude Koch, a native of Germany, who died in 1883. They were the parents of five children: John (deceased), William, Mrs Allen S. Heckman, Mrs Mary Jenkins, and Mrs A. E Seyfried. On October 9, 1883, he married his second wife, Sarah A (Trollinger) Miller, widow of John P Miller of Allentown

JOSEPH MATCHETTE Captain Joseph Matchette, Gentleman, Christian, Soldier, was born in Seacombe, Cheshire, England, on March 18, 1841 He was one of nine children born to Joseph and Susanna (Truman) Matchette The genealogy of the family runs back to one of the men who crossed the Channel with William the Conqueror and at the Battle of Hastings took England from the Saxons He was baptized in the Episcopal Church of his native shire and attended its school.

With his father's family in the spring of 1852, he set sail from Liverpool and after an eight weeks' voyage landed at Philadelphia. The trip to Allentown was made in a stage coach Here his father made a home for the family

During the winter months of the next three years he went to school and shipped on a canal boat through the summer The boat carried coal and iron to Philadelphia One day, while steering, he fell overboard and was taken out of the water by his brother Richard

At fourteen years of age he came to Catasauqua and drove a mule cart which carried ore to the furnaces Because of his interest in machinery he was given the care of a pumping engine In 1856 he began firing the first locomotive (Hercules) used to carry material to the furnaces

After his experience here he was given a position on the Catasauqua & Fogelsville Railroad, where he fired the "Catasauqua," afterwards running this engine and later the "Macungie." In 1860 he began work in the machine shops of the railroad, intending to learn the machinist's trade

The following year the war broke out and he laid the hammer upon the bench and left for the front He enlisted under Captain Arnold C Lewis in

Company C No. 46 Pennsylvania Infantry for three years. Because of his ability to quickly grasp military tactics and his reliable nature, he was soon raised from the ranks. Promotion to Corporal, Sergeant and Lieutenant came in quick succession. By November, 1862, the ranks were greatly thinned and he was made First Lieutenant. In July, 1864, on the battle field near Atlanta, he was made Captain of Company C, 46th Pennsylvania Infantry.

Fifty times during the war he was under fire. Among the battles in which he took part are: Winchester, Antietam, Chancellorsville, Gettysburg, Kenesaw

JOSEPH MATCHETTE

Mountain. His company was at the siege and capture of Atlanta and with Sherman on his march to the sea.

On July 16, 1865, Captain Matchette was mustered out. Returning home he resumed work upon the railroad and was soon placed in charge of the Catasauqua & Fogelsville Railroad In 1868 he resigned from this position to go into the contracting business That year he moved to Gadsden, Ala, where he remained for one year Upon his return to Catasauqua he began working the limestone quarry at Iron Bridge After the limestone of this quarry was condemned, he was given an agency for the Dupont de Nemours Powder Company. He served in this capacity until 1906, when, on account of age, he was retired by the Company.

Since that date he, with his son, has been selling the products of the Ingersoll Rand Co, dealers in quarry supplies

April 8, 1863, while on a furlough from the South, he married Fannie E Lazarus To them were born eleven children, nine of whom lived to maturity Charles L, Assistant Master Mechanic of the Carnegie Steel Co, Rankin, Willard, with the L V. R R at Philadelphia, Minerva Lydia (Matchette) Miller, Allentown, Adah Susie (Matchette) Walters, Lynn, Mass, Joseph D, who is in business with his father in Catasauqua, Blanch T (Matchette) Wolf, Kreidersville, Pa, Thomas T, Walnutport, Pa, Fannie May, Sophia, John Logan, Tecumseh, who are at home, and two daughters, who died in infancy On December 20, 1910, his life partner passed away

When he returned from the war he joined the First Presbyterian Church As time passed he was elected a trustee and later an Elder of that Church He was a faithful attendant at the Sunday School, and, after the death of Mr. John Williams, in 1893, he was elected Superintendent He has served in this capacity ever since.

He has been a life long Republican His interest has been very large in the school life of his home town, acting as a member of the school board prior to his residence in Alabama After his return he was a director for two terms of three years

His life has been one of earnest helpfulness and active usefulness to his home and to his country Captain Matchette has a large place in the hearts of all with whom he has associated on the battle field, in the business world, in Church work, and the social activites of his home town

JAMES C. BEITEL There is no man living to-day who has conducted a profitable business for so many years as James C. Beitel, who on December 8, 1913, celebrated the Golden Anniversary of the opening of his jewelry store at 215 Front Street. Mr. Beitel descends from an illustrious family. The Rev. Heinrich Beutel was a native of Adamsthal, formerly called Mundorf, Austrian Silesia, being born January 18, 1711. He served as missionary in Berbice, Guiana, S. A., from 1740 to 1748 and 1751 to 1763. He married Miss Elizabeth Paschke, October 8, 1739. Mr. Bentel died at Hernhut, Saxony, December 4, 1763. His wife was born January 23, 1714, and died at Hernhut August 10, 1783.

His son Johann Renatus Beutel was born at Pilgerhut, Berbice, Guiana, S. A., December 21, 1740. He married Juliana Schmidt, a daughter of the pioneer settler of Nazareth, and died at Nazareth, September 27, 1840. His wife was born January 3, 1751, and died February 15, 1824.

The next in the line of this family tree was John Beitel, the son of Johann, born at Nazareth July 18, 1782. He married Miss Anna Magdalena Romig and died at Nazareth August 15, 1870. His wife was born at Emaus, Pa., February 22, 1792 and died August 7, 1849. John's son, Josiah Oliver Beitel, was born at Nazareth in 1811 and died in 1898. His wife was a Miss Maria Sophia Kern, born at Bethlehem in 1814 and died in 1895.

JAMES C. BEITEL

From this union proceeded our townsman, James C. Beitel, who was born at Nazareth, June 15, 1842. His wife is Emma C., a daughter of Solomon Koehler and his wife Mary Ann, nee Ehret, and was born August 16, 1845. Mr. and Mrs. J. C. Beitel were married December 29, 1863.

Mr. Beitel was educated in the Moravian school at Nazareth, and at the same time learnt the clock-making business with his father. When President Lincoln issued his third call for volunteers, Mr. Beitel came forward, October 7, 1862, and was mustered in as a private in Captain Owen Rice's Company A, 153rd Regiment Pennsylvania Volunteers. He was detailed as a member of the regimental band He saw service at Chancellorsville and Gettysburg and was honorably discharged July 23, 1863

He now found employment at his trade in Doylestown On December 8, 1863, he opened his store at 215 Front Street, where he continued for over forty-five years. After Robert J Beitel, his son, graduated from High School, Mr. Beitel admitted him in 1900 into the business, and the firm title became J C. Beitel and Son. New lines were constantly added to the stock so that for larger and more commodious quarters the firm moved into their beautiful store in the National Bank Building during 1909.

The public estimate of Mr Beitel has been attested repeatedly He held public office in town at various times His record as Burgess and school director do him credit He was a director of the National Bank of Catasauqua for years; and a charter member of the Lehigh National Bank, whose honored president he has been since its beginning He is also president of the Electric Laundry Company, at Fountain Hill, Pa He is a veteran member of Porter Lodge, 284, F. and A M, since 1874, and a comrade of Lieut Geo W. Fuller Post, 378, G A. R His name is enrolled among those who held office in St Paul's Ev Lutheran Church to which the family belong and which they liberally support Their children are. Mrs Mary Louise Bender, Laura E., a trained nurse in Philadelphia, Gwennie, deceased, former wife of Rev J W. Lazarus, Annie K wife of Dr. J C Lonacre; Robert J, Otilla G, and Mabel O, wife of Charles Edwards

CHARLES GRAFFIN The man and his devoted helpmate who rear a family of sons who bear a truly fraternal spirit to one another, are gallant and devoted to father and mother, manly and honorable in business, ready to toil, and above all alive to their relation to God and their own souls' highest welfare, are a people who are really great True worth is measured by blood, wherefore he who contributes an honorable type of manhood to a community leaves that community far more richly endowed that he who shines before his fellows in the glitter of large possessions, not a crumb of which he is willing to share

Charles Graffin is the son of Thomas and Rachel Graffin. He was born near Howertown, April 17, 1830, and received his education in the "Peoples' Colleges" of Allen Township.

CHARLES GRAFFIN

When a young man of sixteen, he came to Catasauqua and learnt the trade of cobbler at which he toiled for seven years. In 1856 Burgess David Thomas appointed him as the first policeman of Catasauqua. During the Civil War he served as an emergency man in the 38th Regiment of Pennsylvania Volunteers. After his honorable discharge from the Army, he was employed as time and store-keeper at the Crane Iron Works, where he served for thirty-four years. In 1893 he was elected to the office of Justice of the Peace. President McKinley appointed him Post Master of Catasauqua in 1900, and in 1904 President Roosevelt re-appointed him. The Free Delivery System was established during his administration, for which a grateful people pay him a cheerful tribute. His son Samuel S. succeeded his father in the Post Office and is carrying out many details which his father had planned.

Charles Graffin entered into wedlock with Miss Maria, daughter of Felix Snyder and his wife Lydia, October 31, 1854. This union was blessed with ten children, seven of whom survive: Alvin J., Montclair, N. J.; Robert T., Easton, Pa.; George W., Allentown, Pa.; William F., Germantown, Pa.; Harry E., Catasauqua, Pa.; Walter E., Allentown, Pa.; and Samuel S., Catasauqua, Pa. As a member of the M. E. Church, Mr. Graffin is leading in the way of a Right Life."

JOSHUA HUNT. Joshua Hunt was of English descent, his great-grandfather having come from Birmingham, England, at the time when the Penn Colony was established in America, and settled in Chester County, Pa. He married Esther Aston and had among their sons, Samuel, grandfather of the subject of this biographical sketch Samuel Hunt was married to Mary Beale and from this union came five sons and three daughters Thomas, one of this number, was born December 19, 1791, and married Rachel, daughter of William and Elizabeth Evans, of Lancaster County, Pa They had three children among whom was Joshua, born May 13, 1820, in Chester County, Pa For the first ten years of his boyhood he lived in the country, and later he lived for six years in Philadelphia While living here, he attended the Quaker Boarding School at Westtown, Pa

He began his active business career at Harrisburg, Pa., as superintendent of a rolling mill owned by his father When this property was destroyed by fire, he again went to Philadelphia and obtained employment in the rolling mill operated by his father Later he came to Catasauqua for the purpose of acquiring a knowledge of the operations of an iron furnace He spent a brief period in Poughkeepsie, N Y, after which he became assistant superintendent of the Crane Iron Works At the outbreak of the Civil War, Mr Hunt was made Captain of the Pennsylvania Emergency Militia Co B In 1867 he was elected superintendent of the Crane Iron Works and held this position until January 1, 1882.

When he severed his relations with the Crane Iron Company, he was presented with a beautiful and elaborate silver service as an expression of appreciation for his valuable and efficient services rendered to the company

Mr Hunt was identified with the Lehigh Fire Brick Company, Limited, was president of the Catasauqua Gas and Light Company, chairman of the Baker Lime Company, president of the C & F Railroad and was connected with the Bryden Horse Shoe Company.

He was married August 13, 1844, to Miss Gwenllian, daughter of David and Elizabeth Thomas This union was blessed with eleven children Mrs Hunt died October 25, 1875 Mr Hunt was married a second time, May 4, 1880, to Mrs Hannah L Mays, daughter of Dr John Romig, of Allentown. He died July 18, 1886

In public affairs in his own town Mr Hunt was prominent and influential and always took an active and helpful interest. He enjoyed to a remarkable degree the respect and confidence of his fellow townsmen. He was a faithful and consistent member of the First Presbyterian Church in which he was an Elder for nearly forty years

DAVID HUNT David Hunt was the fourth son of Joshua and Gwenllian Thomas Hunt, born in Catasauqua, August 26, 1854, and died February 26 1898. He descended from prominent families, his father being a son of an eminent iron manufacturer, and his mother the favorite daughter of David Thomas of world-wide fame as an iron master and inventor In his early years he attended the public schools of town, and spent three years in Swarthmore College in Chester County and one year in Lafayette College, Easton, Pa In 1876 he went to Oxmoor Furnace, Alabama, then under the management of James Thomas In 1878, he joined the Mackey, Scott & Co expedition to Brazil as a mechanical engineer to construct a railroad along the Madeira River This enterprise proved a failure and Mr Hunt returned to Catasauqua, and, in 1879, entered the employ of the Lehigh Fire Brick Company as manager Under his supervision the works were remodeled, modern machinery introduced and electric power substituted for that of steam

He was a member of the Southwark Hose Company from its organization to the time of his death In political views he was a Republican and was firm in his allegiance to party principles

Mr Hunt was married April 7, 1880, at Mobile, Ala , to Miss Anna L Manning, daughter of Hon Amos R Manning, who as for many years Judge of the Supreme Court of Alabama Seven children blessed this union, three of whom died in childhood Those living are Roger, in Arizona , Gwenllian Thomas, Martha Manning, and Grace Manning, all of whom live in Bethlehem, Pa

As a citizen Mr Hunt was wide-awake and progressive and his support was given to those enterprises which he believed would prove a public benefit His affable manner and the many excellences of his character gained for him the high regard of all with whom business and social relaitons have brought him in contact

HERMAN KOSTENBADER. As we contemplate the personality of Herman Kostenbader, we behold in our mind's eye a polished and cultured gentleman who was real throughout and bore no veneer He was a native of Wurtemburg, Germany, being born in Pfullinger, near Stuttgart, April 9, 1842 His parental grandfather, John F, was a paper manufacturer His father Frederick, was a Restaurateur for some years, after which he became a Forester in the government employ, which office he held until his death which occurred at the age of seventy-five years. His mother was Maria, daughter of Martin Keppler, a butcher by trade. His mother died at the age of thirty-six years, leaving him and two sisters as the fruits of her life. One of the sisters was Mrs August Kiesele, deceased, in Newark, N J and the other is Miss Charlotte W. Kostenbader, whose home is with her brother's family at number 131 Front Street

Mr. Kostenbader attended the public schools of his native town until he was past fourteen years of age. Four years of this time were devoted to sciences and languages, especially Latin, of which he was a master When but a lad he took passage for America in the "Bavaria," at Havre, under Captain Baily. After a rough voyage, which lasted for thirty seven days, he landed at New York August 7, 1856. He proceeded at once to Philadelphia where he served an apprenticeship in the brewery of Schnitzel and Smith Later he was in

HERMAN KOSTENBADER

the employ of Bergner and Engel, and John Klumpp In 1860 he went to Toledo, Ohio, where he wrought at his trade for two years, after which he drifted to Cincinnati, Ohio, and later returned to Philadelphia, Pa. In 1864 he came to Bethlehem, Pa., where he worked for John Schilling for three years In 1867 he came to Catasauqua where he joined Conrad Schaffer in erecting the Eagle Brewery Mr Kostenbader insisted upon making a pure beer and transacting a clean business, by which methods he succeeded admirably and made many and lasting friends

Mr Kostenbader's first marriage was with Maria, daughter of Peter Wagner, in 1868 Mr Wagner was the proprietor of a bakery in town After only four years of happy wedlock, his young wife departed the scenes of this life In 1874 he entered into matrimony with Miss Matilda Strickler, a native of the Canton of Zurich, Switzerland This union was blessed with ten children, seven of whom survive Dorothy, wife of Rev Charles J Gable, Pastor of the Lutheran Church in Melrose Park, Pa , August F , Herman A , Charlotte O , Cecelia M , Mai ie F , and Helen M , all living in Catasauqua Mr. Kostenbader was a man of retiring disposition and quiet manners He was offered a number of public offices all of which he courteously declined He consented to serve as Director in the National Bank of Catasauqua, and, when the Lehigh Bank was founded, he accepted a directorate there He never declined to serve in an official capacity in his Church St Paul's Lutheran Church enrolled him as Trustee in 1897 and felt favored to retain his services until his death He cheerfully supported his Lord's cause, and his name is written upon many gifts and memorials in his church He died December 15, 1909, in the 68th year of his life, and his body lies buried in the family plot in Fairview Cemetery. Mrs Kostenbader followed him into eternity, June 11, 1914

EDMUND RANDALL The Editor and Publisher of the Catasauqua Dispatch for forty-four years. Edmund Randall, is the son of Lawrence H and Mary Jane (nee Dunlap) Randall and was born in Newville, Cumberland County, Pa , September 2, 1844 After his rural schooling he entered the printery of Merklein and Frey, as an apprentice, in 1861 When a lad of less than 18 years age he enlisted in the army as a private in Company A, 126th Regt , Penna Vols , and served in the Fifth Corps of the Army of the Potomac

After Mr Randall had been honorably discharged and was mustered out of military service, he went to Philadelphia again to engage in his typographical art. Upon the expiration of three years he went to Minneapolis, Minn , where he was compositor for two years Later he returned to Philadelphia, where he worked for Col John W Forney. On the 1st of September, 1870, he opened a printing house on Front St., Catasauqua, and began the publication of a paper which he called "The Country Merchant." What was originally but a little more than a business prospectus was soon evolved into a weekly newspaper called the Catasauqua Dispatch.

EDMUND RANDALL

The Catasauqua Dispatch played a long and important role in the life and development of a town of ceaseless activity. It advocated wholesome and progressive measures and often played the part of a terror to evil-doers. When the Municipal Water-Works, which the Dispatch so unceasingly urged, had been completed, a unanimous vote of thanks was tendered Mr Randall by a well attended citizens' meeting held in the Phoenix parlors On account of failing health he sold the Dispatch and his well equipped outfit, April 5th, 1914, to a firm of young men who do business in the name of the Dispatch Printery

Mr Randall is the amiable husband of Maria E (nee Williams), having been united in marriage by the late Dr C E Earle, in Fullerton, October 9, 1873. Their only child is Miss Allie E Randall

In 1889 he was appointed post-master of Catasauqua by President Harrison and served four years and two months. So well did he perform the duties of his office and make improvements to facilitate the distribution of mail matter, that the Postmaster General wrote him a personal letter complimenting him upon his efforts in behalf of the public good

Mr. Randall was made a Mason in 1868 and, upon locating at Catasauqua, affiliated himself with Porter Lodge, No 284, F and A M, and served the fraternity twenty-seven years as secretary Upon the institution of Catasauqua R A Chapter, No 278, in 1894, he was elected secretary and continues in that office ever since He is one of the oldest Past Grands of Catasauqua Lodge, No. 269, I O O F, served as financial reporter of Iron Lodge, No 1964, K of H, until it consolidated with Allen Lodge, No 1764, and is still holding the office to this date He was one of the men who was instrumental in reorganizing the Geo. W Fuller Post, No 378, G A R and is one of the forty-five survivors of the Post, which at one time numbered two hundred sixty comrades, and is the Senior Past Commander.

DAVID DAVIS David Davis, the subject of this sketch, was born in Pottsville, Pa, April 5, 1845 He is a son of Noah and Margaret (Gwynne) Davis, natives of Glamorganshire, Wales, both of whom came to America in their youth, the former, a blacksmith by trade, settled in Carbondale, Pa, where he lived for several years, working at his trade He then went to Beaver Meadows where he was married In 1846 he and his family moved to Catasauqua, where he accepted the position of boss blacksmith for the Crane Iron Works

Mr. David Davis attended the borough schools to the age of eleven years, when he began to work in the shops of the Crane Iron Company. After four years' service, January 1, 1860, he entered the office of the company as errand boy. He was afterward promoted to a clerkship and from that time received various promotions. For a number of years he was chief clerk and January 1, 1892, he was appointed Cashier to fill the vacancy caused by the death of John Williams.

DAVID DAVIS

In 1863 Mr. Davis enlisted in the 38th Pennsylvania Infantry and served until the expiration of his period of enlistment. He is a memebr of the Porter Lodge, F. and A. M.; Catasauqua Chapter No. 278, R. A. M.; and Fuller Post No. 378, G. A. R; a member of the Southwark Hose Company of which he was president for thirty years. He is a member of the First Presbyterian Church in which he holds the office of trustee.

Politically Mr. Davis always was an enthusiastic advocate of the principles of the Republican party and received high honors at the hands of his party when he was elected in 1905 for a term of three years as Recorder of Deeds of Lehigh County, which has always had a large Democratic plurality. He retained his position with the Crane Iron Company while serving as Recorder. He was elected a member of the School Board by his fellow citizens in 1874 and was re-elected successively until he had served in this capacity for thirty-seven years. From 1878 to 1911 he was the efficient Secretary of the School Board. Mr. Davis took great interest in the schools and gave his heartiest support to every measure that was calculated to conserve their best interests.

In 1869 Mr. Davis was married to Miss Annie McKibbin of Philadelphia. They are the parents of five children: Charles L., Asst. Master Mechanic of the

Carnegie Steel Company at Rankin, Pa.; Willard of Philadelphia, an employee of the L. V. R. R.; Bessie F., Mabel and Mattie, who are at home.

Mr. Davis always has given his best support to the movements which were calculated to promote the various enterprises of the town in which he is one of its esteemed residents. He is no less honored by his fellow townsmen than he is loved in private life.

DANIEL DAVIS. Daniel Davis, son of Noah and Margaret (Gwynne) Davis, was born March 12, 1842, in Hazleton, Pennsylvania. When he was three years of age his parents moved to Catasauqua. Here he attended the public schools and was one of the first students when the Bridge Street Building was opened.

After leaving the town schools he went into the blacksmith shop of the Crane Iron Works. Having a mechanical turn of mind, he soon became an efficient and capable workman. When the Civil War broke out, he was only eighteen years of age, yet he volunteered, and on August 17, 1861, was mustered into Major Arnold C. Lewis' Company C, 46th Regiment, Pennsylvania Volunteer Infantry. At the expiration of three years he re-enlisted and served to the end of the war. He was engaged in the battles of Cedar Mountain, Antietam, and Chancellorsville. In the last battle he was captured and taken to Belle Island at Richmond. After remaining on parole for some months, he rejoined his regiment in Tennessee and was with it in the engagements around Atlanta and on Sherman's March to the Sea. When he was mustered out, July 26, 1865, he had been advanced to the rank of Sergeant.

DANIEL DAVIS

At the close of the war he went into the railroad business and was appointed the first agent of the Central Railroad of New Jersey at Catasauqua. This position he filled until 1879, when the Thomas Iron Company gave him the superintendency of the Keystone Furnace at Chain Dam. Seven years later the company made him superintendent of the Lock Ridge furnaces, where he was a very successful manager for twenty-three years. In 1909 he retired from this position and returned to the associations of his earlier days.

His mechanical skill, his bravery on the battle-field, his grasp of business methods in the iron industry, his civic loyalty, his upright life, and his large heartedness make him a man who stands very prominently in the minds and hearts of those with whom his exceptionally active life has brought him in contact.

Mr. Davis married Miss Gwenny Williams of Catasauqua and to them were born seven children. Walter, the oldest son, has a position with the Westinghouse Electrical Company at Pittsburgh; Margaret and Mary are at home; George, John, Emma, and Gwenny are deceased.

He has been a life long Republican, casting his first ballot on the battlefield for Abraham Lincoln. He is a trustee of the First Presbyterian Church of Catasauqua. His membership in Porter Lodge, F. and A. M., 284, dates back to 1867.

DAVID R. WILLIAMS. David R. Williams, the subject of this sketch, was born in Glamorganshire, Wales, May 24, 1843, and died in Catasauqua, Pa., November 10, 1912, his body being interred in Fairview Cemetery.

He received his training in the schools of his native country and came to America in 1864, at the age of twenty-one. Having had a decided taste for mechanics and railroading, he became a locomotive engineer of great efficiency. He was employed on the C. & F. Railroad and later by the Philadelphia and Reading Company when they leased the C. & F. Railroad. Physical disability compelled him to resign his position after a long period of faithful service.

Mr. Williams was a member of the Independent Order of Odd Fellows, Lodge No. 269, and a member of the First Presbyterian Church. In his political affiliations he supported the Republican party.

In 1864 he was married to Miss Elizabeth James and the issue of this union is one son, John J. Williams, of Catasauqua. Mrs. Williams died October 5, 1900, and her remains rest in Fairview Cemetery. Mr. Williams was an enterprising, public spirited and liberal gentleman. He was highly respected by all who had any dealings with him, either in a business or a social way.

GEORGE DAVIES. George Davies was born in the village of Merthyr-Tydvil, Glamorganshire Wales, April 9, 1836. When he was two years of age his mother, Mary (Philips) Davies, died. Seven years later his father, Daniel Thomas, left his native land and brought his family to New York.

Coming to Catasauqua with his father in 1850, he worked at the trade of moulder for two years and then served an apprenticeship of five years at the machinist's trade in the Crane Iron Company's shop under Hopkin Thomas. In 1861, in company with Thomas Jones, he entered Eastman's Business College at Poughkeepsie, New York, and graduated with honors from that Commercial School. In 1863, while at Parryville, he enlisted in Captain James Thomas' Company, Thirty-fourth Regiment, Pennsylvania Emergency Volunteers, and was made a First Sergeant. He marched with his company to Gettysburg, then to Port Richmond, Philadelphia, and was honorably discharged at the expiration of his term of service.

GEORGE DAVIES

Mr. Davies, prior to the war, was employed as Master Mechanic in Belvidere, New Jersey, Camden and Amboy (New Jersey) shops, the Novelty Works, New York City, and at Parryville, Pennsylvania. At the close of hostilities he returned to the latter place but, in a short time, took up his residence in Catasauqua. With the exception of about five years (1871 to 1876), when he had charge of the Carbon Iron Works at Parryville, he remained here until his death.

In 1879 his brother-in-law, James Thomas, with whom he had been on terms of intimacy from childhood, purchased a one-half interest in the Davies & Sons Foundry and Machine Shop, Catasauqua, and this business relationship continued until the death of Mr. Davies. The two men were devoted companions, the wishes of one being law with the other. The firm was identified with the Wahnetah Silk Company, of which Mr. Thomas was president and Mr. Davies a director. They were also the principal stockholders in the Electric Light and Power Company which was established in 1890. Mr. Davies was a director in the Bethlehem Electric Light and Power Company, established in 1882, and Mr. Thomas was its president. He owned valuable real estate in West Bethlehem, and was a stockholder in the Catasauqua National Bank.

Mr. Davies was identified with the Masonic fraternity, holding membership in Porter Lodge, No. 284. He was a staunch adherent to the principles of the Republican party. As a member of the school board, upon which he was serving at the time of death, he was instrumental in promoting the grade of scholarship in the Catasauqua schools. He was a member of the Methodist Episcopal Church, in which body he served in the capacity of trustee, steward, and class-leader. At the time of the erection of Grace Church and parsonage, he was a member of the building committee, and was one of the most liberal contributors thereto.

On August 4, 1864, in Catasauqua, Pennsylvania, Mr. Davies was united in marriage to Mary A. Evans, who came with her father from Wales. The following children were born to them: John M., who died in 1885; Elizabeth, who became the wife of Harry Graffin of Catasauqua; Rowland T., who lives at the old home in Catasauqua; George, who was for two years Superintendent of the Westchester Lighting Company at White Plains, New York, then was connected with the Davies & Thomas Company's Works and is now serving a responsible position in New York; and two infants who died in Parryville.

Mr. Davies passed away at his late residence, Second and Race Streets, Catasauqua, October 1, 1894. He was a most affectionate husband, a devoted father, a loving brother, a true and excellent citizen, a consistent Christian, a considerate employer, and on all sides are spoken words of praise for the manner in which he acted the part of a true man. His superior is seldom met, and his death was universally regretted.

JOHN MORRISON was one of our oldest and most esteemed residents. He ranked among those citizens who upheld the public stability and moral and intellectual progress of their respective communities. Of a jovial disposition, he was a favorite among his fellow townsmen. He was popular with all classes and highly respected for his genial, humorous and consistent character.

Mr. Morrison was a native of Mauch Chunk, Pa., where he was educated in the public schools. In 1860 he came to Catasauqua and was employed by the Crane Iron Works as locomotive engineer. Later he was yard master for the same company. Few men had a longer continuous service with the Crane Iron Company than had Mr. Morrison. He was a faithful, reliable and conscientious employee.

In 1861, Mr. Morrison responded to the call of President Lincoln for 75,000 volunteers and became a private of Company D., 9th Pennsylvania Volunteers, under Captain H. C. Hand and served his enlistment in the Patterson campaign from Chambersburg to Martinsburg, Va. In 1863 he was commissioned as second lieutenant of Company B, 28th Emergency Militia for State service, mustered at Harrisburg, July 3, and discharged August 7, 1863, the Rebel invasion having failed at Gettysburg. He was one of the few survivors of Allen Lodge No. 1764, K. of H., and a comrade of Lieutenant George W. Fuller Post, No. 378, G. A. R. Just a few days before his death he was installed Surgeon of the Post. Mr. Morrison was an ardent supporter of the Republican party, and served several terms as a town councilman, contributing by his influence and support to the advancement of all public affairs.

In 1862, Mr. Morrison became a member of the Methodist Episcopal Church and continued to be one of the most active, constant, conscientious and faithful members. He served the Church in official capacity for many years.

On December 28, 1864 he was married to Miss Mary Smith, and the issue of this happy union was four children: Mrs. Minnie Morrison, of Catasauqua, William M. Morrison, an electrician residing in Philadelphia, Emily, of Catasauqua, Lily (deceased). In his home Mr. Morriso was idolized. He died January 6, 1914.

VALENTINE W. WEAVER. Valentine W. Weaver was of German descent, his great-grandfather, having emigrated from Germany, settled in Virginia, whence he moved to Lehigh (then Northampton) County His son, Valentine, was married to a Miss Weygandt and had children, among whom was Charles, the father of Valentine W, who was born January 9, 1826, at Richmond, Northampton County His boyhood days were partly spent in Northumberland County, where he enjoyed such educational advantages as the country schools of those times afforded He was a clerk at Berlinsville, Milton, Easton and Catasauqua, all in Pennsylvania At the age of twenty he became an apprentice to the Crane Iron Works, and, having learned the machinist trade, he became an agent of their mining intersts at Catasauqua and vicinity

After Mr Weaver was thus employed for several years, he became assistant superintendent of the Thomas Iron Company at Hokendauqua The Lock Ridge furnaces were erected for the Lock Ridge Iron Company and were successfully operated by him in the interest of the Thomas Iron Company After concluding his labors at this place, he went to Pine Grove, where the latter company had extensive property and remained three years The Millerstown Iron Company secured his services for a time In July, 1879, he took charge of the Coplay furnaces as superintendent Here he remained for a number of years He died in Catasauqua October 11, 1893

Mr Weaver was married in 1848 to Miss Mary, daughter of Jacob Mickley of Whitehall Township, Lehigh County, Pa To this union were born seven children William M (deceased), Valentine W (deceased), Lizzie, married to Mr Yerkes of Hatboro, Pa , Mary, wife of Mr H S Bachman, Catharine M, wife of Dr Berry of Allentown, Emily J (deceased) Mr Weaver was a director of the Macungie Iron Company; a director of the National Banks of Catasauqua and Slatington, and a director of the Hokendauqua Bridge Company In politics he was a Republican, but he never aspired for official position In his religious affiliations he was a Presbyterian He had an active business career in various fields of labor, in which he demonstrated his thorough knowledge of all departments As a citizen, Mr. Weaver was patriotic, enterprising and public-spirited Socially he was a prince of gentlemen The better he was known, the more he was loved

BENJAMIN H. WEAVER. Benjamin H. Weaver traces his origin back to Germany, from which his great-grandfather emigrated, and settled in Virginia and some years later moved to Lehigh (then Northampton) County. His son Valentine was the father of Charles, who was the father of the subject of this sketch.

Benjamin H. Weaver was born in Richmond, Northampton County, Pa., on August 21, 1832. His parents were Charles Weaver and Catherine B. (Hummel) Weaver. His boyhood days were spent on a farm. His educational training he received in the public school of the village. He clerked for two years in the store of Hallenback & Reets in Wilkes-Barre, Pa. In 1859 he came to Catasauqua, and was employed by the Crane Iron Company. In 1861 he responded to the call of President Lincoln for volunteers, and enlisted in the First Pennsylvania Volunteers, Company A, under Colonel Yohe of Easton. After three months—the term of enlistment—he returned to Catasauqua. In the same year he re-enlisted for a term of three years in the 46th Pennsylvania Volunteers under Colonel Knipe. He served one year and a half, when he was wounded in the right shoulder in the Battle of Cedar Mountain, August 9, 1862, and was sent to the hospital at Alexandria, Va., where he was confined from August 9 to October 23, 1862. As a brave and intrepid soldier he was anxious to rejoin his Company but was honorably discharged on account of physical disability. He returned to Catasauqua and was re-employed by the Crane Iron Company as mining agent, which position he held for several years. After he severed his relation with the Crane Iron Company, he continued in the same business for himself to the present time.

BENJAMIN H. WEAVER

On November 4, 1864, Mr. Weaver was married to Miss Mary Duff, daughter of David Duff and his wife Isabella. The issue of this happy union is four sons and four daughters as follows Jessie L (deceased), Harry B, Superintendent of the Allentown Iron Company, Gertrude B (deceased), Ralph S, Superintendent of the Allentown Portland Cement Co, Mary Naomi, who lives with her father, Margaret I (deceased), Adrian B, Sales Agent for Rogers, Brown & Co, of Chicago, Cooper F, draughtsman for American Steel and Iron Co, at Lebanon, Pa

Mr Weaver's affiliations are with the Republican party, to whom he has given his allegiance and support since attaining his majority He is a consistent member of the First Presbyterian Church He is faultless in honor, fearless in conduct, and stainless in reputation He is always the same honorable and honored gentleman whose worth well merits the high regard which is uniformly given to him

WILLIAM YOUNGER William Younger was born November 25, 1825, and died in Catasauqua, Pa, December 13, 1906 He was the son of Casper Younger and his wife Catherine (Fink) Younger Casper Younger was born in Bavaria in 1790 and emigrated to America, settled in Lehigh County and served as an officer in the War of 1812 He was a carpenter by trade and died in 1869

When William Younger was an infant, his parents moved from Upper Saucon to Philadelphia where he was educated in the city schools He was apprenticed to a silversmith, but at the age of eighteen he returned to Upper Saucon and, with his uncle, John Berger, engaged in the milling business When he became twenty-one years of age, he returned to Philadelphia and enlisted in 1847 in Company B, Third United States Dragoons, under Captain Butler, for the Mexican War The work of this Company was to guard the supply trains along the Mexican border After eighteen months' service the company was discharged and Mr Younger returned to Lehigh County For a short time he followed his trade but, the love of adventure and travel predominating, he made two trips to California, the first from 1850 to 1852 and the second in 1853. He removed to Catasauqua in 1855 and entered into partnership with Milton Berger in the milling business When his partner died in 1871, he purchased the remaining interest of the mill. He equipped it with modern machinery and enjoyed an extensive and profitable trade.

In 1857 Mr. Younger married Miss Isabella, daughter of Henry Kurtz, of Hanover Township, and to them were born the following children: Amanda L., wife of Clifford H. Riegel, of Catasauqua; Emma J., deceased; Grant R., de-

WILLIAM YOUNGER

ceased; William, deceased; Henry C., of Catasauqua; Ada I., wife of Samuel Gemmel; Esther A., and Ralph, of Catasauqua.

Mr. Younger was an advocate of the principles of the Democratic party. He was a member of St. Paul's Lutheran Church. He was a man of influence in the community and took an active interest in everything pertaining to its welfare. He commanded the respect and confidence of all with whom he was associated.

WILLIAM McCLAIN KILDARE. William McClain Kildare was born in Chester, Pa., January 29, 1831, and died in Catasauqua, May 26, 1906. His father was William Kildare, who came to Catasauqua with his family in 1841. William McClain Kildare was but ten years of age when his parents became residents of Catasauqua, and he resided in town to the time of his death, at which time he was considered the oldest resident of town.

He enjoyed such educational advantages as the public schools afforded. He learned the trade of moulder at the Crane Iron Works and later was employed at the Union Foundry and Machine Shop. For thirty-three consecutive years he was a faithful and efficient employee of the Catasauqua and Fogelsville Railroad, first as fireman, next as engineer and finally as conductor.

WILLIAM McCLAIN KILDARE

Mr. Kildare was married to Miss Amanda E. Sellers, August 20, 1853. From this union there issued four children as follows: Laura Virginia, wife of Irwin H. Ritter, Philadelphia, Pa.; Rose C., who resides with her mother in Catasauqua, Pa.; Albert E., of South Bethlehem, Pa.; and William II., of Catasauqua, Pa.

In his political affiliations, Mr. Kildare's support was given to the Republican party.

He was a devoted and consistent member of Grace Methodist Episcopal Church, serving the Church in an official capacity as Trustee and Steward, and Treasurer of the Sunday School for many years.

Mr. Kildare was one of the most highly esteemed residents of Catasauqua. He was of amiable disposition, kind heart and noble character, who was to his neighbors a true friend and to his wife and children a devoted husband and father.

JOHN WILLIAMS. The subject of this sketch was a native of Landore,

Wales, and was born November 20, 1824. When but a little over eight years of age, he was brought to America by his parents and located at Schenectady, N. Y. At the age of fourteen he entered the employ of John Fullagar of that city, as a clerk. In 1845 he followed the rest of the family, who were then living at Catasauqua, and at once entered the office of the Crane Iron Company. His first duty was to weigh the ore and limestone that was hauled hither by team, to feed three furnaces. Those were busy days, for team was followed by team all day long. In 1849 he was promoted to the position of Assistant Cashier; and, after the death of Owen Rice, he was promoted in 1856 to the office of Cashier. He performed the duties of this office with signal fidelity throughout the remainder of his life.

Mr. Williams was actively connected with many local enterprises. He participated in the organization of the Catasauqua Manufacturing Company in which he held office until his decease. He served as Passenger Agent for the C. & F. R. R. Company for many years, and was Director and later the President of the Catasauqua Gas Company. He was a Director and at the time of his death Vice-President of the National Bank of Catasauqua. He was also a Director in the Lehigh Valley Trust and Safe Deposit Company of Allentown, and President of the Farmers' Fire Insurance Company of Upper and Lower Saucon Townships, and President of the Fairview Cemetery Association. Since man's acts are more eloquent than his words, it is but necessary to point to the many associations in which his counsel and encouragements were sought to show the shrewd and pleasing character of the man, and his earnest endeavor to promote the welfare of his fellow townsmen.

JOHN WILLIAMS

She, whom he led to the bridal altar, September 14, 1852, was Emma Caroline Heilig, daughter of Rev George Heilig, a Lutheran clergyman Her mother's maiden name was Susannah Hook They began housekeeping on Church Street in one of the Company homes Mrs Williams repeatedly declared the happiest period of her life was the season of her housekeeping on Church Street For a while the family lived in Fuller's Block After David Thomas left the "Mansion" on Front Street, John Williams and family occupied it During 1870 he erected the beautiful home on Bridge Street which he occupied until his death, May 24, 1892, and his widow after him, until her death, September 29, 1913 The hospitality of the Williams home was as genuine as its surroundings, which being adorned with palms, ferns and many rare plants, were beautiful and inviting The fruits of this union were eight children, four of whom survive· Lizzie S , Mrs. Frank M Horn, Annie, Mrs. Edward D Boyer, and Messrs John T and George H Williams

In 1852 Mr. and Mrs Williams took up their membership in the First Presbyterian Church, in which he was elected an Elder in 1872, and he served his people as Superintendent of the Sunday School for many years—until his death With an intermission of one year he served the Borough as Burgess from 1861 to 1873

ROBERT E WILLIAMS Robert E Williams was born November 2, 1836, in North Wales He was educated in the schools of his native land The call of America rang loud in the ears of the youth of nineteen and he set out for the land of opportunity In 1855 he located in York County, Pennsylvania, and two years later came to Catasauqua. His first work was with the Crane Iron Company for whom he ran a blast furnace.

Six years after coming to America Mr. Williams answered Lincoln's call for volunteers His inherent patriotism went out to the new land and he was among the first to offer his life, if need be, to preserve her during those crucial days On April 3, 1861, he was mustered into Company D of the Ninth Regiment under Captain Hand of Allentown, Pa. His regiment was engaged at Martinsburg, Harper's Ferry and Harrisonburg, and at these places he proved himself a brave soldier Upon the expiration of three months, the period for which he had enlisted, again offering his services to the nation, he was mustered into Company C of the Forty-sixth Regiment, Pennsylvania Volunteer Infantry He served with this Regiment in all its engagements, including the Battle of Winchester, until he was wounded in the battle of Cedar Mountain A bullet passed through his body and he lay on the battle field for forty-eight hours before medical aid could be given him After this experience he was cared for in Culpepper Court House for two days and then was taken to a hospital in Alexandria, Virginia Three months later he was able to leave and in November, 1862, was mustered out of service. The effects of the wound and the delay in its care kept him in ill health for almost ten years

In 1864 the Catasauqua & Fogelsville Railroad made him a weighmaster. After nine months in this position he was transferred to the general office at Catasauqua, where he was chief clerk Soon after he was made general freight agent and cashier When the railroad was sold to the Philadelphia and Reading Railroad Company in 1890, the general freight agency in Catasauqua was discontinued After nearly thirty years with the Catasauqua & Fogelsville Railroad, he became, in 1891, head bookkeeper for the firm of Davies & Thomas. He was a stockholder in the National Bank of Catasauqua

In 1864 he married Miss Maggie Price, daughter of David Price of Millersville, Pennsylvania To the family circle was added an adopted daughter, Cora B (Williams) Wade, who for some years taught in the Catasauqua public schools and, at the present time, resides in East Orange, New Jersey He died February 18, 1903.

Mr Williams was a member of the First Presbyterian Church of Catasauqua and became an Elder. His political convictions were Republican, and he acted as Burgess for two terms, his first election having been in 1885 He was a Past Master of Porter Lodge, No 284, F and A M , Past Grand of the Independent Order of Odd Fellows No 269, Allen Commandery No 20, K T , the Allen Council No 23, R & S M at Allentown, and Past Commander of Fuller Post No 378, G A R.

OLIVER WILLIAMS To Mr and Mrs David Williams, in South Wales, was born a son, named Oliver, April 23, 1831 When an infant of two years, his parents brought him to America and located in Schenectady, N Y His father traveled extensively in this country and Mexico and published a series of articles entitled "Cymro in Mexico." These articles gained for him a national reputation.

Oliver received his early training in rural schools. During 1843 he attended the old Allentown Academy, then under the care of Prof. McClenachan. Later he spent one session under the tutorage of Prof. Bleck of Bethlehem, Pa. He learnt the trade of an iron moulder at which he worked until 1849, when he entered the optical establishment of McAllister and Company, of Philadelphia, which he served for three years. In 1853 he joined James W. Queen, one of the McAllister firm, in establishing the J. W. Queen Company.

In 1855 Mr. Williams went to Milwaukee where he came in contact with Chester A. Arthur through whom he met R. L. Hardenburg, who induced him to enter the leather business in Chicago in 1858. He remained in Chicago until 1867, when his life long friend, David Thomas, offered him the position of manager of the Catasauqua Manufacturing

OLIVER WILLIAMS

Company. He served this company for 25 years, during which time this plant became the largest merchant iron mill east of the Alleghenies. He was also one of the originators of the Bryden Horse Shoe Works, serving as President and Treasurer of the Company for many years. He was President of the Union Foundry and Machine Company, Vice-President of the Whitehall Portland Cement Company at Cementon and President of the Cement National Bank at Siegfried, Pa. He was President of the National Iron Association, of the Eastern Bar Iron Association, and was a member of the American Institution of Mining Engineers.

Mr. Williams was united in marriage with Anna, daughter of Mr. and Mrs.

John Heilig of Germantown, Pa. Three daughters were born to them: Mrs. D. L. Emanuel, Mrs. R. O. Koehler and Mrs. George E. Holton. He was an active Church worker and was Superintendent of the Sunday School of Trinity Ev. Lutheran Church at the time of his death. His activities and interest in musical circles was marked by his liberal support of the local Amphion Choral Society and the Oratorio Society of Allentown, Pa. He was a close student, a rare conversationalist, an observant traveler, a ready speaker, a graceful writer, a liberal giver and an energetic business man. He died September 17, 1904, and his body was interred in the family plot in Fairview Cemetery.

BENJAMIN F. SWARTZ. On April 7, 1838, at Swartz's Dam, one and one-half miles north of Catasauqua, Pa., Benjamin F. Swartz was born, and died April 8, 1909, at his home in Catasauqua. He was a descendant of one of the oldest and most prominent families in Northampton County. His father's name was Christian Swartz and his mother's name was Catherine Heller. Benjamin F. was next to the youngest of the family and was reared to manhood in his native county. He obtained a fair education in the district schools. After clerking in stores for several years, he entered Wyoming Seminary, where he carried on his studies during 1856 and 1857. In the fall of the following year he went to Ohio, where for two and one-half years he clerked in a store in Wyandot County. He was a successful business man and in partnership with Mr. Park conducted a general store in

BENJAMIN F. SWARTZ

Carey, Ohio, until the fall of 1865, when he disposed of his interest and formed a partnership with his brother, the firm being B. F. & C. Swartz, and engaged in the dry-goods business in Kenton, Ohio.

In 1869, Mr. Swartz came to Catasauqua and was engaged by McKee, Fuller & Co as their traveling salesmen. In 1883 he was taken into the company as a stockholder and was connected with it to the time of his death.

On November 27, 1861, Mr. Swartz was married to Miss Anna L. Dow of Carey, Ohio. Mrs Swartz was educated in Wesleyan University at Delaware, Ohio, and by her union with Mr Swartz has become the mother of two children, Maud O., the wife of Mr. George Graffin of Allentown, and Benjamin F. D., who died April 17, 1886.

Mr. Swartz was a devoted member of Grace Methodist Episcopal Church. He served the Church as Trustee and Treasurer for many years, and was one of the most liberal contributors towards the current expenses of the local Church as well as to all the benevolent enterprises of the Church. In politics he was an ardent Republican never failing to aid any measure for the betterment of the community. His gentlemanly courtesies won for him a host of friends.

JONAS F MOYER One of the citizens of the Borough who has always taken an active interest in its welfare, politically, socially, and morally, is Jonas F Moyer He was born at Macungie, Lehigh County, Pa June 2, 1850, being a son of Samuel and Elizabeth (Mertz) Moyer, the father, a native of Upper Milford, and the mother, of Macungie. The paternal grandfather was born in this State, but his father was a native of Holland, who was one of the early settlers in this county.

Mr Moyer is the fourth in order of birth in his parents' family, there being eight children He was reared in the place of his birth and attended its public schools On June 21, 1877, he graduated from the Keystone State Normal School, Kutztown, Pa., and commenced teaching at the age of eighteen, and followed this profession for eighteen years He clerked in stores in Philadelphia, Allentown, and Macungie For about twenty-eight years he represented the Mutual Benefit Life Insurance Co of Newark, N J Mr Moyer was postmaster of Town from 1894-1898 and also acting postmaster during the sickness of his successor. Henry Davis, from July 1899 to March 1900 It was in 1898 that Mr Moyer was elected to the House of Representatives, serving during the three sessions of 1899, and 1901, and 1903 Three years later, when the Lehigh National Bank of Town was organized, he was selected as its first cashier, which position he has held very creditably to this time.

Mr. Moyer was married in 1878 to Celia R. Troxell, who was born in Washington Township, and is a daughter of E. A. Troxell, who was a merchant of town for many years. To Mr. and Mrs. Moyer were born nine children, seven living:

JONAS F. MOYER

Samuel E., William A., Ida E. (Mrs. A. Keenan), Russell F., Ellen M., Clarence T., Paul W., and, Mamie E. and Solon F. (deceased).

Mr. Moyer is an Odd Fellow, a Past Officer of the Knights of the Golden Eagle, and a Past Officer of the Patriotic Order Sons of America, being one of the founders. He is an active member of the Reformed Church, Superintendent of the Sunday School, and has been in many ways before the public in leading roles.

WILLIAM W McKEE This biographical record would be incomplete if within its pages a sketch of the above named gentleman should fail to appear He occupied a high social position in this community and was deservedly respected by those who were favored with his friendship The simple record of an honorable life is the finest monument which can be reared by any citizen, and it is therefore unnecessary to enlarge upon his history

He was the second son of James H and Mary (Thomas) McKee, and was born December 27, 1852, in Jersey City, and died June 27, 1905, in Catasauqua His parents moved to Philadelphia where he spent his boyhood days After graduating with honors from a Polytechnic School in Philadelphia, he went to Germany where he was enrolled in the University of Freiburg as a student in mining engineering After two years' study he was graduated from this University.

In the meantime his parents had moved to Hazleton Upon his return from Germany, McKee was employed by the Eckley Coxe Coal Company as mining engineer After some years of efficient service with this enterprising Company, he associated himself with the Lehigh Car, Wheel and Axle Works at Fullerton

On April 8, 1890, Mr McKee was married to Miss Ruth Thomas, daughter of Mr and Mrs James Thomas This happy union was blessed with the following children Ruth T James H , and Mary, all of whom reside at home

Politically Mr McKee was a staunch Republican Socially he affiliated with the Porter Lodge No 284, F and A M , and was a Grand Master He was also a member of Lu Lu Temple, Philadelphia, and of the Catasauqua Club.

D. GEORGE DERY D George Dery, one of the most widely known citizens of Catasauqua, has demonstrated that, within the brief span of a quarter of a century, a man possessed of integrity, ability and magnanimity, may rise to lofty heights in the business world. He has had a large part in making the Lehigh Valley a silk manufacturing centre His skill in the methods of silk weaving and his organizing powers have placed his name among the leaders in his field He is the owner of fourteen ever-growing silk manufacturing plants and employs more than three thousand workers Because of his justice and liberality in dealing with his employees, labor troubles have been entirely unknown

He was born in Austria and received his college education in Vienna Obedient to the wish of his parents he entered the army In 1887, having become a Lieutenant, he resigned and came to America

Before leaving Europe, Mr Dery had become most skillful in the processes of silk weaving Because of his reputation as an expert, he was given the superintendency of a mill in Paterson, New Jersey Realizing the opportunity for the silk manufacturer, he started, in 1892, a factory in his own name

A rapidly increasing business demanded other mills In 1897 he chose Catasauqua as the location of his second mill About one year later, deciding to make this place the centre of his business, he moved the Paterson plant and established his home in this place Since the building of this plant, the demands for the Dery Silks have necessitated the erection of thirteen other silk weaving mills and three large throwing plants They are located at the following places Catasauqua, Pa , East Mauch Chunk, Pa , Allentown, Pa , Mills A B and C , Emaus, Pa , Scranton, Pa , Bethlehem, Pa , Mills A and B , Marietta, Pa , Olyphant, Pa , Forest City, Pa , Northampton, Pa , Wind Gap, Pa , and Taunton, Mass Among his other business interests are Directorship in the Catasauqua National Bank and in the Allentown National Bank

Mr Dery is not only a man of large business and intellectual attainments but is gifted with a fine and discriminating artistic taste He has been a zealous collector of fine artistic productions of paintings, among them are some of the works of the old masters, and represent a small fortune in themselves In his spacious green house and about his home he has a large variety of plants and flowers

He is a member of the Lehigh Country Club, of Allentown, the Northampton Country Club, the Livingston Club of Allentown, the Manhattan Club of New York City, the Manufacturers' Club of Philadelphia, and the Elks Fraternity of Allentown. In these organizations he is a leading member

DAVID R GRIFFITH In David R Griffith Catasauqua owns a citizen of whom she may well be proud. He has been in the employment of the Crane

Iron Company ever since his arrival in this country in September, 1869. He began as a patternmaker, and was promoted from time to time until he became the head of the carpenter department at the furnaces. Mr. Griffith, aided by his devoted wife, raised five sons and two daughters, every one of whom reflects credit upon the sublimity of a true home and a God-fearing parentage. Our friend served twelve years as president of the School Board, and six years as its treasurer. When the Welsh people of the town desired preaching of the Word in their native tongue, and "Mother Thomas" made it possible for them to have a church, Mr. Griffith, who possesses rare, natural endowments as a public speaker, especially along sacred lines, studied hard so that by the fall of 1881 he was ordained at Slatington as a Congregational clergyman. Since this time he has waited upon his countrymen with the Word of Life in a most acceptable manner.

DAVID R. GRIFFITH

Rev. Griffith was born at Neath, Glamorganshire, South Wales, January 8, 1845, and is the son of John Griffith and his wife, a born Davies. He was educated in the National Schools of Wales, and was licensed to preach before he was nineteen years of age. Four years before he emigrated to America, March 25, 1865, he entered into matrimony with Miss Hannah, daughter of Mr. and Mrs. John Thomas. The children whom they brought to maturity are: John P., of Port Henry, N. J.; David, Joseph T., Oliver, and George R., of Catasauqua; Edith M., wife of Henry Van Middlesworth of Siegfried, Pa.; and Elizabeth A., wife of Elbert Green, of Catasauqua.

HENRY H. BUCK. All the people of true sensibility and a just regard for the memory of those who have departed this life cherish the details of the hisotries of those whose careers have been marked by uprightness and truth, and whose lives have been filled with acts of usefulness. Such a man was Henry H. Buck, one of Catasauqua's best known and most prominent residents.

He was born October 20, 1838, near Danielsville, Northampton County, Pa., and died in Catasauqua, November 26, 1913. He was a son of Jacob and his wife Elizabeth (Berlin) Buck. His boyhood days were spent with his parents and he enjoyed such educational training as the village school afforded. A part of his time he spent on the farm and in early manhood he learned the wheelwright trade with Thomas Royer, Cherryville, Pa.

Early in the sixties he went to Parryville, Pa., and in 1863, he enlisted in the Thirty-fourth Regiment, Pennsylvania Volunteers, under James Thomas, the superintendent of the Carbon Iron Company at Parryville. Mr. Buck was also a member of the emergency corps which participated in the Battle of Gettysburg. When the Civil War came to a close, he was honorably discharged and located in Catasauqua where he followed his trade as a wheelwright. He lived retired for the last eight or ten years of his life.

HENRY H. BUCK

Mr. Buck was a consistent member of Emmanuel Evangelical Church and took a deep interest in its welfare. He gave the congregation efficient service as an elder, trustee, and Sunday School superintendent, which last office he held for many years.

He was Judge of Election in the Second Ward for many successive terms. He was a Republican in his political affiliations.

He was a citizen of whom any community can well be proud and was held in high esteem by all who knew him.

Mr. Buck was married September 10, 1867, to Miss Emma Oplinger of Danielsville. The issue of this happy union was two sons: Abner H., Principal of the High School, South Bethlehem, Pa.; and Harry E., an employee of the Central Railroad of New Jersey at the local office.

JACOB ROBERTS. Jacob Roberts was born in Marbletown, Ulster County, New York, October 3, 1832, and died in Catasauqua, Pa., November 18, 1905. He enjoyed such educational advantages as the common schools of his boyhood days afforded, a few months during the winter. This training was supplemented by reading standard works on various subjects, chiefly mathematical and mechanical. Having had a mind that was bent on investigation, he filled it with facts which he utilized in a practical way in later years.

Like many prominent men of the country, he taught school for several years, after which he entered the ranks of mechanical scientists and spent fifteen years of his life in acquiring a practical knowledge of blacksmithing, carpentering, carriage-building, painting and machinery. He was engaged for some years in the carriage-building business, also indoor blind and sash manufacturing, in Brooklyn, New York. For a time he was employed as a mechanical expert and consulting engineer in the cities of New York and Brooklyn.

In 1883 he purchased the Hudson River Rolling Mill at Poughkeepsie and, in company with Charles Miller and the Crossman Brothers of New York City, organized the Phoenix

JACOB ROBERTS

Horseshoe Company and began the manufacture of horse and mule shoes. These products found a ready market and the business was a success. In August, 1889,

Mr. Roberts severed his connection with the Phoenix Company and became superintendent of the Bryden Horseshoe Works. He came to Catasauqua and took charge of the Bryden, manufacturing the Boss horse and mule shoes. The manufacture of these shoes has met with phenomenal success, having found ready sales in the market of the world. More than once has the Company been obliged to double the capacity of their works in order to meet the demand of the trade while Mr. Roberts was superintendent of the Bryden.

September 18, 1855, Mr. Roberts was married to Miss Catherine L. Relyea of Clintondale, New York, and their married life was blessed with five children, Mrs. Frances D. Simonson of Newark, N. J., William Roberts of Easton, Pa., Mrs. Austin A. Glick of town, Eva M. and Ida T., both of whom died in infancy.

Mr. Roberts was a devoted member of Grace M. E. Church and one of its most liberal contributors. He was a man of commanding presence and fine social qualities. It was always a pleasure to meet him. He possessed to a marked degree the faculty of making a person feel at ease in his presence.

RICHARD O. KOHLER. Richard O. Kohler was born in Chemnitz, Germany, October 27, 1872, and died October 30, 1913. He was educated in the schools of his native town. These afforded him great educational advantages by which he profited to such an extent, that, when he started in life for himself, he was intellectually well equipped for the vocation of his own selection, that of a business career. In June, 1893, Mr. Kohler came to America and found employment as clerk in the Unicorn Silk Mill. He subsequently engaged with the Bryden Horse Shoe Company, and for several years he was general manager of the Catasauqua Casting Company. For a short period he acted as general sales agent of the Lehigh Clutch Company and traveled extensively in locating their sales. He and his family spent three summer months preceding his death in traveling in Europe and in visiting his brother, who resides in Chemnitz.

Mr. Kohler was married October 31, 1902, to Miss Grace Williams and their home was graced with an only daughter, Anna H. He was a prominent official of the Trinity Ev. Lutheran Church and a member of Porter Lodge No. 284, F. and A. M., and of the Catasauqua Club. Mr. Kohler enjoyed the esteem and confidence of an extended circle of social and business acquaintances.

HENRY J SEAMAN The pioneer of the Seaman family in this country came from an English stock and located on Statan Island, N Y, at some time ante dating the Revolutionary War The father of our townsman was Henry J Seaman His mother, Maria A, a daughter of Charles Augustus Luckenbach, was a descendant of an old Moravian family Mr Luckenbach was an organizer and the first president of the Thomas Iron Company, and an early director of the Bank of Catasauqua

Henry J Seaman, the subject of our sketch, was born in Trinity County, California When he was past three years of age his parents came to Bethlehem, where he attended the Moravian Parochial School He took a course in Chemistry at Lehigh University and was graduated in 1879, when he went to the mining district of Leadville, Colorado, where he served as chemist of a large Smelting Company On account of severe illness he returned home in December of the same year In February, 1880, he succeeded James Gayley as chemist at the Crane Iron Works He was promoted to Furnace Manager, January, 1886 In June, 1889, he accepted the position of Superintendent of the Carbon Iron and Steel Company at Parryville, Pa In February, 1892, he became Superintendent of the Atlas Cement Company, which was in process of organization

HENRY J SEAMAN

At a later date he was elected to the position of General Superintendent of the Atlas Portland Cement Company, of which he has been a director since its organization He was largely instrumental in perfecting the rotary process of manufacturing Portland Cement, and invented and commercialized a process of burning pulverized fuel, now used almost exclusively in the manufacture of Portland Cement

Mr Seaman is Vice-President and General Superintendent of the New York and New England Cement and Lime Company, and a director of the National Bank of Catasauqua   He holds membership in The Engineers' Club, of New York, The Railroad Club, of New York, The Livingstone Club, Allentown, Pa   The Lehigh Country Club, Rittersville, Pa , The American Institute of Mining Engineers, The American Society for Testing Materials, and The American Concrete Institute

He entered into matrimony with Miss Minnie Boyer, daughter of Mr and Mrs Reuben Boyer, in 1885   Their children are. Louise, wife of Paul Miller, and Harry J , both of Catasauqua

GEORGE E HOLTON   George E. Holton was born in London, England, April 24, 1868, son of George and Hope Mary Holton, and died February 10, 1913   He was educated in the schools of Norwood and London, England   He came to America in 1886 and was naturalized in the early 90's.

Mr Holton entered the employ of the Pencoyd Iron Works   In 1889 he became inspector for G W G Ferris & Co of Pittsburg, in the eastern territory, and had charge of the inspection and testing of the cast iron segments used in the construction of the first tunnel under the Hudson River, now known as the Hoboken Tunnel, originally undertaken by Pearson & Co of London, England   His abilities as an iron expert was easily recognized by the late Oliver Williams, the president of the Bryden Horse Shoe Co , who employed him as a salesman for the company. Mr Holton established sales agencies in all parts of the country and secured large orders for them   During stagnation in the American market, he secured large orders from England in competition with English manufacturers during the English-Boer War in Africa, and thus kept the local works steadily employed

Upon the death of Mr Williams, he succeeded him as president of that Company and general manager of the Works   At the time of his death, he was president and treasurer of the Bryden, president and treasurer of Emanuel & Company, a director of the National Bank of Catasauqua and a director of the Cementon National Bank of Siegfried

Mr. Holton was married to Miss Jessica Williams, youngest daughter of

Oliver Williams, and the issue of a happy union is a son Oliver, and two daughters, Catherine and Jessica.

Mr. Holton was a member of Town Council from the Second Ward; a member of the Catasauqua Club; vice-president of the Lehigh Country Club; vice-president of the Lehigh Valley Symphony Society; a member of the Northampton Club, Bethlehem; Livingston Club, Allentown; Bryden Gun Club; Engineer's Club, New York City. He was a member of Trinity Ev. Lutheran Church. In all of these organizations he took a prominent part and is greatly missed.

Mr. Holton was a man of splendid executive ability, personal magnetism, pleasant address, greatly attached to his home and friends. He enjoyed the confidence and esteem of his employees as well as of all who knew him.

LEONARD PECKITT. A citizen who is wide awake and truly interested in the welfare of the community which he has chosen as his home, is Leonard Peckitt. He is the son of Leonard F. Peckitt and his wife, Frances, a born Quickfall. He was born at Carlton Hall, Yorkshire, England, April 17, 1860, and was given his early training by a private tutor. Later he matriculated at the Masham Grammar School, which was followed by a four years' course in Chemistry under Prof. W. F. Stock, County Analyst of Darlington.

He came to America in 1882 and accepted a position as chemist at the Reading Iron Works, where he remained six years. For two years he was chief chemist at the Crane Iron Works, and, since 1890, he was successively Assistant Superintendent, Superintendent, General Manager, Vice-President, and President of the Crane Iron Company. In 1899, Mr. Peckitt took an active part in the formation of the Empire Steel and Iron Company, which took over

LEONARD PECKITT

the Crane Iron Works and other properties in New Jersey and Eastern Pennsylvania He was the first President of the Company and is still serving in this capacity.

The interests of Mr Peckitt are large and varied and his judgments, being well matured, are constantly solicited. He is related as follows· Director, National Bank of Catasauqua, Vice-President and Director, Pottstown Iron Company; Director, Catasauqua and Fogelsville Railroad; President and Director, Victoria Coal and Coke Co, Capetton, W Va ; President and Director, Crane Railroad Co , President and Director, Davies and Thomas Company, Vice-President, Mt Hope Mineral Railroad Co, Wharton, N J , Director, Bryden Horse Shoe Company, Director, Consolidated Telephone Co of Pa , Hazleton, Pa.; Trustee, St Luke's Hospital, So Bethlehem, Pa , Trustee, appointed by Gov. Tener, Homeopathic State Hospital for the Insane, Rittersville, Pa , Fellow of Chemical Society of London, England, Member of the Iron and Steel Institute of Great Britain, Member of the American Iron and Steel Institute, Member of the American Institute of Mining Engineers, Vice-President, Lehigh Country Club, Rittersville, Pa , President, Old Home Week Association, Catasauqua, Pa.

Mr. Peckitt entered into matrimony with Miss Hattie Madeline, daughter of Emanuel Weidler and wife of Stony Creek, near Reading, Pa , in 1899 Their son, Leonard Carlton, is now in Arizona

MRS ELLEN CAROLINE GILBERT At the time of her death, but fifteen days before the beginning of the Old Home Week Celebration, Mrs Ellen Caroline Gilbert was the oldest native resident of Catasauqua She was born in the lower section of the town when it was called Biery's-Port, January 25, 1831 Her father, Daniel Tombler, was a native of Hope, N J , while her mother, Catherine, nee Hartzell, was born at Wind Gap, Pa These parents moved to Biery's-Port in 1821. Mr Tombler conducted the old mill that stood on the site of the present Mauser & Cressman property, and for twenty-three years collected toll at Biery's Bridge. During the re-erection of the bridge, destroyed by the flood of 1841, Mr Tombler met with an accident which resulted in his death

In the days of Ellen's childhood all the children of the Burg attended

Deily's School located near the old Taylor residence. Mrs. Gilbert also attended the old Presbyterian Church on Church Street, in whose Sunday School Allie Thomas, daughter of David Thomas, was her teacher. Sylvester Tombler, now of Allentown, is the only surviving member of that family of ten children.

She was married by Rev. Eberhard February 6, 1855, to Edwin Gilbert. Edwin Gilbert was also a native of town; and, during the Civil War served his country as Captain of Company F., Forty-seventh Regiment, Pennsylvania Volunteers. He died, January 2, 1894, as a member of St. John's U. E. Church to which the family belonged.

Mrs. Ellen Caroline Gilbert

Nine children were born to Mr. and Mrs. Gilbert, of whom the following survive: David W., of Catasauqua; Alice C., wife of Sylvester Minnich of Allentown, Pa.; Edwin D., of Philadelphia, Pa.; Euphemia, widow of Wm. Ritter of Catasauqua; Ellen C., who lives with her brother David.

CHAPTER XII —REMINISCENCES-

Conditions have changed since the balmy days of long ago In 1853, while David Thomas was Burgess, an ordinance to this effect was deemed necessary, "No person shall erect any hog pen on that part of any lot within the Borough adjoining any street or alley thereof without enclosing and separating the same from the street, by a close fence of boards, at least seven feet high " Hogs, as of the *suilline* genus, were banished altogether by Council, June 13, 1893, while hogs as genus *porci* are still admitted

In 1853 it was also declared that the sale of cakes and beer, strong drinks, cordials or cider, on any "public day" in any of the public streets of the Borough, was a nuisance and punishable by fine

The Ordinance from which we are quoting also sets forth that, "If any person or persons shall travel on horseback or in a vehicle faster than at the rate of six miles an hour through any of the streets, lanes or alleys of this Borough, every person or persons so offending shall forfeit and pay one dollar fine "

Town Council passed an Ordinance under Burgess John W Hopkins, August 6, 1888, declaring that there "shall be a Public Street Market on the south side of Bridge Street, from Front to Second Streets, between the hours of four and eight o'clock A M, every Tuesday, Thursday and Saturday of each and every week during the months" of April to October, inclusive The Chief of Police was constituted Market Master, and was directed to collect ten cents per day from every "wagon, hand-cart or vehicle" from which produce was sold, and five cents per day from a person who brought produce in a basket which he carried Children were exempted from making payments It was unlawful to buy or sell any produce except meat, milk, ice, and bread in any part of the town during market hours on market days, except at the established markets

Crane Iron Works, Dec 11th, 1839

Mr David Bowen, Aberdare, South Wales, England

My Dear Friend —I have taken my pen in hand to write you a few lines from this wide western hemisphere I am in perfect health and good spirits and all my family are the same who join me in hoping this brief letter will find you and your family also enjoying good health and happiness I suffered much on the voyage and after I came here from sickness, which you no doubt have heard, but my health and strength have now recovered amazingly, and I am now flattered by those who knew me before that I look better than I did some years ago

We have been treated here with much kindness My employers have done everything in their power for my comfort, they have built me a very good house, with garden and every convenience that one could wish, and I have reason to believe they are satisfied with me I have under my care about 100 men with proper foremen to look after every department, I give the orders and pay them

We live in a very fertile country where every sort of grain, vegetable and fruit is very abundantly grown The climate is very healthy, and the weather has been hitherto very good The people are hospitable and kind, chiefly from German origin There is much of that language spoken here, which I am learning very fast The children can talk it better than I can

Places of worship and schools are numerous Many denominations are supported by voluntary contributions, the schools by a tax, every State appropriating so many thousand dollars for the use of schools There is one built in my neighborhood where every one can educate his children for almost nothing, to any branch of science or literature

The government is Democratic, and chiefly in the hands of the most numerable part of the community, which in my opinion is the worst part of their policy, and the most likely to injure the permanent progress of America Your radicals, with riotous chartists, I think would have enough of universal suffrage only for them to witness the abuse of that suffrage as applied here I have seen with regret the riotous affair of the chartists at Newport, and I am afraid from the appearance of the English newspapers that you are going to have more of it

The population of this district is not very thin It is peopled as thickly as Carmarthenshire The towns are six to ten miles from one another and some of them have from 3,000 to 12,000 people Philadelphia is 54 miles and New York 93 miles, to either of which places we can go from here in one day Traveling here is very expeditious, as there are canals and railroads in every direction The town nearest to us is Allentown which is three miles from our works

The natural resources of this country are numerous All sorts of minerals are very abundant, provisions are very cheap, in fact, everything for the use of man is very moderate except woolen cloths, which are about double of those bought in England Calico and cotton prints are as cheap here as you can get them there, and cotton goods of every sort are very cheap

I do not think the cattle in this country are as good as in the old country, but horses are equally as good, if not better generally Pigs are very cheap and abundant Pork is very cheap, selling in the market at 9 shillings 1 pence per cwt and the best bacon fed upon Indian corn (which is very plentiful here) for 12 shillings 6 pence per cwt of your currency, best flour is $5 50 per barrel or 550 half pence of your currency, weighing 196 pounds I had a barrel last week which makes bread pretty nearly as white as this sheet of paper I am writing upon, good black tea 1 shilling 6 pence to 7 shillings 6 pence per pound; coffee, best, 15 shillings, ½ pence, but very good for 4 shillings ½ pence per pound, loaf sugar is 7 pence, if good season, 6½ pence, burnt sugar for 3½ pence to 5 pence per pound of your currency, and indeed everything in that way is very cheap.

The people here only eat three meals a day, breakfast at 6 in the morning, dinner at 12, and supper or tea at 6 in the evening. They have plenty of meat on the table for each meal whatever house you go into. All classes eat very much alike and about the same times.

Poverty is rarely known here except among the intemperate or idle. Old people, widows and orphans are very well taken care of. The law of the land is very lenient to the actual poor, but very much otherwise to impostors. I have only seen three people begging, two of them Irish and one a German.

Since the time I left, is there any fresh duty? They do not know what duty is here, only on goods imported. The farmers in this country are usually free-holders. There is not one farmer out of a hundred but what lives on his own land, and they are generally very wealthy. Manufacturers are increasing very fast here, they are short of hands and capital, both increasing very fast. We have had some very bad times this autumn in the money market, but it is improving again very fast.

In about three weeks from this time our furnace will have fire in it. We are going to build another in the spring.

John Thomas is here and he is a good boy, very strong and industrious. He sends his best regards to his mother.

Please address your letter to David Thomas, Crane Iron Works, near Allentown, Lehigh Co., Pa.

I am, my dear old friend,

Your sincere old friend,
DAVID THOMAS

Some day long ago, Morgan Emanuel heard that a countryman by the name of David Thomas was running the Crane Works at Catasauqua, and so he determined to come to town in quest of a job. When he walked down Front Street he met Mr. Thomas some where near Lawall's Drug Store and accosted him in Welsh, "Are you Mr. Thomas?" Mr. Thomas replied, "Yes, and who are you?" "I am Morgan Emanuel and came from the coal regions, in the hope that you would give me a job." Mr. Thomas said, "I am sorry, my friend, but we do not have much work at present." "Oh, that is all right, I do not need much work." Upon this rejoinder Mr. Thomas employed him at once.

A few years ago, when steam vapor or hot water heating systems were rapidly supplanting antiquated methods in use, a contractor in his line as steam fitter called upon a certain clergyman in town to interview him with reference to the introduction of a steam heating plant in his church. The contractor asked, "What do you have in your church?" The parson said, "Hot air."

This reminds us of gas-bags. Catasauqua has always produced a great deal of gas, as is especially noticeable on sultry days   The top fillers at the furnaces have always had some wood aglow by which escaping gas was quickly ignited and consumed and thus prevented from doing any harm   In this we have a good object lesson when gas escapes ignite it   There was a time, however, when gas was bought, first in Philadelphia, and later in Bethlehem, and shipped to Catasauqua in bags for use in the Bridge Street Presbyterian Chuich   The bags were attached to a pipe system in the church and weighted so as to give proper pressure to the flame   This was done from the time the original church edifice on Bridge Street was completed in 1852 and continued until the Catasauqua Gas Plant was put in operation in 1856   Dr Danowsky and Nathan Laudenschlager also filled bags with gas at their plant near the old Lehigh Valley depot at Allentown and sold them for the illumination of private homes and public buildings

Miss Esther Pritchard Hudders was one of the prominent landmarks of the village   She was of New England origin, born in Susquehanna County—her ancestors coming from Wales   She was a woman of education ad an expert with the needle   She taught school in the church basement and on two days of the week gave sewing lessons to the girls   Every woman with daughters was a patron of Miss Hudders and the latter, with that calm and dignified manner, would cut a big apple pie for her pupils as willingly as she would a switch from the limb on which the apple had grown   For many years Mrs Hudders lived at Second and Pine, the home erected by her husband shortly after the town became a borough   The house was always a favorite one for the younger element to congregate in

The Rev John Jones left a family of exceptional children, gifted in mental endowment and full of the tricks of healthy youth   A daughter Maggie spent much time under the training of Rebecca Mickley Thomas   A circus came to the outskirts of the village and Maggie wanted to go   Mrs Thomas refused unless she went in the company of a grown person   At noon, a chaperon had not been found and Maggie disappeared leaving the dinner dishes untouched   Nightfall came and the search began   With the last vestige of daylight, Miss Margaret Jones was discovered sitting close to the old church bell, high up in the fork of the big oak tree on Church Street. It took some persuasion to make the climber come down and she washed no dishes that day. The entire village was out on scout, the crowd at the circus had undergone a sharp inspection, but when the next big circus came to Allentown, Mrs Thomas saw that Miss Margaret Jones, daughter of the deceased Welsh divine, was on one of the best seats in the ring.

George Breinig, the father of our late townsman, Simon Breinig, was a shrewd financier. He managed to secure a farm for each of his children as rapidly as they married and started life for themselves. In public he usually wore a silk hat, a pair of calf-skin boots, and while one leg of his trousers was down the other was drawn up and hung over one ear of his boot. On a certain occasion he heard that a farm in the direction of Guthsville was to be sold at auction. Mr Breinig went to the sale and offered the highest bid for the farm. The auctioneer and some gentlemen at the sale gazed at the man with blank amazement. Finally he was asked whether he could pay for the farm or bring security for the price. Mr Breinig said, "I own several farms in Northampton County which are paid for, and I think I could pay for this, but since you hesitate I shall go home and you may keep your farm." After some inquiry it was learnt that Mr Breinig's statement was correct. Then they came and begged him to take the farm at his bid by which he had offered a good price. After some persuasion Mr Breinig took the farm.

Arthur W Hamilton related that matches were first used in England in 1680, that they were sold in small boxes containing about three dozen, for 15 shillings each, or $3 65 in U S money. Matches were made in Paris in 1805. Pocket matches were made by John Walker, an English druggist, who sold eighty-four for a shilling. When Frederick Eberhard settled at Dry Run in 1832, very few people knew anything of the luxury of a match.

The most inflammable substance commonly known was punk. In every home was found a piece of flint rock, a piece of steel, and some punk. To start a fire the dry punk was laid down and the steel and the fire stone struck together in such a manner as to cast the sparks upon the punk. At times sparking was required until one's elbows tired before the punk caught. People used to cover the last glowing embers of their fires at night very carefully with ashes in order to keep them alive and have a start for the next day. If, perchance, the fire was found to be out in the morning (great misfortune) and Mary was awkward with striking sparks, she would take a crock and quickly run to the neighbors a half mile across the fields to borrow some fire as kindling for the breakfast blaze. Often the crock would get so hot before she reached home that she burnt her fingers.

Mr. Eberhard dried small squares of pine wood and, with a knife, split them open in cross cuts about one-eighth of an inch apart, each way, so that the block looked like a checker board. To keep the ends apart he laid slivers both ways between the rows. Then he dipped the slivered ends of the blocks into sulphur and phosphorus by which process he made the first sulphur matches used in this community. He sold them in the block to the merchants at Weaversville, Siegfrieds, Laubachs, Catasauqua, and Allentown.

The employees of the Crane Iron Company, for whom houses had been built on Wood and Church Streets, formed a type of community life which was beautiful so long as a homogeneous people occupied those homes. Besides a common pump on Front Street, there were two old fashioned bake ovens, one on each street named, devoted to the use of the community. The individual in charge of the oven heated it by split wood every day from Monday morning until Saturday evening. At a given hour of each day the ashes were drawn and the ovens wiped clean with a "Huddle-lumpen." Then the busy housekeepers would hasten thither with well raised loaves of bread in straw baskets, with cakes, pies, etc. The dough loaves were dumped out of the baskets upon a large wooden paddle with a long handle, "Backoffen-schieszer," by which they were placed with great skill into the oven. That was mother's bread indeed! A half hour later the whole community was fragrant with the breath of freshly baked goodies. When a cake fell it was, of course, the oven's fault.

We often hear of the strict school discipline of former years and sometimes of the laxity of it in public schools of the present day. On the 17th of March,

1869, a great parade of Irishmen from the entire valley appeared on our streets The Stars and Stripes headed the column, then in its wake, the flag of Erin in festive furl, with silk hats and green ribbons galore. Brass bands alternated "Yankee Doodle" with "Wearing of the Green," and shamrocks and shillelahs flourished in peaceful force A greater than Barney McNulty played the fife and long columns of men kept soldier step to the beat of the drum, while along the line came the clear echoes of the Scottish bag-pipes The High School, deep in the mathematical problems of "Brooks," heard the call of the heather, the toot of the horn and the beat of the drum, then the trampling of horses and the tread of marching hosts—and out of the double doors of the Upper Second Street building poured the "well-disciplined" boys and girls of that Catasauqua High School Two teachers sat helpless at the desk. The ringleaders near the door had ventured and pell-mell after them, like a flock of sheep, went every pupil of the school It was ten o'clock on that early spring morn and at the afternoon session each desk had its usual occupant What punishment could be meted out to this illustration of the power of the mass against the elect? And some of the leaders were girls who took to the banisters and rode down the stairs to make time, those not being the days of the limited skirt

During the winter of 1855 and 1856 a number of young people of town organized a Dramatic Club Meetings and rehearsals were held in the Bridge Street school house After the parts had been well worked out, nights for the exhibition were appointed Thomas Jones and Samuel Davis were the curtain boys Mrs Kate Fuller, Mrs Mary A Thomas, and Mrs Dr Daniel Yoder impersonated some of the chief characters in the play William R Thomas was stage manager. The Rev Dr Earle and David Thomas looked upon the hilarity with suspicion and attempted to stop or prevent the performance from coming off. But their efforts helped the thing along, and crowded houses greeted the amateurs whose performance was a great success

The wife of the late Dr Frederick W. Quig, who was for over sixty-three years a member of the Bridge Street Presbyterian Church and in her girlhood of the Mauch Chunk Presbyterian Church, often related how in the primitive days of "Bierysport" the Presbyterians of the "Old School" doctrine held service in Kurtz's grove. The grass was raked clean the day before and at three o'clock on Sunday afternoon, Rev Leslie Irwin cantered in from the Bath Settlement. His members, some twenty odd, carried wooden stools, hymn books and Bibles. A tuning fork set the pitch and long metre was the favorite tune. In this day of cant and question and religious sensations, it is a relief to pause a moment and contemplate such old-time worship.

George, the son of Jacob Deily, served his father on his large farms for fifteen years after he reached his majority. The father sold his potatoes to people of town and among them a number of bushels to David Thomas. His constant admonition to the boys was, "Be sure you give good measure." When George reached the Thomas home with the number of bushels ordered, Mrs. Thomas insisted that not a potato be put into her cellar until all the bags be emptied and the potatoes remeasured. George explained that the potatoes were measured at home, good measure was given and that he did not have a half-bushel measure with him. But Mother Thomas insisted upon her demand. By this time George grew earnest and said, "I will go home to fetch the measure, and will measure your assignment on condition that you pay extra for what is over the amount at which we intend to give you this load." Mrs Thomas agreed to this. After the load was measured Mother Thomas paid for three pecks of potatoes more than for which Mr Deily meant to charge her. Mr Thomas tantalized his madam quite a bit about good measure in potatoes.

Levi Kraft, a tinsmith who worked for C G Schneller, and Horatio Good from up the valley, went to Mauch Chunk, where they joined their company designated for the Mexican War. The company proceeded to Wilkes-Barre, whence they were transported by canal to Harrisburg, by rail to Pittsburgh and by river-steamer to New Orleans. Both these men lived to return, wearing the peculiar uniforms of that day, with coal-scuttle shaped caps decorated with metal chains. Kraft served three years (1861-1864) in the 47th Pennsylvania Volunteer Regulars, and died a few years ago in the Soldiers' Home at Dayton, Ohio. Good went to California where he was killed by the Indians.

After the Mexican War others returned to their homes at Allentown. John Kuhn, however, was missing. A year later he returned, but the cruel severities of the Mexican Prisons caused him to become insane. He found a home in the Lehigh County Poor House. For twenty-five years he made his annual summer visits to Allentown and Catasauqua in his old uniform with his hat bedecked with flowers and a cavalry sword swinging at his side as he marched along. People generally knew him as "Mexico John," and no one ever thought of molesting him, but rather showed him respect and encouraged him in his innocent amusement.

Very few Indian relics have been found in the vicinity of Catasauqua. During the construction of the Lehigh Valley R. R. a skull, surrounded by boards, pipes, Indian tools, etc, was found a short distance below the station. Many arrow heads of flint were found opposite the mouth of the Coplay creek, while the canal was being dug, showing that the Indians had a sort of factory for arrow heads at the spring that empties into the river at this point. Shortly before his death in 1866, Joseph Miller related to William H. Glace, Esq., that he heard his grandfather say that there was an Indian burying ground on the lowlands, that the elder Miller, who lived in the old stone house above the Cemetery gates, on the road to Hokendauqua, peering through the heavy underbrush at different times, saw parties of Indians bury their dead on the lowlands.

The following important item is quoted from the recent publication of William H. Glace, Esq:

Gentlemen —I am from good authority informed that the enemy Indians have attacked the Frontiers in Northampton county and that intelligence has been given to an officer of credit by a Friend Indian that a considerable body of French and their Indians design again to invade the Province and a number are on their way to fall afresh on the Minnisinks or parts adjacent. The particular view of the Ohio Indians at this time, as it is reasonably supposed, is to obstruct the Susquehanna Indians in their treaty with the English and to prevent thereby a well-established peace between them.

How the forces, within the battalion I have the honour to command, may be disposed of, upon the expected incursion of the savages and the French who prompt them with a cruelty equal to that of the barbarians, I cannot say, but you may depend on it that I shall ever endeavor to serve the country by doing all in my power to succour every distressed part as soon as possible.

But, gentlemen, you must know that the number of forts which are on the east side of the Susquehanna will require a very large part of the First Battalion to garrison them and to allow of scouting parties to watch the motions of the barbarians It will therefore be necessary that the inhabitants should do all in their power to defend themselves and neighbors against an enemy whom we know by experience to strike great terror wherever they commit their ravages.

I recommend it to you to persuade your neighbors to associate themselves immediately into companies under discreet officers of their own choice, that we may be able to preserve our own and the lives of our tender wives and children Great must be the advantage we shall give the enemey if we are unprepared upon their sudden invasion

It needs not much reflection upon what happened about 16 months ago to bring to your minds the amazement and confusion with which the spirits of our people were affected upon a sudden incursion of Indians of whose numbers we were never well informed It would appear as if I had an ill opinion of the disposition of my countrymen to suggest any special motives upon this occasion.

I only pray that Divine Providence may direct you to proper measure and then you can not fail of success in an endeavor to serve your country In which service you may depend on my promise that you will be ever joined by

Your most humble servant
CONRAD WEISER, *L Col*

Attest WM PARSONS.
Reading, April 27th, 1757

George Charles is a family name among the Schnellers, whose progenitor in Germany was George Charles Schneller, a native of Dresden As a youth he went to Herrnhut, Saxony, and studied theology Later he came to Fairfield, England, where he was married to Miss Hannah Meller From Fairfield he was sent as a missionary to the Isle of St. Kitts, one of the West Indies The Islands being an undesirable place to educate their children, they sent their sons, George Charles and David, and their daughter, Rachel, to the Moravian schools at Nazareth and Bethlehem The George Charles at the Nazareth school was the great-grandfather of our townsman Charles G Schneller It will be refreshing to read the appended letter of the father to his son This letter is but a sample of many similar epistles written in the name of the Lord, by parents and friends to loved ones.

St Kitts, March 27, 1807

Dear and beloved Son,—

We your parents, hope you are well It is a long time indeed since you sent us a letter. We do often, not only think, but speak of you Brother Lancaster calls you the little Englishman He loves you, and out of love has sent to you the present of half a guinea which, before this comes to you, undoubtedly you will have received.

On your birthday we considered both the Watch-Word and the text for that day, and prayed our dear Saviour to give to you a cheerful, a willing and obedient heart to love Him, for He will never leave you nor forsake you, doubt it not.

Give our kind salutation to your Master and Mistresses, to your Labourers, yea to all the Christian Brethren and Sisters.

We expect soon to receive a letter from you. When you see your brother David give him two kisses: one from me, one from his mother; and salute your sister, Rachel.

We remain your poor yet tender affectionate parents,

GEORGE CHARLES AND HANNAH SCHNELLER.

CHARLES G. SCHNELLER, ONE OF CATASAUQUA'S EARLY SETTLER

The first excursion to Biery's Port was on an "Ark" run from Allentown, June 26, 1829. Ogden E. Frederick relates with warm enthusiasm the narrative of his mother-in-law, Mrs. James W. Fuller, who was a member of that merry party. She was then a child, Clarissa Miller, eleven years old. She told of how the "Ark" was decorated with U S. flags, how crowded it was and that it was drawn by two horses. The scenery along the water course in those days was truly rustic, and in the month of June must have breathed upon the quiet air a sweetness unalloyed by the many gases that now stain its borders and fade its foliage

The day on which the first train arrived at Catasauqua on the L V R R, July 4, 1855, brought great excitement to the stately community of the Iron Burg There was then a beautiful rustic park along the east bank of the Lehigh, where we now behold the picturesque cinder tip. A cannon was stationed in the park ready to fire when the train rounded the curve above Fullerton. All the people of town flocked to the park in their best Sunday bonnets and gowns. When at last the engine came snorting around the bend to which all expectant eyes were directed, the deafening roar of the cannon shocked every nerve After the train had stopped and the magnates, barons and other great men alighted and formed a procession toward the Eagle Hotel for the banquet, a shrill call of the furnace whistles of Hokendauqua announced that a fire had broken out at that plant. The crowd promptly swung its gaze and directed its hastened steps toward Hokendauqua. In the rush for positions on the barges two of them were over-loaded and, when about mid-stream on the Hokendauqua dam, one of them tipped so as to slide a number of people overboard Although no one got water into his lungs, the principals of the tragedy lost all their starch The blaze shot up the hoisting shaft and destroyed the buckets and rigging When Mr Thomas looked upon the conflagration he dolefully said, "Now we are ruined"

Let it be said, however, that those old boys were an ingenious set They ran a bannister over the steps leading to the cab of the top-filler and by means of a rope and pulleys worked by a horse hoisted buckets to fill the furnace

A local sport of the original Fire Company of the Borough was the Water Fight One part of men played the hose attached to a plug supplied by the furnace pump upon their fellows, who returned a stream from the old hand fire engine The engineer at the furnace regulated the pressure so as to give the hand engine men a vantage from time to time The fighting parties swayed forward and back until at last one or the other party, drenched and exhausted, yielded to their victors and cried "Enough." The onlooking crowds shouted with laughter and applauded while the men were struggling in the combat. Thus the water-fight Saturday became a great day of sport

It is quite natural to suppose that the Iron Works attracted visitors from near and far Prominent among the visitors of the past were Sir Morton Peto, Simon Cameron, Horace Greeley, and Dom Pedro, Emperor of Brazil The bridge-house was repeatedly crowded with people. It was the custom of the villagers to come out at eventide to see the men cast pig-iron

When the girls of the Moravian Seminary were brought for their annual inspection of the works, those young men who were detailed to escort them through the plant were deemed lucky They never forgot to take the sweet lassies by the water-house and the horizontal cylinders, driven by water power, which lifted ponderous doors and dropped them with a bang and a splash which caused the ladies to shriek and jump into the expectant arms of the young men who lead them safely on

> Oh, sentiment so sweet,
> Thy charm can never cease!

Two interesting curios were placed beside the laboratory of the Crane Company on Front Street in 1907 They look like the mouths of two projecting cannon They are discarded tuyers of the furnaces A tuyer is a tube through which hot-blast is forced The one next the street did service in the first furnace erected by the company

Relative to the flood of 1841 we quote from the records of the Crane Company, "On Thursday, January 7th, at nine o'clock in the evening, the river rose so that the back water prevented the wheel from turning at half after ten covering the tow-path of the level above lock 36 At twelve it was two feet over the banks, and was one foot over the bottom of the hearth of the furnace At 1 20 the water was at its height, and 34 inches in the furnace It was at its height until 3 30 o'clock when the river began to fall The water wheel was muddied all over and the water was nine inches over its top The dam and canal bank was broken so that when the water fell in the river it was too low to turn the wheel though every effort was made to fill up the bank, but they could not succeed and were obliged to throw the furnace out on Monday, the 11th of January

David Thomas,
Thomas S. Young ''

The furnace was blown in again on May 18, 1841

The flood of June 4 to 5, 1862, caused the water to rise from twenty-four to twenty-seven feet above its ordinary level, or four and one-half feet higher than the flood of 1841. Bridges, buildings of all descriptions, canal boats, timber, trees, and household furniture floated down the river Miraculous escapes, and rescues were made Uriah F Koehler, at the risk of his own life, rescued the Hockenberger family Dr. William A , his wife, and sons William, Joseph and Henry. He ventured into the water on horse back and brought his neighbors from the house at the lock to the old Koehler school house, where they lived until their home was habitable again. On the last trip the horse swam to shore The roar of the onrushing current was terrible; it could be heard for miles around And the agonizing shrieks of many victims on logs and floating buildings can still be heard in the memory of our old people

For a number of years a corn-whiskey distillery stood where the blacksmith shop of the Davies and Thomas Foundry is located This afforded the farmers of the community a good market for their corn, and a very desirable place for hog feeding Farmers marked their pigs and brought them to the distillery where they were fattened and when they were fit for the slaughter they were brought home and the happy butchering day began. During the fall and winter seasons there were as many as a thousand hogs in the pens at the distillery at one time. This is why some years ago the unkind nickname of ''Hogtown'' was given to the Third Ward At one time cholera broke out among the hogs, and they died like flies Their carcasses were hauled to an old ore mine shaft near Schoenersville Exorbitant taxation and growing restrictions caused the proprietors to desist from distilling any more ''Bolinky,'' the hog yards were turned into lumber yards by John Knauss, who also ran a planing mill After this plant was burnt to the ground, Daniel Davies acquired it for foundry purposes.

When Mrs Wells became organist in the First Presbyterian Church, in 1870, a Choral Society was formed and the first attempt to render classical music in Catasauqua was made James Prescott succeeded Mrs Wells in 1876 and developed the society to such a degree that people from all over the Lehigh Valley journeyed to Catasauqua to hear concerts that were worth while The Iron Borough still enjoys a lofty distinction for good taste and great skill in the rendition of high class music The only noticeable feature to-day is the fact that many places once proudly held by the Welsh and the Irish are now meekly occupied by the Germans

Solomon's doctrine of "spare the rod and spoil the child" was emulated to a giddy height in the early days of *school-keeping* Many an offending child, or a friend of the offender, was sent out to the old apple tree with instructions to cut down a stout water sprout for use upon his own back If the friend went for the whip, there was something for two youngsters to settle that night on the way home from school If he refused to fetch the rod, he too fell under the ire of the school master. Rulers were thrown at scholars who whispered to their neighbors in the next seat, and, when they brought the ruler to the commanding master, he would slap the palms of their hands, or the tips of their fingers bunched together, until they would sting for hours Failures in lessons were rewarded by hand ear-pulls, or by being chased to the foot of the class where, as umpires, they were compelled to enumerate all errors made by their class mates An omission of errors meant some more slaps with the black ruler.

Before the introduction of the Joseph Gillotte Pens, which were made in England, and sold in this country at two pens for three cents, quills were used for penmanship Young teachers usually had the time of their lives until they had acquired the skill to properly point and split a quill The large tail feathers of geese or turkeys made the best quill pens.

Friday afternoon used to be the great time at school. A wide awake teacher usually spent most of his time on Friday afternoons in giving exhibitions which patrons attended in large numbers The program consisted of singing, essays, declamations, dialogues, debates and geographical or spelling matches For a match two persons, usually a boy for one side and a girl for the other, chose alternately until practically the whole school was divided into two companies and ready for the fray The teacher pronounced words which were spelt by pupils on alternate sides in regular order If a word was misspelled on one side it was passed to the other, and then back again, and so on until some one spelt it correctly All who erred were out and took their seats The last one standing won the match

The last day of school was a great day in the life of the child of fifty and more years ago Recitations were heard until noon, when an iron kettle was brought and rigged up by the big boys It was filled with water and the fire started The smaller children were sent home Books, papers, pencils, slates and ink-bottles were nicely packed together (pupils furnished their own books and material in those days) When the water was hot enough the boys carried water while the girls washed desks, benches, windows, and finally scrubbed the floor, ending up at the door, which the teacher locked and the fun was over. Boys and girls who could not be sent home, but were banished from service in the scrubbing party, put in the afternoon by playing in the school yard and watching the big boys and girls coquet A large hogshead was placed into the basement (cellar) of the Bridge Street School Building, which was kept filled by means of buckets from the spouting by the boys on rainy days so that when scrubbing periods came the water was on hand

The game of ball back in the fifties and sixties was not a scientific contest between the pitcher and a batter, but rather an all-around sport The ball was usually made of a piece of rubber or cork wound over with wool or yarn of a worn out sock until it was large enough to handle and then a soft leather cover, cut like an orange rind, sewed over it If the game was "Corner Ball" four fellows stood on spots about fifteen or twenty feet apart The ball was thrown from one to the other, around the square or diagonally across it He who failed to catch or who dropped the ball was obliged to go into the square as a target to be thrown at, and another fellow took his place on the corner. If a fellow on the corner threw at the man in the square and missed him, or if he dropped the ball, he too had to go into the centre. Thus the game continued until all the players were in the centre save one. Now he took the ball and ran from corner to corner, the only spot from which he dared throw the ball, so as to get near some one whom he might hit by throwing. If he could hit them all and thus discharge every one from the box or center he had won the game.

"Gickley-over" was another game which was played around some wagon shed, corn crib, or wood house. The boys would divide, or choose sides, so that an equal number was on each side of the shed. One of the principals on a side would start the game by throwing the ball over the roof of the shed and call out "Gickley-over." If a fellow on the other side of the shed saw and caught it, the fellow who threw the ball was won over to that side. Then the first man on side number two threw the ball to side number one calling out the words which mean 'watch out it is coming over." If in this instance no one caught the ball, but it rolled on the ground, then there was a general scramble for it, and he who got it ran around the shed either way as far as the corner on the other side and threw it at the fellows. If he hit one that man also came over. Thus the game continued and men were won from side to side until at last one or the other side lost its last man, and the game belonged to the side that had won all the men.

"Long-town" came into vogue a trifle later and was really in a manner a fore-runner of base ball. Sides were chosen. One set of men were batters and the other set selected their pitcher and catcher and the rest of the fellows were fielders. Long-town had only one base which usually was a stone, stump or tree about twenty-five strides from the batting point. He who batted the ball over the fence was out. A flying ball caught by some one put a man out. If the ball was batted over or through the bunch of fielders the batter ran to the goal twenty-five steps away. If a fellow picked up the ball before the runner reached the tree or stump, and threw the ball so as to hit the runner then the runner was out, if he missed the runner so that the ball flew far away, the runner could touch the tree and run "home." When all the batters had safely reached the tree, but none dared risk to run home, and a last man would bat the ball far over the crowd, then there was merriment when everybody ran home In case all the batters reached the tree so that there was none to bat, pitcher and catcher would throw the ball to each other a certain number of times in which time somebody must risk and run safely home else the game is lost

In the game of "Round-town" were four or five bases, placed in the form of a square, diamond, or pentagon, and basemen guarded these safety spots. The ball was thrown to the basemen who touched a runner and he was out. If a fielder caught a fly and touched a runner, he put two men out. In Round-town more than one man was privileged to share safety at the same base; and a whole bunch was permitted to run bases simultaneously The bat was a piece of a rail or clap-board, seldom a whittled paddle.

"In ye good and olden times" loved ones did not understand the art of preparing and laying out a corpse so as to conceal the horror of death and the sting of its consequent sorrow When Owen Frederick began to direct funerals in 1848, it was a common practice, in order to keep a body for a day or two until arrangements for burial could be made, to lay a board on two chairs, cover the board with fresh clumps of wet sod and then lay the body on the sod, grass up and cover it with a sheet Later the undertaker brought a rectangular box, two by seven feet and about six inches deep, into which the body was laid and ice packed around and on it The water was drained from the box by a small spout into a bucket that stood on the floor. Still later the ice-box was coffin-shaped, about six and a half feet long, thirty inches wide at the shoulder and twenty-four inches deep The sight of that box caused many a shudder The body, wrapped in a sheet, was laid into the bottom of the box, and a metal tray filled with cracked ice and resting on catches in the box was placed over it, and a close fitting lid was shut down tight. A small spout carried the water from this refrigerator The face and hands of the corpse were washed with saltpeter and water The process of embalming was put into practice in this community in 1884.

Years ago, pall-bearers at funerals were called grave-makers. Sextons in cemeteries were unknown. When some one died, four men were sought who were willing to serve as grave-makers. A day or two before the funeral the grave-makers filled a "stuetze" with water, cider or some other consoling quencher, went to the graveyard together and dug and walled-out a grave for the deceased. Having completed their task by evening they returned to the house of mourning for a good dinner which neighbor ladies prepared. The neighbors also prepared meals for mourners who traveled long distances to be present at the funeral. On occasions when a prominent person died several beef roasts, a whole veal (calf) and two or three dozen chickens were required to form the base of the funeral dinner. It is said that Frederick Biery introduced this custom into this section of the country.

On the day of the funeral the grave-diggers served as pall-bearers, until the committal was ended. Then they donned their overalls and filled up the grave with ground. Thus their office was fulfilled.

Mr. Glace relates William F. Romig was the first physician in Catasauqua. His office was located on lower Front Street. After a practice of some ten years he was succeeded by Dr. F. B. Martin, who admitted Dr. Yoder as partner in 1858. In 1868, Dr. Martin died and Dr. Yoder succeeded him.

Alonzo W. Kinsey, an Englishman, was the first chemist at the furnaces. Kinsey was a scholarly man and manifested a great skill as an experimenter and lecturer. He astonished his friends by washing his hands in a certain solution and then into molten iron which he splashed about him with his hands uninjured. At the request of Capt. Bill Jones, he went to the Carnegie Works, where he married a second time, the mother of the wife of Charles Schwab, now of the Bethlehem Steel Company. He died a few years since at an advanced age.

The first machinist was George Jenkins. He was foreman in the Crane shops. Later he accepted a position as Superintendent of the Boonton Iron Works in New Jersey, where some of his descendants are still living.

Uriah Brunner was the pioneer druggist and newspaper man in town. He titled his paper "The Rising Star of Catasauqua." He moved to West Point, Nebraska, where he became a State Senator of that State.

John Swartz, a brother of the late B Frank Swartz, was the first photographer in town. Pictures were then taken on glass and were called daguerreotypes Mr. Swartz died in 1852

The first barber was Samuel Romig who died early in the fifties James W Fuller, 1st, induced William E Welsh, a colored barber, to come to Catasauqua where he conducted a shop for many years A son of Mr Welsh now conducts a shop at Coplay

Joseph Troxell mended shoes and had a small store on Front Street where Kemp's Clothing Store is now located His son, Alfred M Troxell, is in the business at Front and Chapel Streets

The first stone mason was Charles Breisch, who assisted in the erection of the first furnace One son and a number of grandsons are still in town

Nathan Fegely, formerly of Mauch Chunk, conducted the first lumber yard on Church Street, the present site of the Town Hall His yard ran to Middle Alley and Front Street, which accounts for the right angle in Railroad Street in the rear of Lawall's Drug Store

The David Tombler brick yard was located at Howertown Avenue and Wood Street Later it was moved to the Third Ward where it was abandoned Neighly Brothers made brick on Howertown Avenue near the Hunter farm The Kurtzes ran a brick yard in the Third Ward, which became the property of Franklin Goldsmith who closed out the business over a year ago

The Union Foundry on Front and Pine Streets was opened by John Fritz and his brothers at the close of the forties His brother-in-law, Isaac Chandler, ran a black-smith shop on Front and Bridge Streets, the site of the Crane locomotive house. After a brief tenure they all went to Johnstown, Pa

Mr Glace remembers the first rocking chair brought to Biery's-Port in 1847 Two men brought it on a boat from Bethlehem Many people came to see and try the great curiosity

The first carriage was brought hither from Bath, Pa, in 1849, by John Boyer, father of our townsman, Eugene J. Boyer. This was also a curiosity.

A young man by the name of John Thomas, a relative of the Superintendent, fell from the top of the first furnace, soon after its completion, and his body was buried in the rear of the Presbyterian Church on Fifth Street in Allentown. He was borne on a bier on the shoulders of relays of fellow employees, who wore high hats draped with long streamers of crepe as was the custom in Wales in those days. A long procession of men and women, among whom were "Mother Thomas" and Mrs Lackey, followed the cortege on foot to the grave. After the completion of the Thomas vault by David Thomas the body was deposited in it.

It will be interesting to locate some of the old buildings of Town.

THE STONE BARN, still a part of the Francis J Deily estate, and erected about 1760, stands north east of the Wahnetah Silk Mill.

THE GEORGE TAYLOR RESIDENCE, which is the farm-house belonging to the barn just mentioned, was erected in 1768. Three iron plates bearing the inscription "G T 1768" were found in the open fire-places and kitchen of the building. The large plate in the kitchen was removed and presented by the Deily heirs to the Historical Society of Lehigh County, in 1910.

THE BIERY FARM-HOUSE, at Second and Race Streets, now the house of August Hohl, was erected about 1800.

THE BIERY HOTEL, on Race Street, in the rear of the American Hotel, was erected in 1826, and is now the property of George Deily.

THE BIERY HOME, now owned by Frank B Mauser, on the corner of Race and Canal Streets, was erected in 1830.

THE BIERY STONE-HOUSE, used for many years as a store, at the Canal bridge on Race Street, was erected in 1835. It is now the property and residence of George B F Deily, and the residence of Mr and Mrs Peter J Laubach.

THE THOMAS HOME is the large frame dwelling opposite the furnaces on Front Street, erected by the Company during the fall of 1839. The stone building on the front lawn was the ice house used by Mr Thomas.

THE KURTZ FARM-HOUSE, east of the Rubber Works, was erected about 1800 and is now owned by John Yeager

THE FREDERICK MANSION was so named after George Frederick who owned it for many years. It stood on the West Side, a few rods south of the Hercules Metal Works. It was one of the oldest houses in the Lehigh Valley, having been erected in 1757. When the Lehigh Valley R. R. was built, this house was sold to Asa Packer. It was also known for years as "The Fort" because it was used as a place of refuge from the Indians.

CHAPTER XII

BOROUGH OFFICIALS, OLD HOME WEEK PROGRAM AND VIEWS

BOROUGH OFFICIALS

Dr C J Keim, Chief Burgess
Francis G Lewis, Solicitor
Lewis J H Grossart, Engineer
Daniel Gillespie, Overseer Water Dept
William McNabb, Receiver of Taxes
James H Harte, Street Commissioner.
Henry Zeaser, Fire Marshal
C E Scheckler, Sr, Chief of Police
Andrew Smith, Alvin Roth, Patrolmen.

TOWN COUNCIL

Rufus W G Wint, President.
Reuben C Weaver, Secretary
Ralph C Boyer, Treasurer

COUNCILMEN.

C D W. Bower	Harry B Smith
Robert G Dougherty	Harvey W Snyder
Samuel P Gemmel	Robert H Steinmetz
Joseph M. Kane	Howard V Swartz
Samuel Mitchell	William H Wentz
Oscar H Schugar	Rufus W G Wint.

BURGESSES

Names and Years Served

David Thomas, 1853
John Boyer, 1854
Uriah Brunner, 1855
David Thomas, 1856-57
William Goetz, 1858-59
A C Lewis, 1860
John Williams, 1861-69
James C Beitel, 1870-71
John Williams, 1872-73
M H Horn, 1874
George Bower. 1875.
William H Glace, 1876.
F W Wint, 1877

Henry Davis, 1878-80.
Philip Storm, 1881-84
Robert E. Williams, 1885-87.
John W. Hopkins, 1888-89.
Thomas Jones, 1890-91.
W A Borger, 1892-93.
Charles R Horn, 1894-96
C D W Bower, 1897-99.
Rufus M Wint. 1900-02
Henry W. Stolz, 1903-05
C. J Keim, M. D., 1906-09
H H. Riegel, M. D., 1909-14
C J Keim, M D, 1914-18

CENSUS—The population of the Borough, according to the United States enumeration since its incorporation, has been as follows:

1860	. . 1932	1890	.	.3704
1870	2853	1900		. 3963
1880	3065	1910		. 5250

OFFICERS OF THE OLD HOME WEEK ASSOCIATION

President,
 Leonard Peckitt.

  Secretaries,
   Harry H Aubrey,
   Daniel B Quinn

    Treasurer,
     James S Stillman

EXECUTIVE COMMITTEE

J S Elverson, Chairman Finance Committee
William H Glace, Esq , Chairman Historical Committee
Rev David R Griffith, Chairman Memorial Committee
Capt Joseph Matchette, Chairman Parade and Music Committee
Edmund Randall, Chairman Publicity Committee.
Albert B Lee, Chairman Fireworks Committee
Thomas Deemer, Chairman Decoration Committee
John L Schick, Chairman Entertainment Committee
Harry B Weaver, Chairman Educational Committee
Wilson Scott, Chairman Concessions Committee

PUBLICITY COMMITTEE

Edmund Randall, *Chairman* William T Scanlin
Harry H Aubrey, *Secretary.* John S Matchette
Reuben C Weaver Daniel B. Quinn
Eugene T Quinn.

PROGRAM

SUNDAY, JUNE 28TH

Religious Day.

Special Thanksgiving and Commemoratory Services in all Churches Receptions to former pastors

MONDAY, JUNE 29TH

Reception Day.

General reunion of families and Social and Fraternal societies

Band concert in the evening at 8 45 o'clock Concert by the Catasauqua Choral Society on St Paul's Lawn, at 7 45 P. M Address by Dr John A W. Haas, President of Muhlenberg College, Allentown, on a Civic topic.

TUESDAY, JUNE 30TH

Educational Day

Parade of Public and Parochial School children and Alumni 4 P M

Reunion of the Alumni Association of the Catasauqua High School and Concert by Bethlehem Steel Co Band in High School Auditorium 8 P M Band concert in the evening

WEDNESDAY, JULY 1ST

Sport Day

Registered shoot by Bryden Gun Club Many of the most prominent marksmen in America will participate in the events Extra attraction, the Topperweins, the foremost shooters in the United States to-day. Fancy shooting by Mrs Topperwein

Athletic Tournament, 3 30 to 6 P. M

THURSDAY, JULY 2ND

FRATERNAL DAY.

Grand parade of all Fraternal, Patriotic and Social Organizations
Grand display of fire works in the evening   Band concert

FRIDAY, JULY 3RD

FIREMEN'S DAY

Parade of Catasauqua and North Catasauqua Fire Departments and invited guests

Band concert in the evening

SATURDAY, JULY 4TH

HISTORICAL DAY

Grand historical, patriotic and civic pageant.
Magnificent display of fireworks in the evening   Band concert

* * * * * * *

The series of pictures of some fine buildings and beautiful scenes of Catasauqua, here appended, were printed from cuts loaned the Editors through the complaisant liberality of the firm of Geo V Millar and Company of Scranton, Pa, and the earnest mediation of Messrs A J Etheredge and Company of Catasauqua

GEORGE TAYLOR RESIDENCE—1768.

THE FAUST HOME.

RESIDENCE OF MRS. KATE M. FULLER.

Typical Residence, Catasauqua, Pa.

RESIDENCE OF EDWIN THOMAS.

RESIDENCE OF FRANK M. HORN.

RESIDENCE OF MRS. JESSICA WILLIAMS HOLTON.

RESIDENCE OF J. W. FULLER, 3RD.

RESIDENCE OF LEONARD PECKITT

RESIDENCE OF D. G. DERY.

PINE STREET BRIDGE.

RESIDENCE OF MRS. GRACE WILLIAMS KOEHLER.

VIEW OF CATASAUQUA.

RESIDENCE OF OSCAR J. STEIN.

FRONT STREET, LOOKING SOUTH FROM BRIDGE.

RESIDENCE OF H. J. SEAMAN.

SCENE ALONG LEHIGH RIVER.

RESIDENCE OF MRS. SARAH HUMPHREY PATZINGER.

RESIDENCE OF C. R. HORN.

EAGLE HOTEL.

CATASAUQUA NATIONAL BANK AND EMPIRE OFFICE BUILDINGS.

SCENE ON UNION STREET.

BETHEL WELSH CONGREGATIONAL CHURCH.

SCENE ON HOWERTOWN AVENUE.

FOURTH STREET, LOOKING NORTH FROM BRIDGE.

FRONT STREET BELOW MULBERRY.

SCENE ON CHURCH STREET.

BRYDEN HORSE SHOE WORKS

SCENE ON THIRD STREET.

FRONT AND BRIDGE STREETS.

ENTRANCE TO FAIRVIEW CEMETERY

SOLDIERS' MONUMENT.

LEHIGH VALLEY DEPOT.

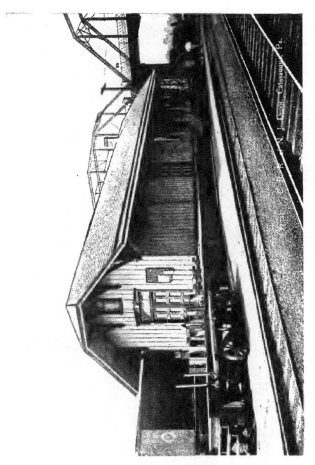

C. R. R. OF N. J. DEPOT.

LOCK AT THE CRANE FURNACES.

CRANE IRON WORKS.

LOWER CATASAUQUA.

LEHIGH RIVER AND CANAL.

THIRD AND WALNUT STREETS

CORNER HOWERTOWN AVENUE AND BRIDGE STREET.